English in Australia and New Zealand

To both our dads—John and John

English in Australia and New Zealand

An Introduction to Its History, Structure, and Use

Kate Burridge
and Jean Mulder

OXFORD
UNIVERSITY PRESS
AUSTRALIA & NEW ZEALAND

OXFORD
UNIVERSITY PRESS
AUSTRALIA & NEW ZEALAND

253 Normanby Road, South Melbourne, Victoria 3205, Australia

Oxford University Press is a department of the University of Oxford.
It furthers the University's objective of excellence in research, scholarship, and education by publishing worldwide in

Oxford New York

Auckland Bangkok Buenos Aires Cape Town Chennai
Dar es Salaam Delhi Hong Kong Istanbul Karachi Kolkata
Kuala Lumpur Madrid Melbourne Mexico City Mumbai Nairobi
São Paulo Shanghai Taipei Tokyo Toronto

First published 1998
Reprinted 1999, 2001, 2002, 2004, 2005, 2010

National Library of Australia Cataloguing-in-Publication data:

Burridge, Kate.
English in Australia and New Zealand:
an introduction to its history, structure and use.

Bibliography.
Includes index.
ISBN 0 19 553813 7.

1. English language—Australia.
2. English language—New Zealand.
I. Mulder, Jean Gail, 1954- . II. Title

427.994

Typeset by Desktop Concepts P/L, Melbourne
Printed in Hong Kong by Sheck Wah Tong Printing Press Ltd

Table of Contents

Preface

A LINGUISTIC ADVENTURE

As the celebrity cook Ian Parmenter says, 'most of us are passionate about good food'. Most of us are passionate about the English language too. For this reason we have blended these two themes into a 'feast on English'. Our examples are culled from culinary texts: cooking books throughout the centuries, food and wine magazines, books about food, health, diet, and even etiquette. Can you imagine a more pleasant way of grappling with the English language than over knives, forks, and a bottle of good wine?

There is, in fact, a serious intention behind our feast. Not only does the metaphor of food help to give the book a nice consistency, but also, and even more importantly, it draws on everyday experiences. We want to bring English alive and to encourage you to wallow in the day-to-day language that is all around you—everything from the instructions on the back of your Wheaties packet to the language of hangover cures. This is especially important when encountering texts from earlier periods of English. There is continuity in the history of English: the language has evolved and it continues to evolve. We want to show that speakers and writers of the past were part of a living, breathing speech community, and that the language they spoke and wrote is the language we speak and write today. We figure that a tenth-century recipe for curing hangovers or removing unwanted body hair helps to convey exactly this—that some of the needs, the desires, even the obsessions of people of the tenth century were not so different from those we have today. Through these food- and health-related texts, the speakers become more real, as does their language. The texts themselves are more natural too, being free from any literary ambition and stylisation.

A GUIDE TO THE MENU

We have served up a smorgasbord of topics, but as sumptuous as the feast may seem, we have had to be selective in our offerings and frugal with the portions. You can explore the themes further in the practical exercises and questions for discussion at the end of each chapter, as well as through the suggested further readings offered at the end of the book.

The focus is English down under—a conspicuously absent variety in the descriptions of English already available. We use the label *Antipodean English* to refer to the assortment of Englishes spoken in Australia and New Zealand. The term *antipodean* actually comes from Greek and means literally 'having the feet opposite'—a particularly hemispherist view that life in the Antipodes was out of the question given that we'd all be standing upside down! We also use the abbreviations *OZ* and *NZ English* to cover the varieties of English spoken in Australia and New Zealand. We realise that some people might find *OZ* a bit slangy, but we feel it has gained enough currency recently to earn it a place in our 'learned' language. After all, it has been around since early this century (*Oz(zie)* made its first appearance in Australian diggers' slang). We realise it's not customary to capitalise the word in the way we have, but we like the symmetry of OZ and NZ.

Now something about the organisation of the book. There's been a lot of discussion recently about what parts of the language you introduce first. Traditionally linguists have taken a bottom-up approach, starting with the smallest units (sounds) and progressing to the largest units (texts). Or do you jump in with words and work in both directions? What we've done here is to keep the traditional bottom-up layout, but we have written the chapters so that they can be read with either approach in mind.

METHODS

The book emphasises a combination of theory and description, and aims to introduce you to the major theoretical and methodological issues in modern linguistic study. At the same time, it provides an overview of the structure and history of the English language in its many different varieties, especially those close to home.

Necessarily, in our view, the book integrates both a synchronic approach (a 'snapshot' of the language at a particular point in time) and a diachronic approach (a series of snapshots or a 'moving picture' of the language over time). In order to understand where English is currently, you need to know where it's already been; each aspect of present-day English—be it vocabulary, sounds, or grammar—is followed by a discussion of its historical development.

Our approach is purposefully eclectic and draws upon many different traditions and areas in linguistics. This includes typology, descriptive grammar, discourse-pragmatics, diachronic syntax, grammaticalisation, sociolinguistics, and generative grammar. It does not follow the restrictive rituals that are necessarily part and parcel of any prepackaged framework.

WHAT WE MEAN WHEN WE SAY 'ONE MEDIUM ONION'

Because this is a linguistic account of English, we need to introduce appropriate terminology. Unfortunately, in a discipline such as linguistics, technical vocabulary often comes across as being particularly mystifying, even offensive, simply because we're dealing with the familiar. Everyone, of course, knows about English, and ordinary vocabulary has itself a host of linguistic terms: *word*, *sentence*, and even *language*, for example. But when applied to the actual study of a language such as English, these labels turn out to be very imprecise, and a more accurate terminology is needed. When a technical term is first introduced and defined, we have presented it in bold type. We have also included a glossary at the end of the book, enabling you look up the definitions of technical terms and to refresh your memory when required. We hope that the terminology does not induce heartburn, and that the book remains entertaining and approachable, offering something of interest to students and lovers of English alike.

Abbreviations

LINGUISTIC TERMS

A	adverbial
AC	adverbial complement
Adj	adjective
AdjP	adjective phrase
Adv	adverb
AdvP	adverb phrase
C	consonant
Det	determiner
dO	direct object
iO	indirect object
N	noun
NP	noun phrase
O	object
oC	object complement
PP	prepositional phrase
P	preposition
Pred	predicator
sC	subject complement
S	subject
S(entence)	sentence
SVX	subject + verb + everything else (basic sentence order)
V	vowel or verb (depending on context)
VP	verb phrase
X	everything else in a sentence (other than subject and verb)

OTHER ABBREVIATIONS

ABC	Australian Broadcasting Corporation
ACOD	The Australian Concise Oxford Dictionary

AND	Australian National Dictionary
ASEAN	Association of South-East Asian Nations
BBC	British Broadcasting Corporation
DAC	A Dictionary of Australian Colloquialisms
DNZE	Dictionary of New Zealand English: A Dictionary of New Zealandisms on Historical Principles
EFL	English as a foreign language
ENL	English as a native language
ESL	English as a second language
HRT	high rising terminal
IPA	International Phonetic Alphabet
MD	The Macquarie Dictionary
NSOED	The New Shorter Oxford English Dictionary on Historical Principles
NZ	New Zealand (English)
OAWD	Oxford Australian Writers' Dictionary
OED	The Oxford English Dictionary
OZ	Australian (English)
RP	British Received Pronunciation

1

Sampling the Varieties

INTRODUCTION

We begin by posing a question: what is English? Just a glance at the following is enough to show you that this is not the straightforward little question that it at first might seem.

> Fair fa' [Good befall] your honest, sonsie [comely] face,
> Great chieftain o' the puddin' race!
> Aboon them a' ye tak your place,
> Painch [paunch], tripe, or thairm [intestines].
> Weel are ye wordy o'a grace
> As lang's my airm
>
> Scots poet Robert Burns, 'Address to a Haggis'

> To hold one box, open at cooling
>
> Instructions on a French tin of snails to keep the open can in the fridge

> And she said, with that you got, your dinner, a lovely dinner, bed 'n breakfast. And she said the dinner was, the woman cooks, does all the cooking herself. But she said you got heaps of, ya know, courses 'n, really really lovely food.
>
> Part of a conversation, Melbourne speaker

> I were only about five and I were staying to school dinners—and she made me eat a big load of mashed potatoes.
>
> Part of a conversation, Lancashire speaker

> We used to cook our trotters out there—all come up in trays, all jelly—they used to nosh 'em there like. It was really beautiful.
>
> Part of a conversation, London speaker

> In a mixing type bowl, impact heavily on brown sugar, granulated sugar, softened butter and shortening. Coordinate the interface of eggs and vanilla.
>
> Twentieth-century adaptation of a recipe for *Chocolate Chip Cookies* in bureaucratese

> Sod Egges: Seeth your Egs almost hard, then peele them, and cut them in quarters, then take a little Butter and put it in a platter upon your egges.
>
> Seventeenth-century recipe for *Sod Egges*, as quoted in Black 1977:49

> Fygges doth stere a man to veneryous actes, for they doth auge and increase the seede of generacion. And also they doth prouoke a man to sweate: wherfore they doth ingendre lyce.
>
> Sixteenth-century warning on the dangers of eating figs, as quoted in Furnivall 1868:200

> All maners of egges waken a man to the worke of lecherie, & specialli sparowes egges.
>
> Fifteenth-century warning on the dangers of eating eggs, as quoted in Furnivall 1868:222

> Wiþ þon þe mōn hine fordrince. Genīm swines lungenne gebræd 7 on neaht nerstig genim fīf snæda simle. [In case a man overdrinks himself. Take a pig's lung, roast it, and at night fasting take five slices always.]
>
> Tenth-century hangover cure, as quoted in Cockayne 1865

> Yu mas putim hatoro long wara pastaim, long tripela de. Bihain yu kukim na kaikai. [You must put hatoro in water first, for three days. After that you can cook it and eat it.]
>
> Tok Pisin (Papua New Guinean Creole) instructions for preparing hatoro (type of cyclad palm), as quoted in Dutton 1985:32

These few samples of texts alone demonstrate the extraordinary assortment of varieties encompassed by the label 'English'. The diversity, as you can see, takes many forms—from exotic vocabulary to some structures that look very un-English indeed. For a few of the passages, we even had to supply full 'translations'.

The kind of variation we see represented here has two dimensions. The first is variation across space. There are two types of space involved: geographical and social. Both geography and society influence language. At any given point in time, English will differ both between countries and within the same country. And socially significant groups of people will differ in their linguistic behaviour. There's another aspect to the social dimension, and that's personal variation. People influence language too. All of us are marked out as individuals by our unique linguistic behaviour. No two people use language in exactly the same way.

The second dimension is variation across time. Time influences language. Shifts in grammar, words, and pronunciation occur even within one's own lifetime. And if the time-span is long enough, the changes can be truly spectacular, as some of the examples above illustrate.

As you can see, 'English' as such is fictitious. There is no one English, no one monolithic entity with a fixed set of linguistic features. Rather, the English language is more like a bag of mixed linguistic allsorts: a variety of flavours and features. What they have in common is a shared history. All have links of some sort with the group of continental Germanic dialects that ended up in the British Isles sometime in the fifth century. And most are, to a greater or lesser extent, mutually comprehensible.

So which variety of English have we chosen to describe in this book? In later sections, which deal with the structural properties of English, we examine the characteristics of the so-called 'standard varieties', as well as those features shared by the majority of other varieties. Wherever Antipodean usage is distinctive, we draw this to your notice. In the other sections we pay more attention to variation and diversity, focusing on who uses what features, where they're being used, and when. Let's begin, then, by sampling the sort of variation that occurs across space.

VARIATION ACROSS SPACE

Very few Australians or New Zealanders really think of their countries as being linguistically diverse. This is probably because in both Australia and New Zealand there is little need in most contexts for anyone to speak anything other than English. This does not mean that they are linguistically uniform, however. It's true, we tend to use labels such as OZ English or NZ English as if each were a single immutable language, but this is not the reality. The reality is that speakers from different regions, from different social classes, of different ages, of different occupations, of different gender identification, and of different sexual orientation will all talk differently. People talk differently in different contexts too, whether it be an informal chat, an interview, a lecture, and so on. Labels such as OZ English or NZ English are convenient cover terms for what are really clumps or clusters of mutually intelligible speech varieties.

To simplify our discussion, it's useful to make a broad distinction between the type of variation associated with speakers (**user-related**) and the type of variation associated with occasions of use (**use-related**). User-related variation includes regional variation (the geographical background of speakers), social variation (the age, gender, sexual orientation, socio-economic class, and education of speakers), and even personal variation (the linguistic details of individual speakers, including social and geographical features, but also personality, physique, and physical condition).

Use-related variation has to do with the way that we alter our language to suit the situations in which we find ourselves. Our language varies constantly in response to a complex of different situational factors; if any one factor is changed, our language changes accordingly. These factors include:

- the relationship between speakers and their audience, and even others who might be within earshot (are we chatting to a chum or to our local priest?)
- the setting (are we at a football match or in church?)
- the subject matter (are we debating who will win the Grand Final or the existence of God?)
- whether a spoken or written medium is used (are we talking on the phone or writing a letter?)

For the moment we will confine ourselves to user-related variation, focusing in particular on the relationship between variety and regional or social context. We will also address a number of questions that arise from this type of variation. What are the different varieties that exist? How do we assess these different varieties? Is one necessarily better than the rest? What are the educational implications? Should students be encouraged to be fluent in more than one variety? In chapter 10 we return to variation but look at the other side of the coin: the varieties of English viewed according to how they are used.

Languages, dialects, and accents

When we start to talk about linguistic variation, we very quickly hit problems of terminology. Terms such as *language*, *dialect*, and *accent* are often loosely applied. For a start, the distinction between language and dialect is not at all clear cut, and all sorts of factors enter into people's judgments about what makes something a dialect and what makes it a language. Unfortunately, too, terms such as these often acquire extra associations along the way, and these can very easily prejudice the issues involved. For example, for many people *dialect* brings to mind something rather quaint and rustic. For others the term is pejorative: dialects are varieties that don't come up to scratch. They're haphazard, vulgar, and provincial aberrations of the real language. Let's start, then, with the technical sense of *dialect* as we'll be using it here.

Most people are aware of pronunciation differences. For example, some NZ English-speakers in Otago and Southland pronounce their *r*'s in words such as *curd* and *first*, whereas other New Zealanders and all native OZ English-speakers don't. But these differences are matters of accent, not dialect. ***Accent*** refers to the pronunciation a speaker uses. ***Dialect*** refers to a speaker or writer's vocabulary and grammar.

People are generally fascinated by vocabulary differences. For example, if you want to buy a certain type of large, smooth sausage in Auckland, you'll find it's called *polony*. In Christchurch, though, it's *saveloy*, and in Southland it's *Belgium* or *Belgium roll/sausage*. Both *polony* and *saveloy* are familiar terms for some Australians, but people in Adelaide are more comfortable with *fritz*, and Brisbanites and Sydney-siders with *devon*. If you're journeying around New Zealand during strawberry season, you'll soon notice that the fruit can be sold in *punnets* (something that Australians can relate to), *pottles*, or *chips*—it depends where you are in the country. People from Melbourne and some New Zealanders call that round yeasty cake with pink or white icing and desiccated coconut on top a *Boston bun*. But in other places in New Zealand, it's a *Sally Lunn*; in New South Wales it's a *teacake* and in South Australia a *yeast bun*. Variation of this kind is undoubtedly significant for speakers; for example, Melburnians who order *scallops* in a fish shop in Sydney will understandably feel cheated when, in place of the expected serve of succulent marine bivalve molluscs, they are handed slices of potato dipped in batter and fried.

Perhaps less obvious are grammatical differences. These can involve, for instance, differences in verb forms (*I done all the cooking* versus *I've done all the cooking*); negative constructions (*I'm not gonna eat it no more* versus *I'm not gonna eat it any more*); and pronouns (*Are youse eating?* versus *Are you eating?*). Differences in grammar can sometimes result in miscommunication across dialects. For example, speakers who make the distinction between singular *you* and plural *youse* might well be confused if they were part of a group addressed by someone who used *you* for both singular and plural; they'd be trying to figure out which individual in the group had been referred to.

And imagine the potential misunderstanding when an Aboriginal child says to the teacher—'You gotta gimme paper?'. *Gotta* in this variety of Aboriginal English functions as a marker of future time (much like *gonna*). A teacher unaware of this would interpret the sentence as a directive—and a rather impolite one at that (see Eagleson et al. 1982 on Aboriginal English). Canberra linguist Harold Koch (1985) has shown that much miscommunication in land rights claims occurs because the Aboriginals involved speak a non-standard form of English and/or a creole lexically related to English—in other words, separate linguistic varieties that are not properly recognised or understood outside their speech communities. Misunderstandings such as these can have serious consequences.

English dialects, then, are all the regionally, socially, and temporally defined varieties that fall under the label of *the English language*. Technically, pronunciation differences alone do not make a variety a distinct dialect. In reality, though, if speakers have a different accent (as we both do), then they will probably show differences elsewhere in their speech. (Jean Mulder, for example, has *drug* as the past for *drag*. Kate Burridge uses *peanut paste* rather than *peanut butter*.) Although some linguists insist on a sharp demarcation between accent and dialect, you'll find that most varieties that differ in pronunciation also show differences in other respects.

The standard dialect

One thing to remember is that we are all dialect-speakers. Everyone speaks at least one dialect of English. The most important dialect (in terms of the way society operates) is **Standard English**. It might surprise you that we call this a dialect, because people tend to talk about a 'standard language', but this is a misleading label. Standard English is one of many different dialects of English; it just happens to be the dialect with the most clout. Standard English is what is promoted in schools; it's what is taught to foreign learners; students are expected to use it in essays; broadcasters are expected to use it on radio (although this requirement is often relaxed now); dictionaries and grammars foster it. How it got to this elevated position is a geographical and historical coincidence. As we discuss in the next chapter, Standard English was originally a local dialect of the London–Central Midland region that just happened to be in the right place at the right time. If a city other than London had had the same non-linguistic advantages (let's say Liverpool or Manchester), the dialect of that region would have been subject to the same spread. This is typically how standard 'languages' arise. It has nothing to do with a variety being perfect, but it has everything to do with economic, political, and social context.

Because the standard variety has been codified (that is, recorded in grammars, dictionaries, and style guides), people feel that it is the variety they should use, especially if the situation is a formal one. Because of the way our society is structured, the standard is the dialect with the greatest prestige, being associated with education and with higher income groups. This does not mean, however, that it is intrinsically better than any other dialect. **Non-standard** (or **vernacular**) must never be equated with substandard. All dialects are equally good for the purposes they serve. They all have their own particular rules; they just do things differently. So when you hear people complain about 'bad English', it's probably not bad English at all. Sentences like *I done all the cookin' meself* or *I don't want nothin' to eat* are not errors in English, but rather errors in Standard English.

Since they are codified in grammar books and dictionaries, standard varieties of English used in different countries are more like each other than non-standard varieties are. For example, if we think of OZ and NZ English, their distinctive character is to be found largely in differences of accent and of some vocabulary, but the two are not strikingly different from other standard varieties at the level of grammar. Speakers of non-standard varieties from these two countries, however, show not only differences of accent and vocabulary, but also significant grammatical differences. A distinctively OZ or NZ English is much more apparent in these varieties, especially in colloquial or informal usage.

Once again, labels such as *Standard* and *Non-standard English* imply that we're dealing with a clear-cut distinction here. As always, labels such as these obscure a reality of flux and variance. It's really only in the context of the written language that we can talk sensibly about a coherent standard. The spoken language is much less uniform, with variation occurring at all levels, especially in sounds and vocabulary. But even in writing, we'll never achieve total homogeneity. First, our language is always changing, but it takes a while before a new usage is totally accepted, especially in formal contexts. For example, a construction such as *usedn't* is frequent in the speech and writing of many educated Australians and New Zealanders, and yet it still hovers on the border between standard and non-standard. There's a lot of disagreement between speakers too. Some maintain that *I usedn't to cook* is 'correct'. Others prefer *I didn't used to cook.* The rest are fence-sitters regarding which they feel is more acceptable. It's also the case that, until recently, both Australia and New Zealand based their standard on the British standard (that is, the standard variety of the United Kingdom). In fact, even today there are still many who defer to British norms, as opposed to OZ or NZ usage, although the appearance of Antipodean style manuals (such as *The Cambridge Australian English Style Guide* by Pam Peters, 1995) and distinctly NZ and OZ dictionaries (such as those published by Oxford University Press) are helping to establish a distinctive standard for Australia and New Zealand.

Regional variation

Linguistic variation that is associated with geographical location is probably more obvious to people than other types of variation. A person in York in the United Kingdom will have different linguistic patterns from someone living in, say, New York, Wellington, Kitchener (Canada), Johannesburg, or Brisbane. What we have here are different **regional** or **geographical** dialects. These geographical dialects can include both standard and non-standard speech forms.

Linguists generally make distinctions between geographical dialects, which are in a sense national varieties such as OZ English, NZ English, Canadian English, Irish English, American English, British English, and South African English. This textbook, for example, focuses on what is distinctive about NZ English and OZ

English. Within these national varieties there can also be distinct regional geographical dialects—for example, Birmingham English in the United Kingdom, Waterloo County English in Canada, Boston English in the USA, and Southland English in New Zealand.

Speakers of distinctive regional dialects will always have a distinctive regional accent as well. But the opposite is not necessarily true. Namely, it is possible for speakers to have a regional accent but write a dialect of English, such as Standard English, that conveys no information at all about what part of the country they come from. Standard English is used and understood by people all over the world, and its grammar provides little or no information about geographical background. This is largely true with respect to vocabulary too, although there can be some lexical items that are regional. There's nothing strikingly Antipodean about the grammar used in this book, for example. Only the nature of the vocabulary might give the game away.

In order to see just how uniform Standard English is globally, the British linguist David Crystal (1995) collected samples from forty English broadsheets from countries all over the world. They were collected on the same day—6 July 1993—and covered the same range of topics. He claims that on purely linguistic grounds it was impossible to tell which paper belonged to which country. There was next to nothing in the way of an obviously regional use of grammar. The only occasional clue was in the form of a distinctive lexical item or spelling. Clearly, we're already well on our way to attaining a worldwide Standard English, at least for writing.

There are accents that are homeless too. For example, British Received Pronunciation (or RP, as it is known) can be found all over the United Kingdom. It will convey information about a person's social and educational background, but nothing about where that person might be from (except that she or he probably comes from the United Kingdom). Originally spoken by the upper classes and courtiers in the south of England, RP became the British accent most associated with wealth, power, and prestige, and was adopted by anyone anxious for social advancement.

The fate of RP is now unclear, however. Certainly it's no longer exclusively the domain of the social elite, but has become more an 'educated' accent. More significantly, though, talking 'posh' doesn't seem to have the same prestige that it once had. Growing egalitarianism and social democracy is now causing the solidarity function of accents to gain precedence over the status function. Many people are now trying to speak more 'down to earth', more 'ordinary', wishing to avoid the *crème de la crème* connotations of pure RP. Variations on RP are springing up too—in other words, accents with an RP base but with clear regional characteristics. Even more telling is the rapid spread in the 1990s of something called 'Estuary English'. This is essentially London speech with distinct Cockney elements. It has now extended well beyond the Thames estuary and is on the way to taking over from RP as the regionally neutral accent.

Certainly in Australia and New Zealand you often encounter hostile (or amused) reactions to RP and the local so-called 'cultivated' accents that fall closest to RP. There's a kind of social tug of war going on between those who see RP and its home-grown variants as affected and artificial ('la-di-da talk') and those who still see it as the 'best kind of English' spoken by the 'best kind of people'. In Australia, the first group now have more of the rope; solidarity and 'down-to-earthness' are winning out over status. In New Zealand, RP used to be rated highly on the prestige scale, but Elizabeth Gordon has told us that this is no longer the case (pers. comm. 3 April 1997). It seems that, in both countries, 'general' NZ and OZ accents have now become more desirable. (Later in this chapter, we discuss accent labels such as 'general', 'cultivated' and 'broad'.)

Regional variation down under

Regional variation within and between Australia and New Zealand probably consists mainly of lexical differences. For instance, at the beginning of the chapter we gave a number of examples relating to food. However, popular claims that people can identify someone's place of origin purely on the basis of how that person speaks are exaggerated. Accent differences are more likely to be a matter of statistical tendency, with a certain pronunciation occurring more in one place than another. With a word such as *plant*, Melburnians are more likely to say [æ] (as in *bat*), and Sydneysiders are more likely to say [a] (as in *cart*). Adelaide and Perth speakers are even more likely to say [a]. But, as linguist David Bradley (1989; 1991) shows, this variation is actually quite complex, and you don't find the vowel uniformly across words that could potentially have the same vowel (for example, *grasp* and *clasp* nearly always have [a], but *plant* and *dance* are variable). So you might find people in Melbourne saying *c[æ]stle* but *d[a]nce* and *pl[a]nt*. There are also complex social and stylistic factors involved here. For example, if you went to a private school, you are more likely to say *d[a]nce* and *pl[a]nt*. And if the situation is a more formal one, the likelihood of [a] is even greater. (Note that the interesting [æ]–[a] variation also occurs in Southland; see Bartlett 1992 on the Southland variety of NZ English).

Certainly some of these accent differences have existed from the beginning of European settlement in Australia and New Zealand. They evolved because of the slightly different dialect mixes in each region. For instance, the Melbourne pronunciation of words like *castle* represents an older pronunciation and is more likely to be found in the north of England. It's assumed that more people from the north originally settled in Melbourne. Earlier we mentioned the Southland 'burr' found in the pronunciation of *r* in words like *curd*. This difference can be explained by the significant number of Scots who settled in these southern regions. Many of the distinctive words (for example, *crib* versus *bach* in the rest of New Zealand for 'holiday home') and some distinctive syntactic structures (for instance, *my hair needs washed*) also have Scottish ancestry.

Although regional diversity is limited now, we might expect that, over time, both physical and social distance will have the effect of increasing regional differences in Australia and New Zealand. Also, the fact that there's no prestige regional variety of English in either country means that varieties will be freer to go their separate ways; in other words, speakers won't want to shift towards a distinctively Canberra or Wellington usage because it has more status.

The separation of urban and rural communities probably creates the richest regional diversity. In Australia, for example, we already find significant differences, particularly with respect to speed and to broadness of accent. As Bradley (1989) reports, Melburnians tend to speak faster than people in rural Victoria of the same socio-economic background. You'll find a greater proportion of broad-speakers in rural Victoria too. This is one popular stereotype that does appear to have some basis in fact.

It's largely the rural areas in Australia and New Zealand that are preserving the distinctive dialect varieties in these places. Rural speakers of non-standard varieties, for example, show not only differences of accent and vocabulary, but also significant grammatical differences. Consider the 'Australianness' of what Australian linguist Andy Pawley (1995; forthcoming) has called 'Tasmanian Vernacular English'. This variety shows a number of distinctive grammatical features, including:

- irregular verb forms

  The last Percy *seen* of 'im was they *was* goin' over the brow o' the hill, y'see.

- plural *you*

  Y's woulda took it off 'im.

- marking of familiar noun phrases with *old*

  And on the corner was this *old* mountain duck.

- general negator *never*

  I *never* [didn't] 'ad 'er.

- gender-marking on both animate and inanimate nouns (for example, items of food and drink are always feminine)

  I put *'er* [the bottle of beer] down that bloody quick that I blew the top off *'er*. And [he] took *'er* [leg of lamb] in and put *'er* on the plate!

A number of these features can be found in various other non-standard varieties around the world, and some presumably are conservative features that were once widespread in Britain (in the eighteenth century and earlier). Taken together, systematic grammatical differences such as these, along with lexical differences, are sufficient to make Tasmanian Vernacular English a distinctive non-standard regional dialect.

But social factors are going to be crucial here too; it's difficult to talk about regionally defined variation without appealing to social aspects of the area. Vernacular Englishes like the Tasmanian variety, for example, are non-standard varieties typical of the lower socio-economic classes in a speech community. Basically, the higher up the social scale you go, the less remarkable the regional differences tend to be. We'll be looking more closely at socially defined variation in a moment.

The 'global village'

Many people now believe that the global village signals the end of this sort of regional variation. In other words, travel opportunities, mass media, and global communication networks spell the spread of Standard English at the expense of local dialects. This may be the case if language were solely for the purpose of communication, but there's the solidarity factor too. This solidarity function is important and should never be underestimated for its potential to intensify linguistic differences. Regional chauvinism evident in the strong rivalry between Sydney and Melbourne, for example, is a major incentive for people to start highlighting their distinctiveness linguistically. Front-vowel differences are already distinguishing Sydney from

Melbourne (with Sydney-siders apparently moving more towards New Zealand usage; see chapter 4).

Certainly, some remote dialects have been overwhelmed by Standard English and have died out, but diversity within English is actually on the increase. Wherever you look, new brands of English are springing up, to the extent that English is now frequently designated in the plural as 'Englishes' (see chapter 12). Language is a powerful symbol of group belonging. Like cream in a sponge, it binds members of a group together and, at the same time, serves as a barrier to keep the non-members out. Differences to do with pronunciation, vocabulary, and grammar serve as badges of identity for different groups, whatever that identity may be. As we've seen here, groups can be defined regionally. But they can distinguish themselves on the basis of various social factors as well.

Social variation

> You're an educated man—it shows in your cleanliness and your vowel sounds.
>
> Tramp to Oliver Priest in 'Oliver's Travels' (BBC comedy)

As we mentioned at the start of this chapter, social parameters to do with the age, gender, sexual orientation, socio-economic class, education, and occupational status of speakers will typically correlate with the way sounds, vocabulary, grammar and communicative patterns vary. For example, if we find a group of people who share the same socio-economic characteristics as well as the same linguistic repertoire, then we must recognise the presence of a social dialect. This association is always coincidental rather than causal. Although, of course, individual members may chose to speak differently from other groups, there is nothing about the way of life in these various groups that produces these differences.

Observing social variation

The American linguist William Labov was the first to show that the relationship between society and linguistic variation could be studied in a systematic way. People had always realised, of course, that different social classes had different linguistic behaviour, but it was Labov's 1966 study of New York English that showed for the first time that these differences could be quantified. He started out by identifying a number of linguistic features that were used variably within the New York speech community. These were called **'sociolinguistic variables'** and included features such as the pronunciation of *r* after vowels in words such as *beer* and *pork*, the pronunciation of *-ing* in words like *cooking* and *eating*, and the pronunciation of *th* in words like *thirty* and *this*.

What Labov did was interview a random sample of the population in New York, trying to elicit a range of different speaking styles: from informal conversation, through a more formal interview, to reading styles (the most formal of all). By this he was able to show a clear interaction between speakers' social backgrounds and the formality of their speaking styles. All the linguistic features he looked at varied significantly according to the social group of the speaker. For example, particular accents (such as the pronunciation of *r* after vowels) were especially associated with speakers higher up on the social scale, and all speakers adjusted their usage towards these more prestige accents in their more formal styles. When people felt the situation becoming more formal, they pronounced the words in ways that they perceived to be more 'correct'. Women appeared to be the most sensitive to the prestigious forms. They showed, on the whole, greater shifts towards the prestigious patterns in their formal styles (see discussion below on p. 13).

Wherever you find similarities of social structure within the English-speaking world, you can expect to find similar patterns of distribution for linguistic variables. Labov's methods are now used extensively in OZ and NZ sociolinguistic research, and a large number of quantitative variation studies have appeared in recent years. The list of works in the further reading at the end of the chapter will give you an idea of the growing importance of this field of study in both countries.

Within all this regional and social variation, we also find sub-varieties defined by variables such as ethnicity, gender, age, and profession. If we really want to be accurate in our descriptions of OZ and NZ English, we should use very specific labels, such as 'the English of a Greek-Australian working-class heterosexual adult female journalist'. Below we give examples of each of these different dimensions, with the exception of 'profession', which we examine in chapter 10.

The dimension of socio-economics

In places such as the United Kingdom, where the class lines are still quite rigidly defined and people tend to be more class-conscious, the features of class dialect will be easier to identify, and people will be linguistically more attuned to these differences. Many people in Australia and New Zealand believe that this sort of marked class system does not exist in their countries. It's probably true that divisions are less rigidly structured and less explicit than in the United Kingdom, in that people are less class-conscious and are able to cut across class boundaries with greater ease. Nonetheless, we all tend to associate with those who are similar to ourselves in terms of educational background, occupational status, and income, for instance. Even in Australia and New Zealand people fall into different social groups, and this will inevitably have consequences for the language they use. In short, all countries show social stratification to some extent, and all languages show socially defined linguistic variation to some extent.

In the last section, we saw that both standard and non-standard variation can be regionally defined. Within the social context, we find this kind of variation as well, although the differences between standard and non-standard social varieties tend not to be as great as those between standard and non-standard regional varieties. For any given region, what you typically find is that, the higher up the social ladder someone is or the more formal the education that person has received, the more likely he or she is to speak Standard English. Non-standard dialects are associated with speakers who fall towards the other end of the social scale.

But there's a lot of variation, even within the one social dialect. People's use of particular forms is generally more a question of frequency than of absolute use or non-use. For example, much can depend on the setting. Non-standard usage is more usual in informal contexts. In more formal circumstances, when people typically pay more attention to their speech, they tend to avoid these forms. Speakers will adjust their accents or their grammar 'up' or 'down' the scale, depending on the situation they find themselves in. It's natural; we all do it.

In New Zealand and Australia, social variation is most obvious in accent differences. Generally speaking, it's possible to classify NZ and OZ English into three overall varieties: broad, general, and cultivated (with RP as a minor fourth). These varieties are distinguished largely on the basis of vowel pronunciations (see chapter 3). The use of one variety over another is governed by a complex of different factors, but principally education, gender identification, and location (urban versus rural). In Australia, another category—ethnic broad—has recently been added to encompass the Migrant Englishes (see discussion in the next section). Some of these varieties are characterised by distinctive grammar as well. For example, those falling closer to the broad end of the spectrum strongly correlate with non-standard grammatical features.

The dimension of ethnicity

Ethnicity is an important part of social identity and is something that people often want to demonstrate through their use of language. For instance, as sociolinguists such as Howard Giles (1977) have shown, different ethnic varieties of a dominant language (in this case English) can become important markers of ethnic group membership.

Certainly, the indigenous populations in both New Zealand and Australia have contributed significantly to linguistic diversity in these two countries. For example, significant phonological and lexical differences exist between Maori English and other varieties of NZ English. Interesting differences also exist with respect to naming and addressing. As Lorraine Johnston and Shelley Robertson (1993) show, Maori-speakers often transfer terms and rules from the Maori address system to their English—for example, a three-way distinction in second-person pronouns *you*, *youse*, and *youse fullas*, and address forms such as *cuz*, *sis*, *bro*, *aunty*, and *uncle*, which reflect Maori kinship relationships. So far, grammatical differences are minor, but this can change of course. It's likely that the lively Maori subculture in New Zealand will mean the eventual genesis of an even more distinctive Maori English. Especially in the face of the possible extinction of Maori itself, Maori features in the English of these speakers may well become important markers of their distinctiveness as a group. As we've already seen, the solidarity function of language has an important part to play in creating variation. In chapter 12 we focus on Maori English and especially on Aboriginal English as varieties that are providing an interesting new dimension to 'Extraterritorial Englishes' (Roger Lass's term; see Lass 1987).

Other ethnically defined varieties of OZ and NZ English come from the large numbers of migrants, in particular those from non-English-speaking backgrounds. These speakers have enhanced the overall variety by retaining, for example, aspects of their own Migrant English accents and foreign accents. To illustrate the extent of the diversity, consider that, over the last 30 years or so, speakers from well over forty different ethnic groups have migrated to Australia. These different ethnic mixes are now adding a vibrant, new, socially relevant aspect to Australian English. In Melbourne and Sydney, for example, the Italian and Greek communities are of particular interest because of their size and also because they have been there long enough to have teenage children who were born in Australia.

It'll be interesting to see whether the second generation will continue to accentuate their ethnic identity by way of distinctive linguistic features. We find, for instance, that ethnic accents of Australian English (what has been labelled 'ethnic broad') feature strongly in media stereotypes (with characters such as 'Con the fruiterer', 'Effie', and the 'Wogboys'). Barbara Horvath's 1985 study of Sydney speech, however, suggests that here the trend may be going in the other direction. Her results indicate that Italian and Greek teenagers are actually moving away from the broad end of the spectrum (characteristic of the first generation of migrants)—perhaps because ethnic broad has become so highly stigmatised. In other words, ethnic groups can end up choosing to distance themselves from the linguistic patterns of their parents in order to assimilate linguistically to the mainstream. Migrant English (or, more accurately, Migrant Englishes) is an area crying out for greater linguistic attention. Migrant populations in both Australia and New Zealand will undoubtedly be a great force for change in the English of these two countries.

The dimension of gender and sexual orientation

Gender is another important social division in cultures. Not surprisingly it is also a part of our identity that is reflected in (and reinforced by) our linguistic behaviour. This is another growing area in sociolinguistic research, especially in Australia and New Zealand, and we suggest that you follow up some of the references in the further reading at the end of the chapter. We'll mention just a few aspects of gender variation here.

One entrenched stereotype (which does have some empirical backing) is that women's speech is more 'proper' and more 'correct'. Studies based on Western communities in the USA, the United Kingdom, and more recently Australia and New Zealand suggest that there is a sort of tug of war going on between the sexes, with women pulling one way (towards prestige forms) and men the opposite way (see references in the further reading at the end of the chapter). In these studies, women (when compared with men of the same social class, age, and educational level) chose forms closest to Standard English. On the other hand, use of non-standard forms correlated not only with working-class speech, but also with male speech. Women also showed, on the whole, greater shifts towards the prestige patterns in their formal styles (as compared with more informal styles).

The speculative explanations for these differences between women and men are numerous and varied. Suggestions include the status-consciousness of women, the influence of their social networks, their social powerlessness, their role in society, and their tendency to speech accommodation (see Coates 1993, 1997; Holmes 1992; Trudgill 1995 for general discussions of these; see also Further Reading). New Zealand sociolinguist Elizabeth Gordon, for example, points out that society expects 'better' behaviour from women, especially sexual behaviour, and women may be speaking more prestigiously so as not to appear promiscuous (as cited in Trudgill 1995:72). Janet Holmes also points out that women are generally more cooperative conversationalists and may well be accommodating to the speech of the middle-class, well-educated interviewers in many of the sociolinguistic studies (see discussion on p. 14).

Other linguists look more to men's behaviour, alluding to the function of vernacular speech as an expression of masculinity (of roughness and toughness). Take the image of the ocker, for example. It can act as an important norm-enforcer for Australian men who don't want to appear effeminate and weak to their peers. In this way, non-standard forms—a broad Australian accent and the use of conventionally tabooed language—become desirable macho markers of gender identity. The solidarity factor, as we've seen, can be very important. We also shouldn't underestimate the power of cultural stereotypes to influence linguistic behaviour by shaping our perception of what are and what are not appropriate ways of speaking.

All of these views have something interesting to offer with respect to the linguistic behaviour of the sexes. But one thing they all agree on is the fact that language is a social phenomenon. As Peter Trudgill (1995:71) so neatly puts it, 'Men and women are socially different in that society lays down different social roles for them and expects different behaviour patterns from them. Language simply reflects this social fact'.

We might also mention here that significant differences between women and men emerge in conversation management too. Basically the research findings paint a picture in which men pursue a style of interaction based more on power, competition, and giving information, while women pursue a style based more on solidarity and support. This is evident in a number of aspects of interaction, such as air-time, patterns of interruptions, linguistic 'hedges', listening noises, and paralinguistic responses such as smiling (see Holmes 1995). The difference between women's cooperative conversational style and men's more competitive style has been interpreted negatively as a reflection of the subordinate status of women in our culture. New Zealand linguist Janet Holmes, however, points out that it could also be viewed more positively: the greater attention that women pay to the needs and feelings of their conversational partners could be seen as evidence of their interactional maturity. Nonetheless it is true that inequality exists in these different styles. Men's competitive style gives them distinct advantages in conversation, particularly in public settings such as the classroom or the workplace. It allows them to dominate, while women do more of the interactional work. These different ways of talking are not insulated from society's power structures.

Linguistic communities are also formed by social groupings such as lesbian, gay, transsexual, and bisexual men and women, with each community using linguistic features to identify group membership. Unfortunately, with the exception of a few collections of gay men's vocabulary (for example, Rodgers 1972; Dynes 1985; Chesebro 1981), detailed studies are few. It's an area still plagued with stereotyping and folk-linguistic notions.

The dimension of age

Age is an important social division in all cultures, and again it is something that people demonstrate through their use of language. As you might expect, the speech of older generations is generally more conservative than that of younger generations. As we'll see in chapters 4 and 11, linguistic changes take a while to catch on, and this fact is reflected in the Englishes of different age groups. New forms that are on the increase will be more prevalent in the speech of younger people, whereas forms on the way out will be more prevalent in the speech of older people.

But age variation doesn't necessarily signal change in progress. In the case of slang, for instance, we find a high turnover rate without necessarily any long-term impression on the language. Teenage slang, for example, includes lexical features (for example, *wicked, sick, mad, zesty*, and *groovy*, which all mean 'good'), grammatical features (for example, sentence-final *not*, as in *You're doing a terrific job—*

not), and discourse features (for instance, conversational particle *like*, as in *like I met this guy, y'know, and he's like totally feral*). However, this sort of usage is usually confined to the domain of 'teenspeak'. It's typically very ephemeral too; for slang to be slangy it must be picturesque, it must be dramatic and it must startle, but above all it must be new.

There are many types of variation that we could include here. People in different professions distinguish themselves by their speciality languages. Pop singers, for instance, demonstrate their identity through pronunciation and even some grammatical forms in their lyrics. Any group of people that can be identified as socially significant will show differences of some degree in their linguistic behaviour.

ATTITUDES TO VARIATION

Are there dialects that can be described as linguistically superior? Our culture tells us that the standard is the best form of English. Non-standard dialects are, by comparison, held to be deficient, incomplete, debased, slovenly forms of the language. But in many respects you could argue that non-standard dialects actually function better than Standard English. For example, the pronoun system of Australian Aboriginal English makes much finer distinctions than Standard English pronouns are capable of. Even if the standard eventually adopts plural *youse*, it still comes nowhere near the complexity of the Aboriginal system (as you will see in chapter 12). Does this mean speakers of the standard are linguistically deprived in this area?

These sorts of evaluations get us nowhere. All varieties have the same potential for complexity and richness of expression. There are no linguistic grounds for saying one is better than another. The choice between good and bad is totally subjective; it is not based on any evidence, but rather on gut feeling or sentiment. A non-standard dialect is as valid a communication system as the standard; *standard* should never be regarded as an evaluative term. On the basis of pure linguistics, all dialects are equal.

From a social point of view, however, things work differently. Non-standard dialects are often disparaged and devalued simply because they don't have the same prestige or status as the standard 'language'. (They don't have the backing of an army or navy, to adapt a phrase usually attributed to Max Weinreich.) They do, of course, have a prestige within the group, but not one that's acknowledged outside the group. Despite our current era of so-called 'equal opportunity', language continues to function to socially disadvantage people, and many in different language communities are still discriminated against—both consciously and unconsciously—for using non-standard dialects and low-status accents.

But attitudes to different varieties can often become confused. For instance, speakers of the standard dialect can be quite tolerant of regional non-standard dialects, especially if they happen to be spoken in picturesque rural parts of the country. These are often described in nostalgic (and rather condescending) terms as attractively quaint or rustic forms of the language. In sharp contrast, where social dialects are concerned there is often strong hostility. Here non-standard is typically equated with substandard, and the speakers of these varieties are condemned for their accent, their use of slang, and of course their grammar (or so-called 'lack of grammar').

These sorts of value judgments typically arise from personal associations and prejudices. Those who approve of a rural lifestyle, for example, or who are attracted to what they see as beautiful unspoiled rural regions, will probably also be attracted to the varieties of English spoken in these places. Varieties spoken in heavily industrialised urban centres, however, are often judged harshly as 'bad' or 'ugly sounding'. If you disapprove of someone's social background, then you'll probably also disapprove of their way of speaking. We might think we're judging an accent of the basis of pure aesthetics, but typically these sorts of judgments have a much deeper social basis. Language is so closely bound up with the life and culture of its speakers that it's very difficult to separate them. Social judgments of this kind appear to be deeply ingrained in the human psyche.

EDUCATIONAL IMPLICATIONS

All this, of course, has important educational implications, especially for those teaching English to students whose home-grown variety is non-standard. It's widely seen as the job of schools to eradicate all signs of these non-standard blots on the English-language landscape. Because of the way our society is structured, using sentences such as *I done it* can put people at a disadvantage. And this is, of course, why teachers have to give students access to Standard English, in order to protect them against this sort of prejudice. But educators are in a difficult position.

First, the standard language does not necessarily have prestige in all contexts. As implied earlier, prestige is a relative term, and the status of a dialect is going to vary from situation to situation. If the standard is not the speech of the people we most closely identify with, then speaking the standard in an intimate setting with family or friends is out of place. It would be inappropriate and offensive, and could be likened to breaking a social convention. People would accuse us of trying to 'speak posh' or of 'putting on airs'—or they may just laugh.

We see this very clearly in both Australia and New Zealand, particularly where ethnic varieties are involved. For example, the linguists Robert Eagleson, Susan Kaldor, and Ian Malcolm describe the animosity felt by some Aboriginal groups towards Standard English when it is used in the company of other Aboriginals—they call it 'flash language'. An Aboriginal teaching assistant describes it this way: 'If you talk...you know, *flash* as they call it at home, that's what they think you are trying to be: stuck up or something you know, and you've got to talk on their level' (1982:155).

In addition, teachers have to make sure they are not pushing the school language in a way that's demeaning to children. Getting someone to give up their linguistic behaviour and adopt another is not like getting them to give up their brand of breakfast cereal. You're also asking them to give up their allegiance to their own social group—to reject the values, aspirations, and accomplishments of those people they most closely identify with. As this chapter has demonstrated, it's through our use of language that we make our social identity known. Teachers have to be sensitive to this. To disparage a child's dialect is to disparage that child's family and friends, as well as that child's sense of self. We know it's linguistically unjustified. And it certainly isn't educationally sound either; it does nothing to encourage a positive attitude towards school.

Children can, in fact, develop two accents, two vocabularies, two dialects even: one for school and one for home. Another Aboriginal teaching assistant comments: 'it's not good going home and talking the same way as we do at school. You've got to have two lots of English in other words: one for home, one for school' (Eagleson et al. 1982:155). Many Aboriginal speakers are, in fact, bidialectal. They might be native speakers of a non-standard variety and have learnt the standard as a second variety in school. Generally they're skilled at switching between varieties according to context.

A bidialectal policy makes sense all round. For a child, there are personal benefits in retaining the home language, and there are also advantages to learning the language of the wider community. Pedagogically the policy is sound too. Teaching the school language will be much more effective if it builds on what children already know about their home language. And approaching this home language as a legitimate and rich variety, and not as a collection of endless mistakes, will help children to learn the standard more effectively. From a scientific point of view, we're better off as well: maintaining vernacular varieties ensures greater linguistic diversity, and this diversity benefits us all.

Language is a culturally transmitted system. Even if one of the scientifically engineered languages, such as Esperanto, were ever accepted and used worldwide, it would change in precisely the same way that a natural language changes. There would soon be different regional and different social varieties springing up all over the place. Speakers do not stop wanting to signal their aspirations, their adherence to certain lifestyles, and their allegiance to different social or ethnic groups. We see a striking example of this in chapter 12 when we look at the effect of the worldwide spread of English as the new global Esperanto.

POINTS TO REMEMBER

- Language varies along two dimensions: time and space. This latter category can be divided between user-related and use-related variation. User-related variation focuses on the speaker and includes regional variation, social variation, and even personal variation. Use-related variation concerns the way we alter our language to suit the occasion in which we find ourselves.
- Accent refers to a speaker's pronunciation, whereas dialect refers to a speaker or writer's vocabulary and grammar.
- Dialects are not fixed entities with clearly defined labels. Even Standard English, which is ideally regionally neutral, shows considerable internal variation. There are, for instance, regional variants (such as NZ and OZ Standard English, the focus of this book).
- The dominant or prestige dialect is Standard English. It's used and understood by writers and speakers all over the world. Standard English can be identified by its grammar, vocabulary, spelling, and punctuation, but can be spoken with a wide variety of accents.
- Standard English tends to be spoken by the educated and those higher up the social scale. It's also the variety codified in grammars and dictionaries, and used by important social institutions (government, education, and the media). While

it's generally considered the variety with the greatest prestige, this doesn't mean it's linguistically superior.

- Many speakers are unfairly discriminated against, both consciously and unconsciously, for using non-standard dialects and low-status accents.
- Non-standard is not substandard. Forms that conflict with the standard are not mistakes of English grammar but form part of a speaker's linguistic repertoire. Any non-standard English variety has its own particular rules, and has the same potential for complexity and richness of expression as a standard variety.

EXERCISES

1 Dialects and standards

The following dialogue is an example of dialectal forms found in rural Tasmania. It illustrates variations in the grammar of English that we can categorise as non-standard. Rewrite the passage in standard written English. Compare the two pieces and describe the differences. Which constructions would you classify as non-standard? Also identify any constructions that you are familiar with, and say whether or not you find them 'acceptable' usage.

Speaker 1 Bill's bachin' there in the camp
and 'e went an' cut 'imself a big, Dagwood sandwich...
and Bill...made the mistake of putting 'is sandwich down
and that old Shep of Leppet's, that one-eyed dog 'e used to have
...'e comes up and 'e grabs...Bill's Dagwood.
...and Shep's o'course 'e's a cunning old fella,
'e don't run away with it, y'see,
'e just walks off with it, y'see,
an' 'e's got this big lump—this Dagwood stickin' out each side of 'is whiskers
an' 'e's pattin' 'imself on the knee and he says
'Come on, little doggie...You've got my sandwich.'
But...the faster...old Bill walked towards 'im, y'see
the faster Shep went...
'e'da et the Dagwood if 'e'da caught it,
if 'e couda got it off the dog.
He wouldna seen anything wrong with that.
Talk about eatin' it after the dog went under the house...

Speaker 2 Y's woulda took it off 'im.

As quoted in Pawley 1995

2 Individual variation: Idiolects

In this chapter we concentrated on social and regional variation. But there's personal variation as well. None of us use language in exactly the same way. We all have our own idiolects. Make a list of some of the special ways in which your friends use language (for example, special words and pronunciation). Ask them whether you have any different ways of using language.

3 **What can we learn from graffiti?**
Gather as many examples of graffiti as you can. Discuss the linguistic aspects of the examples you find—for example, any deviation from the norms of spelling (as a guide to pronunciation); taboo words; grammatical aspects (non-standard plural and past-tense forms, for instance); language-based humour; and so on. Say which aspects of the language are manipulated to provide the humour—for example, sounds or meaning; word boundaries (as in *Be alert—your country needs more lerts*); grammar (in the case of ambiguity); or deliberate misspellings (*phallusy*, for example). You may also consider which language is used (not all graffiti are in English), choice of style, subject matter, and layout and style of writing used. You might even be able to comment on any differences you find between women's and men's graffiti.

4 **Slang**
a In schools and universities you will find that different groups and different years have their very own slang, which members use when talking together. Make a list of your own slang and explain what it means. Why do you think it is that people use slang? Are there different kinds of slang?
b The slang that you use is probably much more international and less distinctively local than, say, the slang that was used 40 or 50 years ago. Can you give examples of this? Why do you think this change has come about?

5 **Women and broadcasting**
Today we just take it for granted that there will be both female and male announcers on television and radio. But this isn't always the case. Some people still think that women's voices lack solemnity and authority. As British linguists David Graddol and Joan Swann note:

> In the media, TV and radio producers are notoriously circumspect about using women for 'serious' work, such as news bulletins. It was years before female news readers and continuity announcers were heard, and when they were, only 'suitable' voice qualities were selected. Producers play a much more active role than might be suspected in such matters. We know how difficult it can be to persuade BBC producers who make Open University programmes to let women provide commentaries or voice-overs, for example (1989:39).

Similar views have been heard in New Zealand and Australia. 'Shrill strident sibilants', 'baleful', and 'lugubrious' is how one listener describes the voices of the female newsreaders on New Zealand radio (as quoted in Gordon & Deverson 1989:86). Why do you think people have these opinions? Do you agree that women's voices lack solemnity and authority?

6 **Nice girls don't talk dirty**
There is a strong stereotype that men swear, and that women are polite and typically do not use swearing and abusive language. Your task is to investigate this assumption. (If you are interested, see Risch 1987.)

a Do women have terms to refer to men in a derogatory fashion? Survey ten women about the derogatory terms that they themselves use and those that they have heard others use in reference to men. Present each 'volunteer' with a questionnaire along the lines of:

Foul language has long been considered the domain of men, and men have at their disposal an abundance of derogatory terms for referring to women (for example, *broad, chick, skirt, piece of...,* and so on). Can you think of any similar terms or phrases that you or your friends use to refer to males?

Terms that you yourself use:

Terms that you have heard others use:

b Are there imbalances in the insulting terms for the sexes? Discuss whether you feel that there are any differences between the terms that are used in reference to women and those used in reference to men. Are the terms referring to women more derogatory? Can some terms be used for both sexes, and if so, are there any differences in meaning depending on the sex of the person referred to (for instance, compare *he's a dog* with *she's a dog*).

7 A global standard?

This is a chance to reproduce Crystal's experiment. Collect samples from as many English newspapers as you can find from countries all over the world. Make sure that you collect them all on the same day, and keep the range of topics as constant as you can. See if you can tell, on purely linguistic grounds, which paper belongs to which country. Can you find any clues about their geographical origins? On the basis of your study, what can you conclude about the possibility of a future worldwide Standard English?

8 'Occupational' dialects

To prepare for chapter 10, find an example of a particular occupational or recreational variety of written or spoken English. You could take a sample of legal English, television or press advertising, bureaucratic language, scientific English, football talk—whatever. Describe what makes it distinctive. For instance, does it have special vocabulary? Do you notice anything unusual about the grammatical structure? If it's spoken, are there any special features of pronunciation (for example, sports announcers will show extraordinary fluency)?

2

The Making of English

INTRODUCTION

The following sample comes from some of the earliest written material we have in English.

> Genim hundes micgean 7 muse blod meng to somne smire mid þa weartan hi gewitaþ sona aweg [Take dog's urine, and a mouse's blood, mingle together, smear the warts therewith, they will soon depart away]
>
> Tenth-century cure for warts, as quoted in Cockayne 1865

There is no doubt that English has changed (and wart remedies too). The further we go back in time, the stranger the language appears to us.

English has been changing throughout its lifetime, and it's still changing today. Paradoxically, we can be curious about word origins and the stories behind the structures we find in our language, but we experience a queasy distaste for any change that might be happening right under our noses. There's kind of double-think involved here. Even some language critics are convinced that English is dying, or if not dying, at least being progressively crippled through long years of mistreatment.

As we begin this chapter, we want to emphasise, with fanfare and with trumpet blast, that flux and variance are natural and inevitable features of any language. The only languages that don't change are dead ones. With 350 million first-language-speakers and about the same number of second-language-speakers, English is well and truly alive; the future has never looked so good.

In this chapter we offer you snippets from the history of English, focusing on those developments that have done most to shape the language. In order to understand what sort of a language it is, you have to understand what sort of language it has been. We'll also be considering how English fits in with the rest of its family. We trace its origins as a Germanic language and follow its development from Old through Early Modern English to the establishment of the standard language in the eighteenth century. But let's begin with the general concept of genetic relationship and see how English got stuck with the relatives it has.

DETERMINING GENETIC RELATIONSHIP: WHO'S RELATED TO WHO(M)?

Compare the following versions of a split pea soup recipe given in Modern English, Modern Dutch, and Modern German. Compare sets of words such as *soup/soep/Suppe*, *pound/pond/Pfund, milk/melk/Milch, water/water/Wasser, white pepper/witte peper/ weisser Pfeffer*, and so on. (Note that all German nouns have initial capital letters.) Compare whole clauses such as *cook them in the same water with the pork hocks*; *kook ze in hetzelfde water met de varkenskluiven*; and *koch sie in demselben Wasser mit den Schweinshaxen*. Even without knowing the other two languages, the similarities in vocabulary and grammar between the three languages leap out at you.

Pea soup	*Erwtensoep*	*Erbsensuppe*
1 pound split peas	1 pond spliterwten	1 Pfund getrocknete Erbsen
20 cups water	20 kopjes water	20 Tassen Wasser
2 tablespoons milk	2 eetlepels melk	2 Esslöffel Milch
2 pork hocks	2 varkenskluiven	2 Schweinshaxen
4 onions	4 uien	4 Zwiebeln
3 or 4 leeks	3 of 4 preien	3–4 Lauche
3 large carrots	3 grote wortelen	3 grosse Wurzeln
1 bunch celery	1 bos selderij	1 Bund Sellerie
½ pound smoked sausage	½ pond gerookte worst	½ Pfund geräucherte Wurst
2 teaspoons salt	2 theelepels zout	2 Teelöffel Salz
white pepper	witte peper	weisser Pfeffer
1 pinch curry	1 snuifje kerrie	1 Prise Currypulver
Soak the peas one night and cook them in the same water with the pork hocks, the salt, the pepper, the milk, the curry, the carrots, the chopped celery and the leeks. Stir now and then, cook till the soup becomes thick and the meat falls off the bones. Cook the sausage for a half an hour in with the soup.	Week de erwten een nacht en kook ze in het-zelfde water met de varkens-kluiven, het zout, de peper, de melk, de kerrie, de wortelen, de gesneden selderie en de preien. Roer af en toe, kook tot de soep dik wordt en het vlees van de beenderen valt. Kook de worst een half uur in de soep mee.	Weich die Erbsen eine Nacht ein und koch sie in demselben Wasser mit den Schweinshaxen, dem Salz, dem Pfeffer, der Milch, dem Curry, den Wurzeln, dem geschnitte-nen Sellerie und den Lauchen. Rühr ab und zu, koch bis die Suppe dick wird und das Fleisch von den Knochen fällt. Koch die Wurst eine halbe Stunde in der Suppe mit.

Original Dutch recipe supplied by Eve Oakley; translated and adapted by K. Burridge.

Of course none of these resemblances are coincidental. English, Dutch, and German are all closely related languages. Their striking similarity is because they share a common ancestor—a parent language or **proto-language** (*proto* means 'original' or 'first'). In this case, the parent is **Proto-Germanic**. It must have developed shortly before the Christian era, but unfortunately we have no written evidence of it. Either no one was writing during this time or, if they were, nothing survived of it.

Let's go back in time. Here's a comparable recipe from the fifteenth century. It describes how to make cherry pottage (one of the hundreds of mushy porridge-like dishes from this period). You'll notice the recipe is non-committal about amounts required; cooks at this time would have been scornful of our modern obsession with exact quantities. We've tried to make the Modern English translation closely follow the original English; so don't be surprised if it reads a little oddly.

> Tak cheryes and do out the stones and grynde hem wel and draw hem thorw a streynour and do it in a pot. And do therto swete botere and wyte bred, and cast therto good wyn, sugre, and salt and stere it wel togedere, and set theryn clowe gilofre and strew sugre aboue, and serue it forth.
> [Take cherries and take out the stones and grind them well and draw them through a strainer and put it in a pot. And add thereto sweet butter and white bread, and add thereto good wine, sugar, and salt and stir it well together, and set therein cloves and strew sugar on top, and serve it up.]
>
> Based on Black 1992:78

As speakers of Modern English, you might initially have found this piece difficult to understand. The language is medieval English, or **Middle English**. Just this simple recipe is enough to show you the enormous changes that have taken place during the last 500 years.

Below we've given a medieval Dutch version of the same recipe alongside the medieval English. As you can see, the languages were even closer at this time.

Neemt kersen ende doet die steen uut ende grynde se wel ende slaet se door enen stromijn ende doet se in eenen pot. Ende doet daertoe soete boter ende witte broot, ende doet daerto goeden wijn, suker, ende sout, ende roert se wel tesamen, ende set daerin groffel nagelen ende stroiter suker op, ende dient se op.	Tak cheryes and do out the stones and grynde hem wel and draw hem thorw a streynour and do it in a pot. And do therto swete botere and wyte bred, and do therto good wyn, sugre, and salt, and stere it wel togedere, and set theryn gilofre clowe and strew sugre aboue, and serue it forth.

Adapted from recipes in Black 1992; Cockx-indestege 1971

Through ordinary processes of language change, a single language can split into dialects and ultimately into distinct languages. Over time, Proto-Germanic did exactly this; eventually it diverged into English, Dutch, and German. Because there is less time-depth separating medieval Dutch and English, the languages have had less time to diverge—hence the more striking similarities between the two. As you turn the clock back, you undo the changes and the closer languages become. Go back another thousand years and they'd be just varieties of the same language.

Let's do just that; let's go back a thousand years to the English we now call '**Old English**' or '**Anglo-Saxon**'. There are no pottage recipes from this time (in fact, there are no cookery books at all). Instead we offer two delicious suggestions from one of the famous physicians of the tenth century. These are among the many extraordinary 'health' recipes from the leech books of this period.

But first we need to point out a few things about the Old English script. The symbol 7 was used in manuscripts at this time for 'and', much like & is used today. We've modernised the alphabet except for two of the runic symbols: *þ* (thorn), representing 'th' sounds, and æ (ash), representing something like the vowel sound in the word *ash.* (Again we've made the Modern English translation follow the original fairly closely.)

> Nim henne æg gnid on ealu hreaw 7 sceapes tord niwe swa he nyte sele hem drincan godne scenc fulne

[Take a hen's egg, rub it up raw into ale, and a sheep's turd new, so that he doesn't know, give the person a good cup full to drink]

Recipe from Cockayne 1865

Bærn swealwan to duste 7 meng wiþ feldbeon hunig sele him etan gelome
[Burn a swallow to dust, and mix with field bees' honey; give that to the person to eat frequently]

Recipe from Cockayne 1865

Small wonder the first recipe advises not telling the man what he's eating. The remarkable ingredients aside, there's probably very little of these recipes you could actually follow. As English was handed down to each successive generation, so more and more changes crept in: new words were added; new pronunciations appeared; and new grammatical structures emerged. About forty generations of speakers have gone by since these recipes were written down, and the original language doesn't even look English any more.

Unfortunately, we have no written Old Dutch to compare here. Well that's not strictly true; one sentence of original Old Dutch has survived today. Scribbled in the margins of a Latin manuscript sometime during the eleventh century (we like to imagine by a lovesick scribe), it reads:

Hebban olla uogola nestas bigunnan hinase hic eende thu uuat unbindan uue nu
[All birds have begun nests except me and you; what are we waiting for now?]

—not a bad line, even by today's standards. Dutch texts only start to appear during the Middle Ages. But we can deduce that a thousand years ago the languages were so close that they would have been mutually understandable; in other words, if the scribe's intention had indeed been to put the hard word on someone, then the proposal would have been well understood had the intended lover been Dutch or English.

But let's continue with this question of genetic relationship. How can we justify the claim that certain languages are related while others are not? Have a look at the Modern Latvian version of the pea soup recipe given earlier.

Zirņu zupa
1 mārciņa skaldetie zirņi
20 krūzes ūdens
2 ēdamkarotes piens
2 cūkas kājas
4 sīpoli
3–4 puravi
3 lieli burkāni
1 bunte selerija
½ mārciņa žāvēta desa
2 tejkarotes sāls
baltie pipari
naža gals karija pūders
Zirņus izmērcē vienu nakti un vāra tanī pašā ūdenī ar cūkas kājām, sāli, pipariem, pienu, kariju, burkāniem un sakapātu seleriju un puraviem. Pa bri-

žam apmaisot, vāra kamēr zupa paliek bieza un gaļa atdalās no kauliem.
Žāvetu desu vāra zupā pus stundu.

It might surprise you to learn that Latvian is also a relative of English. Close scrutiny (and considerable phonological imagination) might reveal some similarities, like the words for 'salt', 'pepper', and 'celery'. But on the surface there's nothing familiar-looking about it at all. The reason it looks so strange is that it's a more distant relative than Dutch. There's a much greater time-depth separating English and Latvian, and more changes have crept in. We can show this as follows:

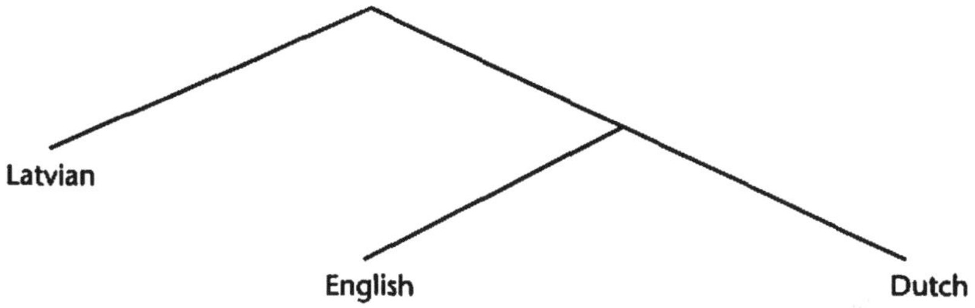

Sound correspondences

What confirms the fact that languages are genetically linked are not only the similarities (which, of course, in the case of Latvian aren't all that apparent anyway) but also, more importantly, the existence of systematic differences. We'll show you what we mean with a simple example. Below we've taken a number of words from the pea soup recipes given earlier.

English	*Dutch*	*German*
white	witte	weiss
water	water	Wasser
cook	kook	koch
milk	melk	Milch
pepper	peper	Pfeffer
pound	pond	Pfund

What's very exciting about this group of words are the systematic differences (which are in bold). German *ss* corresponds to Dutch and English *t*; German *k* (at the beginning of words) and *ch* (elsewhere) corresponds to Dutch and English *k*; German *pf* (at the beginning of words) and *f* (elsewhere) corresponds to Dutch and English *p*. These are **sound correspondences**. Those of you who have learnt either Dutch or German have probably already figured out many of these correspondences for yourselves; they can be useful when it comes to learning vocabulary.

The only way we can account for systematic differences of this kind is to assume that these words are connected historically and that they have evolved from a common source. We call these related words '**cognates**'. *Cognate* means 'sharing an ancestor'. In fact, we have a good idea of what the ancestral words looked like. On the basis of many more of these sorts of correspondence sets, we can work out the sound changes that have taken place. We can even reconstruct the items themselves;

for example, *white* and *water* go back to earlier **hwīt* and **watar*. (We use an asterisk here to signal that the forms are reconstructed.) In a discipline called 'historical linguistics', you learn techniques for reconstructing proto-vocabulary in this way. For the moment, though, you'll just have to accept the forms on faith.

It's because sound change is orderly that we are able to reconstruct ancestral stages of languages in this way. If sound change weren't regular—if sounds could change willy-nilly into other sounds—we would have trouble even establishing genetic relationship.

Hunting for cognates

Just a quick note about cognates: if you are seriously going about the business of collecting the cognates of languages that you suspect are genetically related, it does require a fair amount of sleuth work. Take a very simple example from our illustrative text here: the humble pea soup recipe. English has the word *carrots*; German has *Wurzeln*, and Dutch has *wortelen*. Even with the greatest phonological imagination, it seems unlikely that *carrots* is cognate with the German and Dutch words. So this example is no help to our investigation and would have to be weeded out, along with other obvious non-cognates.

The question is: does an English cognate exist for *Wurzeln/wortelen*? A little detective work will uncover the rare English word *wort*, a kind of plant used in medicine (often the second element in plant names like *butterwort*). It therefore shares an element of meaning with the other two (the idea of 'root') and is indeed a cognate.

During your investigation you need also to be wary of imposters such as the English *mangel-wurzel*, a kind of beetroot fed to cattle. The *wurzel* bit looks cognate, but it is in fact borrowed from German.

Cognates or a question of chance

How can we be sure that our correspondences above are really the result of a shared history and not the result of borrowing, like the *wurzel* example just given? We know that languages borrow words from each other. In fact, English is one of the greatest filchers of all time when it comes to other languages' vocabulary. But borrowing is unlikely here. First, we're dealing with huge numbers of words, not just the small handful we've given here. Second, they are common-usage words. Languages will borrow if they need expressions for new concepts; but why borrow terms for basic ingredients such as milk, water, and pepper?

If it's not borrowing that causes these correspondences, could they be the result of chance? This isn't likely either. Because words are symbols, this means that the relationship between their sound and their meaning is totally arbitrary. In other words, there is no natural connection between the physical make-up of a word like *rose* and its meaning 'beautiful fragrant flower'; as Shakespeare wrote in *Romeo and Juliet*, 'that which we call a rose / By any other name would smell as sweet'. Bearing this in mind, then, when we come across sets of words like those above, what are the chances that speakers of these languages will independently arrive at the same arrangements of sounds to represent each item? These sets of words permeate the entire vocabulary of these languages; there are literally hundreds of them showing similar systematic correspondences. This could not be accidental.

But what about sound symbolism? A rooster's crow will come out remarkably similarly across the languages of the world. In English they go *cockadoodledoo* and in Japanese *kokekokko*. Certainly there are echoic words of this sort, but they're largely limited to imitations of natural sounds; even then, many of them are just as conventional as ordinary words. (English pigs go *oink oink*, and Japanese pigs go *boo-boo*—so much for imitation!) Calls of nature aside, then, when we encounter sound correspondences between languages, no matter how slight they are, we have no choice but to assume they are the result of a shared history.

The Proto-Indo-European language family

The concept of genetic relatedness between languages had been bandied about for a long time, but it really wasn't until the middle of the eighteenth century that the idea properly took off. During a famous lecture in 1786, Sir William Jones argued that Sanskrit, Ancient Greek, and Latin were related and could be traced back to some 'common source, which, perhaps, no longer exists' (as quoted in Crowley 1997:22). Jones was arguing for Proto-Indo-European, the parent of most of the languages of Europe, south-western Asia and northern India. It's a little unfair to give all the credit to Jones here, but it's certainly true that, up until then, most scholars spent their time arguing that one of the existing classical languages was the parent. It was Jones who helped to advance the idea of a proto- or ancestral language that no longer exists. Proto-Indo-European has left us no written records, because writing hadn't been invented then. But we know that it must have existed because of the regular correspondences between the sound systems of these languages. It's assumed to have been spoken sometime around 3000 BC.

Jones's ideas were enthusiastically taken up by other scholars, and before long the systematic study of language evolution was undertaken for the first time. The work carried out by European linguists during the nineteenth century led to the classification of all the Indo-European languages into the sort of genealogical tree shown in Figure 2.1. As you can see, all the modern Germanic languages represent the diverse continuation of Proto-Germanic, and if you follow the bold line, you can trace the development of English through to modern times. In the next section, we examine exactly how the Germanic languages evolved from their prehistoric parent, Proto-Indo-European.

SNIPPETS FROM THE HISTORY OF ENGLISH

Ancestral snippets from the history of English

Let's imagine the sorts of conditions that would have given rise to the Germanic group of languages. For some reason, around 1500 BC the Germanic group left the Indo-European homeland. Who knows why: disputes perhaps, or maybe just an adventurous spirit. All languages change, but when they're in different places, they don't have to change the same way. What happened here was that the Germanic

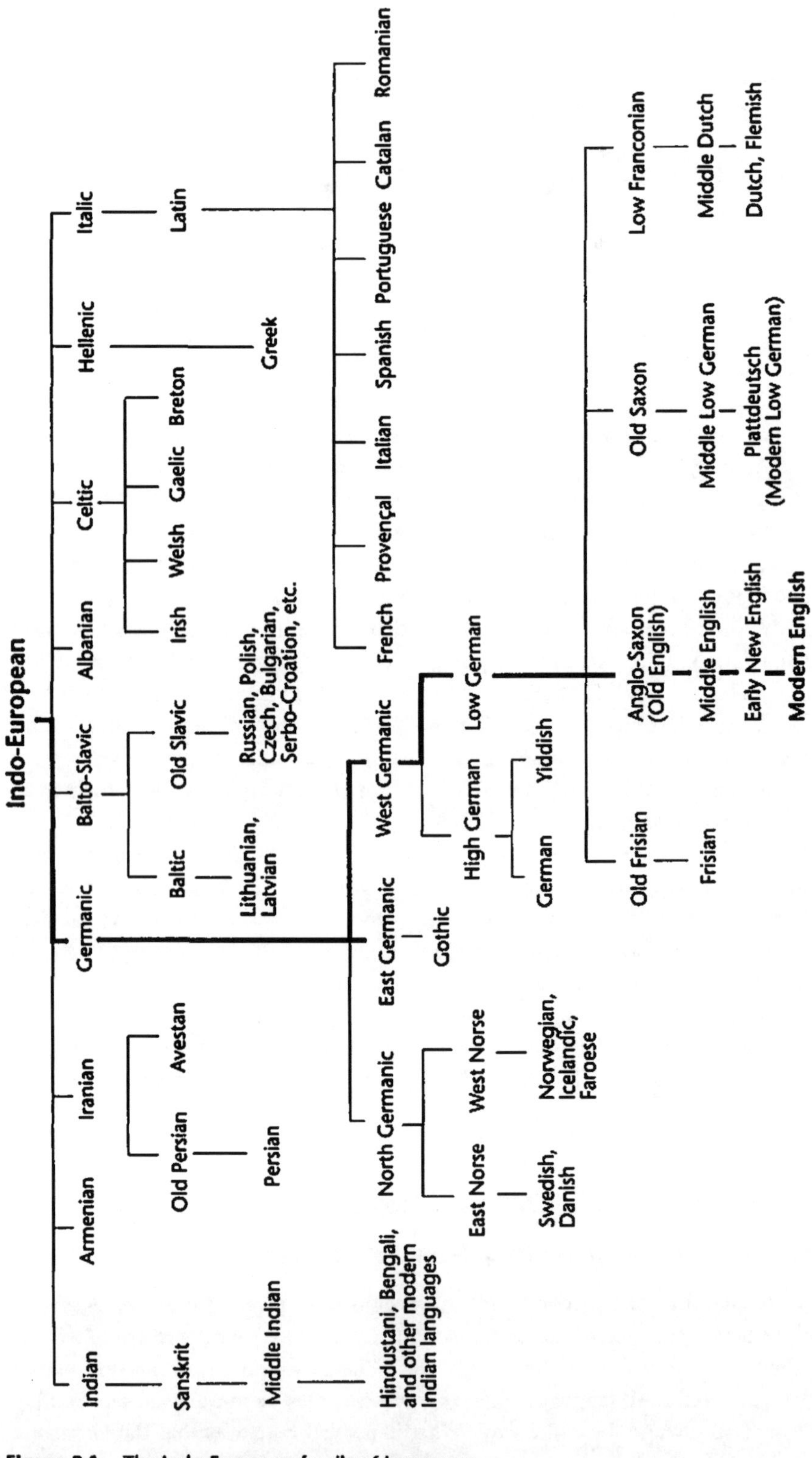

Source: Adapted from Myers & Hoffman 1979:46.

Figure 2.1 The Indo-European family of languages

group developed a number of distinctive characteristics, which then set it apart from the other Indo-European groups. The most significant of these Germanic innovations was something we now know as the **'First Germanic Consonant Shift'** (or **'Grimm's Law'**, after one of the famous brothers Grimm). The following is a basic description of what happened (the phonetic details are explained in chapter 3). Remember that these consonant shifts occurred before Germanic split up into all the different branches. They are what served to make Germanic distinct from the other Indo-European languages.

Proto-Indo-European		*Germanic*
(voiceless stops) p, t, k	*became*	(voiceless fricatives) f, θ, x(h)
(voiced stops) b, d, g	*became*	(voiceless stops) p, t, k
(breathy voiced stops) bh, dh, gh	*became*	(voiced stops) b, d, g

Table 2.1 shows some cognates from Latin, Sanskrit, and Old English to illustrate these innovations. The Latin and Sanskrit represent the original sounds; the Old English represents the Germanic innovations. The sound correspondences are given each time in bold, and the ancestral phonemes from which they derive are given in the first column. As you can see, the beginnings of words are more stable than the ends of words, and they generally provide better clues for establishing genetic relationship.

Table 2.1 Latin, Old English, and Sanskrit cognates

Proto	*Latin*		*Old English*	
*p	piscis	'fish'	fisc	
*t	trēs	'three'	thrēo	
*k	cord	'heart'	heorte	
*b	bursa	'purse'	pursa	
*d	dent-	'tooth'	tōth	
*g	genus	'race'	cynn	'kin'
	Sanskrit		*Old English*	
*bh	bhára-mi	'I carry'	beran	'bear'
*dh	bándhanam		bindan	'bind'
*gh	ghánti	'he strikes'	gūth	'battle'

There were many more sound changes than just the ones represented here. There were many grammatical changes too. For example, Germanic developed it own class of verbs that indicated past with some sort of dental suffix, as in English *chew–chewed*. With time and more and more changes, Germanic eventually split off from Indo-European. As we mentioned earlier, the combination of time, geographical separation, and the processes of change can cause a single language to ultimately split into a number of distinct languages.

After Germanic split off from Indo-European, the number of speakers increased in size. And as the language spread geographically, it changed in different ways in the different parts of Europe, giving the three main branches you can see in Figure 2.1: North, East, and West Germanic. North Germanic is the parent of the modern Scandinavian languages (except Finnish, which isn't Indo-European at all). East

Germanic is the parent of Gothic and its descendent Crimean Gothic (both long dead). West Germanic underwent a number of additional splits, eventually sprouting all the modern groupings you can see in Figure 2.1.

English didn't come into its own until the middle of the fifth century, when it was brought across to the British Isles by various Germanic tribes (the infamous Angles, Saxons, and Jutes). During the following five centuries it developed into an independent language, distinct from any of its Germanic relatives spoken on the Continent.

To illustrate the sorts of changes that inspired the splits within West Germanic, let's return for a moment to the different versions of the pea soup recipe given earlier. On the basis of just a few words from these recipes, we established the sound correspondences shown in Table 2.2. These represent part of a series of changes known as the **'Second Germanic Consonant Shift'** (Grimm's Law was the first). Here the English and Dutch consonants represent the earlier sounds. German is the innovator. At some stage during the medieval period, the High German spoken in the southern part of Germany distinguished itself by undergoing a number of consonant shifts, and these, together with changes elsewhere in the language, had the effect of splitting if off from the rest. English escaped these particular consonant shifts because it had already migrated to Britain by this time; the other West Germanic languages (Dutch, Flemish, and Frisian) were north of the area where the changes took place.

Table 2.2 Second Germanic Consonant Shift

English	*Dutch*	*German*
t	t	ss
k	k	k (initially) / ch
p	p	pf (initially) / ff

More snippets from the later history of English

With the exception of a few inscriptions from the fifth and sixth centuries, our earliest evidence of English dates from the eighth century. Most of the extant texts, however, are later: from the tenth and eleventh centuries. The gripping tale of *Beowulf* is the earliest piece of literature—the surviving manuscript is dated around AD 1000, but the language is probably earlier, from around AD 750. Books during this period were enormous, heavy, and prodigiously expensive items, costing (according to one estimate at the time) roughly the equivalent of a ship. Pages were made from animal hides with very elaborate binding, and everything, of course, was written by hand. Needless to say, the reading audience was small, largely confined to the religious educated elite. Dating the language in manuscripts can be difficult. Even if we had knowledge of the authors (which we usually don't), it's likely that plagiarism and paraphrasing figure strongly in the works handed down to us; there's always the lingering possibility that a text is, in fact, a copy of an earlier work that has since been lost.

You can see in Figure 2.1 that linguists have identified various stages in the development of English: Old English or Anglo-Saxon (450–1100); Middle English (1100–1500); Early New English (1500–1800). We should stress that stages such as these are arbitrary. They don't always correspond to significant linguistic developments. For example, the start of Early New English, according to some scholars, is earlier than we've stated here. They argue that it should coincide with the death of Chaucer and the beginning of some major sound changes in the language (see, for example, Strang 1974:ch.3 and discussion in Crystal 1995:56). We prefer a later date, however—one that coincides with the advent of printing (see below). Determining the end of the Early New English period is more straightforward. Since the language after 1800 doesn't present any real difficulties for modern readers (think of Jane Austen's novels), it seems appropriate to make this the start of Modern English.

Clearly what we're really dealing with here is a continuum, and the dates for so-called 'Old, Middle, and Early New English' are just convenient labels for describing the language. If we had the benefit of a time machine and could arrange a get-together of English-speakers from, say, the fifteenth and sixteenth centuries—so-called 'Middle English-' and 'Early New English-speakers'—the differences in their speech wouldn't be any more remarkable than those that we witness today between older speakers and teenagers.

You will find some texts describe Old English as a dead language. Now languages can certainly die; perhaps the speakers are killed (as in the case of Tasmanian Aboriginal languages), or perhaps they simply give up speaking the language in favour of another (as in the case of Manx and Cornish). But obviously Old English didn't die; it just evolved.

WHEN DO DIALECTS BECOME LANGUAGES?

We want to make a small detour in the discussion here and talk about when a **dialect** becomes a **language**. The difference between related languages and dialects of one language is very unclear, and linguists often disagree about where to draw the line. We've been suggesting here that if the differences between dialects become great enough—or, more particularly, when speakers stop understanding one another—then we have separate languages. But let's think about this some more.

Mutual intelligibility is not always easy to determine. For a start, how do we approach English in its various stages? On the one hand, we can think of Old, Middle, and Modern English as one language. But on the basis of mutual intelligibility, we have at least two, perhaps even three, languages.

Furthermore, it's possible for varieties to merge with one another to produce a kind of cline or continuum of variation. As we'll see in chapter 12, 'Aboriginal English' involves such a cline, ranging from, at one end, varieties that are no different from English elsewhere in Australia (except perhaps in accent) to, at the other end, those that are not mutually comprehensible.

There are geographical clines too (sometimes called '**dialect chains**'). Here speakers in closely situated speech communities can understand one another (perhaps they live in neighbouring villages), but speakers located at the geographical extremes of these chains cannot. You can find examples of dialect chains stretching across Europe. Near the German and Dutch border, for instance, German-speakers using their own 'home-grown' varieties can communicate better with neighbouring Dutch-speakers than with German-speakers in the south of Germany, who speak southern varieties of German. So where does German end and Dutch begin? There's so much variance and indeterminacy here that any attempt at dividing up such a continuum on the basis of purely linguistic criteria (like mutual intelligibility) is problematic.

We hit other problems too, because notions such as language and dialect are not exclusively linguistic. Just as relevant are extra-linguistic factors, and these can include a range of different geographical, political, and socio-historical concerns; all are interrelated and none are immune to change. For example, language differences are an important part of what distinguishes one nation from another, and over time it's possible for national frontiers to become linguistic frontiers. This means that some varieties will be thought of as separate languages simply because they come to be spoken in different countries. For example, we think of Norwegian-speakers and Swedish-speakers as using separate languages, and yet they can understand each another. Conversely, we think of Mandarin and Cantonese as one language—Chinese—because they're spoken in the same country and use the same writing system, and yet they're not mutually intelligible.

Mutual intelligibility is not always a linguistic concern either. For example, the small North Frisian dialect area in western Germany divides into a number of individual village varieties, which are by reputation mutually incomprehensible. The recent pro-Frisian language movement, however, appears to be overcoming this diversity. Suddenly Frisian-speakers from these different villages can understand one another; it seems that psychological factors such as motivation and solidarity can encourage comprehension.

While recognising these exceptions to the rule, we'll draw the traditional distinction here: dialects are mutually comprehensible, whereas languages are not. Just remember that individual labels such as German, Dutch, and English give the impression of easily identifiable and neatly compartmentalised entities, but such tidy classifications are not necessarily the reality.

THE DEVELOPMENT OF STANDARD ENGLISH

In chapter 1 we first introduced the notion of Standard English. Before we offer you a potted account of its development, here are some of its most important characteristics:

- Standard English is a variety without a home. Anyone can speak it, no matter where they live.
- It's the variety promoted in schools, recorded in dictionaries, style guides, and grammars, and used in law courts, government institutions, and the media. For all these reasons, it has a lot more social clout than other varieties.
- Standard English is more uniform in writing. All over the world, people are writing in Standard English, and there's very little variation. People speak it too, but because of the nature of speech, there is always more variation.
- Standard English is a variety that involves vocabulary and grammar, but not pronunciation; it can be spoken with any accent.

Standard English is a recent arrival on the scene. From the Old English period to the end of the Middle English period, the English language existed without very much attention paid to it at all. It wasn't until well into the sixteenth century that a standard emerged, but even then it took several centuries to stabilise.

The beginning: Old English

During the Old English period, the country was divided into seven kingdoms: Kent, Essex, Wessex, Sussex, East Anglia, Mercia, and Northumbria. And there were four principal dialects (although dialect differences at this time would have been slight): Kentish, Mercian, Northumbrian, and West Saxon. There may have been more, but no documentation survives. Most of the extant manuscripts are in the West Saxon dialect, and consequently it's this dialect that is the basis of our current grammatical descriptions of Old English. West Saxon came very close to being a literary standard at this time. There was even some normative activity going on, with traditional West Saxon spelling conventions gaining ground. This is not, however, the predecessor of our modern standard. Mercian, as it turns out, happened to be the dialect in the right place at the right time.

The unfolding: Middle English

The four major dialects of Middle English developed out of the earlier Old English divisions: Northumbrian became the Northern dialect; Mercian became the Midlands dialect (comprising East and West Midland); West Saxon became the Southern dialect (south of the Thames); Kentish retained its name.

As we just discussed, Old English West Saxon looked ripe for standardisation, but its career was interrupted by the arrival of the French in 1066. For several centuries after the Norman Conquest, English was well and truly under the Norman French thumb. The prestige languages were French and Latin, and these were what people typically wrote in. And when writers eventually abandoned French and wrote in English again, they wrote in their local variety, using their own home-grown forms and spellings. West Saxon had lost its edge. French scribes ignored traditional English conventions, and spelt the language much as they heard it. They also introduced a number of their own conventions, giving the language a new look. But there was no single prestige model that people were under pressure to follow. There were no dictionaries, no grammars, and no spelling books, and variation was rampant. People's attitude to English also revealed that it was a long way off being standardised. For example, they still didn't consider it respectable enough for serious literature and continued to use Latin for this.

To give you a brief idea of the diversity in this period, have a look at the following variant spellings. These all come from the earliest cookery manuscripts in English (fourteenth century) (as reproduced in Hieatt & Butler 1985:1).

coneys	'rabbits'	connynges, conynges, conyngs, connynges, conynggys, conyes, conynggis
cranes		cranys, cranes, crunes
crustards	'open tarts'	crustardes, crustedes, crostudes
frumenty	'another pottage'	furmenty, frumente, formenty, furmente, formete, furmynte
ginger		gyngeuer, gyngyuyr, genger, gynger, gyngere, ginge, gyngeuyr, gyngyuer, ginger

Some of this variation is scribal, but a lot is dialectal too. Manuscripts of this time often show a mixture of different dialect forms. For instance, although this particular manuscript is basically in the dialect of the south-west Midlands, it also contains a smattering of northern features, such as *ane* for *one*, *qw* for *wh*, and *egges* in place of *eyren* 'eggs', as well as some south-eastern features, such as *z* for *s*.

By the late Middle English period, however, regional variation of this type was becoming less common as the dialect in and around London started to move to centre stage. Because of the influx of different dialect-speakers to the big city, London English was itself a kind of dialectal hybrid. Basically it was Southern, but with a strong East Midlands flavour. Some Modern English words reflect this mixture: *busy* has a London pronunciation ('bizzy') and *bury* a Kentish pronunciation ('berry'), but the spelling is West Midland.

The 'success' of the London dialect was not because of any linguistic advantage it had over the other players. It was not a conscious choice. When varieties come to dominate in this way, it is never for linguistic reasons. London English piggybacked on a series of geographical, cultural, economic and political episodes. These had the effect of putting it in such a position that standardisation was inevitable. Here are some of the main events:

- The emergence of London as a political and commercial centre, and as the seat of the court and the judiciary, meant that huge amounts of manuscript copying was already coming out of this area.
- Chaucer's literary genius helped give prestige to the London dialect, as did London's proximity to the major universities of Oxford and Cambridge.
- London was at the heart of a rich agricultural area and a growing wool trade.
- In one sense, London English did have an advantage over its rivals. In terms of the three main dialects, London English was both geographically and linguistically midway between the two dialect extremes: Northern and Southern. It was a natural compromise.
- When William Caxton set up the first printing presses in 1476, he did so in Westminster in London, thus pushing London English even more into the limelight. Books could be reproduced at a fraction of their former cost, and in the course of the next 150 years, something like 20 000 publications appeared—all in London English.

The golden age of prescription: Early New English

A sure sign that standardisation was well under way was the fact that people suddenly started to talk about their language in a different (more moralistic and judgmental) fashion. Certainly people had been making judgments about other people's speech for centuries. For example, observations about regional diversity (mostly disparaging comments about rural speech) were commonplace. But at the beginning of the sixteenth century, there suddenly appeared a real vocabulary of abuse, of the type that you find in complaint literature today. On the one hand, there was the right sort of language (described as 'pure', 'true', 'natural') and, on the other hand, the wrong kind of language (described as 'corrupt', 'foul', 'false'). These labels hint at the idea of an approved standard; to stray away from it was to stray from what was pure and good.

But we're still not at the point at which we can talk of an identifiable Standard English. For a start, English still lacked the support of reference books such as grammars and dictionaries. In other words, it was not yet codified. And although printers such as Caxton had a normative influence (by promoting certain usages), spelling and punctuation remained inconsistent for some time yet. Printers in those times had to justify their lines, and variant spellings were extremely handy for this.

To give you some idea of the variation that persisted, consider some language samples from etiquette manuals at this time. As you can see, the problem of how to pick one's teeth in a genteel fashion was a hot topic in these handbooks. (While you're trying to imagine a society without dictionaries and grammars, you might also try to imagine a society without toothpicks or dental floss. The arrival of the toothpick at the dinner table was probably as welcome as the first reference work on English; they actually roughly coincided.)

Thi teth also thow pike nat with no knyf
þy tethe be no pikynge, grisynge [grinding], ne gnastynge [gnashing]
Noþur at þy mete þy toth þou pyke
þi teeþ also at þe table picke with no knyf
Pyke not þi tethe with thy knyfe
Ny at þe mete þy toþe þou pyke
Pick not thy teeth with thy Knyfe
Pycke not thy tethe with thy knyfe nor fynger end

Based on etiquette texts in Furnivall 1868

As you can see, creative spelling continued to thrive. For the two simple words *pick* and *teeth*, we find the following variant spellings: *pyke*, *pycke*, *pike*, *picke*, *pick* and *tethe*, *teth*, *teeþ*, *teeth*. People didn't even agree on the alphabet. Around this time, the Old English symbol *þ* (thorn) was in the process of being replaced by *th*, but there was much inconsistency. Even personal names showed variation. William Shakespeare's signatures are variously spelt *Shakspere*, *Shaksper*, and *Shakspeare*. Other versions at the time include *Shagspere*, *Shackespere*, *Shake-speare*, and *Shakespeare*.

English was still overshadowed by the classical languages. For example, it was well into the eighteenth century before English truly ousted Latin as the language of learned and technical writing. Isaac Newton wrote some of his works in Latin: *Principia Mathematica* (1687) and *Arithmetica Universalis* (1707). In contrast to the classical languages, English seemed unregulated and unrefined. Of course these languages were written, which meant that they lacked the natural flux and variance of a living breathing language. Against these ossified linguistic paragons, it was small wonder that poor old English appeared 'copious without order, and energetick without rules' and 'perplexity to be disentangled, and confusion to be regulated' (Samuel Johnson in the preface to his dictionary, as reproduced in Bolton 1966:130).

The cry went out for an academy to do some regulating, polishing, and refining, and to stop the language from slipping into further decline. Writers fretted that if they couldn't stop the changes, their works would not be understood by future generations. Italy and France had their academies; English looked even more unruly without one.

The eighteenth century became the high water mark of authoritarianism. In 1755, Samuel Johnson published the first complete dictionary of English. His intentions were perfectly clear: to rid the language, as he put it, of 'barbarous corruptions', 'licentious idioms' and 'colloquial barbarisms' (*The Rambler*, 15 January 1752). The writer Jonathan Swift was also clear in his aim: he wanted to fix the English language forever. One of the greatest pieces of complaint literature is his *Proposal for Correcting, Improving and Ascertaining the English Tongue* (1712, as reproduced in Bolton 1966:107–23). He was one of the greatest proponents for setting up a regulating body to 'ascertain' the language (that is, to determine correct usage and settle the English language for good).

Despite enthusiastic support for such an English Academy, nothing came of the idea. Even so, large numbers of regulating handbooks continued to appear, setting out how the language should and should not be used. Following on from Johnson's dictionary, more dictionaries were produced. And in the second half of the century, grammar books abounded. Notions of 'right' and 'wrong' became a popular topic of English grammar, and we owe many of our current prescriptions to the grammatical debates of this time. For instance, the popular abhorrence of double negatives can be traced back to one individual: Robert Lowth. His *Short Introduction to English Grammar* (1762) had a remarkable influence, probably because the time was ripe for such a book, and probably also because he was the Bishop of London (as Jean Aitchison 1991:121 suggests, perhaps people felt his grammatical insights were divinely inspired). Because of Lowth and his imitators there appeared a much stronger 'prescriptivist' approach to the language than ever before, and the effect of this is still clearly evident in attitudes and educational practices today.

THE DEVELOPMENT OF ENGLISH DOWN UNDER

The arrival of English down under

Towards the end of the eighteenth century, the population of the British Isles was only about 15 million. As many as one-third of these people spoke their own Celtic languages and little or no English. And not all the native English-speakers spoke the standard either; a good many spoke only their regional dialects, and the dialect differences could be striking. We are, after all, talking of a time when horses and sailing vessels were the most efficient means of travel and communication.

This, then, was roughly the state of the language when exploration southwards established the first English-speaking settlers in the Antipodes. For Australia, the date coincides with the arrival of Captain Cook in 1770. Over the course of the next 20 years or so, Great Britain established its first penal colony in Sydney. The first arrivals were largely prisoners, prison officers, and their families. Non-convicts, or free settlers as they were known, didn't reach significant numbers until the middle of the nineteenth century.

On the other side of the Tasman Sea, English got off to a later and somewhat slower start. Cook charted the islands at around the same time that he visited Australia, but it was almost the middle of the nineteenth century before the official colony was established. Before then the number of English-speakers in New Zealand was very small. In the second half of the century, however, immigration from Australia and the United Kingdom increased dramatically.

The rise of Antipodean accents

Much discussion has focused on the origins of OZ and NZ pronunciation, and at times the speculations have been wild. Some have maintained that these accents are caused by climate, by a national nose inflammation as a result of pollen or hay, and even by a fear of opening the mouth on account of dust and flies; other accounts look to carelessness, laziness, some kind of gross national inferiority complex, a free-wheeling and adventurous spirit, or an outlaw heritage. Even ill-fitting dentures have been suggested as a likely cause. Certainly speakers can use linguistic differences to highlight their ethnic character, but different ways of thinking and behaving are never directly related to linguistic features such as accent. Language change is not caused by ethnic character, anatomy, or climate—or even by bad dentistry. You might think these theories bizarre, but they still surface from time to time in the popular press.

As we've just seen, both Australia and New Zealand have a relatively recent history of European settlement in common, and both share transplanted Englishes. Currently there are two basic schools of thought regarding the relationship between the relocated accents and the dialects back in southern England. One is that they represent an amalgam of the various relocated dialects; the other is that they are basically Cockney English with a dash of the others (Gordon & Deverson 1985:17–19, in reference to the origins of the NZ accent, label these the 'mixing bowl theory' and the 'single origin theory' respectively).

The OZ accent

Many people have remarked on the geographical uniformity of the OZ accent. Although there's some socially marked variation, there's remarkably little in the way of regional variation, especially given a country that is some thirty times the size of the United Kingdom.

When dialects come together, a kind of melting pot effect is usual, and it's likely that the uniformity of OZ English grew out of a blending of the original British dialects that first came into Australia (from south-east England, Ireland, and Scotland). In a short period of time, all the different varieties spoken by convicts and free settlers underwent a general levelling process to produce what we now know as OZ English. (See Trudgill 1986:29–40.) We can look to the relative homogeneity of Canadian English (or further afield to a language such as Pennsylvania German, which is spoken in parts of North America) to see similar results from this kind of melting pot effect.

G. R Cochrane (1989) tells a different story. He argues that London English alone is the basis for the main features of the OZ accent. Certainly there are considerable similarities between OZ and London English, even in the range of social variation: the three socially relevant accents (Received Pronunciation, popular London, and Cockney) roughly correspond with cultivated, general, and broad Australian (see chapters 1 and 3). Cochrane suggests that the London accent was established early, with other influences (such as the Scottish and Irish accents) appearing later.

We'll probably never get the whole picture. In truth, both theories are compatible. We can accept that there was a London dominance, and this is reflected today in the striking congruence between London and OZ English. We can also accept that some levelling out of differences would have occurred during these early times and that this would have contributed to the overall homogeneity of the language.

There are two points that all linguists seem to agree on. First, the uniformity of the language was enhanced by the high mobility of the population during the early years. With New South Wales as the point of departure, settlement was largely by sea, and the rapid population spread meant that the language was able to remain uniform. (Compare this to the USA, where people spread out more gradually by land, producing much greater diversity.) Second, the range of socially relevant variation would have been present from the time of early settlement. In other words, both the cultivated and broad ends of the spectrum would have been transplanted to the colony. The accents of officials and clergy would have represented an early form of Received Pronunciation, the modern prestige accent, and those of the convicts would have demonstrated the low prestige features. Subsequently, the greater social mobility in Australia and the movement of linguistic features both up and down the social scale would have had the effect of bringing these two extremes closer together.

The NZ accent

Many have argued for the early dominance of London Cockney in New Zealand too. Unlike Australia, however, early immigration figures for New Zealand do not show a great influx of settlers from around London. Early settlers came from all over the British Isles, especially Scotland and Ireland, and to a lesser extent Wales. This suggests that the reports of a London English presence in New Zealand are exaggerated.

As Elizabeth Gordon and Tony Deverson (1985) argue, however, there was always a strong Australian presence, and OZ English is undoubtedly an influence here. There can be no doubt that, by the time Australians started to flood into New Zealand, an OZ accent had already become distinct. As unappealing as this might sound to New Zealanders, OZ English would have had a certain prestige for newcomers, being, as Gordon and Deverson (1985:19) neatly put it, 'the mark of the Antipodean'. Certainly there were close ties with Australia, even well before organised settlement from the United Kingdom began. And these ties were made stronger with continued immigration from Australia to New Zealand during the nineteenth century, especially to the gold-mining parts of the country.

It's likely that both the single dominance theory and the melting pot theory have something to contribute to the New Zealand question as well. If links with Australia were well established before the main influx of immigrants from the United Kingdom, it's feasible that there was time for 'colonial' children to establish their accents before the overlay of regional varieties from the different parts of the United Kingdom. The country then would have experienced an intermingling of varieties and the subsequent levelling predicted by the melting pot effect. This would account for the fact that NZ English falls linguistically somewhere in between OZ English and British English.

TO PRESCRIBE OR DESCRIBE?

Linguists in this century have tried to distance themselves from the prescriptive movement of the eighteenth and nineteenth centuries, emphasising the important distinction between a prescriptive and descriptive approach. The prescriptive approach is one that tells you how you ought to speak. Prescriptive grammar books comprise a hotchpotch of 'dos' and 'don'ts' about sentence structure, word meaning, and word usage. Much like etiquette books, which outline rules of polite behaviour, rules such as the following outline the 'best' sort of language:

- Do not use *youse.*
- Do not use *data* as a singular noun.
- Do not begin a sentence with *but.*
- Do not end a sentence with a preposition such as *to.*
- Do not use more than one negative in a sentence.
- Do not say *between you and I.*
- Do not use *impact* as a verb.
- Do not use *disinterested* to mean 'uninterested'.

On the other hand, the descriptive approach describes how we actually speak. Introductory books such as this emphasise the need for linguists to retain this sort of objectively descriptive stance. Linguistic science must found its theories on observed behaviour. To construct a theory about Modern English grammar based only on sentences such as *It is I* and *The data are misleading* would be about as sensible as constructing a theory of gravity based on the premise that only apples fall downwards. In English we encounter sentences such as *It is I* and *The data are misleading*, as well as those such as *It's me* and *The data is misleading.* Both alternatives are used, but in different contexts. Imagine saying *It is I* on the phone to a good friend. You'd be laughed at or accused of putting on airs. But there are contexts—say in a very formal piece of prose—where you might well imagine writing something like *It is I who am responsible.* Most of us would write *The data is misleading*, except perhaps in a piece of academic writing, where *data* is used as a plural with a singular *datum.*

What linguists are interested in here is which factors motivate one construction above the other—hence their attempts to replace absolute labels of prescriptive grammar, such as 'right', 'wrong', 'mistake', and 'error', with relative labels, such as 'appropriate' and 'suitable'. Language isn't absolute; it's not a matter of putting a tick or a star beside a sentence. It's much more interesting than that.

But linguists are in a tricky position here. As Deborah Cameron shows so clearly in her 1995 book *Verbal Hygiene* (chapter 3), there is no popular belief that linguistic scientists so vehemently wish to displace as the fixation on prescriptive grammar; nor is there a popular belief so resistant to their efforts at displacement—hence the current gap that exists between linguists and the wider community. The feeling is definitely one of mutual distrust, with linguistic experts refusing to address lay concerns and lay speakers showing absolutely no interest in listening to linguists. We can still recall an article in a newspaper a number of years ago in which the editor of *Verbatim*, Laurence Urdang, described linguists as 'categorically the dullest people on the face of the earth—rather than trying to present and explain information, they seem to be going in the opposite direction. They try to shield people from knowing anything useful about the language' (*Washington Post*, 13 January 1992, p. D5). Clearly something must be done to bridge this gap.

Linguists study language, just like zoologists study the physiology, anatomy, and behaviour of animals, botanists look at plants, sociologists research the nature and laws of human society, and so on. A linguist who condemns a native speaker for saying *youse* rather than *you* is a bit like a zoologist who condemns a dromedary for having two humps and not one. You can't have zoologists describing the structure of certain animals as defective. You can't have biologists denigrating certain species in the plant world simply because everyone else views them as weeds. You can't have sociologists ignoring some aspects of human society simply because others consider them deviant. And yet this is precisely the sort of activity that the wider community expects linguists to engage in.

The problem is that linguists can argue until they're blue in the face that all constructions are equally good and that change is a natural and inevitable feature of a thriving language, but popular beliefs about language are difficult to shift. Let's give you a concrete example. Some time ago, one of us suggested publicly that English would be better off if it abandoned the apostrophe to signal possession and retained it only for its other functions. As you can see from a sample letter below, the idea was not met with wild enthusiasm:

> How disappointing it is that those who direct the nature and structure of our language should be so accepting of outright errors and misuse of our language.
>
> First John Hajek, Melbourne University, and now Kate Burridge (Burrage?) of Latrobe [sic]. I should like to know why the misused and incorrect English of the ignorant, the ill-informed, the apathetic and the lazy should be acceptable? If this continues we shall have no formal structure of our language: it will become unteachable, unintelligible, and eventually, useless as an accurate means of communication. Can you imagine the French, the Italians, the Germans allowing gross abuse being acceptable to their academics.
>
> 3LO listener to Peter Clarke, 3LO 'Breakfast', pers. comm., 21 March 1996

Can we bridge the gap?

Earlier we might have given the impression that these prescriptive urges grew out of the great authoritarianism of the eighteenth century. Certainly the dictionaries and handbooks of that time gave them a much more public arena, but linguistic prescriptivism has been with us for centuries and is much more ingrained than that. It's also underpinned by much deeper social concerns. Even speakers from oral cultures with no written standard feel strongly that certain ways of saying things are better than others. Humans would have to change beyond all recognition before these urges to improve and clean up their language disappeared.

So what's really going on when people object to words and word usage in this way? The point is that it's not a language matter we're dealing with here, but more a social issue. Words and word usage carry with them a lot of social baggage, and that's typically what people are reacting to. Rules of usage such as 'don't use *impact* as a verb' don't count for much as they are; they get their meaning from their cultural and social setting. People aren't objecting to *impact* as a verb as such. It's just that it sounds like a bit of pretentious gobbledygook, and maybe they don't want to be identified with the kind of people who use that sort of jargon. Similarly, people don't care about the apostrophe as such (in fact, many of the complaint letters actually get the prescriptive rules wrong), but there is this perceived link in people's minds between bad grammar and bad behaviour. If you don't give two hoots about the placement of the apostrophe, then you're not likely to be a good person in society. It's not cleanliness that's next to godliness, but good grammar.

Take some examples from the past. Early condemnations of the English language are as commonplace and as passionate as today's. What is interesting are the sorts of things they complained about. In 1653 John Wallis railed against the use of the word *chicken* as a singular noun. In 1755, when Samuel Johnson wanted to rid the language of 'colloquial barbarisms', he was referring to the use of words such as *novel* in place of *new*, and *capture* in place of *take*. Jonathan Swift, like others at the time, complained bitterly about contemporary shortenings, such as *mob* from the Latin phrase *mobile vulgus*, and *pozz* from *positive*. Swift blamed changes such as these on the 'loose morals' of the day. But the social significance of all these usages are lost to us today, and the objections to them now seem puzzling and trivial.

As Cameron argues (rightly in our opinion), making value judgments is an integral part of using language, and 'verbal hygiene', as she calls it, forms part of every speaker's linguistic competence. By dismissing it as unworthy of attention, linguists are failing to meet their own descriptive ideals. Studying the way people like to intervene in language is crucial to a proper understanding of what human language is. This is not to say that linguists should suddenly start embracing pointless rules such as 'don't end a sentence with a preposition' and 'don't split an infinitive'. But they must make a greater contribution to public debates about English grammar, and must focus critically on the particular standards and values being invoked.

Surely, the way to change unjust laws is to introduce more enlightened ones. This is how we must view prescription. We won't go into details here, but in the case of the possessive apostrophe mentioned earlier, what we have is a long history of bewildering inconsistency, beginning with the possessive apostrophe's introduction into English from French during the sixteenth century. Small wonder many twentieth-century writers of English are confused about where to put it. Signs like *Nomination's for Director* (National Art Gallery of Victoria) and *Canva's Hat's* (Melbourne store) are commonplace. Now if it can be shown that the possessive apostrophe speeds up linguistic processing, for instance, then a case can be made to hang on to it. But if a rule offers no advantages (which we suspect is the case here), why keep it? (A case could be made for potential ambiguities between singular and plural possessors, although context is usually sufficient to overcome any confusion. Afterall, in speech we seem to cope alright.)

Many prescriptive rules are totally unjust; they don't allow for language change; they don't allow for stylistic variation. And many have been artificial for English from the start, stemming from a time when regulating English meant making it look more like Latin. The rules can hurt too. Despite our current era of equality for all, linguistic prejudices go unchallenged in the public arena. People openly argue that non-standard usage is inferior to standard. Even well-intentioned corrections can belittle and demean. There's nothing wrong with wanting to set standards in the use of language. But people must be sensitive to the social harm that can come from it. It's not prescription that's the problem really, but the misuse of it.

Prescription and non-discriminatory language

Some recent usage books are now managing to steer a sensible course between prescription and description. In *The Cambridge Australian English Style Guide*, for example, Pam Peters makes recommendations but does this using principles of linguistic science, as well as the wonderful usage evidence that's now available via huge data banks of actually occurring language.

There are other areas too where the activities of linguists are straightforwardly—and legitimately—prescriptive. For example, in multicultural societies such as Australia and New Zealand, linguists play an important part in the implementation of national language policies. Australia leads the way in this regard, having had an explicit language policy as early as 1987. Linguists have also been involved in helping to establish home-grown OZ and NZ Englishes as legitimate varieties by promoting reference literature such as the new *Oxford Australian Writers' Dictionary* (OAWD), *The Dictionary of New Zealand English* (DNZE), *The Australian Concise Oxford Dictionary* (ACOD), and *The Macquarie Dictionary* (MD). Many are involved in formulating guidelines for preferred language use to do with inclusive language and Plain English (see the discussion in chapter 10).

As a case in point, consider discriminatory language. This is language that targets a range of different facets of identity, including sex and gender, race, ethnicity, class, sexuality, age, political or religious beliefs, and physical, intellectual, or psychiatric disability. Whether intentional or otherwise, it creates or reinforces a hierarchy of difference between people. It affects everyone.

With surprising elasticity, language can be used to express one point, while obscuring another—to normalise one perspective, while alienating or negating the experiences and perspectives of others. Language can often appear to be a 'neutral', 'unbiased' representation of 'fact'. But language can also be discriminatory when we fail to consider the assumptions that inform the words we use. It expresses cultural norms and belief systems that are often so entrenched in language as to appear 'normal' or 'true'. Take the example of a questionnaire that asks for an individual's 'first' or 'Christian' name. This may not be designed to offend or discriminate, but both the terms *first name* and *Christian name* suggest a bias towards Christian, Anglo-Celtic culture. This wording overlooks and alienates people from cultures in which the 'first name' is the family name, as well as people who are not Christian.

Guidelines for non-discriminatory language encourage a rigorous and ongoing examination of the language we use, and a consideration of the needs and feelings of others when we choose the words through which we convey meaning. Laying down ethical guidelines in this way is very different from outright prescriptive handbooks, with their superficial notions of correctness and their narrow definitions of grammatical excellence. Guidelines for non-discriminatory language do not call for a closing down of options for speech, but for a more precise and accurate use of language. Employing inclusive language works to ensure that different opinions, lifestyles, choices, and experiences are recognised, validated, and reflected. It is not enough to adopt a new set of words. Rather, it is a matter of examining habits of speech and writing in an attempt to convey meaning accurately (for a fuller discussion, see Banks & Mulder 1996).

POINTS TO REMEMBER

- English has been constantly changing throughout its history.
- The process of change and geographical separation inevitably gives rise to regional variation. Over a long enough period of time, regional dialects will diverge further to become mutually unintelligible or, in other words, distinct languages.
- Sound correspondences are said to exist when sounds regularly occur in corresponding positions in sets of words that are similar in shape and meaning.
- Words that are historically related are cognates. Cognates represent the continuation of a single lexical item in the parent (or proto-) language.
- The symbolic nature of language and the orderliness of sound change are what give us the license to compare languages and establish genetic relationships.
- Standard English is the variety that is understood by writers and speakers all over the world, and is supported by authoritative literature such as dictionaries and grammars.
- Standard English developed out of the London dialect. This had nothing to do with the dialect being linguistically perfect for the job; all along the way, it piggy-backed on a number of geographical and historical events that pushed it onto centre stage.
- The prescriptive approach is one that tells you how you ought to speak and write. The descriptive approach describes how you actually speak and write.
- Linguistic science must remain objectively descriptive and avoid anything that smacks of moral and aesthetic judgment. It is, however, appropriate for linguists to focus critically on the particular standards and values being invoked in the prescriptive debates.

EXERCISES

1 Sound Correspondences

Listed below are sets of cognates from four early Germanic languages as well as Modern English. Consider just the consonants, and state the systematic sound correspondences they reveal.

Old English	*Old Norse*	*Old High German*	*Gothic*	*Modern English*
ān	einn	ein	ains	one
wæter	vatn	wazzar	wato	water
etan	eta	ezzan	itan	eat
þrī	þīir	drī	þreis	three
þū	þū	dū	þū	you
stān	steinn	stein	stains	stone
weorþ	verþ	werd	wairþ	worth
pund	pund	pfund	pund	pound
weorpan	verpa	werfan	wairpan	to throw
īs	īs	īs	–	ice
hleāpan	hlaupa	hlaufan	hlaupan	leap
drincan	drekka	trinkan	drigcan	to drink

2 **Cognates: Modern Germanic**
Go back to the German, Dutch, and English versions of the pea soup recipe given in this chapter (p. 22) and do the following tasks:
a Compare the three and list the words that you suspect are cognate.
b List those words that you suspect are not cognate.
c Are there cases where a cognate does exist in English, but the word's current meaning makes it no longer appropriate for this recipe? We discussed one example in the text. Another is *smoked/gerauchte/gerookte*. *Smoked* isn't cognate. The English cognate is, in fact, *reeked*, which now means 'smelt unpleasant'.
d List any differences in grammar (for example, word order) between the three languages.

3 **Cognates: Early Germanic**
Repeat exercise 2, but using the medieval pottage recipes (Middle Dutch and Middle English) given in the text (p. 23). The similarities between the two texts are more striking. Why?

4 **Sound symbolism**
We all associate certain sound sequences with particular meanings. Such sound sequences are called 'phonesthemes'. They either occur at the beginning of words or they're rhymes, and they symbolise certain meanings. Identify the phonesthemes below, and try to describe the meaning that is characteristic of them. Add any other words that you can find. Can you think of other phonesthemes?
a crash, dash, flash, gush, rush, smash, swish, whoosh
b bump, chump, dump, hump, lump plump, rump, slump
c swagger, swash, swat, sway, sweep, swerve, swill, swing, swipe, swirl, swish
d glare, gleam, glimmer, glint, glisten, glitter, gloss, glow
e snaffle, snafu, snag, snare, snarl, snort, sneak, sneer, sneeze, snipe, snivel

5 **Grimm's Law**
In each of the following pairs, one word is native (Germanic) and the other is borrowed from Latin or Greek. On the basis of Grimm's Law, identify the native and the borrowed items. (Hint: the borrowings preserve the original Indo-European stops.) Do you notice any stylistic differences between the members of each pair? Are some more characteristic of a higher style?

father/paternal, triad/three, heart/cardiac, hemp/cannabis, tooth/dental, generic/kin, pedal/foot, purse/bursar

Here are some trickier ones. Explain how it is that these words can be traced back to a common Indo-European source. (You will have to check an etymological dictionary.)

eat/edible, vehicle/wagon, pluvial/float, cram/agora, sediment/sitter, foam/spume, erode/rat

6 **Acceptability**
Read each of the following sentences. Your task is to make a judgment on the relative acceptability of each sentence. Answer as honestly as you can. Indicate your judgment by placing a number (1–5) by each of the sentences. If you do find sen-

tences are wrong, unacceptable, awkward or even odd, try to say why you feel this. The scale of acceptability is as follows:

1 totally unacceptable
2 relatively unacceptable, but not as bad as 1
3 uncertain as to acceptability
4 relatively acceptable but not as good as 5
5 totally acceptable and natural

a I aren't bothered.
b I ain't bothered.
c I'm right, aren't I?
d You and me must get together some time soon.
e The cake will have to be made by John and I.
f The mission of the USS *Enterprise* is to boldly go where no one has gone before.
g He's fatter than me.
h He objected to my baking the cake.
i He objected to me baking the cake.
j Who were you talking to?
k (Who's there?) It's only me!
l It is I who am to blame.
m He's basing it on data which are not reliable.
n I don't want nothing to eat.
o There's two men waiting for you.
p Everyone can vote as they wish.
q See youse later!
r Hopefully, it's going to be a fine day.

7 What is grammar?

What do you understand the term *grammar* to mean? Often speakers of English can be heard criticising their fellow speakers for not having any grammar. What do you think they actually mean by this?

8 Change: is it for the better or for the worse?

Below are two extracts that present very different attitudes towards change in language. William Caxton, in his preface to the *Eneydos* (1490), describes how he came upon an old book in his bookshelf. It caused him to reflect upon changes that have occurred in English and on change in general:

> I...toke an olde boke and redde therin / and certaynly the englysshe was so rude and brood that I coude not wele vnderstande it...And certaynly it was wreton in suche wyse that it was more lyke to dutche [German] than englysshe I coude not reduce ne brynge it to be vnderstonden / And certaynly our language now vsed varyeth ferre from that whiche was vsed and spoken whan I was borne / For we englysshe men / ben [are] borne vnder the domynacyon of the mone [moon], which is neuer stedfaste / but euer wauerynge / wexynge [growing] one season / and waneth & dyscreaseth another season

As reproduced in Bolton 1966:2

Many years later, in 1712, Jonathan Swift published *A Proposal for Correcting, Improving and Ascertaining the English Tongue*. Here he wrote the following:

> The English Tongue is not arrived to such a Degree of Perfection, as, upon that Account, to make us apprehend any Thoughts of its Decay: And if it were once refined to a certain Standard, perhaps there might be Ways to fix it for ever...I see no absolute Necessity why any Language should be perpetually changing; for we find many Examples of the contrary...But what I have most at Heart, is, that some Method should be thought on for Ascertaining and fixing our Language for ever, after such Alterations are made in it as shall be thought requisite...What Horace says of *Words going off, and perishing like Leaves, and new ones coming in their Place*, is a misfortune he laments, rather than a Thing he approves: But I cannot see why this should be absolutely necessary
>
> As reproduced in Bolton 1966:117–18

Compare the two attitudes to language change expressed in these extracts. Discuss the goal that Swift sets up. How desirable is it? How practical?

3

What's in a Sound?

INTRODUCTION

She'll be right, mate. Frequently uttered, this distinctly OZ and NZ phrase offers assurance that all is well; life's problems will be resolved. (But if you are an efficiency expert, it may drive you into a frenzy when given as a promise that the job will be finished, the deadline will be met.) As Henry Williams in *Australia: What is it?* expresses it:

> If the madmen triumph and the button is pressed and this earth is reduced to a smouldering radio-active cinder, maybe, out on the old Barcoo or somewhere out west, there will be a survivor, a lone battler to emerge from his timber-and-corrugated shack, look out across the ruined planet, roll up his sleeves and roll himself a smoke, and say, 'She'll be right, mate'.
>
> As quoted in Wilkes 1996:316–17

It is a short, simple phrase to say; it's only four words. But what you have probably never stopped to worry about is just what you are doing when you say it. In this chapter we look at what it takes to actually say this phrase, and you'll see that it is far from simple. In the following sections we focus on how we produce spoken English by looking at precisely how many different sounds there are in OZ English and NZ English, and how we might best describe and transcribe them. We consider how the sounds fall into patterns and how they can change in connected speech. The discussion is rounded off by exploring the use of stress and intonation for different ways of saying things.

THE SOUNDS OF OZ AND NZ ENGLISH

Before you can appreciate the complexity of uttering *She'll be right, mate*, we need a run-down on the necessary equipment: air from the lungs, a larynx, an alveolar ridge, a hard palate, a velum, a tongue, lips, teeth, and a nose.

The speech organs

The lungs

Let's start from the bottom with the lungs. When we speak, we do not follow a rhythmic breathing pattern. Instead we take in quick breaths of air, but exhale slowly, so that we can speak as the air flows out. The actual rate and timing of breathing follows the patterns of speech with pauses for breath usually coming at the ends of clauses, sentences, and paragraphs.

Air coming out of the lungs is the power source for all the sounds in English. We can, of course, talk while we're actually breathing in. Give this a go. You'll find that you are producing a loud whisper, not ordinary speech, and that it is a much more inefficient approach than speaking on an outgoing breath.

The vocal folds

Now the air from the lungs travels out through the trachea (windpipe) into the **larynx** (Adam's apple, voice-box—it's all the same). Put your fingertips against your larynx. It is actually a valve with an elaborate set of muscles, and it feels hard because the main piece of cartilage that forms the outer shell of the larynx is in front. All the air that comes up from your lungs flows through an opening in the larynx called the 'glottis'. Along the sides of the glottis there are two small muscular folds called the '**vocal folds**' or 'vocal cords'. (They're not actually cords, but in 1741, Ferrein, a French scientist, gave them that name because he thought they produced a sound like the strings of a violin. They don't, but the name has stuck anyway).

The vocal folds are retractable, and as you're reading this, your vocal folds are probably apart, roughly forming a triangular opening through which you are pulling air in and pushing it out as you breath. But the muscles in and around the larynx can pull together the small pieces of cartilage attached to the back ends of the vocal folds, and narrow or close the space between them. When you swallow, you actually close the vocal folds (among other things) to help direct food and drink to the stomach, bypassing the lungs.

When we speak, the vocal folds can be adjusted so that there is only a narrow passage between them, and the pressure of the air that is flowing out will cause them to vibrate or buzz. Lightly put your fingertips on your larynx and make the cartoon noise for sleeping: z-Z-Z-Z-Z. You'll be able to feel it with your fingers as well as hear it. Sounds produced when the vocal folds are vibrating are said to be **voiced** and those produced when the vocal folds are apart are said to be **voiceless**.

The difference between voiced and voiceless sounds is an important distinction in English; it is important to know whether you are being asked for a *sink* or *zinc*. The only difference between the initial consonant in each of the pairs of words *zip/sip*; *thy/thigh*; and *vine/fine* is that the first consonant is voiced and the second is voiceless. To hear this difference say just the consonant at the beginning of each of these words and hear and feel the difference with your fingertips against your larynx. Another way of hearing the difference is by putting your fingers in your ears to plug them up. (Give it a go.) Returning to *She'll be right, mate*, all the initial sounds are voiced, except *sh* which is voiceless.

The vocal tract

The air then runs out through the vocal tract (which includes your larynx and the whole airway from the top of your larynx), up the back of your throat, over your tongue, past your teeth, and between your lips, as well as through your nostrils. The different sound qualities of the consonants and vowels of English are produced by

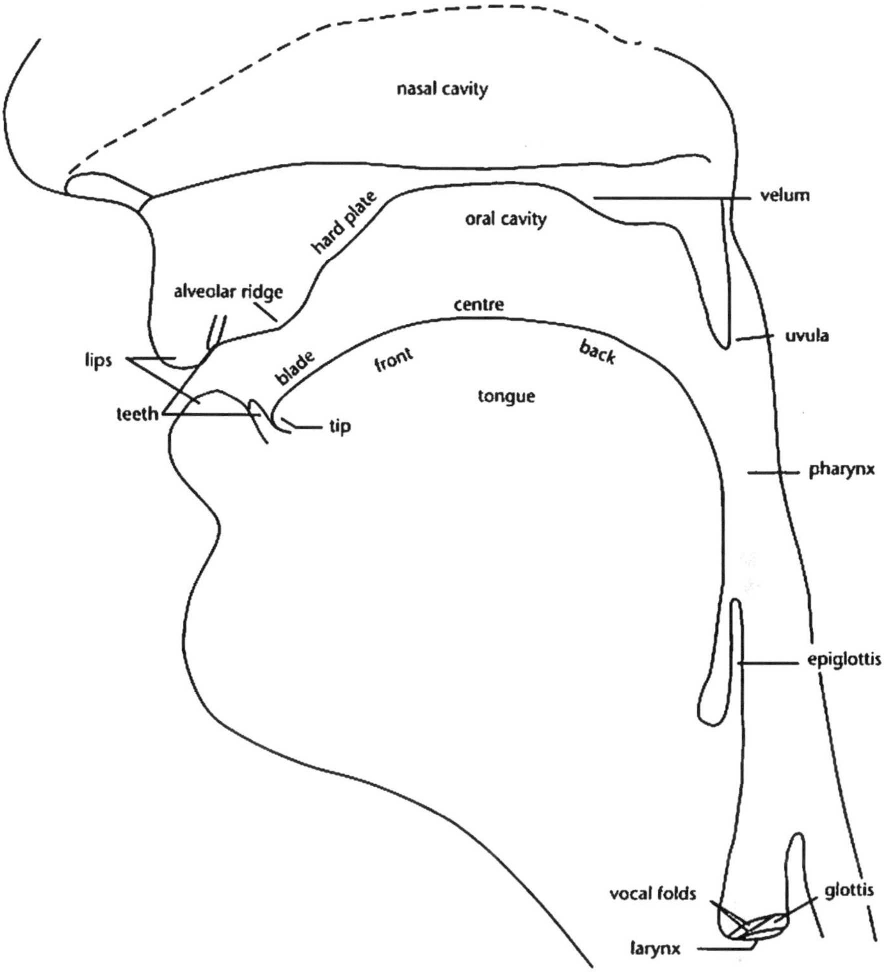

Figure 3.1 The vocal tract

constricting or varying the shape and length of the tract through which the air passes. The major parts of the vocal tract are shown in Figure 3.1.

As the air moves up through the pharynx, which is the name for the cavity above the larynx, it passes into the oral cavity. That air can also move into the nasal cavity if the velum is lowered. The **velum** or **soft palate** is a muscular flap forming the back half of the roof of your mouth, and from it dangles the funny little tear-drop-shaped uvula. The name *velum* comes from the Latin word, which has among its meanings that of 'covering'. In effect, the velum does act like a cover in that, if it is raised, air can only escape through the mouth, whereas if it is lowered, then air can flow out of both the mouth and the nose. When we speak, the velum is in constant motion, moving up and down. On the basis of this, we divide sounds into oral sounds, which are uttered with the velum raised, and nasal sounds, with the velum lowered. The initial consonants in ***she'll be right*** are all oral, while the initial consonant in ***mate*** is nasal.

Continuing along the roof of the mouth, the **hard palate** is a bony partition that divides the oral cavity from the nasal cavity. It and the velum are important in producing sounds. The tongue touches or comes close to them in the production of consonant sounds such as that at the beginning of ***she'll***.

Next there is a ridge in the very front of the hard palate just behind the upper teeth which is known as the **'alveolar ridge'**. You can easily feel it with the tip of your tongue. Again in the production of sounds like those highlighted in ***she'll be right, mate*** the tongue touches or comes close to the alveolar ridge. The initial sounds in ***be*** and ***mate***—the remaining consonants in our phrase—are made with the lips.

Finally, there is the tongue, which is perhaps the most important of the speech organs, reflected in the saying 'language is the gift of tongues'. It is made up almost entirely of a large number of muscles that operate as a whole to allow the tongue to move forwards and backwards, and up and down, to lengthen and shorten itself, and to otherwise assume various shapes. The tongue can actually be divided into five different regions that are relevant in producing the sounds of English: the tip, blade, front, centre, and back. Say the vowels in *she'll* and *mate* repeatedly: *e-a, e-a, e-a*. Feel your tongue moving forwards and backwards (if you put a finger between your teeth, you can feel it with your finger). When your tongue moves, it changes the shape of the space in the vocal tract, creating different sounds.

While it may not take much thought (or commitment) to utter the phrase *she'll be right, mate*, we can see that it is far from a simple task for our speech organs to actually produce it, and even more complex to describe all the movements that our speech organs make. In the next sections we look more closely at the terms for describing the different sounds of English.

Describing consonants

English, like all other languages, makes a distinction between vowels and consonants, based on the amount of obstruction encountered by the air flowing from the lungs. With vowels, the air flows relatively freely through the oral cavity, with the different sound qualities being created by varying the shape of the space through which the air is flowing. With consonants, on the other hand, the air flow is obstructed, for example, by closing the lips or jamming the tongue across the airway to completely block the flow, or by making a narrow opening that forces the air to hiss its way through. However, rather than a sharp division between vowels and consonants, there is really a continuum of obstruction. Some consonants, such as those at the beginning of *yet* and *wet*, are rather vowel-like in that they are sounded continuously without any audible hissing. Because of this, these two consonants are sometimes called 'semi-vowels'.

In describing the twenty-four consonants of English, we need to ask these questions: Where in the vocal tract is the obstruction? How (and to what degree) is the airflow obstructed? Are the vocal folds vibrating? Is the velum raised or lowered?

Places of articulation

By identifying which parts of the vocal tract are involved, the following terms describe the different places of articulation in English:

- **bilabial**: using both lips. Look in a mirror and say ***my big pud***. See and feel how the lips come together for the first sound in each of these words.
- **labio-dental**: using the lower lip and the upper teeth. Again look in a mirror, but this time say ***five very fine vines***. When you make the first sound in each of these words, notice how your lower lip is raised until it almost touches the upper front teeth.
- **dental**: using the tongue tip between the teeth, or the tongue tip or blade close behind the upper teeth. Say ***these thick things*** and feel where your tongue is when you make the first sound in each of these words. Does your tongue position vary from between the teeth to behind the upper teeth or is it consistently one or the other?
- **alveolar**: using the tip or blade of the tongue and the alveolar ridge. Say ***ten deadly donuts*** and again feel which of the two possibilities your tongue uses in making each of the highlighted sounds in these words.
- **palato-alveolar**: using the blade of the tongue and the back of the alveolar ridge. Say ***she shipped short sheared sheep***. To feel the place of articulation more easily, hold the position of the first sound in each of these words and breathe in. You can feel the incoming air cool the blade of your tongue and the back of your alveolar ridge.
- **palatal**: using the front of the tongue and the hard palate. Now say ***yes you yammer***, hold the position of the first consonant, and breathe in. This time you will feel the incoming air cool the front of your tongue and your hard palate.
- **velar**: using the back of the tongue and the velum. Say ***come consume kebabs*** and feel how the tongue touches the velum when you say the first sound of each word.
- **glottal**: using the space between the vocal folds. Finally, say ***he had hairy hands*** and hear the friction as the air rushes between the slightly open vocal folds and resonates through the vocal tract.

Manners of articulation

Now we need to look at how the different consonants are made at the various locations in the vocal tract. We can divide the consonants into six different manners of articulation based on the degree of obstruction of the airflow, which varies from a total closure to a narrowing. With one manner of articulation—the nasals—the velum is lowered, whereas with all the others it is raised. With respect to the vocal folds, we will see that, in English, the stops, fricatives, and affricates can be voiced or voiceless, whereas the nasals, laterals, and approximants are all voiced. The six manners of articulation are as follows:

- **stop**: a complete closure in the oral cavity with the velum raised. Feel where the closure is made as you say the initial sounds in ***pat, bat*** (bilabial closure); ***tale, dale*** (alveolar closure); and ***came, game*** (velar closure). In each of these pairs, the initial sound of the first word is voiceless, whereas the initial sound of the second is voiced.
- **nasal**: a complete closure in the oral cavity with the velum lowered so that air escapes through the nose. The three nasals in English are all voiced and you can hear them at the beginning of the words ***meal*** (bilabial closure) and ***neat*** (alveolar closure), and at the end of the word ***bring*** (velar closure).

- **fricative**: two speech organs come close together to partially block the airflow and create a turbulence in it that we can hear. Focus on the bolded sounds as you say the words ***feign***, ***vein*** (labiodental); ***thin***, ***then*** (dental), ***seal***, ***zeal*** (alveolar); and ***mesh***, ***measure*** (palato-alveolar). Again, in each pair the highlighted sound in the first word is voiceless and in the second it's voiced.
- **affricate**: first a complete closure or stop is made in the oral cavity, and then, rather than being fully released, it is slackened so that a fricative sound is made. There are two affricates in English: both are palato-alveolars, but they differ in voicing. We find the voiceless affricate at the beginning and end of the word ***church*** and the voiced affricate at the beginning and end of ***judge***. Feel the series of movements involved in making an affricate as you say these words.
- **lateral**: a partial closure is made by the blade of the tongue against the alveolar ridge so that air can flow between one or both sides of the tongue and the roof of the mouth. In English there is only one lateral: it is an alveolar and is voiced. You can feel how the air flows around your tongue by saying ***limo leaping lion*** and holding the tongue position of one of the initial sounds while you breathe in. The tongue will feel cold on the side or sides not in contact with the roof of your mouth.
- **approximant**: two speech organs come close to each other, but not so close that an audible turbulence is produced. The three sounds in English that can be listed as approximants are all voiced and are found at the beginning of the words ***you*** (narrowing between the front of the tongue and the palatal), ***woo*** (narrowing the lips by rounding them and by creating a narrowing in the velar region), and ***roo*** (narrowing in the alveolar region for most OZ and NZ English-speakers).

The terminology varies somewhat here with some linguists including laterals in the category of approximants. The initial sound of ***woo*** is also sometimes referred to as a labial-velar since it involves both a narrowing of the lips and of the velar region. Later in this chapter, and in the next chapter as well, we discuss some of the regional variation in the production of the initial sound in ***roo***.

To summarise, we can describe the consonants of English in terms of three factors, which are generally listed in the following order:

1 state of the vocal folds (voiced or voiceless)
2 place of articulation
3 manner of articulation

It is not necessary to specifically state whether a consonant is oral or nasal, given that the velum is raised for all the manners of articulation, except for nasal (and nasality is already encoded in the name of this term). Likewise voicing is only mentioned for those places and manners of articulation in which a voicing contrast occurs, such as with an alveolar stop. Thus the sounds at the beginning of each of the words in ***she'll be right, mate*** can be described as:

she'll	voiceless palato-alveolar fricative
be	voiced bilabial stop
right	alveolar approximant
mate	bilabial nasal

Describing vowels

When saying an English vowel, the air escapes through the mouth in a relatively unimpeded way, and the different vowel sounds are created by varying the shape of the tongue and the lips. This causes the shape of the space through which the air is flowing to vary, producing different vowel qualities. So in order to describe the vowels of English we need to specify the position of the tongue and the shape of the lips.

Tongue position

In making a vowel sound, the tip of your tongue is down behind your lower front teeth, and the body of your tongue is domed upward. What is important in describing the different vowels sounds is locating the top of that dome—that is, the highest point of the tongue—and determining how high or low that point is in the oral cavity, and how far forward or back it is. To see how both of these parameters are important in the description of vowels, stand in front of a mirror and say *he* then *ham*. Watch as your jaw drops down as you say the vowel in *ham*. With both vowels the tongue is in the front of your mouth, but with the vowel in *he* it is fairly close to the roof of your mouth, whereas with the vowel in *ham* the tongue is much lower. We can describe the vowel in *he* as a high vowel and that in *ham* as a low vowel.

To help feel where the highest point of your tongue is, put a Smartie, Lifesaver, or some other small sweet on the centre of your tongue. Now say the vowel sound in *he* followed by the vowel in *pud*, and feel your tongue (and the sweet) move back in your mouth as you say the second vowel. In both vowels the tongue is close to the top of the vocal tract, but in the first vowel the tongue is towards the front of the mouth, whereas in the second it is towards the back. Correspondingly, we can describe the vowel in *he* as a front vowel and that in *pud* as a back vowel. Combining the tongue height with the relative front–back position of the tongue, we can say that the vowel in *he* is a high front vowel, the vowel in *ham* is a low front vowel, and the vowel in *pud* is a high back vowel. Finally, say *pot* and feel where your tongue is as you say the first vowel; we can describe it as a low back vowel.

Taken together, the tongue height and its front–back position give us a way of locating the highest point of the tongue, and this is traditionally displayed using a quadrilateral as in Figure 3.2. Very roughly, the quadrilateral represents the area of the mouth that the tongue moves around in, with the lips, or the front of the mouth, to the left. The relative positions of the highest point of the tongue are given for the highlighted vowels in the words *he*, *ham*, *pud*, and *pot*. As you can see, the front–back or horizontal dimension can be divided into front, central, and back areas, while the tongue height or vertical dimension can be divided into high, mid, and low.

Lip shape

You may have noticed as you said the vowels in *he* and then in *pud* that not only did the tongue move further back, but the lips also changed shape. Look in the mirror as you say these two vowel sounds; notice that the lips are unrounded for the vowel in *he* but rounded for the vowel in *pud*. Now say the vowels in *ham* and *pot*, and look at the shape of your lips. In each case they are unrounded.

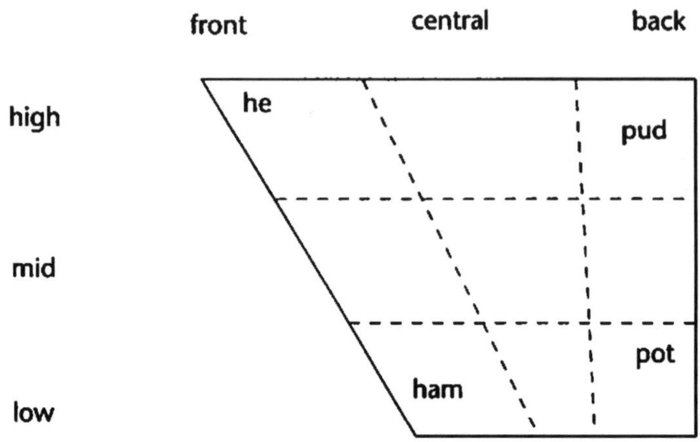

Figure 3.2 The vowel space

To summarise, we can describe vowels in terms of three factors, which are generally listed in the following order:

1 height of the body of the tongue
2 the front–back position of the tongue
3 degree of lip rounding (rounded or unrounded)

And the highlighted vowels in the words *he*, *ham*, *pud*, and *pot* can be described as:

he	high front unrounded vowel
ham	low front unrounded vowel
pud	high back rounded vowel
pot	low back unrounded vowel

Vowel length

At this point you may be thinking: Isn't there more to describing vowels? What about long and short vowels? There are indeed several pairs of vowels in English that are made in roughly the same part of the mouth but that differ in length. For example, say the words *fit* and *feet*. If you give each word the same amount of emphasis, you can hear that the vowel in *fit* is much shorter than that in *feet*. Some linguists see this difference as being a tense/lax contrast. But no matter what you label the distinction in vowel pairs such as this, it is not just a matter of length: a different place of articulation is involved. The vowel in *fit* is lower and slightly further back than the vowel in *feet*. In other words, length isn't the only difference between these two vowels, and the difference in the position of the tongue is sufficient for differentiating them.

Diphthongs

At this point let's return to the phrase *she'll be right, mate*, which we were trying to describe at the start of this whole discussion of sounds. If we look at the vowels, we see that the vowel in *she'll* and *be* can be described as a high front unrounded vowel, and we say that it is a simple vowel, or a monophthong, since the tongue does not move significantly when saying it. The vowel sounds in *right* and *mate*, however, can be described as diphthongs since, in each case, the tongue moves from one position to another during the production of the vowel sound. Feel the movement of your tongue as you slowly say the vowel in *right* (see Figure 3.3). If you are having a hard time feeling the movement, another Lifesaver may help, or try laying a finger on

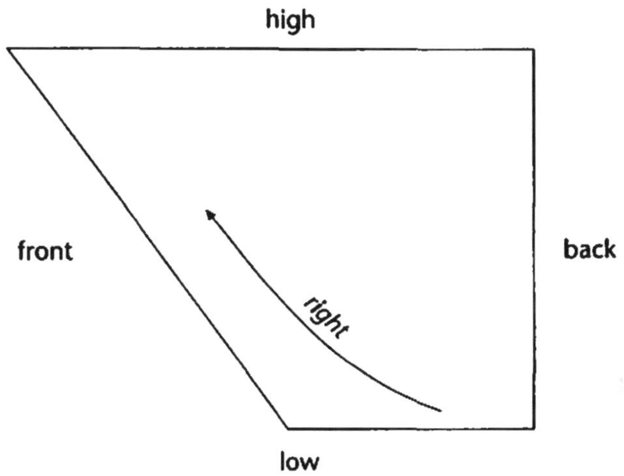

Figure 3.3 A dipthong sample

your tongue as you say *right*.

Diphthongs are a distinctive identifying feature of both NZ English and OZ English, and historically, they were some of the first sounds to be noted as part of the 'colonial twang' in each country. A typical reaction to the emerging NZ accent is found in the following extract from an address given in 1910 by E. W. Andrews of Napier Boys' High School to a Conference in Wellington of the Secondary Schools' Assistant Teachers:

> New Zealand speech is very eccentric in some of its vowel sounds, especially the diphthongal ones. It is the broad continuous vowels and diphthongs that give to the English language its musical beauty, and an incorrect rendering of them is very distressing to the English ear...The broad 'a' of father and the narrow 'a' of fat appear to cause great difficulty, and are advanced in the mouth almost to the sound of 'e' in 'pen', so that 'last' becomes 'least', 'camp' 'kemp'. This difficulty naturally causes the broad 'a' diphthongs to diverge, 'ah-oo' into 'e-oo', and 'ah-i' into 'aw-i'; so that 'noun' becomes 'ne-oon' and 'mile 'mawill'. Ask a colonial child to say 'I went down to the town to buy a brown cow', and you may almost make sausages out of the mangled beef.
>
> As quoted in Gordon & Deverson 1989:32

Transcribing sounds

Linguists use a phonetic alphabet such as the International Phonetic Alphabet (IPA) to provide a unique written representation for each sound that occurs in any of the languages of the world. Using a phonetic alphabet such as the IPA allows us to adopt a method of transcribing sounds that is completely consistent, where a particular symbol always refers to the same sound and a particular sound is always represented by the same symbol.

OZ English and NZ English each have forty-four contrasting sounds (though for an increasing number of New Zealanders there are only forty-three because they make no distinction between the vowel sounds in *ear* and *air*). Given that the English alphabet has only twenty-six different letters and that the spelling system is full of inconsistencies (see chapter 4), it is not possible to represent each of the forty-three or forty-four different sounds with a unique letter. However, a system such as the IPA allows us to accurately transcribe the sounds of Englishes down under. It is important to remember that the symbols of a phonetic transcription system such as the IPA are not the same as letters, and that they represent the sounds of language, not the letters of a writing system. To answer the question 'How many sounds are there in the word *thought*?', we have to forget about spelling and listen to the sounds. There are three sounds.

The sets of characters that are commonly used for representing the sounds of NZ English and OZ English are drawn from the IPA, and the majority of these characters are already familiar to you since the IPA is based on the Roman alphabet. Dictionaries such as the MD, ACOD, and the *Collins English Dictionary*, as well as most OZ and NZ linguistics textbooks, use IPA symbols in their pronunciation guides. While the question of which set of IPA symbols to actually use is not without controversy (particularly in Australia), a relatively standard list of IPA symbols for representing the sounds of NZ and OZ English is provided in Tables 3.1–3.3.

Keep in mind that any major regional dialect area, such as OZ English or NZ English, is made up of many variants reflecting differences in age, social background, sex, smaller regional localities, and other factors, and so not all speakers of OZ English, for example, will pronounce the vowel sound in *pool* with the same vowel quality. As we will see in the next section, the set of symbols that is listed below represents a broad transcription of the sound system of Antipodean English.

Table 3.1 Symbols for transcribing English consonants

Stops		*Fricatives*		*Nasals*	
p	pin	f	fat	m	mat
b	bin	v	vat	n	no
t	tin	θ	thing	ŋ	ring
d	din	ð	then		
k	curl	s	seal		
g	girl	z	zeal		
		ʃ	shoe		
		ʒ	beige		
		h	hat		
Affricates		***Approximants***		***Laterals***	
ʧ	choke	r	rat	l	leaf
ʤ	joke	j	yes		
		w	win		

Table 3.2 Place and manner of articulation of English consonants

Manner of articulation	*Place of articulation*							
	Bilabial	*Labio-dental*	*Dental*	*Alveolar*	*Palato-alveolar*	*Palatal*	*Velar*	*Glottal*
Stop								
Voiceless	p			t			k	
Voiced	b			d			g	
Nasal	m			n			ŋ	
Fricative								
Voiceless		f	θ	s	ʃ			h
Voiced		v	ð	z	ʒ			
Affricate								
Voiceless					ʧ			
Voiced					ʤ			
Lateral				l				
Approximant	w			r		j		

Table 3.3 Symbols for transcribing OZ and NZ English vowels

Simple vowels (monophthongs)		*Diphthongs*	
i	peat	aɪ	buy
ɪ	pit	eɪ	bay
ɛ	pet	ɔɪ	boy
æ	pat	aʊ	how
ə	apart	oʊ	hoe
ɜ	pert	ɪə	here
a	part	ɛə	hair
ʌ	but	ʊə	tour
ɒ	pot		
ɔ	port		
ʊ	put		
u	pool		

SOUNDS AND SOUND SYSTEMS

Let's return to our phrase *she'll be right, mate.* Using the symbols we introduced in the previous section, we can transcribe the phrase as /ʃil bi raɪt meɪt/. While this simple phrase is often uttered, no two speakers are going to say it with exactly the same sound quality, tone of voice, timing, and emphasis. Yet we can understand the phrase each time we hear it uttered. How is this? Shouldn't these differences in pronunciation be captured in how we transcribe the phrase?

Phones, phonemes, and allophones

When we listen to an utterance, what we are really focusing on is how the sounds convey differences in meaning. We are concerned with the significant aspects of the sounds, not a total awareness of how each sound is made. For example, when saying the initial sound in *roo*, speakers of many varieties of American English will have the tongue tip curled back, whereas in some Scots English varieties it will have a trilled sound as in words such as *rye* and *raw*. The articulation of this sound can also vary depending on the types of sounds that precede or follow it: the shape of the lips can be influenced by the following vowel (spread in *read*, rounded in *rude*), and in rapid speech, the tongue may make a quick tap against the back part of the alveolar ridge between vowels and after some consonants (as in *very*, *sorry*, *three*). These variations in how the sound is actually produced do not affect the meaning of the word and are not reflected in the transcription system given in the previous section.

What we are seeing is that the sounds of English can be examined from two perspectives: the **phonetic** and the **phonological**. Phonetics is the study of the way we make, transmit, and receive speech sounds, whereas phonology is the study of the sound systems and patterns of sounds that occur in a language. Phonetics is concerned with describing the physical units of sound produced by the speech organs, and such sound units are called '**phones**'. In contrast, phonology is concerned with identifying the distinctive sound units in a language by identifying the sound units that determine differences of meaning within that language. These abstract sound units are called '**phonemes**'. What we listed in Tables 3.1 and 3.3 as the forty-four sounds of OZ English and NZ English are actually the phonemes of each of these English varieties.

To help separate the two ways of looking at the sounds of a language, square brackets [] are used when sounds are being discussed from a phonetic point of view (that is, as phones or concrete speech sounds) and slashes // are used when they are being discussed from a phonological point of view (that is, as phonemes or as part of the sound system of a language). For the most part, transcriptions in this book are phonological; they show the phonemes and use slashes, as in /ʃil bi raɪt meɪt/ 'she'll be right mate'.

Now let's return to our discussion of the initial sound segment in *roo* and look at the relationship between phones and phonemes more closely. As we noted above, this sound may be pronounced differently depending on, for example, the regional variety of English that's being spoken (Scots English versus OZ English, for example), the stylistic variety (for instance, slow, careful speech versus faster, more casual speech), or context (where it occurs in a word). However, each of these phones or different pronunciations would still be recognised by a speaker of English as representing the same phoneme /r/. We can speak of the phones or variant pronunciations of a phoneme as **allophones** of that phoneme. The term allophone comes from Greek: *allos* 'other' + *phone* 'sound'. Thus, in our example, the different pronunciations of *r* are allophones of the phoneme /r/.

On the other hand, except for the initial consonants, the sounds of the words *roo*, *zoo*, and *loo* are identical. Since these are all different words, we can see that these initial consonants are distinctive sounds in English and are thus phonemes (/r/, /z/, and /l/ respectively). In short, phonetics gives us a way to describe the phones of English and how they differ, whereas phonology identifies the phonemes of a language and how the phones arrange themselves as allophones of these phonemes.

Determining phonemes

Given that not all the phones in English signal differences in meaning, how do we determine just what are the significant sounds? What method can we use to show, for example, that there are forty-four phonemes in NZ English and OZ English? The general procedure that linguists use is to look at the distribution of the phones.

Minimal pairs

The first step is to search for pairs of words, such as *peace* and *peas* or *feet* and *foot*, that differ in only one sound, with the differing sound occurring in the same position in each word. Such pairs are known as **minimal pairs**. As the difference between the two sounds in such a pair signals a difference in meaning, this is direct evidence that the two sounds represent different phonemes. Thus *peace* and *peas* are a minimal pair illustrating that [s] and [z] are phonemes in English, and likewise, *feet* and *foot* show that [i] and [ʊ] are phonemes.

Unfortunately, it is not always possible to find minimal pairs, as there may be accidental gaps in the vocabulary, where a minimal pair could exist but doesn't actually occur. For example, we are not aware of any minimal pairs for [ʒ] and [ʤ]. Yet we find that each of these sounds contrasts with other sounds in English, such as in the minimal pairs *measure* [ʒ] and *mesher* [ʃ] and *judge* [ʤ] and *fudge* [f]. Because of this we can consider /ʒ/ and /ʤ/ to be phonemes in English.

Complementary distribution

Now it may turn out that, when we are looking at where a particular pair of sounds can occur, we find that the two sounds are always used in different contexts. This is termed '**complementary distribution**', and the two phones are said to be allophones of the same phoneme.

Let's take as an example a sentence such as *Liver is wonderful.* (It's just an example!) In NZ and OZ English there is a very clear audible difference between the initial sound of *liver* (which is known as a 'clear' *l*) and the final sound of *wonderful* (which is known as a 'dark' *l*). In each case, a partial closure is made by the blade of the tongue against the alveolar ridge. However, for a clear *l*, the body of the tongue then runs down and back, as in the production of a front vowel, whereas for a dark *l* the body of the tongue is higher and shaped, as in the production of a high back vowel. If we look at where these two sounds are found, we see that the clear *l* occurs at the beginning of a syllable, as in *lean* and *Bologna.* In contrast, a dark *l* occurs at the end of a syllable and when it is a syllable on its own, as in *full* and *fiddle* respectively. Since the clear *l* never occurs in the same context as the dark *l*, they are allophones of the phoneme /l/. That is, the clear *l* is the allophone of the phoneme /l/ found at the beginning of a syllable, whereas the dark *l* is the allophone of /l/ found at the end of a syllable or as a syllable in its own right.

In this example the complementary distribution of the allophones is a matter of position in the syllable. In other cases the complementary distribution may be dependent on the adjacent sounds, the morpheme or word structure, or a combination of these.

Free variation

The final possibility in considering the distribution of two sounds is that they may appear in the same context without causing a change in meaning. In this case they are said to be in '**free variation**' and are allophones of the same phoneme. As we noted above, in pronouncing the *r* in words such as *very*, *sorry*, and *three*, the same speaker may sometimes make a quick tap of the tongue against the back of the alveolar ridge, particularly in rapid speech. However, at other times, as in slower, more careful speech, the *r* in the same words will be pronounced with a narrowing in the region of the alveolar ridge. In this case, the two phones are found in the same context and do not signal a difference in meaning. We therefore cannot say that they represent different phonemes, but instead say that they are allophones of the phoneme /r/ and are in free variation. The variation is free in the sense that we aren't able to anticipate from speaker to speaker, or even from circumstance to circumstance, which phone will occur.

Sounds in connected speech

So far in our discussion of the sounds of English, we have been focusing on the individual sounds, with the transcription of a phrase such as *she'll be right, mate* /ʃil bi raɪt meɪt/ showing how the sentence would be said 'sound by sound' and 'word by word'. Viewing spoken English as a sequence of single sounds broken into words is further reinforced by writing, since language is represented as a sequence of letters separated by different amounts of space. However, in reality, spoken language isn't like this at all. We do not make first one sound, then move on to the next sound in the word, then the next, until we reach the end of the word. Likewise, when we speak, we do not just speak in single words but in groups of words. These groups are continuous, and they may or may not have pauses between them. Because we speak in a (semi-)continuous flow of sounds and words, this can change the shape of the words. Some sounds might drop off. Some sounds might be added. Some sounds might blend into one another, creating transitions from one sound to another.

Let's consider in more detail some of the most common processes found in connected speech.

Loss of sounds

Deletion occurs when sounds are left out, as frequently happens in ordinary, casual, rather quick, everyday speech. Unstressed vowels may be deleted, as in *p(o)lice*, *b(e)live*, *t(e)rrific*, and *g(o)rilla*, whereas with consonants, the deleted consonant is most often made at the same place of articulation as one or other of its neighbours. *Grandmother*, for instance, is generally pronounced as [grænmʌðə] with the /n/ and the deleted /d/ both being alveolars.

Entire syllables are even deleted, as is the case when the suffix *-ly* is added to an adjective stem that already ends in *-le*; for example, *gentle* + *ly* becomes *gently*, not *gentlely*. Typically, the deleted syllable is identical or similar to a neighbouring syllable, as is the case with *library*, which can be heard pronounced with three syllables, [laɪbrəri], or with two, [laɪbri].

Many of the pronouns, auxiliary verbs, prepositions, conjunctions and determiners in English are particularly prone to the process of deletion. For instance, in speech and increasingly in writing, the verb *be* forms a contraction with the preceding pronoun: *I'm*, *you're*, *she's*, *he's*, *it's*, *we're*, and *they're*. The labels ***strong form*** and ***weak form*** are used to describe the two distinct ways of pronouncing common English words such as these. The strong form occurs when the word is said in isolation or is being emphasised, whereas a weak form is used in the normal flow of connected speech. In the weak forms, consonants may be deleted and vowels reduced to [ə], or sometimes [ɪ], or deleted altogether, as the following examples illustrate:

	Strong form	*Weak form*
them	[ðɛm]	[ɪm, m]
was	[wɒz]	[wəz]
to	[tu]	[tə]
and	[ænd]	[ən, n]
the	[ði]	[ðə]
must	[mʌst]	[məs, ms]

Addition of sounds

A sound may be added as the various parts of the vocal tract move from one sound to another, and this is known as '**epenthesis**'. In the case of consonant addition, most examples are the result of some kind of 'mistiming'. Say the words *mince* and *mints*. You probably think you pronounce them differently, but in fact you don't. It's just the spelling that suggests this. For both, you would say something like /mɪnts/. Whenever we have a cluster of a nasal and a following consonant, as in the word *mince*, we usually insert an oral stop that is produced at the same place of articulation as the nasal. It's difficult not to. What happens is our soft palate is lowered for /n/ and the air passes through the nose. Because the following consonant, /s/, is oral not nasal, we need to raise the soft palate to stop the air escaping through the nose. But if the soft palate is raised too early, in other words before the tongue position has changed, you produce an oral stop made in the same place of articulation as the nasal.

The addition of vowels has quite a different motivation. There's a lot of evidence to suggest that speakers do actually prefer a consonant–vowel syllable structure, and in keeping with this, we often find vowels being inserted between consonants, usually to help the pronunciation of what are otherwise difficult clusters. It's a kind of consonant cluster simplification. You've probably encountered non-standard pronunciations such as *umberella* 'umbrella', *ellum* 'elm', *fillum* 'film', *athalete* 'athlete'.

Modification of sounds

Perhaps the most obvious aspect of connected speech is that a sound may change its shape depending on the company it keeps. And by far the most likely way that it will change is to become more like a neighbouring sound (known as '**assimilation**'). Alternately, a sound may become unlike its neighbour (not surprisingly, called '**dissimilation**'), or it may swap order with a neighbouring sound (**metathesis**). In this chapter, we will focus on the process of assimilation, and in the next chapter we will look as some examples of dissimilation and metathesis that have occurred in the making of English.

To begin with, you may recall that earlier in this chapter we said that English consonants are described according to three parameters: state of the vocal folds (that is, voiced or voiceless), place of articulation, and manner of articulation. When sounds change to become more like other sounds, they change according to one or more of these three parameters. For example, say the word *pancake* in a sentence and you most probably will have said something that sounded more like *pangcake*. What happens here is that the [n] is anticipating the following velar [k] and assimilating to it in place of articulation; in other words, it becomes velar [ŋ]. This type of assimilation, called **'anticipatory assimilation'**, is by far the most frequent, and our nasals are notorious for doing it. Think of words in English with an *in-* or *con-* prefix. You will find that the nasals always anticipate the place of articulation of the following sound and convert to it—for example, *impossible* and *indent*, and *compel* and *contend*. This kind of assimilation even works across word boundaries: *handbag* becomes *hambag* [mb]. We can represent it in a kind of formula: AB → BB.

Assimilation can also work in the opposite direction; in other words, a sound can take on one or more features of the preceding sound. This is called **'lag assimilation'**. The formula would look like this: AB → AA. This process is less common, but plenty of examples exist in English, especially in rapid speech pronunciations such as [sɛvm] and [əlɛvm] for *seven* and *eleven*. In fact, in these two words, what you often hear is mutual assimilation, whereby the sounds borrow from each other—that is, [sɛbm] and [əlɛbm] (the labial quality of [v] is transferred to the following nasal, which then gives its stop and labial qualities to the [v], converting it to a [b]).

Another type of assimilation that you commonly hear in both OZ and NZ accents is called **'voicing assimilation'**. This involves the voicing of voiceless consonants when they occur between vowels in a word such as *atom* or a sequence such as *get it*. Think about it; your vocal folds are vibrating for the vowel sounds, and it's much easier not to shut off the voicing for the intervening consonant. Hence, we pronounce these as if they were spelt with a *d*: *adom* and *gedit*. In fact, what we are pronouncing here is really a very fast [d]. This is something called a **'flap'**, because what we're actually doing is 'flapping' the tongue against the alveolar ridge.

A final type of assimilation that we will illustrate is one that is so common that it has its own label: **'palatalisation'**. This sort of change affects consonants that occur before front vowels such as [i] and [e], and also the palatal approximant [j] (which, if you remember, is very like the high front vowel [i] and is sometimes even called a 'semi-vowel'). What happens here is that the tongue position of the vowel or approximant gets transferred onto the preceding consonant. Take a word sequence such as *can't you* [kant ju] or *did you* [dɪd ju]. The vocal tract is constricted for the articulation of [j], and the consonant [t] or [d] shifts into the vowel area, producing the palatal affricate [tʃ] or [ʤ], giving the pronunciation *can't you* [kanʧu] and *did you* [dɪʤu] respectively. It's as if a palatal pronunciation gets superimposed upon the consonant.

Variation in OZ and NZ English

When we first looked at the symbols for transcribing OZ and NZ varieties of English, we noted that vowel differences make up most of the distinctiveness that we associate with a particular accent and that, in addition, any major regional dialect such as OZ English or NZ English is actually made up of many variants. In this section we return to the discussion of vowels and consider two aspects of the variation within our Englishes down under.

We noted in chapter 1 that we can think of OZ and NZ English as a continuum of cultivated–general–broad and ethnic broad varieties, and that they are primarily differentiated by allophonic variation in the vowel phonemes. The vowels in Table 3.4 show the most interesting differences in OZ English. The diacritics indicate a modification to the starting point of the vowel: y̞ lower, y̝ higher, y̟ fronter, y̠ backer. As we can see, in moving from the cultivated end of the continuum to the broad end, the vowels become longer and more drawn out, in that the distance between the endpoints of the diphthongs increases. The vowel variation you see here is solely a matter of pronunciation. In other words, it is purely allophonic and doesn't affect the system of phonemes; the same set of contrasts is maintained.

Table 3.4 Allophonic variation in the vowel phonemes of OZ English

		Cultivated	*General*	*Broad*	*Ethnic Broad*
/i/	beat	[i]/[ɪi]	[əɪ]	[ə̞ɪ]	[ə̞ɪ]
/eɪ/	bait	[ɛɪ]	[ʌɪ]	[ʌ̞ɪ]	[a̝ɪ]
/oʊ/	boat	[oʊ]	[ʌʊ]	[aʊ]	[ə̞ʊ]
/aɪ/	bite	[aɪ]	[a̠ɪ]	[ɒ̝ɪ]	[ɒɪ]
/aʊ/	bout	[aʊ]	[æʊ]	[æ̝ʊ]	[ɛʊ]

Source: adapted from Horvath 1985 and Mitchell & Delbridge 1965

We discuss NZ English vowels in greater detail in chapter 4. For the moment, we confine ourselves to one interesting feature. As we mentioned above, there are generally either forty-three or forty-four phonemes in the various varieties that form NZ English. For many New Zealanders, the front centring diphthong /ɛə/, as in *chair*, and the high front centring diphthong /ɛə/, as in *cheer*, are actually merging. This means that the contrast between the two phonemes is not being maintained and that pairs of words such as *cheer* and *chair*, and *rear* and *rare* are being pronounced the same. While this merger seems to have been going on for some 40 years, the question of which phoneme they are merging on appears to be controversial. In two studies, Elizabeth Gordon and Margaret Maclagan (1990; Maclagan & Gordon 1996) have found that the direction of the merger is on /ɪə/. However, Janet Holmes and Allan Bell (1993) have found that, for the speakers they surveyed, the direction of the merger has reversed in the last 20 years and is now on /ɛə/. This is a case in which variation looks like a possible sound change in progress (we take this up in more detail in chapter 4). Only time will tell whether the two phonemes will completely merge and which phoneme will win out.

SOUNDS IN CONTEXT

As we have seen from briefly looking at connected speech, the vowels and consonants of English do not act alone. Likewise, as we will discuss in this section, they are not organised simply as a sequence of sounds within a word. Instead they are arranged in terms of syllables, which are in turn arranged into words. In this section, we will first consider the structure of English syllables and then the features of spoken English, such as stress and intonation, that apply to syllables, words, and phrases.

Syllable structure

When we simplify our speech to 'use words of only one syllable' to make a point 'perfectly clear', we are drawing on our knowledge about the relationship between words and syllables. For example, a 'monosyllabic' word, such as *corn*, only contains a single syllable, whereas 'polysyllabic' words such as *salad*, *cucumber*, and *avocado* contain two, three, and four syllables respectively.

Just as a word can consist of a single syllable, so too can a syllable consist of a single sound. For example, the word *I* has one syllable that contains one sound, whereas the single syllable of *squash* consists of five sounds. The structure of English syllables can be divided into four parts: the **onset**, the **nucleus**, the **coda**, and the **rhyme**. Each syllable has a nucleus or peak, which is usually a vowel (V) but can be certain consonants (C), such as /l/, /r/, or a nasal. The nucleus may have one or more consonants preceding it, which make up the onset, and it may also have one or more consonants following it, which make up the coda. In a syllable such as *salt*, /s/ is the onset, /ɒ/ is the nucleus, and /lt/ is the coda. The nucleus and the coda combine to give the rhyme of the syllable, and it is this property that we make use of in rhyming slang such as *stop thief* for 'beef', *soft as silk* for 'milk', *Mother Machree* for 'tea', *kerb and gutter* for 'butter', and *Anna Louise* for 'cheese'.

The structure of the syllable can be represented as:

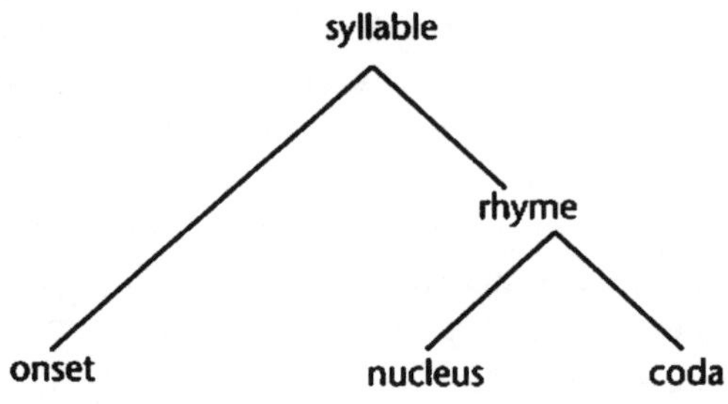

Now while the nucleus is generally a vowel, there are a few consonants—/l/, /r/, or a nasal—that can act as the syllable nucleus, and in these cases they are called 'syllabic consonants'. For example the second syllable in *little* /lɪtl̩/and *mutton* /mʌtn̩/ is a syllabic consonant (/l/ and /n/ respectively), and this is shown by a small vertical mark beneath the consonant.

We find that people generally agree on the number of syllables in the majority of words in English. There are a few cases, however, where people disagree, and some of these are because of dialectal differences in the way that particular words are pronounced. For example, pairs such as *grown/groan*, *mown/moan*, and *thrown/throne* are not homophonous for many speakers of NZ and OZ English, the first member of each pair being disyllabic. Similarly, some people maintain that they make a distinction between *lightning* (in the sky) with two syllables /laɪt$nɪŋ/ and *lightening* 'making light' with three syllables /laɪt$n̩$ɪŋ/, and between *codling* 'a little codfish'

/kɒd$lɪŋ/ and *coddling* 'a way of cooking an egg' /kɒd$l̩$ɪŋ/. (The $ marks a syllable boundary).

The speed of speech, degree of formality, and context of use can also influence the number of syllables that people assign to a word. For example, if words such as *meal*, *feel*, and *heal* are carefully read aloud as distinct words in a list, many people will say that they contain two syllables, but when they occur in connected casual speech, they are likely to be counted as having only one syllable. English has an unusually large range of different types of syllables, including onsets of two or three consonants. The monosyllabic words in Table 3.5 illustrate this range.

Table 3.5 Syllable types

Syllable type	*Example*	*Onset*	*Nucleus*	*Coda*
V	eye		/aɪ/	
VC	all		/ɔ/	/l/
CV	bee	/b/	/i/	
CVC	fish	/f/	/ɪ/	/ʃ/
CVCC	box	/b/	/ɒ/	/ks/
CCVCC	trust	/tr/	/ʌ/	/st/
CCCVC	string	/str/	/ɪ/	/ŋ/

The rules that describe the possible syllable structures are called '**phonotactic constraints**'. In English there are restrictions, for example, on the combinations of consonants that make up a two- and three-consonant cluster. The following list shows the possibilities for three-consonant clusters in a syllable onset at the beginning of a word:

/s + p + l, r, j/
/s + t + r, j/
/s + k + l, r, j, w/

Can you think of a word illustrating each of these possible consonant combinations? (Some of the combinations such as /skl/ are quite restricted.)

To sum up, the phonotactic constraints describe the permissible sequences of vowels and consonants in a syllable and thus distinguish the thousands of words that do not exist but could from the thousands more that cannot because they do not have permissible English syllable structures.

Prosodic features

So far we have focused on the segments of speech or 'what we say'. But as an oft-quoted adage highlights, 'it ain't what you say; it's the way that you say it'. For instance, the meaning of what is being said can be altered just by using a different 'tone of voice': a whisper can convey secrecy or conspiracy; nasality can imply anxiety; and breathiness can convey deep emotion or sexual desire. In examining the different 'ways' of saying things, the most significant properties to consider are tempo, loudness, and pitch. These properties, referred to as **prosodic** (or **suprasegmental**) features, are features not of individual sound segments but of syllables, words, and phrases. First we will illustrate each of them individually, then consider how they combine to produce the stress and intonation patterns of English words and sentences. We finish this section with a discussion of the functions of high rising intonation in NZ and OZ English.

Tempo

Varying the tempo or speed at which we talk can serve a number of functions. Differences in feeling can be conveyed. For example, a fast tempo can show excitement, and a slow tempo can convey a pondering reflective tone. As any child standing in front of a display of lollies knows, a parent's response of *No-o-o*, said with a long drawn out vowel, is possibly open to negotiation, whereas a short, clipped *No* is unlikely to be.

The tempo of an utterance can also signal grammatical boundaries: a quicker tempo marks that a phrase is functioning as a parenthetical aside (*That cake they brought—**you know the one I mean**—was really rich*), or that it is functioning as a single word (*a **devil-may-care** approach to life*).

Loudness

As with tempo, a range of feelings can be expressed by differences in loudness: friendliness can be signalled by a soft voice, whereas anger is often expressed in a loud voice. Loudness, along with other prosodic features, is an important marker of our personal identity and of various occupational varieties. In sports broadcasting, for instance, snooker commentary is characterised by a soft voice, while rugby play-by-play announcers use a loud voice.

Pitch

When we speak, we also vary the pitch of our voice by changing the rate at which the vocal cords vibrate: the faster they vibrate, the higher the pitch. The pitch range (that is, the difference between the highest pitches and the lowest pitches in an utterance) can also be varied. A wide range is typically used by cricket commentators, whereas a narrow range is found in the monotone or 'drone' of a horse race call. The average pitch height of the 'drone' rises, though, as the race progresses. A person's average pitch height can also be a factor in stereotyping, as illustrated by the complaints of some people that the voices of women broadcasters are pitched too high.

Pitch changes serve an important function in conveying sentence meaning. Listen for whether the pitch of your voice falls or rises as you read out loud a statement such as *They're two snags short of a barbie* and the corresponding echo question *They're two snags short of a barbie?* Typically we say a statement with a falling pitch, but we say a question with a rising pitch at the end. As we discuss below, pitch changes occur in distinct patterns in forming the intonation system of English.

Stress

Stress is the term we use for the syllable that is given prominence in a word or phrase. For example, in many dialects of English, there are word pairs that can be distinguished by their stress pattern—nouns are stressed on the first syllable and verbs on the second:

This brand of juice is an **import**. (noun—stress on first syllable)
They **imported** apples for their line of juice. (verb—stress on second syllable)

For speakers of OZ English, verb members of such pairs tend to be stressed on the second syllable, whereas in NZ English it is common to hear first-syllable stress as in **re**search (verb) and **pro**test (verb) (Elizabeth Gordon, pers. comm., 3 April 1997). In both varieties, it seems that nouns show variation: some can be stressed only on the first, some only on the second, and some on either. The trend is increasingly towards stress on the first syllable.

While in words of three or more syllables, more than one syllable may be stressed, there will still be a single syllable that receives greater stress than the others, and we say that this syllable carries primary stress. Analyses differ as to just how many levels of stress there are in English (some distinguish as many as four), though most dictionaries mark only one or two. In marking stress, primary or main stress is often indicated by a high vertical bar placed before the stressed syllable and secondary stress with a low bar, as in /ˌmʌltəplə'keɪʃən/ 'multiplication'. Alternatively, primary stress is indicated by an acute accent (´) over the vowel of the stressed syllable and secondary stress with a grave accent (`), giving /mʌ̀ltəpləkéɪʃən/ 'multiplication'.

In connected speech, variations in the use of stress produce the speech rhythm of a language. In English there is a tendency for stressed syllables to occur at near regular intervals as we speak, and as a result of this tendency, English can be called a stress-timed language. By this we mean that rhythm is a matter of timing within the sentence, and English syllables vary in the length of time they take to utter. In the stress-timed pattern of English, three syllables do not necessarily take three times as long to utter as one syllable. Instead there is a tendency to stress syllables at regular intervals and jam intermediate syllables between the stressed syllables. In comparison, many other languages, such as French, can be called syllable-timed languages. In these languages, each syllable is perceived as tending to take about the same length of time to utter.

Historically, English has been a stress-timed language. But in some parts of the world, where new varieties of English have developed, these 'New Englishes' are syllable-timed rather than stressed-timed. In Hong Kong English, for example, the emergence of a syllable-timed rhythm can be explained by the influence of various regional Chinese languages, which are all syllable-timed languages. Speakers of syllable-timed languages, whose variety of new English also tends to be syllable-timed, often find the stress-timed rhythm of the more established varieties of English difficult to understand, while speakers of the more established varieties find the new syllable-timed varieties difficult to follow because they reduce the pattern of stress contrast, which is an important factor in identifying a spoken word.

Intonation

Not only are English utterances characterised by their rhythm, but they also have typical patterns of pitch changes, which form the intonation system of English. In analysing the intonation of an utterance, we divide it into one or more intonation phrases. Each intonation phrase has a particular pitch change pattern, which is known as a '**tune**'. Within the intonation phrase, there is usually a single syllable that stands out because it carries the major pitch change, and this particular syllable is called the '**nuclear syllable**'. Consider the following direction from a recipe for meatballs:

If olive oil is not available, || use another oil low in saturated fat.

In this sentence there are two intonation phrases, and the beginning of the second intonation phrase is marked by ||. The major pitch changes in each intonation phrase are represented by lines placed above the utterance, and the nuclear syllable is in bold. The pitch change that starts on the nuclear syllable continues until the end of the intonation phrase. This example also illustrates that, while a word such as *olive* will have a primary stress on the first syllable when it is pronounced in isolation, in connected speech the primary stress may be reduced or downshifted (if it is not the nuclear syllable), as in the intonation phrase *if olive oil is not available.*

As we saw above, one function of different tunes is to distinguish between statements and questions. Another function is to distinguish those parts of an intonation phrase in an utterance that are old or known information from the part that is new. Generally the word with the nuclear syllable signals the part of the utterance that the speaker is treating as new information. To see this, try saying the following sentence with the two different intonation patterns that are indicated:

A frittata is a type of omelette.

A frittata is a type of omelette.

The first intonation pattern would be appropriate as an answer to the question: *What is a frittata?* In this case *frittatas* are what is being talked about, and the new information is that they are a type of omelette. In contrast, the second intonation pattern might be used in answer to someone soliciting help with a crossword puzzle: *What is eight letters long and is a type of omelette?* Here the new information is *frittata.*

To give a sample of the range of intonation patterns in English, let's consider the one-word tone group *yes*:

Utterance	Tune	Possible context of use
Yes	falling	Yes, let's go have a cuppa.
Yes	high rising	I'm not sure I want to agree to this?
Yes	low rising	Keep going, I'm listening.
Yes	falling–rising	I'm not really sure about this.
Yes	rising–falling	I'm telling my cricket team-mate to run.

High rising intonation

A distinctive intonation pattern that occurs in NZ and OZ English is the use of a high rising terminal (HRT) rather than a falling one at the end of a statement. An HRT is similar to the rising pitch found at the end of a yes-or-no question, such as *Do you like anchovies?*, or an echo question, such as *You like anchovies?* Consider the following example from a recent study of HRTs in NZ English (Britain 1992:80–1). Here the italicised clauses end with an HRT, marked by ↑, and a + marks a pause:

Pam: I had another incident of someone in Porirua following me followed me home from the railway station *and tried to cut me off in the park*↑ I was walking home about half past seven at night and I knew he was following me fr- *and I stopped in at the chicken shack*↑ *and bought some chips*↑

Interviewer: mmm

Pam: and everything and m- mucked around *and um when I got out the shop I couldn't see him around*↑ and I w- crossed the cr- road at the crossing walked up to where the bridge is to go over the park

Interviewer: yeah

Pam: and started to walk up the path *well just out of the corner of my eye I say him across the road*↑ *in the bushes*↑ *across the road*↑ and he crossed the road *and started to come up the road behind me*↑ and I ran across the park back down to the shops *and he tried to cut me off the other way*↑ *so I was going like this and he was going like that*↑ and we just sort of met + there and he said don't be scared of me + huh and said F off [laughs] and then I phoned up my father and he came down and got me

Although the use of HRTs also occurs in the USA, Canada, and the United Kingdom, it has been stereotyped (and often stigmatised) as a distinctive pattern of NZ and OZ English since the early 1960s. Given the greater frequency of HRTs reported in studies conducted in New Zealand, it is possible that the use of HRTs has been imported from New Zealand into Australia. Alternatively, it might always have been in OZ English, but has just been slower to take off. However, since there is a 10-year gap between the first systematic data collection in the two countries, and since methodologies of the various studies differ substantially, it is impossible to know for sure.

Questions of geographic origins aside, in both NZ and OZ English this feature is generally believed to mark younger speakers, especially young female speakers and, in New Zealand, young Maori speakers. However, whether this is a linguistic change in progress or simply a feature of the speech of a particular age group remains to be seen. A linguistic innovation that began in the 1960s may be carried through by speakers into their 50s as a permanent change, or it may remain a marker of the speech of the under-25 crowd.

Why use it? In both varieties of English, HRTs seem to have a dual function: they are used to regulate the conversational interaction, and they are markers of (positive) politeness. A speaker might use the first function of an HRT to check that the listener has understood, to ask for the listener's reaction to what has been said, or to seek empathy from the listener. An HRT can also be used to signal that the speaker wants to continue to talk. The second function of an HRT signals positive politeness towards the listener, actively inviting the listener's participation, and emphasising the common ground between the speaker and listener—that is, the in-group nature of their relationship. In short, HRTs provide a way of mutually constructing a conversation and maintaining the engagement of the conversational partners, while also expressing group solidarity.

POINTS TO REMEMBER

- Phonetics is the study of the way we make, transmit, and receive speech sounds, whereas phonology is the study of the sound systems and patterns of sounds that occur in a language.
- Consonants are described in terms of the state of the vocal cords (voiced or voiceless); the place of articulation (bilabial, labio-dental, dental, alveolar, palato-alveolar, palatal, velar, or glottal); and the manner of articulation (stop, nasal, fricative, affricate, lateral, or approximant).
- Vowels are described in terms of the height of the body of the tongue (high, mid, or low); the front–back position of the tongue (front, central, or back); and the degree of lip rounding (rounded or unrounded).
- We use a phonetic alphabet such as the International Phonetic Alphabet to transcribe the contrasting sounds of English, since there are not enough letters in the English alphabet to represent each of the distinctive sounds with a different letter.
- Phones are the physical units of sounds produced by the speech organs, whereas phonemes are abstract units that indicate differences of meaning within a particular language. The variant pronunciations, or phones, of a phoneme are allophones of that phoneme.
- In determining the phonemes of a language, we look at whether the phones occur in minimal pairs, complementary distribution, or free variation.
- In the flow of connected speech, the pronunciation of sounds is affected by the processes of assimilation, dissimilation, deletion, epenthesis, and metathesis.
- The sequence of sounds within a word is arranged in terms of one or more syllables, and the structure of a syllable can be divided into the onset, nucleus, coda, and rhyme. Phonotactic constraints describe the possible syllable structures within a language.
- The prosodic features of tempo, loudness, and pitch combine to produce the stress and intonation patterns of words and sentences.

EXERCISES

1 Reading transcription

The following example is a transcription of a passage in Aboriginal English that has been pronounced carefully. Rewrite it in conventional English orthography.

[ɪn ðə waɪt kʌltʃə nɒt tə lʊk sʌmwʌn ɪn ði aɪ ɔl ðə taɪm ðæt ðɛ tɔkɪŋ tə ju ɪz rud ɪts laɪk jə nɒt peɪjɪŋ ətɛnʃən bʌt tə lʊk æbərɪdʒənəl pipəl ɪn ði aɪ ðə hoʊl taɪm jə tɔkɪŋ tə ðɛm ɪz rud bəkɒz jə stɛrɪŋ æt ðɛm ðæt wɒz rilɪ had tə gɛt just tu ɪt teɪks ə lɒŋ taɪm tu æksɛpt ðæt sʌmθɪŋ jə lɛnd æz gʊd mænəz ɪn wʌn kʌltʃə ɪz rɒŋ ɪn ənʌðə ə lɒŋ taɪm tə bi eɪbəl tə du ðæt ənd fil kʌmftəbəl əbaʊt duɪŋ ɪt]

transcription of passage from Bowden & Bunbury 1990:15

2 Finding errors in transcription

The following transcription is of another passage in Aboriginal English. However, the person who transcribed it has made some mistakes. List the words that contain the mistakes, and for each one, give the correct version.

[wɪθ rəleɪʃənsɪps ðɜra sɛtən θɪŋz ɪn ðə æbərɪgənəl səsaɪjəti ðæt yu dʒʌst doʊnt du, ænd aɪm lɜnɪŋ ðoʊz—wɒt tə du ænd wɒt nɒt tə du. ju kæn rəfjuz ə bɪskət ɔrə pis əf brɛd ɔrə pis əv keɪk u sʌmθɪŋ, but ju nɛvə rəfjuz ə kap əv ti. ðɛra pipəl ðæt ju goʊ and si fɜst ænd pipəl ju spɛnd ə sɜtən əmaʊnt əv teɪm wɪθ. ðɛra sʌm thæt ju kæn tɛk tu əbaʊt sɜtən θɪŋz ænd ʌðəz hu cæn tik əbaʊt ʌðə θɪngz.]

transcription of passage from Bowden & Bunbury 1990:14

3 Describing sounds in tongue-twisters

The effect of tongue-twisters often depends on a pair of consonants that have a similar articulation. For example, in *She sifted thistles through her thistle-sifter,* the two consonants that give difficulties are /s/ and /θ/. While both of these sounds are voiceless fricatives, they differ in their place of articulation: /s/ is an alveolar, while /θ/ is a dental. In each of the following tongue-twisters (supplied by Ivan Uemlianin, pers. comm., 27 January 1996), identify the pair of consonants that create the tongue-twister, and describe their similarities and differences in terms of voicing, place of articulation, and manner of articulation:

a freshly fried fresh flesh
b Ed'd edited it
c preshrunk silk shirts
d tie twine to three tree twigs
e a bloke's bike back brake block broke.
f the sixth sick sheik's sixth sheep's sick (a variant on what the *Guinness Book of Records* considers to be the hardest tongue-twister in English)

4 Transcribing oronyms

In connected speech, there are no silences between words in the way that there are spaces between written words. This is a defining feature of 'oronyms', which are sequences of sounds that can be divided into words in more than one way. For each of the following oronyms (supplied by Patrick Nilens, pers. comm., 23 October 1995), write out your pronunciation using the phonemic notation employed in the text. Are each of these true oronyms in your dialect of English?

a I scream / ice-cream
b grade A / grey day
c iced ink / I stink

- d It's hard to recognise speech / It's hard to wreck a nice beach
- e That's where the sun's rays meet / That's where the sons raise meat
- f night rate / nitrate / nigh trait
- g The stuffy nose can lead to problems / The stuff he knows can lead to problems
- h A girl with colitis goes by / a girl with kaleidoscope eyes (from the Beatles' song 'Lucy in the Sky with Diamonds')
- i I'll never be your pizza burnin' / I'll never be your beast of burden (from the Rolling Stones' song)
- j It's a happy enchilada [Mexican food] / It's a half an inch of water...(from the John Prine song 'That's the Way the World Goes 'Round')

5 The phonology of cartoon characters

One of the most memorable qualities of many of the Warner Bros cartoon characters is their speech patterns: Elmer Fudd chasing 'that wascally wabbit' and Tweety Bird's wide-eyed pronouncement, 'I taut I taw a putty-tat'. Consider the following examples of Tweety Bird's speech from a study by Stephen Cutts (1992:38).

a Describe how Tweety Bird pronounces consonant clusters in initial position. What phonological process is this an example of?

[tɒp]	stop
[tɔrm]	storm

b Tweety Bird (like Elmer Fudd) has trouble pronouncing /l/ and /r/. What phone does Tweety Bird use for each of these two phonemes?

[wɒkin]	rocking
[wʌwi]	worry
[twɪk]	trick
[wɔ]	law
[swip]	sleep

c However, Tweety Bird (again like Elmer Fudd) does correctly pronounce /l/ and /r/ in certain positions. Given these data and those in (b), list the allophones of the phonemes /l/ and /r/ respectively. State the distribution of the allophones for each of the phonemes.

[ol]	ol'
[wəpild]	repealed
[dir]	dear
[tɔrm]	storm
[wɪtl]	little
[pepə]	paper

d Tweety Bird also has trouble pronouncing certain consonants in syllable-initial position. Identify which consonants are problematic, and describe how Tweety Bird actually pronounces them. What general change is occurring in the place and manner of articulation of these sounds?

[dʊd]	good
[do]	go
[dwæni]	granny
[tɔt]	caught
[tʌmz]	comes
[hɪpətwɪt]	hypocrite
[tʌmtin]	something
[tɔ]	saw
[tɔt]	thought
[pʊtitæt]	pussycat
[ætɪdənt]	accident

6 Speech in writing

What do spellings such as the following show about English pronunciation? In each example, describe the phonological processes that have taken place.

a I hafta go.
b Drinka pinta milk.
c a wannabe
d if I had my drothers
e fish 'n chips
f gotcha!
g A nice cold cuppa (ad for Diet Coke)
h Gonna make you sweat (from *The Australian Way*, Qantas in-flight magazine, November 1996)

7 Syllable structure

People differ in their judgments of the number of syllables that the following words contain. Ask several people (including some children if possible) to say these words and then tell you how many syllables there are in each of them. Try to explain, for each word, why people may differ in their judgments, even if the people you ask are all in agreement.

a furore
b medicine
c laboratory
d spasm
e oven
f prisoner
g million
h merrier
i feral
j hire
k hour

8 Sniglets

However many words exist in English, there are still lexical gaps, and people happily create new words to represent unexpressed concepts. American comedian Rich Hall has even created a name for such words: 'sniglets'. The following are some examples from a contest on ABC Radio 3LO that was held in 1995. Notice that these English 'sniglets', like all English words, conform to the phonotactic constraints of the language.

splatchnoff	'just a little' (food, for example)
blamp	'the part of a dog's nose that gets wet and hot'
flobs	'the small amount of tea or coffee left in the bottom of a cup'
wockles	'dusty cobwebs hanging from the ceiling'

Identify which of the following are already words in English (and write them in conventional spelling), which are potential sniglets, and which are not possible words/sniglets in English (and state your reason):

a [θroʊpt]
b [sktiʧʃ]
c [waɪskt]
d [bkli]
e [kwɒdrənt]
f [blæʧʃ]
g [fruit]
h [zɪŋkaɪt]
i [skiʧʃ]
j [gnɒstɪk]
k [blizk]
l [tɪkz]
m [hoʊks]
n [strɛŋp]
o [θɪnk]
p [ʧʃækari]
q [fjuzi]
r [plɒkəl]
s [trɒpoʊ]
t [sŋɪp]

4

Sounds across Time

INTRODUCTION

If only we somehow had access to a time machine and could transport ourselves back to the period, say, of Geoffrey Chaucer (?1345–1400). Other differences aside, the accents we would encounter would sound at once tantalisingly familiar and bizarrely foreign. Or what if we went even further back in time to a performance of the great epic poem *Beowulf* (around the eighth century). To our modern ears, the language wouldn't even sound remotely English, although some of us might recognise it as being Germanic.

In this chapter, we explore some of the major sound changes that have transformed the shape of English so radically over the centuries. Phonological change is probably the most highly developed area in the field of historical linguistics. For a start, we know a lot about speech organs and the mechanics of speech production. So we already have a good idea about what are, and what are not, likely sound changes.

The study of sound variation and change within English has a particularly long history. Until the 1980s, however, Antipodean English tended to be overlooked in the discussion. This was true especially of NZ English, which, if it was discussed at all, was lumped together with OZ English. In this chapter, we illustrate some of the sound changes and variation in NZ English and OZ English.

A hot topic within any study of English phonology is spelling, whether you want to know how to teach it, how to adapt to different conventions, how to reform it, or even just how to cope with an American spell-checker on your computer. Throughout this book we've been illustrating that you cannot understand where English is unless you have seen where it's been. As you'll appreciate by the end of this chapter, this makes even more sense when it comes to understanding the English spelling tradition.

TYPES OF SOUND CHANGE

First, let's look at how some of the usual processes that affect the way we pronounce language can act as triggers for sound change. As we saw in chapter 3, there are three main types of phonological processes: loss of sounds, addition of new sounds, and modifications to already existing sounds. These processes are going on all the time in our language. Some are regular processes; some are irregular or sporadic. And as we will illustrate here, sometimes they lead to lasting change in the language. But before we look more closely at some of the sounds changes that have actually taken place over the history of English, let's consider the question of process versus change.

Process versus change

As we noted in chapter 3, deletions and assimilations are especially frequent in ordinary connected speech, and it's through these sorts of short cuts that we achieve a fluent and smooth-sounding speech style. For example, in everyday speech, it's usual to omit the unstressed vowels and syllables. Words like *arithmetic*, *enough*, and *escape* are much more likely to be pronounced as *'rithmetic*, *'nough*, and *'scape*, with the initial unstressed vowel omitted. People often complain about these reductive processes, describing them as 'sloppiness' or 'laziness'. But imagine just how turgid and long-winded you would sound if you paid attention to every detail and pronounced each individual sound as if it were in isolation? These sorts of reductions are an inherent characteristic of ordinary casual (and usually rapid) speech. We all make them, and we would sound stilted if we didn't.

Sometimes these reductions remain just that: fast speech phenomena. They make no long-term impression on the language but remain a spontaneous feature of connected speech. However, it can happen that the reduced forms become so common that they start to appear with their own spelling, as in the catch phrase *the three r's: reading, ritin' an' rithmetic*. In this way, they exist—usually as more colloquial variants—alongside their full forms. They might even become so established that they make it into the dictionary. The *Oxford English Dictionary* (OED), for example, contains a separate entry for *nuff* ('enough'). Some reduced forms become so successful that they actually oust the original full form: *possum* and *squirrel*, for example, have replaced the earlier *opossum* and *esquirrel*. The full forms and the reduced forms can also end up parting company and pursuing separate paths. In this way, deletions are responsible for the introduction of many new words into the language; nowadays, for example, no one connects the forms *etiquette* and *ticket*, or *acute* and *cute*.

Like deletions, assimilations are also very frequent in normal connected speech. As we saw in chapter 3, most of us would pronounce *miss you* as /mɪʃə/, *can't you* as /kătʃə/, and *did you* as /dɪdʒə/. This is simply a matter of our efficient speech organs taking necessary short cuts. But in this context, the assimilations are just the pronunciations of casual speech and don't have any long-term effect. We're not likely to change to /dʒu/ in other contexts for the pronunciation of *you*. But as we'll see below, assimilation can also have a dramatic impact on the language. In the case of English, it has even been responsible for the introduction of a number of brand new consonants into the language, including /dʒ/ and /tʃ/.

To highlight the distinction between process versus change, the standard practice in linguistics is to use an arrow → when a process is under way in the language and to use an arrowhead, or shaftless arrow, > to represent historical processes (that is, changes that have taken place). In both cases, the direction of the arrow or arrowhead represents the direction of the process or change.

Old sounds drop out

The linguist Ron Langacker once described languages as 'gigantic expression compacting machines' (1977:106). It's an apt description. Through the deletion of sounds, words can be compressed into mere fragments of what they once were. Take Modern English *lady* and *lord*, which are all that are left of the original *hlāfdige* and *hlāfwēard* (literally, 'loaf kneader' and 'loaf warden'). The transition went something like this:

hlāfdige > lafdi > lady
hlāfwēard > hlāford > laverd > lord

Consonants, vowels, and even whole syllables can be deleted over the course of time. And while they may disappear from any environment, they are particularly vulnerable at the ends of words, where articulation is weaker. As we will see in chapter 11, this vulnerability has figured prominently in the disappearance of the inflectional system in English.

Clusters of consonants are also liable to simplify. Compare the following forms. In Modern English, the initial cluster has been reduced each time. In the case of /kn/, the spelling retains the cluster.

Old English	*Modern English*
hlūd	loud
hnutu	nut
hring	ring
cnoccian	knock

Both OZ and NZ English show signs of further cluster simplification. For example, the pronunciation /hw/ in words such as *whales* and *which* has been gradually disappearing, so that *whales*, *Wales*, and *wails* are now pronounced identically for most people, as are *which* and *witch*. In NZ English, the cluster is hanging in a little longer, especially in formal speech, but the fact that it's avoided by younger people suggests that its days are numbered. Note that originally the cluster was spelt *hw* but this changed to *wh* after the Norman Conquest.

The disappearance of /hw/ is by no means confined to the speech of Antipodeans, however. The change to /w/ started very early (probably sometime during Middle English), but for centuries it was considered a vulgarism— in fact, in some parts of the world it still is. Many elocution manuals continue to insist on /hw/, acting much like artificial life-support systems for the pronunciation. Only in Scotland and Ireland does the cluster seem to be maintained, and its survival in Scottish English probably explains its greater tenacity in New Zealand.

The disappearance of /hw/ is actually part of an ongoing trend. As you can see from the examples above, the phoneme /h/ was part of a number of other clusters that no longer exist: /hl/, /hr/, and /hn/ (this last one sounds a bit like a sniff). The only /h + C/ cluster that's now left is /hj/, as in *huge* and *human,* but as you are probably aware, many speakers have lost this cluster as well. In a number of varieties of English, *Hugh* and *you* are pronounced in the same way as /ju/.

Sometimes consonant loss is accompanied by a lengthening of the neighbouring vowel (unless it's already long, in which case it doesn't change). This is called '**compensatory lengthening**'. It's almost as if the space taken up by the consonant is transferred to the adjacent vowel; the length then becomes a kind of ghost of the lost consonant. Have a look at the following examples. As you can see, early English experienced regular loss of nasal consonants when they occurred before voiceless fricatives. In each instance, the loss is accompanied by a lengthening of the vowel (which later changes to a diphthong in Modern English). We've supplied the Modern German here for comparison, because it preserves the original nasal–fricative cluster. Note that length on the Old English vowel is traditionally signalled by a dash above the vowel.

Pre-Old English	*Old English*	*Modern English*	*Modern German*
*gons	gōs	goose	Gans
*fimf	fīf	five	fünf
*munth	mūþ	mouth	Mund

Vowel deletion has occurred so rampantly that a number of impressive sounding labels have been developed to describe the loss of vowels from different parts of the word:

- **Apocope** involves the disappearance of the final vowel. Once upon a time the final silent *e* in many Modern English words such as *tale* was pronounced. In other words: /ta:lə/ > /ta:l/ > /teɪl/. This kind of erosion of word endings is very common.
- **Syncope** involves the loss of medial vowels. These sorts of losses are significant because they can result in new consonant clusters, as in *munecas* > *monkes* > *monks.*
- **Aphesis** is—you guessed it—the loss of an unstressed initial vowel, as in the examples we mentioned earlier, *opossum* > *possum* and *esquirrel* > *squirrel.*

It is also possible for an *entire* syllable to disappear and this is termed '**haplology**'. For example, *interpretative* > *interpretive* and *Englalond* > *England.* As you can see from these two examples, the syllable that disappears is typically identical or similar to an adjacent syllable.

New sounds appear

The opposite strategy of sound loss is sound addition; in other words, segments have been introduced where they previously didn't exist. The label '**epenthetic change**' is sometimes used to describe this type of sound change. It's considerably less common than sound loss, however.

As we discussed in chapter 3, the motivation for new consonants appearing is mistiming: sounds are added as the vocal organs move from one sound to another. In some cases, such as in the following examples, the pronunciation with the epenthetic sound has actually become the preferred form, and in these cases we say that an epenthetic change has taken place. In each instance, note the identical place of articulation of the nasal and oral stop in the Modern English words.

Old English	*Modern English*
brēmel	bramble
ganra	gander (compare related *gannet*)

þunor	thunder (compare German *Donner*)
þȳmel	thimble

We also find instances where a consonant has been added to the end of a word. In these cases the motivation is different, but it still involves a kind of mistiming. When you've finished saying something, your speech organs go back to rest position. But if you do this more abruptly, then somewhere in the vocal tract you get a closure, and this means that you add a stop consonant. The informal (also more emphatic) pronunciation of *no* as *nope* is usually attributed to this process. (*Yep* was formed later by analogy; see chapter 11 for a discussion of analogy.) Usually though, the cause is that the tongue rests against the alveolar ridge before articulation is complete, and this results in an extra alveolar stop. This explains the shift from early English *middes* and *betwihs* to *(a)midst* and *betwixt* (also the dialectal variant *varmint* alongside the standard form *vermin)*. This sort of change is irregular and is much rarer than the type of consonant addition we discussed earlier.

Old sounds are modified

As well as loss and addition, sounds can be modified in various ways. As we outlined in chapter 3, sounds can change their shape to become more alike (**assimilation**) or to become unalike (**dissimilation**), or they can be reordered and appear in another position in the word (**metathesis**). Not only do these processes occur in connected speech, but they are also types of sound changes that have occurred in the development of English. Let's look at some examples of each of these types of historical change.

Assimilation

One type of assimilation—palatalisation—has lead to the current pronunciation of words such as *nation*, *sure*, *sugar*, *measure*, *pleasure*, and so on. Sometimes the spelling gives a clue; for example, the *ti* in *nation* shows the original [i] that triggered the pronunciation [ʃ]. Occasionally it happens, too, that consciousness of the spelling can cause speakers to revert to the original non-palatal pronunciation. For example, during the eighteenth century, the bold letter(s) in words like *presume* and *consume* were pronounced as [ʒ] and [ʃ] respectively; in *hideous*, *Indian*, and *idiot* as [ʤ]; and in *duteous*, *bounteous*, and *plenteous* as [ʧ].

So far, in all of the examples of assimilation that we have seen, either as a process of connected speech or as a sound change, the assimilation has been partial. That is, the sounds that have been changed have still retained at least one of their original features; in other words, they have remained distinct. But it is also possible for a sound to assimilate totally to the neighbouring sound. Consider, for example, the history of the word *wool*. The Proto-Germanic consonant cluster [ln] became a long (or geminate) [ll]:

Proto-Germanic **wulno* > Pre-Old English **wullo* > Old English *wull*

It is also possible (although less common) to find assimilation occurring over a distance. In consonants, it's rare, and is only responsible for sporadic changes such as *orang-utan* > *orang-outang*. In vowels the process is more usual and has brought about some significant changes in the language. Really it involves a kind of vowel harmony. Consider the following changes that gave rise to the Modern English alternation *foot/feet*:

	Singular	*Plural*
	[fo:t]	[fo:ti] (in pre-Old English)
becomes	[fo:t]	[fœ:ti]
becomes	[fo:t]	[fe:t]
becomes	[fʊt]	[fit] (in Modern English)

Originally the plural was signalled by an *-i* ending. In anticipation of the frontness of the vowel [i] in this suffix, the long back vowel [o:] in the stem fronted to [œ:], giving [fœ:ti]. The vowel [œ:] is probably new to you; basically it's just a round [e]; make the vowel sound /e/ and then, instead of spreading your lips, round them. The suffix was later dropped, leaving then the alternation [fo:t/fe:t], which then later changed to the forms we now know today.

This kind of vowel harmony (or '**umlauting**', as it's called) is a feature of Germanic languages and has produced many of the irregular vowel alternations you find in Modern English. For example, the vowels in the second member in pairs like *full/fill, food/feed, lie/lay, fall/fell,* and *drink/drench* are the result of vowel harmony with the palatal semi-vowel [j] in the now lost suffix *-jan*.

Dissimilation

Dissimilation is really the opposite of assimilation; it describes how sounds become less like other sounds in the neighbourhood. Most linguists attribute dissimilation to the fact that we find repetition of the same muscular activity difficult. You've probably all experienced at some time the difficulty of repeating the same action over and over again (whether it be stuffing envelopes, playing the same note over again, or repeating a sound in a tongue-twister like *Betty Botter bought some butter but she said the butter's bitter*). Frequently you suddenly find yourself doing something weird, often substituting a totally different action. In a sequence of repeated sounds, we can avoid the difficulty by substituting one of the sounds, and that's what often happens in tongue-twisters.

The liquids, such as [l] and [r], can be unstable and are particularly prone to this sort of dissimilation process. For example, the Latin borrowings *marmor, turtur,* and *purpur* became the English *marble, turtle,* and *purple* (the second [r] dissimilates to an [l]). But this change is only sporadic: a succession of *r*s won't regularly trigger dissimilation in this way.

Metathesis

Metathesis, or reordering, describes changes in the order of adjacent segments. Like dissimilation, metathesis can be regular, but is usually not. Also like dissimilation, examples of metathesis in English frequently involve liquids. Below are some examples.

Old English	*Modern English*
bridd	bird
hross	horse (compare unmetathesised *walrus*—literally 'whale horse')
bēorht	bright

thridda	third (compare unmetathesised *three*)
wæps	wasp (compare current non-standard *waps*)
aks	ask (compare current non-standard *aks*)

PHONETIC VERSUS PHONEMIC CHANGE

In the previous chapter we made a distinction between a phonological and phonetic description. Just to review, a phonetic description deals with the physical shape of the sounds of a language (in other words, the pronunciation of words and sentences). In contrast, a phonemic description deals with the way in which sounds relate to each other (in other words, the way in which the sounds form a system in a language). A phonemic description tells us what the basic sound units are for differentiating meanings. Looking at the historical changes in both the phonetic inventory and the phonemic system of English not only provides some valuable insights into where English has already been, but also helps us to understand where it is now.

Phonetic change: changes in accent

The history of English shows a number of phonetic changes (in other words, changes where there has been no disruption whatsoever in the number of phonemes or in the relationship between them). For example, the distribution of the allophones of a particular phoneme can change, as can the phonetic realisation of a phoneme (in other words, how it's pronounced). These are simply pronunciation changes; they have no real impact on the overall sound system.

To illustrate, the oral and nasal stops /t d n/, which are now pronounced as alveolar sounds, were once thought to be dental stops; that is, they were once pronounced much more forward in the mouth. From around the time of the medieval poet Chaucer, the articulation of these sounds started to move progressively further back in the mouth. Although the shape of the sounds has changed acoustically, this hasn't done anything to change the phonemic system of English; /t d/, for instance, still contrast with the other stops /p b/ and /k g/. The same words are distinguished as in Chaucer's time. The only difference is that they have a somewhat different phonetic form or pronunciation. This is pure phonetic change and can be represented as follows. (Note that the half moon under the symbols indicates that these sounds were produced more forward in the mouth.)

[t̪ d̪ n̪] > [t d n]

Another example is the phoneme /r/, which as you know, is now generally pronounced as an approximant. Historical linguists think that originally it was pronounced as a flap or trill, not unlike you find in Scots English today. A trill resembles a sequence of very rapid stops, with the tip of the tongue vibrating against the roof of the mouth (a flap is like one of these trills). Again this is just a simple change in pronunciation; nothing has changed in terms of the overall system.

Both these examples involve the phonetic shape of a phoneme in all the environments in which it appears. Changes can also occur in restricted environments. The /r/

phoneme illustrates this sort of change too. We know from spelling and from other sources (for instance, modern dialects) that, at one time, speakers of English pronounced /r/ wherever it appeared in a word. In other words, *her* would have been pronounced [hɜr]. Sometime in the seventeenth century, the pronunciation changed so that /r/ came to be pronounced only in the positions where it appeared before a vowel sound. This was the situation when English came out to Australia. So British and Australian speakers now say *her* [hɜ] *sausage* but *her* [hɜr] *appetite.* We describe these as *r*-less, or non-rhotic dialects.

Compare this situation with the English colonisation of North America, which took place much earlier during the seventeenth century. At this time the colonial settlers pronounced the /r/ wherever it was spelt, and it was this pronunciation, then, that was carried to North America. We describe the American dialects as *r*-ful, or rhotic, dialects. Pockets of *r*-lessness in the USA (such as Boston) are the result of earlier prolonged contact with the United Kingdom.

In New Zealand the situation is different again. Although English arrived in New Zealand later than in Australia, the distinct mix of input dialects, in particular the stronger presence of Scottish and Irish settlers, produced a different outcome. Today there are rhotic speakers still found in the South Island, principally Southland and parts of Otago. Previously, though, they were much more widespread and could be found in places such as Dunedin, Christchurch, and Nelson, which are now *r*-less (Bartlett 1992:5).

As far as the *r*-less dialects of English go, nothing has changed with respect to the phonological representation of the words. The system is the same. All that's changed are the rules of pronunciation—we pronounce *four* as [fɔ], but when followed by a vowel, as in *Four 'n Twenty Pies*, the [r] surfaces again and you get [fɔr ən twenti paɪz]. A possible explanation for why the /r/ is pronounced before vowels is that it is awkward to move from one vowel to another without adding in a linking-*r*, as it's commonly known. Similarly, adjacent vowels are sometimes linked with an /r/ even when there is no *r* in the spelling as in *soda(r) 'n ice* [soudər ən aɪs]. In these cases it is called an 'intrusive-*r*'. The use of an intrusive-*r* is considered to be 'highly improper' by some conservative speakers and is a favourite target of the media watchdogs.

These sorts of changes are going on all the time in the language. Unfortunately, though, they may not be obvious in earlier stages of English. They aren't always reflected in writing, and this was increasingly the case as spelling grew more conventionalised over the years.

Phonemic change: changes that alter the system

In looking at the changes that have lead to some sort of alteration in the phonemic system of English, let's begin with consonants. Table 4.1 shows the consonant inventory for the three major stages of English: Old, Middle, and Modern. Compare the three systems (at each stage, the new phonemes are in bold). What you will notice is that all the changes have had the effect of bringing about greater symmetry within the system. By symmetry we mean that languages tend to align their consonants up in pairs: voiceless sounds are usually matched with voiced ones across the board; oral stops are usually matched with nasal stops across the board. You can see here that most of the gaps in the system have been filled; the system has become more balanced.

Table 4.1 Consonants in Old, Middle, and Modern English

Old English							*Middle English*							*Modern English*						
p		t	tʃ		k		p		t	tʃ		k		p		t	tʃ		k	
b		d	dʒ		g		b		d	dʒ		g		b		d	dʒ		g	
m		n					m		n					m		n			ŋ	
f	θ	s		ʃ	x	h	f	θ	s		ʃ	x	h	f	θ	s		ʃ		h
							v	ð	z					v	ð	z		ʒ		
w		l	r	j			w		l	r	j			w		l	r	j		

One obvious way that symmetry can be achieved is through phoneme loss. One consonant phoneme that has disappeared from English is the velar fricative /x/. This must have occurred sometime between Chaucer and Shakespeare. In some cases it dropped out altogether, as in words such as *night* and *light* (although preserved in the *gh* spelling). Elsewhere it collapsed with /f/ and /k/, giving forms such as *rough* and *elk,* and in some words it was vocalised, as in *sorrow* and *hollow* (Old English *sorh* and *holh*). You can see that, by eliminating /x/, this also eliminated one of the gaps in the system, since /x/ had no voiced partner.

The phoneme that now stands out in the Modern English inventory is /h/. With the loss of /x/, all our voiceless consonants now have voiced partners, except for poor old /h/. In terms of neatening up the pattern, you would expect /h/ to find a mate or to drop out entirely. You can probably guess its fate. First, it doesn't show the sort of healthy distribution that you would expect of a robust phoneme. It has disappeared from all positions except syllable-initial, and is confined to words such as *ham* and *ahead.* Even in this position, though, it's weakly articulated. Some dialects have already lost it altogether—for example, London Cockney (evident in the Cockney rhyming alphabet—*ay is for 'orses; i is for lootin* [high-falutin']*; n* [hen] *is for eggs*). 'H-dropping', as it is sometimes called, is also prevalent in the broad varieties of OZ and NZ English. /h/ probably would have disappeared long ago, except that 'dropping one's *h*s' has long been considered to be bad. So there has been considerable social pressure to keep it. Nonetheless, the prognosis for /h/ is not good.

The English consonant inventory also shows the addition of several new sounds, which you can see have had the effect of filling gaps in the system. Let's look firstly at the appearance of the voiced fricatives /v ð z/ in Middle English. Old English did have the sound [v], it's true, but it was not an independent phoneme. It existed only as an allophone of /f/; in other words, as a variant pronunciation of /f/ whenever /f/ appeared between two vowels. (/f/ is just assimilating here to the voiced vowels on either side.) So in Old English the rule was to voice /f/ whenever it occurred in this environment.

/f/ → [v] between vowels
[f] everywhere else

How did [v] get the status of a phoneme in English? We can regard borrowings from French as at least one source. The influence of French was so great during the time of the French invasion that borrowed items were pronounced close to the original French pronunciation. So when the English borrowed a word such as *veal* from French, [v] appeared in initial position and contrasted then with /f/, as in the minimal pair *feel/veal*. Another source was the loss of final vowels. When the final vowel in a word like *save* disappeared, it meant that [v] occurred in final position, where it couldn't have occurred before. In effect what happened was that /f/ split into two phonemes: /f/ and /v/.

Old English had [z ð] too, but like [v], they were just variant pronunciations of their voiceless counterparts /s θ/. In other words, they didn't exist as independent phonemes but were only ever found between vowels. Their separate status as phonemes also came about because of changes occurring elsewhere in English. You are familiar with pairs of words such as *grass/graze* and *bath/bathe*. These pairs show voiced and voiceless alternating final consonants. The final *e* that is preserved here in the spelling shows the original trigger for voicing these fricatives. With the loss of these vowels, however, the fricatives suddenly found themselves word-finally contrasting with the voiceless set (for example, the noun *grass* /gras/ versus the verb *to graze* /greɪz/. English now had a series of voiced fricative phonemes /v ð z/ to match the voiceless series /f θ s/.

Another consonant addition to Modern English was /ʒ/. Again there are several sources for this phoneme. Initially, the sound was introduced into the language via palatalisation of the cluster /zj/. Words such as *measure* and *treasure* would have once been pronounced as if they ended in /zjur/. But in anticipation of the following palatal, /z/ changed to /ʒ/ (for example, [mɛzjur] > [mɛʒər] > [mɛʒə]. Originally /ʒ/ would have been restricted to medial positions after a stressed vowel, but later French borrowings such as *beige*, *rouge*, *genre*, *garage*, and *aubergine* introduced the sound into other positions.

Another new phoneme in Modern English is the velar nasal /ŋ/. It began life as a variant pronunciation of /n/, occurring only before velar sounds—that is, it wasn't an independent phoneme but an allophone of /n/. Originally a word such as *sing* was pronounced [sɪŋg] (and still is in some British regional dialects). As we mentioned earlier, this sort of nasal assimilation is very common. The pronunciation rule at the time would have looked something like this:

/n/ → [ŋ] before velars
[n] everywhere else

How, then, did the velar nasal acquire its new status as a phoneme? Sometime in late Middle English, voiced stops were lost after nasals in final position. This is why we have those 'silent *b*s' in words such as *climb* and *lamb*. As we've seen so often before, our spelling is conservative and preserves evidence of the original pronunciation. In other words, [læmb] became [læm] and [sɪŋg] became [sɪŋ]. Once we lost final [g] in words such as *sing*, the velar nasal came to be in contrastive distribution with the other nasals in this position; *some*, *sun*, and *sung*, for example, now make a minimal group. The meaning contrast between these words depends entirely on the distinction between the nasals. Notice that in Modern English /ŋ/ still has a fairly limited distribution, only ever occurring word-finally and between vowels; never initially, except in borrowings. These sorts of restrictions are typical of a new phoneme. Of course, a number of Aboriginal and Maori borrowings have /ŋ/ in initial position: *ngowa* 'Australian mallee fowl', *ngoora burr* 'Australian woody burr', *ngaio* 'New Zealand evergreen tree'; *ngara* 'New Zealand lizard'. But as alternative spellings such as *gnow* and *noogoora burr* show, at least some speakers still avoid the velar nasal in this position, pronouncing these two words /nau/ and /nəgurə bɛ/ respectively.

All the changes we've seen, including the loss of the velar fricative /x/ (as well as /h/ in some dialects), have been in the direction of a more symmetrical consonant system. For every oral stop, there is now an equivalent nasal stop; for every voiceless consonant (stops, fricatives, and affricates) there is now an equivalent voiced partner. We can't go as far as saying that all sound change occurs in order to bring about a more symmetrical sound system, but it is true to say that languages typically show remarkable symmetry in their systems. And if there is a gap, they tend to fill it or eliminate it somehow. But this remains a tendency and can never be seen as a cause for change.

SYMMETRY OF CHANGE: THE GREAT ENGLISH VOWEL SHIFT

We'll now see a spectacular example of movement towards symmetry, this time in the long vowels of English. It's a kind of chain reaction change that took place during the time of Chaucer and Shakespeare (sometime between Middle and early Modern English). The Danish linguist Otto Jespersen first dubbed it 'the Great English Vowel Shift'.

In Middle English there were seven long vowels: /iː/, /eː/, /ɛː/, /aː/, /uː/, /oː/, /ɔː/. Basically what happened was that these vowels successively moved up one notch in height—that is, they all progressively came to be articulated with a higher tongue position. The two vowels /iː/ and /uː/ had nowhere to go and so became diphthongs. These changes are represented below:

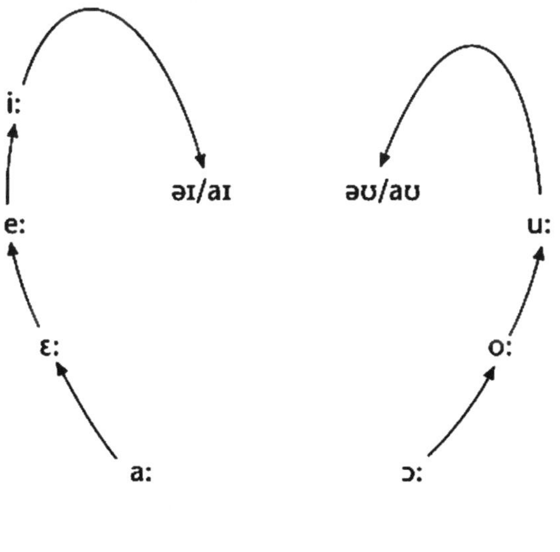

Table 4.2 The Great English Vowel Shift

Middle English	*Chaucer*	*Shakespeare*	*Modern English*	
/i:/	[mi:s]	[məɪs]	[maɪs]	'mice'
/e:/	[me:t]	[mi:t]	[mit]	'meet'
/ɛ:/	[mɛ:t]	[me:t]	[mit]	'meat'
/a:/	[na:mə]	[nɛ:m]	[neɪm]	'name'
/u:/	[hu:s]	[həʊs]	[haʊs]	'house'
/o:/	[go:s]	[gu:s]	[gus]	'goose'
/ɔ:/	[stɔ:nə]	[sto:n]	[stoʊn]	'stone'

Further changes took place in Modern English. In Shakespeare's time the modern diphthongs in *mice* and *house* were not fully realised. They were more like the modern Canadian equivalents /əɪ/ and /əʊ/. Vowels /ɛ:/ and /o:/ later diphthongised to /eɪ/ and /oʊ/, and sometime during the eighteenth century, /e:/ changed to /i:/.

What seems to happen in shifts of this nature is that one vowel moves and this sets off a chain reaction, with the rest of the vowels all shifting in solidarity. Because it happened so long ago, it's difficult to determine which was the rogue vowel out of the seven. One explanation involves what's called a **'pull chain'**. One vowel moves, leaving a gap, and this has the effect of pulling another vowel in to fill the gap, and so on. Alternatively, it might have involved a **push chain**. One vowel invades the territory of another vowel, pushing it into the territory of yet another, and so on. Most historical linguists feel that the evidence (in the way of rhymes, spellings, borrowings) points more to a pull chain, with the high front vowel /i:/ as the possible initial trigger. Of course, determining why it shifted in the first place is still a problem. Whatever the cause, the point to appreciate here is the beautiful symmetry of these changes. What happens in the front of the mouth also happens in the back of the mouth.

One may think that the story ends here, but as linguist Laurie Bauer has observed, there appears to be what he calls 'the Second Great Vowel Shift' taking place in Antipodean English (Bauer 1979; 1992). Like the first Great Vowel Shift, it involves a general raising, but this time of front short vowels. It also involves a movement of the central vowel /ʌ/ into the general front area. Similar shifts are happening in both Australia and New Zealand, but NZ English appears to be setting the pace. We can represent the change as something like this:

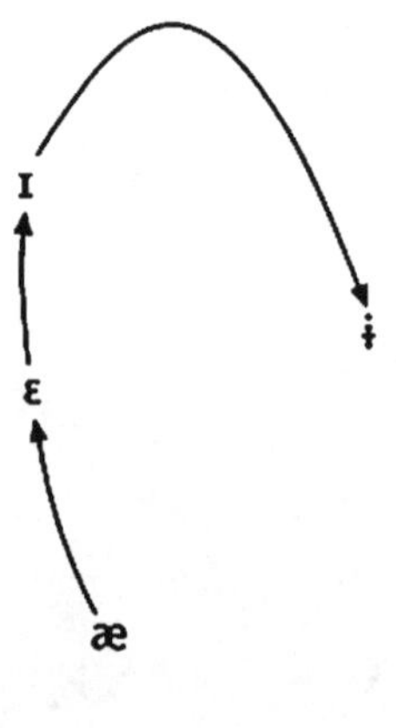

Vowel	*NZ English*	
/ɪ/	[bɨd]	'bid'
/ɛ/	[bɪd]	'bed'
/æ/	[bɛd]	'bad'

Again what is striking here is the remarkable symmetry of these changes. Precisely the same number of contrasts are maintained. NZ vowels in the words *bid*, *bed*, and *bad* are as clearly separated as the corresponding British English vowels.

Linguists also report a general raising of Sydney and Melbourne front vowels /ɪ/, /ɛ/ and /æ/ (see, for example, Bradley 1989). The changes are very reminiscent of what's going on in NZ English, although /ɪ/ is higher and much more to the front than the NZ equivalent. This accounts for a number of popular representations—for example, the claim that Australians think New Zealanders are saying 'fush and chups' and New Zealanders think Australians are saying 'feesh and cheeps'. These particular shifts, together with a number of other vowel changes, especially involving diphthongs (see Further Reading at the end of the book), really form the basis of what have become distinctive accents within these Antipodean varieties of English. As we noted in chapter 3, consonant changes, by comparison, are much less striking.

SOUND CHANGE IN PROGRESS

The progression of sound change is both socially and linguistically structured, and there are two fundamental aspects that we will explore:

- All changes occur in the presence of socially relevant variation.
- Sound changes proceed gradually through the lexicon.

Let's start with the first point. In chapter 1 we looked at some of the dimensions of linguistic variation. By exploring such dimensions we can frequently learn a lot about the progress of language change through a speech community, and we can even tell which group initiated the change. As we also discussed in chapter 1, the American linguist William Labov was the first to show that socially marked variation could be systematically studied (Labov 1966). He identified a number of linguistic features that were used variably within the New York speech community. With respect to the pronunciation of post-vocalic *r*, he made the following observations:

- The presence of post-vocalic *r* is associated with speakers higher up the social scale.
- The presence of post-vocalic *r* is associated with careful speech styles.
- In self-reports, New Yorkers claim they insert more *r*s than they in fact do.
- In word lists (the most formal speech style of all), the lower middle class insert more *r*s than the upper class. They also tend to over-use *r* (pronouncing *God* as [gard], for example). This is hypercorrection.

When people sense that the situation is becoming more formal, they pronounce words in ways they perceive to be more 'correct'. People from the lower middle class are anxious to improve their status and are the most sensitive to prestigious forms. They show their linguistic insecurity by greater shifts to the prestigious patterns in their formal styles and by hypercorrections such as [gard]. The insecurity and social mobility of this class make them important conduits in the spread of change. Those at the extreme ends of the social scale tend, by comparison, to be conservative.

What we have here is an example of a conscious change towards an overtly prestigious form. 'Overt prestige' is based on norms of behaviour set by the upper classes. Not all change is inspired by overt prestige, however. Lower-class varieties inspire changes too, and this involves forms with 'covert prestige'. Let's take an example of one such change currently under way in NZ English.

In chapter 3 we mentioned the flapping of /t/ between vowels as an example of assimilation. The New Zealand linguist Janet Holmes undertook a detailed sociolinguistic survey of flapping in NZ English (Holmes 1994). Her data clearly indicate a change in progress. First, flapping is more frequent in the speech of young New Zealanders than that of middle-aged New Zealanders. When change is under way, you expect younger speakers to use the feature more than older speakers. In addition, the working class use it more than the middle class, and men use it more than women. It is also more frequent in casual contexts (conversation) than formal contexts (interviews); that is, it occurs more often in contexts where people are least aware of their usage. In short, flapping is most established in the conversational style of young, working-class males (who score 82 per cent for flapping), and least established in the interview style of middle-class, middle-aged women (who score 35 per cent).

Curiously, flapping is more frequent in the conversational speech of young, middle-class women than young, middle-class males. These women are not far behind the young, working-class males, scoring a surprisingly high 70 per cent (against the 59 per cent of their male counterparts). As Janet Holmes suggests, these women appear to be acting as a kind of spearhead for this vernacular change to enter into the middle class. These findings indicate a change away from the prestigious pronunciation towards the vernacular or 'non-standard' pronunciation of /t/. In short, flapping entered NZ English via working-class vernacular speech but is now spreading into middle-class speech via young, middle-class women.

In the context of this discussion on variation and change, you might find the following a useful catch phrase to remember: 'Variation is the "now" aspect of change; change is the "then" aspect of variation'. Like many catchy learning devices, it is a little misleading in its simplicity, in that it does suggest that all variation is indicative of change in progress. While it is true that all change does assume the presence of the sort of socially marked variation we've just seen, some variation can exist without ever bringing about change. As we discussed in chapter 1, linguistic features are markers of group identity. Changes won't occur unless people outside a particular group want, consciously or subconsciously, to belong to it. In other words, linguistic forms must first acquire some type of prestige—overt or covert—before change occurs.

The second point at the start of this section states that sound change is not only socially but also lexically structured. By this we mean it's not a purely mechanical process that affects all eligible vocabulary at once, but is lexically gradual, slowly spreading through the vocabulary and affecting different groups of words at different times. This is called **'lexical diffusion'**, and we see it operating here in NZ flapping.

Holmes, for example, investigated the effects on flapping of different linguistic factors, like word position, stress, and vowel length. She discovered the favourite environment for flapping was word-final /t/ as in *get eggs*. Words with /t/ in this position are acting like fronts in the diffusion. Factors such as frequency are also crucial. Frequent items are more susceptible to change. They act much like centre forwards in the diffusion. For example, the common-usage phrase *sort of* is out there in front, leading the advance; it scores very highly for flapping in the data.

All this is interesting for what it says about the role of American influence. Flapping is a widely recognised feature of American English, and it's assumed to represent an American innovation in both OZ and NZ English. The environment stereotypically associated with American usage is that found in the middle of words such as *letter* and *butter*. But, as Holmes shows, this is not where the voicing of /t/ is most established. It is much more frequent across word boundaries, casting doubt on the explanation that American English is the direct source for this change. But since flapping of this sort is such a very common sound change anyway, the chances of parallel but independently motivated change will always be very high.

SOUNDS AND SPELLING CHANGE

The final area of historical development that we explore in this chapter is the English spelling system. It has been evolving for over 1000 years, and the complications we encounter today are the consequence of various linguistic and social events, which have taken place over this period.

The English spelling system

As we noted in the previous chapter, there is hardly a nice, straightforward relationship between the letters in the English alphabet and the sounds of English. This is not to say, though, that there is no correspondence between letters and sounds. David Crystal (1995:272) has estimated that only about 3 per cent of everyday English words are so irregular that they would have to be learnt completely by heart, and that around 82 per cent are spelt according to regular patterns. That leaves some 15 per cent of cases where we could argue about the status of their regularity. But given such statistics, the chief conclusion must be that we should not exaggerate the size of the problem, as some supporters of spelling reform are prone to do. Reports that *foolish* can be spelt 613 975 different ways, and that 50 million school children waste 10 million hours a day learning the system, are clearly over the top (cited in Lingren 1969:3). But we shouldn't minimise it either, for a great deal of confusion is caused by that 3–15 per cent.

Let's begin our look at the history of English spelling by listing the ways that spelling and pronunciation fail to neatly match:

- A letter or letter sequence may have two or more pronunciations: the letter *c* is pronounced as [s] in *ice*, but as [k] in *cream*.
- A sound may be represented by two or more different letters or letter sequences: the sound [k] is spelt with the letter *c* in *candy*, but with the letter *k* in *ketchup*.
- A single sound may be represented by a sequence of letters: the sound [ʃ] is spelt with the letter sequence *sh* as in *shellfish*.
- A single letter may represent a sequence of sounds: the letter *x* stands for the sounds [ks] in *box*.

- A letter may not represent any sound (that is, it is 'silent'): the letter *k* is not pronounced in *knead.*

While each of these points has been illustrated with a consonant example, vowel examples could equally have been used. In each case, whether vowels or consonants are involved, you have to know the whole word to get the spelling right.

To understand some of the reasons for these 'unphonetic' spellings, we will give a thumbnail sketch of how the English spelling system has developed.

The sources of irregularity

Inadequacies of the Roman alphabet

The complications began right at the start in Old English. In devising a writing system, the Irish missionaries of the time had to adapt their 23-letter Roman alphabet for the thirty-five or so sounds that were distinctive in Old English. (The exact number depends on the dialect and whose analysis you use). They added four new letters: þ 'thorn', ƿ 'wynn', ð 'eth', and æ 'ash'. Thorn and wynn were borrowed from the runic alphabet, which was used at that time in northern Europe, Scandinavia, and the British Isles. Eth is thought to be an adaptation of an early Irish letter, and ash came from the Latin script, although its name derives from the runic symbol for the same sound (the runic symbol though is very different). They also resorted to using some letters (such as *c* and *g*) to represent more than one sound, and sequences of letters to represent other sounds (such as *sc*—the equivalent of present day *sh*).

Foreign spelling conventions

The next set of complications was introduced after the Norman Conquest by French scribes, who imposed several new spelling conventions. For instance, since the letters *u*, *v*, *i*, *n*, and *m* were all written in a very similar way, they tried to make it easier for the reader by changing some of these letters when they occurred next to each other. In some sequences, for example, they substituted *o* for *u*, creating *come*, *love*, *one*, and *son*. The effects of the new spelling conventions were so strong that by the beginning of the fifteenth century, English spelling was really a mixture of two systems: Old English and French (see chapter 2).

Printing

The invention of the printing press created yet more complications. As we discussed in chapter 2, line justification was often achieved by shortening or lengthening words rather than by varying the word spaces. As a result, an extra *e* was added to words here and there, or *i* was swapped for *y*. It also turns out that many of the first English printers came from Europe, and they tended to impose the spelling conventions of their own native languages onto English. (Caxton himself introduced a number of Dutch spellings, such as *gh* for words like *ghost* (earlier *gost*) and *ghastly* (earlier *gastlic*).

Gradually the system stabilised. But because of the one-time fluidness of spelling, the spellings that were eventually selected were not always done so with internal consistency in mind. The result is an inherited set of spelling exceptions.

Spelling is conservative

It is quite ironic that, just as spelling was becoming more standardised, the vowel sounds of English began undergoing the set of changes known as the Great Vowel Shift. The change in vowel sounds did not lead to spelling reform, since once the letters had established themselves, people continued to use them, even though their pronunciation had changed. The net result is that thousands of words are now spelt as they were pronounced in Chaucer's time, before all this vowel shifting took place. Many of our modern 'silent' consonants such as in ***kneed*** and ***sword*** have also come about because of the conservative nature of spelling: the pronunciation changed after the word's spelling was already established. If the printer Caxton had been born a couple of centuries later, or if sound changes such as the Great Vowel Shift had occurred a couple of centuries earlier, our spelling would be much truer to pronunciation.

Etymological respellings

Early attempts at rationalising the spelling of various English words have also left their mark on English spelling, often by creating an even greater irregularity. In the sixteenth century, Renaissance scholars tried to indicate something of the history of a word in its spelling. For example, the *b* in *debt* was added to indicate that the word came from *debitum* in Latin. *Subtle* and *doubt* got a *b* this way too. Some analogical recreations also contributed to the irregularity. For example, *coude* was made to look like *would*; *delite* got a *gh* to look like *light*; *rime* was made to look like *rhythm*.

Increasing emphasis on the written word

Some of these fancy respellings actually came to affect the pronunciation. Because of the importance that people began to place on writing (over speaking), they started to pay more attention to spelling, perhaps even to etymology, and many words acquired what are now called '**spelling pronunciations**'. For example, words such as *fault* and *vault* got a new *l* and came to be pronounced that way. The verb *avail* (from Old French *valoir*) acquired an initial *a*, and even an extra *d* (*advail*), to make it look more impressively Latin. Some of the spelling pronunciations caused more discrepancies between spelling and pronunciation (for example, *schedule*, with American English [sk] and British English [ʃ].

As we saw at the start of this chapter, a consciousness of spelling can sometimes lead to the reversal of a sound change, thus restoring an earlier pronunciation. For example, in *medium* and *cordial*, people stopped saying /midʒəm/ and /kɔdʒəl/ and reverted to the non-palatal pronunciations of these words. Lost consonants and vowels have also been restored this way. For example, full forms *epistle* and *apostle* made a reappearance in English, ousting reduced forms *pistle* and *postle*.

Borrowings

A final complication in the history of English spelling is that, with the rise of British imperialism in the late sixteenth and early seventeenth centuries, continuing through to the nineteenth century, thousands of words were borrowed by English, along with their sometimes rather un-English spelling. Examples include *ghetto*, *carnival*, *balcony*, *cocoa*, *gazette*, *pneumonia*, *jungle*, and *sherbet*. And, of course, these borrowings are continuing to flood in today.

And so it is through this haphazard evolution that we have ended up with the spelling system we have. Plagued from the start with an inadequate alphabet, language change, imaginative respellings, borrowed words, and spelling conventions, it's surprising that the regular patterns are as high as 82 per cent.

Whose standard?

While the spelling of most English words is now very fixed, there still remains the question of whose standard to follow. The competition is really between British and American standard spelling, both of which are followed in New Zealand and Australia. In comparing the differences, we find that American usage sometimes preserves an older spelling, as with *check*, which migrated across the Atlantic during the colonisation of the Americas before the *k* was changed to *qu* in Britain. For similar reasons, we find words such as *ensure* and *insure*, which are differentiated in British spelling but have the same spelling in American English.

Let's consider a curious case in point: *-or* and *-our* in words such as *four*, *fourteen*, and *forty*. The inconsistency in the spelling of these words is a headache for many of us. The spelling of *four* naturally helps to distinguish it from its homophones *for* and *fore* (although there is generally no need to distinguish homophones by spelling, since they normally appear in context). But to have the spelling *four* in *fourteen* but not in *forty* seems perverse, especially when records show that it was spelt *fourty* in earlier times and was only displaced by *forty* in the eighteenth century. The problem is compounded, as there are two different ways of spelling a sizeable group of nouns ending with *-or* or *-our*. The most common ones are:

arbo(u)r	favo(u)r	labo(u)r	savio(u)r
armo(u)r	fervo(u)r	neighbo(u)r	savo(u)r
behavio(u)r	flavo(u)r	odo(u)r	splendo(u)r
clamo(u)r	glamo(u)r	parlo(u)r	succo(u)r
colo(u)r	harbo(u)r	ranco(u)r	tumo(u)r
demeano(u)r	hono(u)r	rigo(u)r	vapo(u)r
endeavo(u)r	humo(u)r	rumo(u)r	vigo(u)r

It turns out that the variation between *-or* and *-our* goes back to the seventeenth and eighteenth centuries, when scholars wanted to use *-or* for words borrowed from Latin but *-our* for borrowings from French. The problem was that in many cases it wasn't clear which language a word had been borrowed from, and the choice of *-or* or *-our* was made arbitrarily. And some words, such as *harbour*, were spelt with *-our* even though they were original English words.

Because of this confusion about which word came from where, more and more people began to feel that it would be better to use *-or* across the board, and in the USA this became accepted practice. In Britain, on the other hand, the trend for *-or* was reversed because of the influence of Samuel Johnson's dictionary, which had a mixture of spellings for words in this category. Overall, Johnson's dictionary had a stabilising effect on British English, particularly with respect to spelling. In fact, most of Johnson's choices are still found in modern practice.

In Australia and New Zealand, official usage has followed the British tradition, though both spellings are actually found. For example, the Australian Labor Party has spelt its name without a *u* since early this century; the *Australian National Dictionary* (AND) records *Labor Caucus* in 1911 and the full title *Australian Labor Party* in 1918. In contrast, in both the United Kingdom and New Zealand, the Labor Party's counterparts spell *Labour* with a *u*. Pam Peters's *The Cambridge Australian English Style Guide* records that, in the Australian corpus of English, ratios between *-or* and *-our* vary considerably, depending on the word. For example, *labor* (excluding references to the *Labor Party*) outnumber *labour* by 129:95, whereas *behaviour* outnumbers *behavior* by 99:10. The ratios for the rest lie in between. She has also found that spellings with *-or* are more often used by newspapers and magazines than by book publishers.

One reason that some people prefer *-or* is that, if you use an *-our* spelling, it is actually harder to know how to spell related words. For example, if you spell *humour* with a *u*, you must remember to leave it out in *humorous*. It is the same with *labour* and *laborious*, *vigour* and *vigorous*. Even worse is *honour*, which remains the same in *honourable* (as compared with *honorable*), but changes in *honorary* and *honorific*. If, however, you spell *humor*, *labor*, and the rest without a *u*, you don't have any of these problems.

A question of reform

Because English spelling is neither totally consistent nor globally standardised, it would seem that there is scope for reforming it. Rather than arguing for wholesale change—which would require revision of the entire corpus of English writing from the past several hundred years (not just literature, but also, for example, newspapers, journals, textbooks, and government records)—some spelling reformers argue that perhaps more modest adjustments could be made. For example, promoting more regular spellings wherever they are already used by a group of significant size, or are familiar even as alternate spellings.

Let's consider what Stephen Murray-Smith has to say on the matter of reform in his *Right Words: A Guide to English Usage in Australia* (1990:378–9). The following are some suggestions that, he argues, 'would not cut us off from other users of English but which would make life a bit easier'.

EASY

- Agree on *-or* endings rather than *-our*.
- Agree on *-ise* endings rather than *-ize*.
- Agree that the digraphs *ae* and *oe* become *e*.

A BIT HARDER

- Agree on *-er* rather than *-or* endings for words, so that we spell *advisor* as *adviser*.

HARDER STILL

- Agree on *-able* endings instead of *-ible*, so that *accessible* becomes *accessable*.
- Drop *-e* from the root of all words (with some possible exceptions) before adding suffixes, to give us *blamable* instead of *blameable*, *namable* instead of *nameable*.
- Agree that final consonants of words of more than one syllable not be doubled on adding suffixes, to give us *transfered* instead of *transferred*. If we cannot do this, let us at least agree that the letter *l* follow the same rule as other final consonants, so that we have *traveled* instead of *travelled*.

- Agree that where *ei* or *ie* have the sound of *ee*, they will be spelt *ie*, to give us *sieze*, *wierd*.

Spelling reform is a tricky business. People love to whinge about English spelling, but when it comes to reform, most remain vehemently opposed. (Bear in mind that reforms have been suggested since as early as the twelfth century.) A few sensible reforms, however, along the lines of Murray-Smith's suggestions, could easily be incorporated. As Peters (1995:710) suggests, '[t]hose who wished could continue to use the traditional spelling for each word in the set, but others could use a standardised spelling...without fear of being ridiculed for bad spelling...A few systematic reforms...would tidy up the system, and lighten the load for everyone, without allowing that "anything goes"'. But it's doubtful whether reforms (as sensible as they might be) such as *tung*, *yu*, and *filosofy* will ever catch on. You can only go so far.

POINTS TO REMEMBER

- The sorts of processes that affect the way we pronounce our language can act as triggers for sound change. A historical sound change is a process that has left a lasting imprint on the language.
- There are basically three types of sound changes that have affected the development of English: old sounds have dropped out; new sounds have appeared; and already existing sounds have been modified.
- Some sound changes, such as assimilation and deletion, are regular sound changes. Others, such as metathesis and dissimilation, are highly irregular.
- Languages typically show remarkable symmetry in their sound systems, and many sound changes work to retain or enhance this symmetry.
- Both the phonetic inventory and the phonemic system of a language can change over time.
- The progress of sound change is socially structured: patterns for different age groups, social classes, genders, and styles suggest change in progress.
- Linguistic forms must first acquire some type of prestige—overt or covert—before change occurs.
- Change is also linguistically structured: it doesn't affect all potential words at the same time, but proceeds gradually through the vocabulary.
- The 'unphonetic' nature of the English spelling system can be attributed to language change, different scribal conventions, the idiosyncratic fixing of spellings, the conservative nature of English spelling, and the form of the original alphabet.

EXERCISES

1 Comparison of English and Kriol

a In the following, compare the English words with the Kriol equivalents (Kriol is an English-based creole spoken in northern parts of Australia). What sort of changes are illustrated? Say why you think each change occurs.

English	*Kriol*	*Meaning*
/dɒnəld/	Donal	'Donald'
/ask/	aks	'ask'
/dɛsk/	des	'desk'
/slɪ:p/	silip	'sleep'
/hɒt/	ot	'hot'
/hɒspətl/	ospital	'hospital'
/bɪgəst/	biges	'biggest'
/faɪv/	fipe	'five'
/boʊt/	bot	'boat'
/moʊtəka/	modiga	'vehicle'
/meɪk/	meck	'make'
/pəlismən/	balijiman[1]	'policeman'
/ʃʌtʌp/	shurup[2]	'shut up'

1 *j* in Kriol represents a voiced palatal stop.

2 Kriol *r* here represents a voiced flap.

b The English pronunciation here is typical of careful speech. Do any of the changes you have listed occur in conversational English?

c Why, do you think, do some Kriol-speakers insert *h* in words like *uncle* > *huncle* and *island* > *hisland* /hailənd/?

2 Consonant clusters

a Compare the following standard and non-standard forms. What changes do they illustrate? Are they regular? On the basis of the changes, can you draw any inferences about the permissible or favoured sound sequences in English?

Standard	*Non-standard*
asterisk	asteriks
ask	aks
spaghetti	pesghetti
uncomfortable	uncomfterble
perhaps	prehaps
pervert	prevert
remuneration	renumeration
animal	aminal
anemone	anenome

b Can you think of other examples that you might have heard in colloquial speech or children's speech?

3 The Great English Vowel Shift

a Using a vowel chart, formulate the changes that have taken place in English. The letters in Old English spelling resemble the phonetic symbol. You will have to put the Modern English into phonetics. What do you notice about the modern spelling?

Old English	*Modern English*
tīd	tide
īs	ice
hē	he
dēman	deem
ǣl	eel
ǣlfen	evening
hūs	house
brūn	brown
dōm	doom
hrōst	roost
āc	oak
hām	home

b Now supply the Modern English for the following Old English forms (note that *þ* represents /θ/ and is now spelt *th*; *c* before *e* is pronounced [tʃ]; the verb ending *-an* has disappeared):

cū, sōn, mēd, wīn, gōs, tā, mē, bān, sǣd, þū, dæl, hlūd, bītan, hlāf, cēs, rīsan, wēpan, cniht [knixt]

(Hint: for the last item, think compensatory lengthening.)

4 Phonological processes

a In his *Dictionary of Australian Colloquialisms* (DAC), lexicographer Gerald Wilkes has an entry under the word *beauty* that reads: 'Expression of full agreement and approval, often pronounced "bewdy"' (1996:26). Describe the sound change this illustrates. Why do you think speakers pronounce the word this way? Can you think of other examples?

b A speaker intending to say *discussing shortly* comes out with *discushing*. Why? Name the type of change this speech error illustrates.

c In non-standard speech, you sometimes hear forms such as *fambly* ('family'), *membry* ('memory'), and *younkster* ('youngster'). Explain each of these pronunciations. Name the type of change.

d During the middle ages, some speakers changed the pronunciation of *grammar* to *glamour*. The word *glamour* still survives but with a different meaning. Why would speakers have done this? What type of change does it illustrate?

5 Kiwese and Strine

Kiwese: A Guide, a Ductionary, a Shearing of Unsights by Alex Buzo (1994) and *Let's Stalk Strine* by Afferbeck Lauder (1981) (Professor of Strine Studies, University of Sinny) are both successful books that exploit stereotypical features of the NZ and OZ accents for humorous effect. Most of the humour derives from respellings based on broad vowel sounds, exaggerated assimilations, and deletions. Using the features we have covered in this chapter, describe how the authors arrived at the respelt words below. How faithfully do you think they represent the NZ and OZ accents? Do you find any of these features in other dialects of English? (Hint: you will probably have to read these out aloud).

Kiwese

Bun Button (As in 'I've bun button by a mosquito')
Duck-hid (An insult directed at men)
Kiri Pecker (Australian business magnate)
Sin cherie (What good cricketers like Martin Crowe make)
Jungle Bill's (As in 'Jungle Bill's, Jungle Bill's, jungle all the way')
Turning a truck (What immoral women are to be found doing for money)

Buzo 1994:13, 28, 68, 114, 62–3, 135

Strine

Emma Chissit ('How much is it?')
Gloria soame ('glorious home')
Aorta ('They ought to')
Get chews twit ('get used to it')
Cheque render ('jacaranda')
Where cheque etcher hat? ('Where did you get your hat?')

Lauder 1981:36, 20, 11, 22, 15

6 Transcription practice

Transcribe the following words. What do you notice about the place of articulation of the nasal in each case? How can you explain this?

imbibe, munch, consumption, banquet, gormandise, sustenance, ambrosia, condiments, hamburger, sandwich (give the colloquial pronunciation here too—that is, 'samwich'), Lancashire hotpot, shrimp, mince, pumpkin.

7 Changes in stress

a The words below are given with their earlier stress patterns. In each case we have marked the stress with a high vertical bar before the stressed syllable (see chapter 3). Rewrite each word, indicating the stress pattern that you use yourself. In terms of syllable structure, what generalisations can you make about changes in stress patterns that have occurred? (Words and inspiration for this exercise from Bauer 1994)

ab'domen, bi'tumen, 'formidable, 'hospitable, 'nomenclature, 'pejorative, pre'cedence, quan'dary, se'cretive, so'norous, 'applicable, con'template, de'cadent, eti'quette, re'plica

b Now that you've established the new pattern, where would you expect the stress to settle in the following controversial cases:

kilometre, controversy, comparable, metallurgy

c Some prescriptive texts allow only *'kilometre* and *'controversy*, and many argue that they are the only correct pronunciation. Do you agree with these people?

d The following are also words that are currently in flux. Show where you put the stress in your speech. Then check a dictionary and see what it recommends. Where would you expect the stress to settle?

articulatory, Caribbean, clandestine, irrevocable, lamentable

8 The English spelling system

Using the categories developed in this chapter, identify each of the deviations from an ideal spelling system discussed in the poem below. Comment on the feasibility of making any reforms here.

I take it you already know
Of tough and bough and cough and dough?
Others may stumble, but not you
On hiccough, thorough, slough and through?
Well done! And now you wish, perhaps
To learn of less familiar traps?

Beware of heard, a dreadful word
That looks like beard and sounds like bird.
And dead; it's said like bed, not bead;
For goodness sake, don't call it deed!
Watch out for meat and great and threat,
(They rhyme with suite and straight and debt).
A moth is not a moth in mother.
Nor both in bother, broth in brother.

And here is not a match for there,
And dear and fear for bear and pear,
And then there's dose and rose and lose,
Just look them up—and goose and choose,
And cork and work and card and ward,
And font and front and word and sword.
And do and go, then thwart and cart.
Come, come, I've hardly made a start.

A dreadful language? Why, man alive,
I'd learned to talk it when I was five,
And yet to write it, the more I tried,
I hadn't learned it at fifty-five.

Anonymous, as quoted in Matthew Leditschke, pers. comm., 18 September 1996

5

What's in a Word?

INTRODUCTION

This chapter deals with the formation and internal structure of English words, or what is known as morphology (from Greek *morphe*, meaning 'form, shape'). We begin our discussion of Antipodean English morphology by generally considering the status of the word within linguistic analysis. Does the word form a natural unit for analysis? And if it does, what are the criteria for determining it?

The answer to the first question is straightforward: the word does appear to form a natural unit for speakers. As English-speakers yourselves, you will recognise that George Bernard Shaw's famous sentence *There is no love sincerer than the love of food* (as quoted in Goode 1987:17) has ten words. Even though the sentence could be written as a continuous stream of sound—*Thereisnolovesincererthantheloveoffood*—you all make the same word boundaries. Presumably none of you would be tempted by *The reis nol oves in cererth an thelo veoff ood.* Well, you might argue, this is simply because we know how to write and are therefore familiar with English writing conventions, which group sound sequences into words and put spaces between them. We know how to play word games such as Scrabble and Balderdash; we read. But it seems that there is something natural about the word as a basic unit, since even speakers of unwritten languages share the same intuitions about how to divide utterances into word-units. It's something everyone can do, but saying just how we do it is not easy. There are many different accounts of the word, and none seems to accord with our actual intuitions. It is even more difficult to go beyond English and to find a description that will work across the languages of the world.

IDENTIFYING WORDS

Probably the best definition of 'word' is one offered by Leonard Bloomfield (1933), who characterises words as the smallest units of meaning that are able to function independently in a language; 'minimum free forms' is how he describes them. Let's explore some aspects of his account and see how they apply to the words of English.

Semantics

From the point of view of meaning, we could say that a word constitutes a single meaningful unit. But there are problems. Think of a word such as ***unappetising.***

Surely, it compares to the string *not appetising*, and this suggests that it is comprised of two different units of meaning. Or take a word like *more*, as in *more tasty*. It would seem to be a word, but it has the same sense as the *-er* ending in *tastier*. Does this mean then that *-er* is a word? Finally, consider the string *the delicious food*, where the entire phrase could be said to represent a single concept.

This is where the second part of Bloomfield's account is crucial. For something to be a word, it has to be free and also a minimum form. This would exclude *un-* and *-er*, which can't stand alone, and also the phrase *the delicious food*, which itself can be divided into smaller units. Unfortunately, what it also excludes are parts of words such as *beetroot*, which can stand alone. We need to go beyond semantics to other aspects of this freedom in order to cover compounded word structures such as these.

Structure

There are three aspects to the structural character of a word. The first has to do with position. While it's not possible to rearrange elements within words, words themselves, as single units, show a certain mobility. Words can be permuted, while bits of words cannot. However, words such as *on*, *not*, and *the* are problematic. Although we recognise these as words, they can't move freely at all, because they depend on certain words around them. (As we'll see later, these items are poor examples of words, probably because they're on their way to becoming something else.)

The second aspect has to do with 'uninterruptibility' (if that's an allowable word). With the exception of curiosities such as *kangabloodyroo* (which we consider later), it's not possible to place material within English words. They constitute a single bound unit. On the other hand, it is possible to place material in between words—for example, *platefuls of food* versus *large platefuls of hot and fiery food*. The fact that most of us say *jack-in-the-boxes* rather than *jacks-in-the-box* is evidence that we now think of this string as a single word.

Finally, words are able to stand alone. To the question *What's the staple of life*?, you might reply *meat* or *tofu*. Even words such as *not* or *a*, which can't normally stand in isolation, can be manipulated to do so. For example, a current teenage trend is to strand *not* at the end of the sentence for ironic effect: *I like you—not*. Or you might conceive of a situation where a speaker is driven to ask, *Did you say **a** or **the**?*

Phonology

Additional evidence exists to support a conception of words as units of sound structure. For example, some languages have regular stress patterning and assign it on the basis of word-form. Unfortunately for us, English has a notoriously irregular stress assignment. More useful are pauses and hesitations, which typically occur at word boundaries: *There is ummmmm no love...sincerer than errrr the love of food*. But since speakers can pause in the middle of words too (*un-err-appetising*), pausing potential is only useful up to a point.

These, then, are some of the characteristics that we would expect words to show. In combination, as a set of diagnostics, they enable us to identify most of the words of English. What we'll find, however, is that there are always some segments that fit the diagnosis better than others. From a historical perspective, this is perfectly understandable. Words don't necessarily remain words, but over time may actually lose their independent status. Think of the word *not*. Throughout this book, we've been using contractions such as *don't* and *can't*. We realise that we've done this at the peril of offending certain readers, who will find such contractions colloquial and inappropriate for written English. But, in fact, *not* rarely appears in its full form (unless emphasised). Instead it attaches itself to the preceding auxiliary, as in *didn't*, or even fuses entirely with it, as in *ain't* and *won't*. While these examples appear to be whole words, they yield conflicting results when put to the test. Such rogue items should always make us curious; when forms don't fit nicely into our classifications, it usually means that there is something interesting under way in the language.

Lexemes versus words

We have established that words are viable units of structure; but are they workable units for linguistic description? One difficulty is the imprecision of the actual term *word*. This is often a problem when terms from ordinary language are used in a technical context. We end up having to redefine them and create new words to capture distinctions that aren't covered in their everyday usage. And this is exactly what happens here.

Consider the following: *eat, eats, eating, eaten, ate*. At one level, these are unarguably different words with different pronunciation, spelling, meaning, and grammar. But at another more abstract level, you probably feel they represent one vocabulary item; they're just different forms of it. For this more abstract unit, linguists prefer to use the term ***lexeme***. It's lexemes that are relevant for dictionary-makers. The forms *eat, eats, eating, eaten, ate* are five different word-forms. But they represent one lexeme, and would be listed as such under one heading in a dictionary. Usually lexemes are written in capital letters. We have, therefore, five different physical representations of the one lexeme EAT. We will keep the term *word* for these physical forms, the actual assemblages of sounds or letters that occur in speech and writing. This is really how the term *word* is understood in ordinary language. If you were told to write an essay of '2000 words', it's words that you count, not lexemes—or your essay would be much longer.

Now that we have identified what words are, there are a couple of additional notions that we need to make clear. These relate specifically to the relationship between words and their meanings. Words that belong to different lexemes but that are written and pronounced the same are called '**homonyms**'. For example, the NZ and OZ slang word *grouse* 'excellent' and the more conventional *grouse* 'type of game bird' are different lexemes that happen to be pronounced and written alike. Generally speaking, the word-forms in spoken language (phonological words) correspond to the written word-forms (orthographic words), but they don't have to. For instance, *meet* and *meat* are phonologically the same, but orthographically they are different. Examples like these, which are pronounced the same but have different meanings and different spellings, are called '**homophones**'. Conversely, the words *read*, as in *I read the book yesterday*, and *read*, as in *I do like to read*, are orthographically the same but phonologically different (that is, they have the same spelling but different pronunciation). These are **homographs**. Languages such as English, which do not have a consistent phonemic spelling system, often show examples of this sort of mismatch between lexemes and word-forms. Advertising is quick to exploit this feature of English. A diet clinic called *Weight No More* is punning on the homophony between *weight* 'weighable amount, quantity' and *wait* 'to defer action'. Advertisements for Lifesavers that describe the lolly as 'hole-some' are punning on the characteristic hole in the middle and the product's supposed health-promoting qualities.

A final distinction that we can make involves the grammatical properties of the word. In the example just given of the homographs *read* and *read*, we have two different representations of the one lexeme READ that perform different grammatical tasks—that is, they are two different grammatical words. The first depicts action in the past; the second depicts the general activity of reading. These two different grammatical meanings happen to be signalled by different phonological words, but identical orthographical words. A lexeme such as EAT, given earlier, signals these grammatical meanings with totally different verb forms: *ate* versus *eat*.

For many verbs, the same form is used for a number of different grammatical meanings. An extreme case is the lexeme CUT. The same word, *cut*, can represent habitual action (as in *I cut my finger every time*), completed action (as in *I cut my finger yesterday*), recently completed action (*He has cut his finger*) or the basic action (*It's easy to cut your finger*). Orthographically and phonologically we have one word, but grammatically four words. This collapsing of items, where the same word-form of a lexeme represents different grammatical meanings, is known as '**syncretism**'. In other words, this is homonymy between two or more forms of a lexeme. The history of English demonstrates this kind of collapsing of forms on a grand scale (see chapter 11).

It is also possible that one lexeme has several different but closely related meanings. This relationship is known as '**polysemy**'. At this stage you might be wondering how we tell whether we have separate lexical items, or the same lexical item with different meanings. This is obviously something of great concern to dictionary-makers, who have to decide, for instance, whether the two meanings of *grouse* given earlier are grouped under the one entry (polysemy) or have their own distinct entries (homonymy). In this example, the meanings are obviously unrelated; it is a clear case of homonymy. Yet not all cases are so clear-cut. Just how far do the meanings have to diverge before we regard them as representing separate lexemes. Is the *bug* in your computer the same as the *bug* that attacks your roses, or the *bug* that lays you up in bed for a week? The boundary between polysemy and homophony is a very fuzzy one.

Morphemes versus words

While the word is clearly a valid linguistic unit, it remains an awkward concept for linguistic analysis. Although we increased the precision of the term by distinguishing a number of different types of words, as a unit of description it still has one important drawback: words aren't minimal units (remember the problem with *unappetising*). Although they are meaningful and can be used to form larger structures, they themselves are not basic units of meaning; they can be divided into smaller meaningful parts, or what we call '**morphemes**'.

The morpheme is best described as the smallest unit of meaning in the structure of the language. By this we mean that we cannot divide the unit any more without severely altering the meaning. For example, *pumpkin*, *cardamom*, and *cook* are all words and they are also morphemes. Take the word *pumpkin*. As one complete unit by itself, it has meaning, and while we can apparently divide it into the smaller units *pump* and *kin*, these have meanings that are not associated with the word *pumpkin*. We wouldn't dissect *pumpkin* in this way, any more than we would divide *cardamom* into *card*, *a*, and *mom*. These segments all have meanings totally unrelated to *cardamom*. On the other hand, a word such as *pumpkins* has a meaning as a whole, but we can also divide it into two smaller meaningful units: *pumpkin* and the plural ending *-s*.

One difficulty with morpheme analysis is knowing just how much to acknowledge history in assigning morpheme boundaries. The examples we have just seen are straightforward, but what about a word such as *garlic*. Although we would probably want to classify this as a single morpheme, it actually derives from the Old English *gārlēac* and consists historically of two separate morphemes *gār* 'spear' and *lēac* 'leek'. You could argue that the parts are no longer obvious to modern speakers and therefore should not be analysed as such. But even with more transparently complex forms, such as *breakfast*, it is doubtful whether many native speakers recognise the morphological complexity (that is, the idea of 'breaking a fast'). This poses an interesting theoretical question, and it is something we return to later.

TYPES OF MORPHEMES

For the morpheme to be a useful working concept, we need to make a number of basic distinctions.

Lexical versus grammatical

This distinction relates to the type of meaning involved. Take the sentence *A cauliflower is nothing but a cabbage with a college education* (Mark Twain, as quoted in Goode 1987:258). Some morphemes have meanings that exist outside the language—that is, they relate to aspects of human experience that exist in the world. The items *cauliflower*, *nothing*, *cabbage*, *college*, and *education* are all referrable—that is they have real-world meaning (although they differ in concreteness). We refer to these as '**lexical morphemes**'. Membership of this class is open-ended. English is acquiring new lexical morphemes all the time.

Other morphemes do not relate to items in our experience, but rather deal with the relationships between these items; that is, they tell us something about their fellow morphemes. Their meaning is purely grammatical. Consider *a* in the above. This little word merely tells us that we are referring to any old cabbage and cauliflower. They're not specific items, and they're not already known to us. The class of **grammatical morphemes** is much smaller than the class of lexical morphemes and can be exhaustively listed in any English grammar.

There are three other grammatical morphemes in the above sentence—*with*, *but*, and *is*. *With* shows the relationship between the lexical morphemes *cabbage* and *college education*, while *but* joins the two clauses in the sentence. *Is* is semantically empty, but its form tells us we're dealing with the present tense and that the items involved are singular. It has a linking function to connect the subject with the rest of the sentence and in this way fulfils a requirement of English structure: that every sentence has a verb. You could compare this example with something like *God is* 'God exists', where *is* has more lexical meaning.

There's not always a clear-cut boundary between grammatical and lexical. Again, the reason for the indeterminacy is historical; because grammatical items evolve out of lexical items, periods of fuzziness are inevitable. This is something we explore more fully in chapter 11.

Bound versus free

We can make a further division of morphemes, based on where they can appear. The pattern of phonemes that represents the morpheme *cabbage* can exist in isolation. We describe such morphemes as '**free**'. Other morphemes like plural *-s* cannot exist on their own, but are only ever found in the presence of others. These we describe as '**bound**' morphemes.

Roots, stems, and affixes

The vast majority of English morphemes are **roots**. These are single lexical morphemes, which are usually free (although, as we will see below, they can occasionally be bound). Roots really represent the core of the word, to which bound morphemes may then be added. Most of the bound morphemes occurring with roots are **affixes**. Items such as *bake*, *cabbage*, and *taste* are the centres of words to which the affixes are then attached (for example, *baking*, *cabbages*, and *distasteful*). Affixes are classified according to where they appear with regard to the root (indicated by a hyphen). English affixes fall into two main types. **Suffixes** follow the root (for example, *-ed*, *-s*, *-ing* in *cooked*, *cooks*, *cooking*). **Prefixes** precede the root (for example, *in-*, *non-*, *un-* in *intoxicating*, *nonalcoholic*, *uncooked*).

There is also a third minor type—**infixes**—which, not surprisingly, must occur inside the root. In English the only viable infixes are non-standard intensifiers such as *bloody* as in *fanbloodytastic*. Some secret languages make use of infixes too, but they're generally meaningless, only intended to distort English words in order to baffle potential eavesdroppers. For example, 'Up-up' language involves inserting an *-up-* inside each syllable: *food* becomes *fupood*. Infixes are actually quite rare among the world's languages, and are peripheral to English and to Indo-European languages in general.

Affixes can directly attach themselves to bare roots, as in the above examples, or they can attach to constructions that already contain one or more affixes. Such constructions are called '**stems**'. When a stem has a single morpheme only, then it's a root. (This might seem a fairly trivial distinction to make, but its importance will become apparent below.) Take the example of *mouth*. To form the plural, we simply add *-s* to the stem *mouth*. But *mouth* is also a root, because there are no other morphemes added. However, if we take *mouthful* and form the plural, we add the same suffix, but to the stem *mouthful*. This is not the root, however, because it consists of two morphemes: *mouth* and *ful*.

In chapter 11 we will be discussing items that seem to fall somewhere between free and bound morphemes. These are called '**clitics**'. Although they are bound morphemes in the sense that they attach to other words, they are not affixes (at least not yet), in that they correspond to elements that can be expressed as independent words. Examples include *n't*, *'ll*, *'s*, *'d* as in *didn't*, *we'll*, *he's*, *she'd*. In a way, they 'lean on' other words for support; this is how they get their name (from a Greek word meaning 'lean on').

Compounds and bound roots

The examples we've seen so far all consist of a single root. However, words can also contain two or more roots, and these we refer to as '**compounds**'. For instance, the NZ word *blackball* 'boiled lolly' consists of two free-standing morphemes: *black* and *ball*. Each part is a lexical root. In compounds such as these, one part (typically the first) carries the main stress and is therefore more prominent than the other(s). Compare the stress of *'blackball* with the noun phrase *'black'ball*, where both words carry equal stress. It's sometimes difficult to know how to write these compounds. Do you eat *hot dogs*, *hot-dogs*, or *hotdogs*? Often it boils down to the length of time a compound has existed. Pam Peters, in a 1996 lecture at the University of Melbourne, offered a nice illustration of this. One Australian airline began business in New South Wales under the name *East West*. In 1982 it went national and became *East-West* and then, in 1990, simply *Eastwest*. But there's a lot of inconsistency too. Even dictionaries don't agree on the conventions they adopt, although on the whole, American editors abandon hyphenation quicker than we do.

Compounding can sometimes be used creatively to show that a phrase is actually conceived of as a single concept. For example, *once a year* is normally a phrase and is written as such. And yet in his cooking book, *Consuming Passions*, Ian Parmenter writes it as a hyphenated word. *Turkey*, he explains, *is a once-a-year treat for most of us* (Parmenter 1992:93). Our food texts are full of examples of this kind of creative compounding. Here's a taste of them:

> It's oysters. They do it to me by the dozen, with their mouth-filling freshness, in-your-face saltiness, primal fragrance and strange tangle of textures. They are the S-word on the half-shell.
>
> Dupleix 1996a

> ...aromatic dishes, served on plates adorned with 'quasi-aggressive-in-a-sweet-way' figures
>
> *Vogue Entertaining*, June/July 1995

Just as familiarity typically removes hyphenation in well-established compounds, it can also bring about even further reduction as the morphemes become more closely associated. With familiarity comes phonological change and omission: morpheme boundaries become blurred and the compounds become obscure. For example, many Australians and New Zealanders refer to their respective countries as *God's own country*, but this is typically shortened and is now even spelt as *Godzone*. Spelling is not always affected though (*cupboard* [kʌbəd], for example). Increasing emphasis on literacy, however, sometimes has the effect of restoring the full pronunciation to these reduced compounds (for instance, *grindstone* was earlier [grınsən], and *waistcoat* was earlier [weskət]. Of course, compounds are more prone to spelling pronunciations of this kind when the words become unfamiliar, perhaps because the objects fall into disuse, as in the case of *grindstone*. If cupboards become unfashionable, the word *cupboard* might well revert to its full pronunciation.

With compounding, we encounter a familiar dilemma. When items in a compound drop out of use, or when phonological change obscures them, at what stage do we stop thinking of it as a compound? For example, only the word enthusiast will be aware that *nostril* began life as a compound of two nouns: Old English *nos* 'nose' + *thyrl* 'hole'. Even if *thirl* were not obsolete as an independent item, it has undergone such phonological change in the word *nostril* that it is no longer recognisable. Since the compound is no longer meaningful, it makes sense to treat it as a single morpheme. But let's return to *breakfast*. Probably at some stage in your schooling you were told that this word consists of two parts—*break* and *fast*—but for practical purposes, this is a single item. Some may not even be aware of the compounding, and most of us don't think about it in this way. Are we really justified in saying that this word is morphologically complex? Clearly the morphological analysis of a word can change during its history.

Although the majority of roots are free-standing morphemes, there are some roots that never occur independently (for example, *perceive*, *receive*, *conceive*). The root of these words doesn't have a constant meaning, but there is a core sense there, which is then modified by the affix. Often this can only be determined etymologically; this root is Latinate (*-ceive*, meaning 'take'). Although this is no longer obvious to modern speakers, there are two additional reasons why we must recognise *-ceive* as a root. Segments such as *per-*, *re-*, and *con-* occur frequently and are undoubtedly prefixes. It's their distributional behaviour that forces us to segment these problematic words in this way. Furthermore, the root behaves the same way phonologically with respect to derived forms. For example:

perceive–perception–perceptive
receive–reception–receptive
conceive–conception–conceptive

Only by assuming that *ceive* is a morpheme can we give a uniform account of its derived forms. So while the semantic basis for recognising these morphemes remains shaky, these other pieces of evidence force us to adopt this analysis. What distinguishes these roots from others that we have seen is that they are **bound roots** (that is, they can only occur in combination with other morphemes). Such examples are problematic for our earlier definition of 'morpheme' as a minimal meaningful unit, since we are identifying these not on the basis of their meaning but, rather, according to their distributional behaviour. As Francis Katamba (1994:114) nicely expresses it, these root morphemes are more 'chameleon-like' in their meanings, and they change according to their environments.

Derivational versus inflectional morphemes

Finally, we can distinguish morphemes according to their function. This classification identifies two main groups: inflectional and derivational morphemes. As with other classes of morphemes, however, the relationship between these groups is more that of a continuum than a clear-cut division. So what we will do here is identify some of the classic features of each. Just remember, individual morphemes need not show all of these.

First, consider the inflections in English—or what's left of them. The history of English has seen the unrelenting erosion of what was once a very rich inflectional system, leaving the modest little group of suffixes represented in Table 5.1 (see chapter 11). Despite its small membership, this class remains an important feature of English structure.

Table 5.1 Inflectional morphemes in English

Stem	*Suffix*	*Function*	*Example*
cook	-s	third person singular present	He cooks every day.
cook	-ed	past tense	She cooked yesterday.
cook	-ing	progressive	He is cooking right now.
eat	-en	past participle	She has eaten all the food.
oven	-s	plural	The ovens are new.
oven	-s	possessive	The oven's light is broken.
fast (adj/adverb)	-er	comparative	She eats faster than me.
fast (adj/adverb)	-est	superlative	She is the fastest eater of all.

First, **inflectional morphemes** (or **inflections**) are grammatical morphemes. They modify, but do not change the meaning of an item or its word class; in other words, they never create new lexemes. For instance, *tasty*, *tastier*, and *tastiest* are all adjectives; they are all different forms of the one lexeme TASTY. Second, inflections are changes made in the form of words to express their semantic and syntactic relationships to other words in a sentence. For instance, the agreement morpheme *-s* in *He cooks* indicates that we are dealing with present tense and that the subject of the verb is third-person and singular. Third, inflections show a regular distribution. They occur with all or most of the members of large morpheme classes. In fact, parts of speech are frequently determined on the basis of the inflections they carry. For instance, the majority of English verbs inflect for the third-person singular form. A defining characteristic of English nouns is their ability to take the plural suffix *-s*. Finally, inflections typically occur away from the root at the margins of words. For example, the plural morpheme *-s* appears last in a word after all other suffixes (*flavour-ing-s* and *confect-ion-er-s*, for instance).

Derivational morphemes form new lexical items; that is, when conjoined to roots, new lexical items are **derived** (hence the label 'derivational'). Unlike inflections, then, they can actually change meaning (see Table 5.2). Typically they change the word class. For instance, the verb *drink* (which brings to mind the action of drinking), can be converted into a noun by adding an *-er* suffix. What comes to mind then is a person who performs the action of drinking. However, if instead we add the inflectional *-s* ending to the verb *drink*, we still have the same concept in mind of 'imbibing'(that is, *drink* as an action). The additional information that the inflection provides is 'present tense', and 'third-person singular subject'. *Drinks* and *drinking* are simply other forms of the word—or, more correctly, the lexeme—DRINK, whereas something like DRINKER is a different lexeme with its own set of forms.

Table 5.2 Examples of inflectional and derivational morphemes in English

Lexical item	+ *Inflectional suffix*
glutton (noun)	gluttons (noun + plural)
taste (verb)	tasted (verb + past tense)
pure (adjective)	purer/purest (adjective + comparative/superlative)

Lexical item	+ *Derivational affix(es)*	+ *Inflectional suffix*
glutton (noun)	gluttonise (verb)	gluttonises (verb + present)
taste (verb)	tasty (adjective)	tastier/tastiest (adjective + comparative/superlative)
pure (adjective)	impurity (negative + noun)	impurities (noun + plural)

A second feature of derivational morphemes is that they indicate semantic relationships within words. For example, the morpheme *-ful* in *plateful* has no particular connection with any other morpheme beyond the word *plateful*. It's an affix that derives nouns from other nouns (receptacles such as mouths or containers) and means 'amount that fills X' (here X = *plate*); compare *bellyful* and *pocketful*.

Third, derivational morphemes do not, like inflections, occur across whole classes. Although most nouns take the inflectional *-s* ending, only a limited number take the derivational suffix *-ade* 'drink': *gingerade* and *lemonade*. A notable exception here is the agentive suffix *-er*, meaning 'someone who *verbs*' (*bakers* bake; *singers* sing). As an example of a derivational affix that affects most members of the verb class, it shows a distribution pattern more typical of inflectional suffixes such as *-s* or *-ed*.)

Finally, derivational affixes occur close to the root, before inflectional affixes. A root + derivational affix(es) represents the stem to which additional affixes can then attach. A sure sign that an affix is derivational is its ability to have another affix added to it. Inflections cannot take additional affixes.

BUILDING WORDS: DERIVATION AND INFLECTION

We have already shown that morphemes divide into two major functional classes: derivational and inflectional. This fact reflects the two primary aspects of word-building: the creation of grammatical words (or **inflection**) and the creation of lexical items (or **derivation**). Within these two principal categories fall a number of common morphological processes. Some of these processes—such as affixation, backformation, and stem modification—are applicable to both inflection and derivation. Others—such as compounding, reduplication and conversion—apply only to derivation.

Morphological processes

Affixation

Probably the most common method we have of indicating grammatical distinctions and of forming new words is **affixation**, or the addition of affixes to stems or roots. English has over sixty prefixes and more than eighty suffixes. As we saw earlier, infixing only occurs in expressive colloquial language; colourful 'four-letter' words can interrupt stems to create extra emphasis: *ecofrigginnomics*. We have already listed the inflectional affixes (all suffixes). The rest are derivational. They include native items such as *un-*, *mis-*, *-ish*, and *-ness*, and imports such as *-ise* and *-ese*, and they vary a lot in vitality. Some have died out completely and survive only in relic form; for example, *and-* 'against' is fossilised in a word like *answer*. Others may no longer be productive but survive intact in common-usage words; for example, *-th* once used to form abstract nouns such as *stealth*, *filth*, *wealth*, and *truth*. Others appear to move in and out of fashion; for example, the old suffix *-dom* was brought back from the dead during this century with forms such as *pcdom* 'political correctness', *parentdom*, *stuffed-shirt-dom*, and *yuppydom*—Dennis Baron (1989:154) even cites *lawnmowerdom*. Although some of these may be nonce (one-off creations), it would still seem unwise to declare this particular suffix dead.

For full accounts of modern English derivation, we suggest that you consult substantial works such as Bauer (1983) and Quirk et al. (1985).

Backformation

Affixation relies on pattern extension to form new vocabulary items. So does **backformation**, except that it works in the opposite direction by removing an affix. It can happen, historically, that a complex form (X + affix) exists in the language before the simple form (X) (or sometimes the simple form has simply dropped out of use). For example, OZ and NZ English-speakers have 'backformed' (itself a backformation) the new verb *to bludge* 'to scrounge' from the noun *bludger*, interpreting the final *-er* as the agentive suffix for 'one who does X'; if a *baker* bakes, then a *bludger* must bludge. (Note that *bludger* is actually an abbreviation of *bludgeoner*, meaning 'a person using a bludgeon'). This process has given us common verbs such as *afflict*, *enthuse*, *laze*, *liaise*, *aggress*, *grovel*, *televise*, *gate-crash*, *manhandle*, *eavesdrop*, *house-hunt*, *jell*, and many more. Backformations can have great comic potential. Some may recall the memorable backformation in the television show 'The Nanny': *You're the butler—now butle!*

These sorts of backformations are more likely to occur with very strongly entrenched patterns—to fill an apparent void, as it were. For example, final *s* in a word stem is occasionally interpreted as the plural suffix *-s*, and a new singular is backformed. An example would be the derivation of a new singular form *contact len* from *contact lens*. This process has given rise to a number of 'new' formations in English, like the singular *pea* from original *pease*; recall the old adage *Every pease has its vease* ('fart'), *but every bean fifteen*. Speakers interpreted *pease* as a complex form and created a singular *pea* to fill the vacancy. It's really a kind of pattern-neatening process. Other examples include *cherry* < *ciris*; *riddle* < *raedels*; *burial* < *bygrels*; *sherry* < *sherris*; *eave* < *efes*. These backformations started appearing once *-s* had become firmly established as the plural marker (see chapter 11).

Stem modification

Many languages make use of alternations in stem vowels, consonants, tone, and stress to indicate particular grammatical meanings, and to derive new lexical items. In English, **stem modification** was once a very important process, but it now has a much less significant role to play.

As part of the inflection of modern English verbs, vowel modification is still used to indicate tense. Verbs such as *drink–drank–drunk*, *ride–rode–ridden*, and *eat–ate–eaten* illustrate some of the vowel-alternation patterns that exist, but there are many different classes. This kind of vowel modification is an inherited feature of Indo-European. Over the past millennium, however, more and more verbs have been shifting over to affixation as a way of marking tense distinctions, so that vowel modification is now considered an irregularity of some modern verbs: *stepped* gradually replaced *stope*, *climbed* replaced *clomb*, and so on. (We discuss these more fully in chapter 11, together with nouns such as *man–men* and *foot–feet*, which signal the plural with a vowel change).

Although no longer as productive as it once was, vowel modification still indicates a derivational relationship between some nouns and verbs (for example, *seat–sit*, *shot–shoot*, *drop–drip*, *sale–sell*, *food–feed*, and *blood–bleed*). It also demonstrates a causal relationship between a handful of verbs, such as *fall–fell* 'cause to fall' and *lie–lay* 'cause to lie', (as in *chickens lay eggs*), although the distinction between *lie* and *lay* is collapsing for many speakers. Consonant modification can also indicate differences between parts of speech (for example, noun and verb pairs such as *belief–believe* and *advice–advise*, and adjective and verb pairs such as *safe–save* and *lo(a)th–loathe*, where there is a difference in voice in the stem-final fricative). Some pairs, such as *breath–breathe* and *bath–bathe*, show alternations in both final consonant and stem vowel.

Stems may also vary with respect to stress patterns. Since the sixteenth century, English has used stress to differentiate noun and verb pairs (for instance, *'record–re'cord*, *'conduct–con'duct*, and *'produce–pro'duce*). The change involves a stress shift from second syllable to first syllable in nouns (also causing a change in vowel quality). There are still many pairs that remain unaffected, but we can expect that most of these will eventually fall into line. The public outcries over an initial stress in nouns such as *'research* and *'address* suggest these stress patterns are currently in the process of shifting—not everyone likes change.

Conversion

English is unusual in that so many words can convert to other parts of speech without adding any affix. This is why **conversion** is sometimes called 'zero-affixation'. Typically, conversion involves the major word classes: nouns, verbs, adjectives, and adverbs (see Table 5.3).

There don't appear to be any restrictions on conversion; words can move between classes with extraordinary ease. There are even examples of conversion from minor classes such as prepositions and conjunctions. *Up* and *down* can be more than just simple prepositions—for example, *to up the stakes* and *to down tools* (verb); *to be on the up* and *to have a down on someone* (noun); *up-market* and *a down-drain* or *a down experience* (adjective); and *to set up* and *to go up and down* (adverb). Obscenities are among the most grammatically flexible of all. For example, the word *fuck* has extended from an exclusively verbal usage to every major part of speech (see Allan & Burridge 1991 on flexibility in swearing).

Such elasticity in our words is an offshoot of the loss of inflection, although curiously it's a convenience that not all speakers fully appreciate. A sporting commenta-

Table 5.3 Conversion between word classes

Verb → Noun		*Noun → Verb*	
Established	*Recent*	*Established*	*Recent*
a guess	a think	to bottle	to trash
a call	a read	to bridge	to network
a command	a big ask	to mail	to impact (on)
			to leaflet
Adjective → Verb		*Adjective → Noun*	
Established	*Recent*	*Established*	*Recent*
to better	to total (a car)	a roast	a gay
to empty		a weekly	a given
to open		a regular	a nasty

tor recently reported, *Well, it wasn't gold, but at least he medalled.* More conservative speakers find such individual inventiveness abhorrent, and many are quick to condemn even everyday usages such as *to have a listen* and *to impact (on).* Complaints are commonplace: 'It annoys me very much to hear verbs frequently used as nouns', writes one person from Western Australia. 'I hope *Ozwords* will examine the new trend to use nouns as verbs', writes another from New South Wales (from letters to *Ozwords*, vol. 1, no. 3, 1995, p. 3). As the editor of *Ozwords* rightly points out, this is not a new trend. We've been doing it for centuries, and with time, new examples such as *a big ask* will sound as familiar as venerable oldies such as *attempt* and *fall* (nouns from verbs) and *to chair* and *to date* (verbs from nouns). It wasn't that long ago that people were applying labels such as 'abomination' and 'lubricious barbarism' to the verb *to contact*, a newcomer at the time.

Compounding

Since we've already discussed compounds at some length, we will focus here on the very fuzzy boundary between compounding and affixation. Consider the English suffix *-dom*, which goes back to the Old English word *doom* 'judgment'. At the time when words such as *kingdom* and *Christendom* were created, these were undoubtedly compounds, but in twentieth-century creations such as *Nazidom* and the more jocular *yuppydom*, *-dom* is the perfect example of a derivational suffix. At what stage do we say that it has lost its independent status?

Slang creates problems for us all the time. For example, the word *head* has produced a spate of words, mostly personal insults ascribing mental or physical inadequacy: *egghead*, *dickhead*, *acidhead*, *blockhead*, *blubberhead*, *cheesehead*, *boofhead*, *fathead*, *meathead*, *pinhead*, *dopehead*, *weedhead*, to name a few. Although it's too early to call these derivatives 'affixes', *head* is clearly an affix in the making. What we've got here is a continuum from compounding to affixation; there is no magic point at which a root stops being a root and starts being an affix.

Occasionally it can happen, too, that an affix develops independent status. In chapter 10 we examine a number of the 'super-literate *eses*' of the twentieth century. This label covers varieties of English such as *bureaucratese*, *computerese*, and even *linguisticalese*. Originally a suffix, *-ese* formed adjectives and nouns from place names (*Japanese*, for example). It then developed the sense of 'the language or style of X' (X being the entity described in the stem). At this stage, it also acquired negative overtones (that is, the derogatory associations of jargon). If *ese* does become established as a lexeme in its own right, terms such as *computerese* will technically become compounds. (See also Bauer 1983 for a discussion of *isms* and *ologies*).

Reduplication

Reduplication is a repetition process whereby all or part of the stem is repeated and the resulting form is a kind of compound. It's argued to be a peripheral process in English, and it certainly does seem rather limited compared with those languages in which it is regularly used to convey important grammatical distinctions, such as 'plural' in nouns and 'ongoing action' in verbs. But while reduplication plays no grammatical role in English, it is responsible for producing some 2000 words in the language, and new ones are being created all the time.

There are basically three types of reduplicated compounds. One involves reduplication of the whole stem: *goody-goody*, *fifty-fifty*, *hubba-hubba*, *never-never*, *hush-hush*. Some OZ examples—such as *woop-woop(s)* (in NZ *wop-wops*), meaning 'remote area'—are undoubtedly inspired by the reduplication process in Aboriginal languages (where it's a common indicator of plurality and intensity). Other forms are confined to nursery language: *woof-woof*, *Mama*, *yum-yum*, *ta-ta*, and *gee-gee*.

A second type involves the repetition of the rhyme (that is, the root vowel(s) and following consonant(s)). Sometimes one, and sometimes none, of the elements are independently meaningful: *argy-bargy*, *arty-farty*; *lovey-dovey*, *helter-skelter*, *higgledy-piggledy*, *super-duper*, *namby-pamby*, *hankey-pankey*, *hokey-pokey*, and *hoity-toity*. Occasionally the stems are both existing words: *stun-gun*, *brain-drain*, *flower-power*, *culture-vulture*, and *gang-bang*. This type of reduplication is very productive, particularly in slang; examples from NZ and OZ teenage slang include *tin grin* 'someone with braces' and *sprain(ed) brain* 'crazy person'. Sometimes speakers stop identifying the compounded elements with independently existing forms. This can occur through phonological change, because the words drop out of use, or simply because the meaning relationships become obscure. For example, *hob-nob* derives from present subjunctive forms of two now obsolete verbs *habb(an)* and *nabb(an)* (literally 'have' and 'not have'); *willy-nilly* derives from the expression *will I nill I*, based on the verbs *willen* 'want' and *nillen* 'not want'. Some recent creations such as *hi-fi* from *high fidelity* fit into this category.

The third type of reduplicative compound is rarer than the others. It involves some sort of modification of the stem vowel, typically [ɪ] → [æ] or [ɪ] → [ɒ] (for example, *shilly-shally*, *dilly-dally*, *mishmash*, *riff-raff*, *tick-tock*, *flip-flop*).

Many of these are undoubtedly expressive formations, where the sounds attempt to imitate the sense of the word (for instance, *hurdy-gurdy* is somehow appropriate to the sound of the instrument). Sometimes the sounds or sound sequences come to symbolise certain meanings and spawn new formations. The *-ing* rhyme, for example, has become an expressive pattern for speakers, producing formations such as *ping-pong*, *ding-dong*, *wing-ding*, *swing-wing*, *sing-song*. (See chapter 6 on phonesthemes.)

Productive morphemes

Several times in the course of this chapter we have talked about productive morphemes. What exactly do we mean by productive here? Basically the description covers any morphological process that is frequently or actively used in word-formation.

On the surface, it's a straightforward notion: the more frequently an affix is used, the more productive we assume it is. But as usual, things are more complex than at first they seem. The Scrabble players among you will immediately recognise the ticklish nature of productivity. What do you do when your partner defiantly puts down a word such as *busher*, maintaining quite reasonably that it means 'one who bushes (it)'; (that is, 'camps in the bush'). Do you allow it or not? The *-er* suffix can create agent nouns from most verbs. The word *busher* doesn't appear in any dictionary, but that doesn't necessarily mean the word doesn't exist. Dictionary-makers are constantly having to redraw the admission and exclusion boundary for marginal vocabulary items. For example, the words *belongingness* and *apartness* have now been included in the *New Shorter Oxford English Dictionary* (NSOED) and the MD, but were absent from previous editions. And consider the following example, where Wendy Harmer plays on the productiveness of the *-ism/-ist* suffix.

> And as I confront my unthinking lookism, I begin to ask myself is it possible I could also have been guilty of 'hearism', 'tasteism' and 'smellism'?
>
> Harmer 1995

Now few of the *isms* in her article appear in even the most recent of dictionaries. But you will find them and many others in satirical articles on political correctness. Conversely, dictionaries are full of entries no longer in use (some were never frequent). The NSOED has rarities such as *comer, studier, presider, cycler, raper, supposer*, and *stealer.* Why not *busher*?

There are a couple of aspects that we need to point out here. First, what we are dealing with is another continuum, not a clear-cut division. Processes aren't simply productive or unproductive; it's a matter of degree. Moreover, even the most productive of processes are never 100 per cent effective. For instance, the hugely successful Germanic *-er* suffix we just mentioned is maximally productive, yet there are still exceptions (for example, 'someone who types' is not a *typer* but a *typist*). This is not to say, however, that productivity is a simple matter of numbers either. A limited distribution doesn't necessarily mean a lack of productiveness. It can depend on the nature of the stem. For example, the *-ade* suffix is only productive in forming the names of flavoured softdrinks such as *lemonade, orangeade*, and *gingerade*. Phonology can also affect the likelihood of a process taking place. The suffix *-ise* is extremely productive in forming verbs from nouns or adjectives of more than one syllable (for example, *burglarise, containerise*, and *marginalise*). The noun-forming suffix *-ion* is very productive, but at the same time is limited to verb stems ending in *-ate*, such as *educate*.

Second, productivity is affected over time. Affixes often start off slowly and only subsequently become active. The *-(a/e)teria* suffix first made its appearance in the 1920s in the word *cafeteria* (from American Spanish *cafetería*). It took off slowly as a suffix, initially via the process of blending (see discussion in chapter 6), but eventually became active in designating self-service retail or catering establishments—for example, *bookateria*, *casketeria* 'undertaker's establishment', *chocolateria*, *hatateria*, *healthateria*, *pie-teria*, *valeteria*, *washeteria*. Recent additions, such as the NZ English *calfeteria* 'bowl with multiple teats from which a number of calves may feed', suggest that the suffix is still active.

Some affixes can be productive for a limited period only; with time they atrophy. For example, the once lively plural suffixes *-en* or *-er* are now well and truly dead. They occur only in a handful of living fossils such as *oxen* and *children* (*children* shows both suffixes). Similarly, the now deceased negative prefix *wan-* was once highly productive, forming words with the same ease as the current prefix *un-*. In Old English it was responsible for a large number of expressions, now mainly obsolete or dialectal: *wanton* (originally 'undisciplined' now 'sexually promiscuous'), *wanbelief* 'disbelief', *wancheer* 'grief', *wanchance* 'ill luck', *wancouth* 'uncouth', *wandeedy* 'mischievous', *wanearthly* 'unearthly', *wanease* 'unease', *wanhope* 'despair', *wanhap* 'misfortune', *wanruly* 'unruly', *wandought* 'feeble person', *wanrest* 'unrest', *wanluck* 'bad luck', and many more.

The fashion analogy is a useful one here. Suddenly sun-dried tomatoes, for some reason, capture people's palates, and for a while sun-dried tomatoes appear on the menus of all fashionable cafés. In the same way, affixes get taken up by ordinary language and extend from their specialist usage into other contexts (although obviously without the deliberate manipulation that you find in the fashion or food industry). The *-ise* suffix has become very trendy. Now we *burglarise* not *burgle*, and *prioritise* not *rank*; we even *entitise*, *condomise*, and *incentivise*. *Prayerise, Picturise, Actualise* reads the slogan of one New Age religious group. Like modes of dressing and eating, affixes come in and out of fashion in this way, some achieving almost voguish popularity. The word *buster* has been around in compounds since the mid-nineteenth century, but it was the 1984 *blockbuster* movie *Ghostbusters* that produced a sudden flurry of copycat creations, such as *alley busters* 'bowling balls', *ballbusters* 'sexually demanding women', *cold busters* 'doctors', *line busters* 'queue jumpers', *taxbusters*, *fare busters* 'travel agents', *virus busters* 'vaccines', *bronco busters* 'horse breakers', *crime busters*, *dam busters*, *chart-busters*, *woof busters* (a dog training service), *stress busters* (a masseuse service), *Gutbusters* (a weight-loss program targeting the waists of Australian males), and in American English, even *buster busters* 'people opposed to the proliferation of *buster* terms'.

The *-ette* suffix nicely illustrates the sensitive nature of productiveness. At the end of the eighteenth century, *-ette* had two functions: first to indicate 'small' (as in *cigarette* or *kitchenette*) and second to indicate 'imitation or substitute' (as in *leatherette* or *flannel(l)ette*). In the first sense, it remains productive; recent editions include *dinette* 'small dining room' (1930), *laund(e)rette* (1949), *diskette* 'floppy disk' (1973), and *Veepette* 'insignificant Vice-President' (as applied to J. D. Quayle). In the second sense, however, it is less productive, and recent additions, such as *satinette* and *winceyette*, are few. Robert Burchfield, former editor of the OED, points out that the word *suffragette* (first recorded 1906) heralded another use of the suffix with the meaning 'female'. It triggered creations such as *usherette*, *(drum) majorette*, and even *undergraduettes* (Burchfield 1989, part 1:4). Branded as sexist, however, this usage all but disappeared—except in the world of journalism, it seems. Playing on the suffix's recent fall from grace, male journalists have created forms such as *hackette, hypette, snoopette, awarette, editorette, voguette, whizzette*, all of which are deliberately provocative. Many are probably one-off forms. Nonetheless, they are interesting for what they tell us about the productivity of the suffix. Even if many of these new creations fall by the wayside, they still indicate the vitality of this affix.

REPRESENTING MORPHEMES

So far our discussion has only referred to things called morphemes. But as usual, the situation is more complex than this. You have already come across the concepts of phonemes, phones, and allophones in chapter 3. Conveniently there is also a parallel naming system for morphology.

Morphemes, morphs, and allomorphs

Have a look at the correspondence between the forms on the left and on the right.

phone	morph
phoneme	morpheme
allophone	allomorph

Phones are the physical units of sound produced by the speech organs. In the same way, **morphs** are the actual speech sounds, the physically occurring units (either words or parts of words) to which meaning attaches. On the other hand, phonemes, you will remember, are abstract units; they are what distinguish the meanings of words. **Morphemes** too are abstract; they refer to the actual units of meaning, which are then represented (or realised) by particular morphs. It's only morphs, therefore, that are real. They are the physical forms, the actual fragments of sound, representing the morphemes.

In chapter 3, we saw that phonemes may be pronounced differently, depending on where they occur in the word. This fact gives rise to these things called allophones (that is, variant sounds representing the same phoneme). Morphemes too can have a number of different phonological shapes. These are called '**allomorphs**'. In terms of the linguistic system, they are simply variants or alternative phonetic forms (pronunciations) of morphemes (that is, various morphs representing the same morpheme). The term comes, as you might guess, from the Greek: *allos* 'other' + *morphe* 'form'. As a matter of convention, morphemes are typically represented in { }, and allomorphs in [ ].

Take the example of the morpheme {FOOD} 'substance(s) to maintain life'. What appears inside the curly brackets is the concept or the meaning. Normally, we simply use traditional spellings, as we've done in this case, or we might use a description of the morpheme (for example, {PAST} or {PLURAL}).

The morpheme {FOOD} is represented by the morph (or, in terms of the system, the allomorph) [fu:d], which is the encoding of phonemes of this particular concept. It just happens that this is the only allomorph of the morpheme {FOOD}.

The indefinite article {A} provides a good example of a morpheme with more than one morph. In this case, there are two allomorphs: [ə] and [ən]. Allomorphs typically appear because there is some sort of conditioning factor involved. More often than not, it's related to pronunciation and has to do with the phonological environment. Look at the two columns of words below and try to work out the forms of {A} that you would use, and what might be conditioning them.

lemonade	iced tea
sandwich	open sandwich
main dish	entree
starter	antipasto
Lancashire hotpot	Irish stew
morning tea	afternoon tea
poached egg	omelette

What you will have discovered is that, if the word following *a* begins with a consonant, then the allomorph is [ə], and if it begins with a vowel, it is [ən]. These allomorphs are said to be in complementary distribution. All that means is that they never occur in the same position; there is always something about their immediate environment that acts as a trigger. In other words, [ə] has the distribution 'before consonants' and [ən] 'before vowels'; they never overlap. Their distribution is therefore phonologically conditioned. In this case, the allomorphy is reflected in the spelling.

A less obvious example is the definite article. What you will discover when you try putting {THE} in front of the list of words above is that [ðə] occurs before words beginning with consonants, and [ði] before words beginning with a vowel. This is something we do automatically. Non-native speakers might occasionally substitute the wrong allomorph, but it would only ever sound like a slightly odd pronunciation. It could not alter the meaning, because the difference between allomorphs of the same morpheme is never meaningful.

At this point, we can introduce a further conditioning environment, which involves whether or not the articles are stressed. Consider the following example with the indefinite article:

> I don't just want *an* omelette (that is, any old omelette); I'm after the best there is.
>
> I don't just want *a* sandwich; I want the one with lobster and dill mayonnaise.

When emphasised in this way, speakers generally supply the full vowel [æn] and [eɪ] rather than the reduced (schwa) forms [ən] and [ə]. This gives us four allomorphs: [ən] (unstressed before a vowel), [ə] (unstressed before a consonant), [æn] (stressed before a vowel), and [eɪ] (stressed before a consonant). Try stressing the definite article *the* and see what happens to the vowel in these different environments.

The patterns of allomorphy we have just discussed don't hold for speakers of all Antipodean varieties of English. Speakers of Maori English and many other NZ English-speakers use [ə] and [ðə] before words beginning with both consonants and vowels (Elizabeth Gordon, pers. comm., 3 April 1997). For these speakers, stress will be the only relevant conditioning environment here.

Most allomorphs of morphemes are phonetically very similar, but in the particular treatment that we are assuming here, this doesn't need to be the case. As a final example, consider the plural forms of the following three groups:

Group 1 chip, dessert, cake, rollmop, puff
Group 2 flan, salad, herb, meatball, egg, pie
Group 3 spice, sandwich, cheese, dish

The English plural is spelt *s* (or *es*), but has at least three different phonetic forms. The first is a voiceless fricative [s], the second a voiced [z], and the last [əz]. In other words, {PLURAL} in English has three alternative realisations or allomorphs. The distribution of these different allomorphs (that is, the contexts in which they appear) depends on the phonological characteristic of the stem-final segments. In other words, the morpheme {PLURAL} is realised as:

Group 1 [s] after stems ending in a voiceless segment (excluding sibilants).
Group 2 [z] after stems ending in a voiced segment (excluding sibilants).
Group 3 [əz] after stems ending in a voiced or voiceless sibilant.

The name 'sibilant' is used for the fricatives [s, z, ʃ, ʒ], as they have a higher pitch than the other fricatives. It is stems ending in one of these sounds that take the [əz] allomorph.

The allomorphs of {PLURAL} are phonologically conditioned because we can describe their distribution—the environments in which they occur—in phonological terms. They occur because of phonological processes such as assimilation (in this case, of voice) and epenthesis (vowel-insertion)—both processes make the pronunciation easier. The allomorphs are in complementary distribution (that is, each occurs in certain environments in which the others never occur). This is the established pattern for forming the plural in English, and you can predict when each of the allomorphs will appear. When English acquires new food terms, such as *cappuccino*, *fu yung*, *taco*, *pappadum*, *kebab*, *pilaf*, *mousse*, and *bouillabaisse*, we automatically apply the correct plural, even though we might have never heard the term before. As speakers of English, you automatically select between these alternative forms without realising it. As linguists, you can now isolate the forms and determine their meaning and distribution.

Again NZ English has something interesting to offer here. For some NZ English-speakers there is evidence that the voicing contrast between consonants word-finally is disappearing (Maclagan 1975). This means that the pattern of allomorphy we have just described will not be valid for these speakers. Since only voiceless constants appear in final position, this will reduce our three-way contrast—[s], [z], and [əz]—to only two, [s] and [əs] (of course, this involves not only the plural morpheme, but also the possessive morpheme {s} and present-tense morpheme {s}). As far as we can tell, there is no evidence of this change occurring in OZ English.

Another little glitch for our neat three-way contrast is an example such as *ox* and its plural *oxen*. Here we have a quite different form of the plural morpheme, but there is nothing in the phonological shape of *ox* to account for it. Its irregularity arises from the actual lexical item *ox*. Compare words such as *box*, *fox*, or *axe*, all of which take the regular plural ending. We say, therefore, that this particular allomorph for {PLURAL} is **lexically conditioned**; this is just something about the word *ox*.

So far the allomorphy has involved affixes, but it can involve stems as well. Consider forms such as *house–houses*, *loaf–loaves*, and *wife–wives*. Here we have competing stems, differing with respect to the voicing of the last consonant (a fricative)—for example, [haʊs]– [haʊz]. The pattern is not widespread, however, and there are many more nouns (also ending in fricatives) that do not show this alternation (for instance, *cliffs* and *places*). What we have here is another instance of lexical conditioning. There is nothing in the phonology of these words that is causing the alternation. They are special irregular facts about English that must simply be learnt.

Suppletion

It can happen that historically unrelated forms collide, for some reason, to produce totally irregular and eccentric patterns in the language. For instance, two of the most important verbs in English have mongrel origins, and the result is something called '**suppletion**'. The verb *be* is a totally mixed-up verb, showing a combination of at least three, possibly four, originally distinct verbs: *bēon* 'to become' provides *be*, *being*, and *been*; *wesan* 'to dwell' provides the past tense forms *was* and *were*; and the Indo-European verbal root **es-* 'to exist' provides *is*, *am*, and possibly *are* (although this may involve a fourth source). The verb *go* has most of its forms built on *go*, but derives its past-tense form, *went*, from the verb *wend* 'to make one's way'.

Suppletion then covers those cases where the addition of a grammatical morpheme causes a complete change in the original form. The verb *be* changes to *am*, *is*, *was*, and so on as the various grammatical morphemes of {TENSE}, {NUMBER}, and {PERSON} are added. Similarly, no amount of phonological imagination will ever derive *went* directly from *go*. Yet there is a clear grammatical connection between the forms *go* and *went*, which suggests that we are not dealing with distinct lexemes (although this is controversial). It is usual to treat these forms as inflectionally related via the process of suppletion; for example, the morphemes {GO} + {PAST} are realised as the suppletive form *went*. These words can't be segmented into their various parts in the way that regular forms of the language can be; they must be handled by special rules.

Suppletion when it occurs always affects frequently used items. Common verbs such as *go* and *be* are suppletive in many of the Indo-European languages, as are the most common adjectives; for example, the lexemes GOOD and BAD typically have suppletive comparative, and superlative forms, as in *good–better–best* and *bad–worse–worst*.

POINTS TO REMEMBER

- Morphemes are the smallest units of meaning in the structure of a language.
- Lexical morphemes have identifiable meaning, or they indicate a change in meaning when added to a word stem. All roots (the majority free-standing) are lexical.
- Grammatical morphemes provide information about grammatical function by relating certain words in a sentence to each other. Bound inflectional affixes and free-standing parts of speech, such as prepositions, articles, pronouns, and conjunctions, are grammatical.

- Derivational affixes belong to a large open set of affixes that form new words, change parts of speech, have more lexical meaning, appear close to the stem, show irregular distribution, and occur with only some members of a class.
- Inflectional affixes belong to a small closed set of affixes that don't form new words, have more grammatical meaning, are ordered after derivational affixes, show regular distribution, and are added to every appropriate stem.
- There are two types of word-building: the creation of grammatical words (inflection) and the creation of lexical items (derivation). Common morphological processes such as affixation, backformation, and stem modification are applicable to both inflection and derivation. Others, such as compounding, reduplication, and conversion, apply only to derivation.
- Productive morphological processes are those frequently or actively used in word-formation.
- Morphemes are abstract and refer to actual units of meaning. Morphs are the physical forms representing the morphemes.
- Morphemes are not represented consistently in every environment by the same morph. There are alternative representations called 'allomorphs'.
- Allomorphs are said to be in complementary distribution when they never occur in the same position.
- Suppletion covers totally eccentric forms such as *go–went*, where the addition of a grammatical morpheme causes a complete change in the original form.

EXERCISES

1 Types of 'words'

English has many examples of homophony, homonymy, and polysemy. This mismatch between lexemes and word-forms is the source of considerable humour in English word-play. Examine the following restaurant names, and say whether the word-play involves homonymy, homophony, polysemy, or anything else. Have a look in your *Yellow Pages* and see if you can add to this list of punning eateries.

a Out to Lunch
b Beau Thai
c Thai Me Kangaroo Down Sport
d Relish the Thought
e The Daily Grind (coffee shop)
f The Upper Crust (bakery)
g We are Nuts (nut dealer)
h Wok Inn (North American pronunciation of *wok*)
i Eaternity
j Garden of Eatin'
k I & Joy Bagels
l Just for the Halibut
m Sweet Revenge (chocolatier)

n Higher Grounds Coffee Shop
o Just Desserts
p Lettuce Entertain You
q French Lettuce

2 **Word-building processes**
With cultural expansion comes lexical expansion. For example, according to Dwight Bolinger (1975), a supermarket that stocked 8000 items in 1966 stocked 14 000 items in 1973—and who knows how many more now? All of these new items need names. Go out and browse for yourself through the supermarket shelves and collect examples of product names that illustrate each of the processes we have looked at in this chapter: affixation, stem modification, back-formation, reduplication, compounding, and conversion.

3 **Child language**
Using the word-formation processes we discussed in the chapter, characterise the 'errors' in the following examples that we have collected from child language.
a You're a nidiot!
b It fell offed!
c Look at the hippobottomus!
d Mother: Noway Katie. Child: Yesway!
e Pinocchio longed his nose.
f I've brokened it.
g (In the context of waxing a boat) Give the boat another wack.
h How do you crumpet these? (Later) Look, I'm crumpeting!
i I don't wanna go to the eyedentist.
j (To the waiter) Pour me! (And later) Hop me on!

4 **Word-building and humour**
The following is an extract from a torrid tale of 'requited' love. Using examples, explain what aspect of English morphology this story has exploited for humour.

> It had been a rough day, so when I walked into the party I was very chalant, despite my efforts to appear gruntled and consolate. I was furling my wieldy umbrella for the coat check when I saw her standing alone in a corner. She was a descript person, a woman in a state of total array. Her hair was kempt, her clothing shevelled, and she moved in a gainly way. I wanted desperately to meet her, but I knew I'd have to make bones about it, since I was travelling cognito. Beknownst to me, the hostess, whom I could see both hide and hair of, was very proper, so it would be skin off my nose if anything bad happened...

Winter 1994:82

5 **Suppletion**
a At school we're taught to say *worse–worst* rather than **badder–baddest*. How then do you explain the following famous song lyrics?

> Bad bad Leroy Brown,
> Baddest man in the whole darn town,

Badder than old King Kong,
Meaner than a junkyard dog.

Would *worse–worst* do here? If not, why not?

b In the following pairs of italicised words, identify which have a derivational, and which a suppletive, relationship. Compare the examples in parentheses; is there a difference in meaning (that is, is the relationship between *read* and *readable* the same as between *read* and *legible*)?

i What can be *read* is *readable*. (What can be read is *legible*.)
ii What can be *chewed* is *chewable*.
iii What can be *seen* is *visible*.
iv What can be *eaten* is *edible*.
v What can be *known* is *knowable*.
vi What can be *heard* is *audible*. (What can be *heard* is *hearable*.)
vii What can be *detected* is *detectable*.
viii What can be *done* is *feasible*. (What can be *done* is *doable*.)

6 **Free and bound morphemes**

In the following hangover cure, divide each word into morphemes and indicate whether each morpheme is free or bound. If bound, state whether it is derivational or inflectional. If derivational, state what each affix does (for example, does it change a noun into a verb?). Discuss any problems that you encountered in your analysis.

> It's true, some Americans wholeheartedly swear by the goodly prairie oyster and its beneficial consequences...an unbroken eggyolk on top of which you pour, well mixed, a smallish pinch of salt, a teaspoon each of tomato ketchup, Worcestershire sauce and lemon juice, half a teaspoon of vinegar, a tiny drop of tabasco and a hefty pinch of cayenne. Instructions read:
>
> 'Shut eyes, open mouth,
> Murmur prayers for the soul,
> Pop in and swallow whole'.
>
> Absolutely revolting! It sounds more along the lines of some extraordinarily ancient Roman emetic or a means of exorcising a devil...
>
> Adapted from Goode & Willson 1987

7 **Representing morphemes**

For each of the following verbs, write the final sounds of the past suffix. Then answer the questions below.

> munch, chew, chomp, consume, masticate, gnaw, feast, taste, snack, gulp, gluttonise, nibble, nourish, dine, banquet

a Identify the allomorphs of the morpheme {PAST}.
b State the distribution of the different allomorphs of the morpheme {PAST}.
c Why does your statement fail to account for the past of words such as *drink*, *eat*, and *feed*.

d In Antipodean English, the verbs *buy* 'purchase' and *bring* 'convey, carry' are becoming confused in their past-tense forms—for example, *Mr Eric Grant of Glen Iris bought in a couple of his 1975 Bin 389 for evaluation* (*Age*, 24 August 1994). Why do you think this is happening, and how should we now treat the relationship between *bring* and *bought*?

8 Words over time: classifying morphemes

Using the OED (or another good etymological dictionary), trace the history of each of the following words. Show how an etymologist might divide them into morphemes. How would you classify them now? What difficulties do you encounter?

hussy, werewolf, lord, gossip, cobweb, daisy, lukewarm, digest, prepare, pregnant, quince, news, wiseacre, umbrella

6

Words across Time

INTRODUCTION

Vocabulary is an area of language that fascinates most people, probably because words are more within our reach than other areas of language, but also because they provide us with wonderful windows into a speech community's values and attitudes. In this chapter, we've decided to focus on the dynamic aspects of our lexicon. Those of you who have battled with early English texts will have quickly realised the extent to which vocabulary can change. Words drop out of use; meanings modify. Have a look at the following extract from a medieval recipe for *grete pyes* 'big pies' (and they must have been huge).

> *Grete pyes*. Take *faire* yonge beef, And suet of a fatte *beste*, or of Motton, and *hak* all this on a borde small; and *caste* therto pouder of peper and salt; and whan it is small *hewen*, put hit in a bolle. And *medle* hem well; then make a faire large *Cofyn*, and *couch* som of this stuffur in. Then take Capons, Hennes, Mallardes, *Connynges*, and parboile hem in a boiling pot; And then couch all this *fowle* in the Coffyn
>
> [Large pies: Take good young beef, and suet from a fat animal or from mutton, and chop this up on a small board; and add pepper and salt; and when it is finely chopped, put it in a bowl. And mix them well together; then make a good large pastry case and lay some of this filling down. Then take capons [castrated cocks], hens, mallards [wild ducks], rabbits, and parboil them in a boiling pot; And then lay all this bird flesh in the pastry case.]
>
> Recipe from Black 1992:118

The adjective *fair* originally meant 'fit, suitable' but now has chiefly the meaning 'equitable, just' (or 'light in colour'). In the sense of 'animal', *beast* is generally found in rural contexts, usually in reference to 'stock'. To modern readers, early cooking verbs seem excessively brutal. Nowadays we chop things, but we used to *hew*, *hack*, and *smite* them. All these verbs would now be used in restricted contexts to mean 'sever into pieces with violent cutting blows'; both *hew* and *smite* are archaic and would probably only be used for special effect (for example, *hew asunder*). Not many people *cast* these days, except perhaps in fishing. *Meddle* was once a neutral verb meaning simply 'to mix' but has now become quite negative, suggesting 'mixing unduly, interfering in others' affairs'. Although bakers still talk about *coffin lids* for 'pastry cases', this seems particularly bizarre to general readers, who understand only the very specific sense of 'a box for a corpse'. We no longer use *couch* meaning 'to lay something down', except in the specific context of writing and speech (*he couched his speech in flowery language*) and, of course, the noun meaning 'piece of furniture for reclining'. *Connynges* or *coney* (rhyming with *honey*) was the word for 'rabbit' until the nineteenth century, when it dropped out of use. *Fowl* once included birds of any kind. Spectacular examples like these are easy to find.

LEXICAL CHANGE

When people think of language change, what they often have in mind is, in fact, lexical change. In this section we examine two of the most fundamental aspects: how new words are born and how they die.

Where do words come from?

The verb *to coin* is used generally to refer to vocabulary expansion, but strictly speaking it should include only outright creations or inventions. True coinages are words fashioned out of the blue—words without etymologies, if you like. For example, the word *googol* 'one followed by 1000 zeros' was apparently coined by a mathematician's son and doesn't appear to have any known relatives. Since true coinages are so rare, we'll concentrate on the more usual ways that English goes about getting new words.

Names: onomastics

Most of you can probably think of examples in which brand names have lost their capital letter and have become household words. *Esky* was once a trade name for a type of portable cooler in Australia. Its NZ equivalent is a *chilly bin*. We now use the word *daks* for any pair of basic trousers, but originally it was the exclusive label of Simpson's of Piccadilly. The somewhat less glamorous *stubbies* were a brand of shorts, but now apply widely to any shorts of that style. In each of these examples, the name has extended from a specific case to refer generally to the whole class of items. This process has been dubbed '**commonisation**', and it is responsible for a surprising number of new words. *Blockout, boogie board, dumpster, ethernet, filofax, jet ski, playdough, popper, portaloo, porta-potty, solar film, stackhat, superglue, velcro, walkman, wetbike*, and *whipper snipper* are some recent additions to the MD. The NZ word *zambuck*, meaning 'ambulance person', is slightly different. This word derives from the tradename of an ointment that comes in a black-and-white container, much like the uniforms of the St John ambulance officers (Gordon & Deverson 1985:47).

It can also happen that place names and personal names enter the language as ordinary words. *Jeans* have their origin in the town of Genoa, where a type of heavy cotton fabric (resembling denim) was once made. *Denim* itself derives from Nîmes, the name of a city in southern France (originally *serge de Nîmes* or 'serge (cloth) of

Nîmes'). Most of you will be familiar with *lamingtons* (from Baron Lamington, a Governor of Queensland), *grannies* (from Maria Ann 'Granny' Smith, who developed the Granny Smith Apple), and *pavlovas* (from the Russian ballerina Anna Pavlova)—we won't debate here whether it was an Australian or New Zealand invention. Thomas Crapper, Queen Victoria's plumber and the famous patentor of the valveless water-waste preventer, probably gives us the backformed verb and mass noun *crap* (although there may be additional influences, such as Middle English *crap* 'grain husk' > 'residue'). When Lorena Bobbit cut off her husband's penis in June 1992, the verb *to bobbit* suddenly appeared in newspapers around the world to describe this and similar events. Dictionary editors seem to agree that it is too early to speculate on the word, but the associate editor of the OED states, 'if *bobbit* turns up in several different stories over a period of time, this suggests it should go in the dictionary' (as quoted in the *Age*, 7 February 1993:11).

Personal names become verbal expressions of our personality. Because of this special force, they occasionally enter ordinary language as the generic label for a certain 'type'. OZ *ocker* derives from the proper name *Oscar* (compare *Macca* from *McKenzie*). The original *ocker* was a television character played by the comedian Ron Frazer. In the 1970s the name started to be used generically for any character of that type—typically dressed in *stubbies*, *Chesty Bond* singlet, and thongs, and always cheerful, unpretentious, but not overly intellectual. In many ways he is like *Norm*, the creation of Phillip Adams for the Life Be In It campaign in Victoria in 1975. Designed to spur us all into athletic pursuits, Norm is the supreme couch potato—slumped in front of the television, wrapped around a tinnie, and watching sport. Although he retains his initial capital, *Norm* is already well along the path of commonisation. (Compare *charlie* or *wally*, which have even stronger overtones of stupidity.) One etymology for *Sheila*, OZ and NZ slang for 'young woman', is that it stems from the generic use of the (originally Irish) proper name. At first it applied to any young Irish woman, much like *Paddy* for Irish men, but then extended to include all women. Who was the original Sheila? Though candidates have been suggested, it was just a very popular name at the time. Oddly enough, the immortalisation of names such as these in Antipodean idiom has almost guaranteed that they will never again be used for children's names.

Acronyms and abbreviations

> *From:* The Vice-Chancellor *To:* Deans of all Faculties
> *Subject:* INDUSTRY YEAR SHADOW SCHEME
>
> As you are no doubt aware, 1987 has been designated Industry year by the Government. The DES, through the UGC, have urged the CVCP to ensure that universities throughout the UK—
>
> 'He does love acronyms, doesn't he,' Philip murmurs.
>
> Lodge 1989:84

Acronyms refer to those words that are formed from the initials of other words. For example, *Anzac* 'Australian and New Zealand Army Corps' was first used during the First World War. Other examples include *AIDS* from 'Acquired Immune Deficiency

Syndrome', and *dwems* those 'dead White European males' currently on the top of the political correctness hit list. Some believe that *wowser* 'prude, killjoy' derives from the phrase 'we only want social evils remedied', but this is more likely a clever linguistic invention after the fact. You have to be careful with some explanations of acronyms; they make good stories, but they may not always reflect the true origin of the word.

Acronyms should be able to form pronounceable words. Examples that are pronounced just as strings of letters, like those in the quote above, are not acronyms but simply **abbreviations** (or alphabetisms). Other abbreviations include *BO* 'body odour', *PDQ* 'pretty damn quick', and *TIIC* 'the idiots in charge'.

Although we all seem to be swimming in a sea of acronyms these days, people will probably be relieved to know that the majority remain peripheral to the language. They serve either as proper names, such as *Qantas* 'Queensland and Northern Territory Aerial Services' and *ASEAN* 'Association of South East Asian Nations'. Or they are specific to certain occupations. For example, *SOC* 'staff observation checks' and *PAL* 'personal action letter' form part of the lexicon of McSpeak, the language of the giant hamburger corporation McDonald's. But words such as these are never likely to become a part of our general lexicon.

Some acronyms can become so fashionable that they trigger copycat formations. For example, acronyms describing social types became very popular in the 1980s. The first creation was *yuppie* 'young urban (or upwardly mobile) professional person' (incorporating the suffix *-ie*). It gave rise to a flurry of similar expressions: *dink* 'double income no kids', *pippie* 'people inheriting parents' property', *puppie* 'poncy yuppie', *scuppie* 'socially conscious urban professional', *woopie* 'well-off old people', *zuppie* 'zestful upscale people in their prime', and *nimby* 'not in my back yard'. Many of these die out as quickly as they appear, but they do illustrate how lively these processes can be.

Blends

Blends are words originating from the contraction of two (or more) existing words. The new word then incorporates meaningful characteristics from both. In 1993 New Zealand venison officially acquired a new higher quality image and a brand new name: *cervena*. This derives from the blend of the Latin word for 'deer', *cervidae*, and the name (originally French) for 'deer meat', *venison*.

The blending process has been a part of English for centuries, and examples can be found from way back: *flush* = *flash* + *gush* (1548). More recent examples include *affluenza* 'the disease of being too rich', *cracker* 'credit card hacker', *fottle* 'collapsible bottle', *humongous*, and *ginormous*, both meaning 'shockingly big' (see if you can figure out the component parts), *labradoodle* 'Labrador and poodle cross', and a recent New Zealand product *cashgora*, which is quite literally 'a blend of cashmere and angora'. Lewis Caroll's famous poem *Jabberwocky* is full of wonderful examples and some, like *chortle* (*chuckle* and *snort*) and *slithy* (*lithe* and *slimy*), have made it into ordinary language.

Blends sometimes lead to the creation of new morphemes, which can then become productive new affixes. For instance *-oholic* or *-aholic* 'addict' now means one who habitually indulges in whatever the first part of the word denotes: *chocoholic*, *footballaholic*, *golfaholic*, *newsaholic*, *junkaholic*, *icecreamaholic*, *worrya-*

holic, potatochipaholic, beefaholic, bookaholic, sleepaholic, spendaholic. The source of these new formations was eighteenth-century *alcoholic* 'pertaining to alcohol', which was formed from *alcohol* + *ic*. The sense shifted in the twentieth century to 'person addicted to alcohol', and in the 1970s this lead to the blend formation *workaholic* and *workaholism*. Blends like these allowed for the reinterpretation of *-oholic* as a suffix. This kind of inventive restructuring on the part of speakers demonstrates a type of **folk etymology**. In this instance, speakers have rewritten the history of *alcoholic* and, in a sense, provided it with a new etymology.

Shortenings

Shortenings are simply abbreviated versions of longer words. If they replace the longer form, they can be considered new words. In many dialects of English, *bra* has supplanted *brassiere* (French for 'shoulder strap' from *bras*, meaning 'arm'). We've been shortening words for ages, and older examples are easy to find. For instance, few of us still connect *mob* and *bus* with their Latin originals *mobile vulgus* 'fickle crowd' and *omnibus*, meaning 'motor vehicle for paying passengers'—literally *omnis* 'all' + dative plural *-ibus*.

Other clippings (some with additional affix *-y* or *-o*), such as *breaky*, *stroppy* (< *obstreperous*), *loony* (< *lunatic*), *compo*, *bike*, *flu*, *ad*, and *maths*, coexist with longer versions, but typically characterise more informal usage. As part of slang, these forms can be unstable, varying greatly from region to region and from year to year. New Zealand teenagers, for example, report using *rad* (< *radical*), *shot* (< *good shot*), *sec* (< *second*), *far* (< *far out*), *later* (< *see you later*), *spaz* (< *spastic*), *bro* (< *brother*), *prob* (< *probably*), *awes* (< *awesome*), *dizz* (< *dizzy*), *cuz* (< *cousin*), *pros* (< *prostitute*), *stiff* (< *stiff bikkies*), *stuff* (< *good stuff*) (Smith 1993), but many of these will have become totally passé well before this text book makes it into print.

While we're looking at stylistic doublets of this kind, it's worth pointing out that English has a number of single syllable doublets that differ only in vowel quality: *ass/arse, gal/girl, hoss/horse, bust/burst, tit/teat, sassy/saucy, cuss/curse*. In these cases, the more colloquial member (sometimes also dialectal) has a short vowel and its partner a long vowel. Occasionally the practice of shortening leads to the creation of two different words; for example, *razz* 'to hiss, make fun of' comes from *raspberry* 'sound of contempt, derision', which in turn originates from the end-clipped rhyming slang *raspberry tart* 'fart'. As in this case, the meanings can diverge to such an extent that no one but the keenest etymologist would connect the two words. Compare also *grotty* from *grotesque*.

Morphological processes

As we discussed in the previous chapter, there are a number of morphological processes that are used to create vocabulary. We will summarise the most significant ones here.

Affixation

Affixing is probably the most important means we have of coming up with new words in English. It resembles compounding, except that it involves bound morphemes, such as prefixes and suffixes. As we saw in chapter 5, some affixes are highly productive and achieve almost voguish popularity—for example, *-ise* in *prioritise*, *personalise*, and *diarise* 'to enter something in your diary'. Since the 1950s there has been an explosion of these *-ise* words.

Conversion

This process converts words to other parts of speech with no affixation. For example, the noun *bach* or *batch* as an abbreviation of *bachelor* appeared in the mid-nineteenth century in phrases such as *old bach* 'elderly bachelor' and, later that century, converted into the verb *to bach* 'to live alone and cater for oneself'. In NZ English, early this century, the verb then converted back into a noun, meaning 'holiday house, weekender'.

Backformation

Words can be formed to fill apparent vacancies predicted on the basis of existing words that speakers assume derive from them. For example, by removing the suffix *-ation* from *irritation*, we form a new noun (usually plural) *irrits*, as in *it gives me the irrits.*

Compounding

Compounding involves the combination of two or more free morphemes. Old English was truly remarkable in the variety and flexibility of its compounds, and we continue this tradition. Here are some recent fashionable additions to the lexicon of music: *world music*, *fusion music*, *thrash metal music*, *speed metal*, *techno-pop*, *acid house*, *slamdance*, *breakdancing*, and *headbanging*. As is the case with acronyms, it can happen that certain patterns suddenly become fashionable. In this way, parts of compounds can function almost like affixes in their ability to form new words. Recall the exuberance of the *buster* compounds discussed in chapter 5.

Compounded patterns such as these can also arise through folk etymology. As we saw earlier, speakers often reinterpret boundaries within words to give their structure more meaning. This can create new morphemes, which then get extended to form new compounds. An example close to home is provided by the innovative *ccino* compounds, now often spelt *chino*. It so happens that the first part of the Italian word *cappuccino* collides, at least in pronunciation, with English *cup*. This has prompted some cafés around Melbourne (and probably in other places as well) to advertise, in addition to their regular *cappuccino*, a *mugaccino* 'cappuccino in a mug', *frothaccino*, *bambinoccino* or *bubaccino* 'milk froth with powdered chocolate on top (for children)', *chococcino* 'frothy hot chocolate', *mellocino* 'giant *café latte* with marshmallow froth', *timecino* —'a giant hazelnut-flavoured cappuccino with marshmallows' (named after the *Time* café), and *skinnyccino* and *caroccino* for the health conscious. The bill of fare in one café even reads *cup o' chino.* It seems we are well on the way to creating a new *chino* morpheme. This example is reminiscent of the often cited *burger* creation. *Hamburger* (an adjective derived from *Hamburg*) was a German borrowing. The first part of the word corresponds to a meat in English, and so the word was reinterpreted as a compound: *ham* + *burger* (even though ham was never an ingredient). This false analysis has given rise to a spate of new compounds such as *Aussie burger*, *eggburger*, *cheeseburger*, *chickenburger*, *vegeburger*, and even *burger bits* (a dog food) and *burger rings*.

Word-play: expressive formations

English has many examples of onomatopoeic words such as *whoosh*, *cheep*, and *plop*, which somehow echo their senses. Speakers can also start to associate certain sounds or sound sequences with particular meanings, and these can be used to form new words. Such sound sequences are **phonesthemes**. They occur either at the beginning of words (*tw-*, *gl-*, *fl-*) or their rhymes (*-ash*, *-ump*, *-itter*). Although they symbolise a certain meaning, it's often difficult to pin down exactly what it is. For example, the following words (mainly verbs) show a characteristic *-ump* rhyme and seem to denote 'heavy fall': *bump, dump, crump, clump, flump, jump, plump* (verb), *slump, stump, thump*. Others (mainly nouns) with the same rhyme denote some sort of 'round protuberance': *bump, chump, clump, dump, hump, lump, mump(s), plump* (adjective), *rump, stump*.

We can also include here imitative words, or interjections, such as *ouch!* These refer to the involuntary noisy responses that we make to express some sort of emotion. They also include automatic noises such as *kerchoo, burp, hack, hiccough* (*hiccup* got remodelled to look like *cough*). Comic magazines are good sources for these. The interesting thing about them is that they start life as rather inadequate attempts to represent the actual sound being made; *ho-ho, hardy har, yakety yak, yuk-yuk*, and *te-he* don't sound anything like laughter. They then become conventionalised, functioning as ordinary nouns and verbs with their own pronunciations. For example, *tut-tut* and *tisk-tisk* have spelling pronunciations that don't sound anything like the clicks we make to express impatience. Other expressions of annoyance (many archaic) include *Fie!* (thirteenth century); *Faugh!, Bah!, Pish!, Pshaw!, Pooh!* (seventeenth century), *Humph!* (nineteenth century).

Borrowing

So far we've looked at how English enriches its vocabulary by drawing on sources already available to it. Another way is to look to external sources—to expand the lexicon via **borrowing**. This term refers generally to the process whereby a language takes and incorporates some linguistic element from another language. Lexical borrowing is the most usual, although any part of the grammar can be borrowed. English is a great borrower and has borrowed (or stolen) from as many as 120 different languages. In fact, something like three-fifths of our entire vocabulary is non-native. Two languages in particular have made significant contributions.

From the end of the eighth century and for about 200 years, there were a number of Scandinavian raids on the British Isles. These culminated in twenty-five years of Danish rule, with large settlements of Scandinavians, particularly in the northern and eastern parts of the country, and considerable Scandinavian influence on native English. The nature of the borrowings are unusual in that they include everyday vocabulary. Basic verbs such as *die, get*, and *give*; nouns such as *husband, fellow*, and *egg*; and even grammatical words such as the pronouns *they, them*, and *their*, which replaced Old English *hie, heom, heora*, are just a handful of the hundreds of words that entered the language at this time. Borrowings of this sort suggest two things. First, the two languages existed side by side with more-or-less equal prestige. Second, they were probably mutually intelligible. In fact, their closeness makes it difficult to assess the true extent of the Scandinavian contribution.

Of a very different nature were later French borrowings. For some 200 years after the Norman Conquest (1066), French was the language used among the upper classes, and the effect on English was enormous. Some 10 000 French words were adopted (the majority between 1250 and 1400), 75 per cent of which are still in use today. The nature of the borrowed items reflects the prestige that French enjoyed during this time. The Normans controlled the State, the military, and cultural and intellectual interests, and French words flooded into these areas, sometimes as brand new additions, sometimes ousting the Anglo-Saxon expressions, and sometimes existing side by side, but usually later diverging in meaning and style.

To illustrate the impact of French on our vocabulary, consider its culinary contribution. Here's a medieval recipe for haddock in a tasty sauce. We've italicised the French words.

> *Haddocke* in *Cyuee*. Shall be yopened & ywasshe clene & ysode & *yrosted* on a *gridel*; grind peper & *saffron*, bred and ale *mynce oynons*, *fri* hem in *ole*, and do therto, and salt: *boille* hit, do thyn *haddok* in *plateres*, and the *ciuey* aboue, and ghif forth.
>
> [Haddock in civet [stew]. [It] should be opened and washed clean and boiled and roasted on a grill. Grind pepper and saffron, bread and ale, mince onions, fry them in oil, and combine and salt: boil it, put the haddock on plates and the civet on top, and serve.]
>
> Recipe from Black 1992:60

There are forty-four words in this recipe, and thirteen are French in origin. The everyday vocabulary remains Germanic; grammatical words such as conjunctions (*and*), auxiliaries (*shall*, *be*), pronouns (*hit*, *hem*), prepositions (*in*, *on*), basic ingredients (*bread*, *ale*, *salt*, *pepper*) and basic preparation verbs (*wash*, *open*, *do*, *give*). It is interesting that the French verb *boil* appears alongside the Anglo-Saxon verb *seethe* (here in the participle form *ysode*). Generally when this occurs, the two words end up differentiating in meaning, as has happened in Modern English: *seethe* is now only used metaphorically (*to seethe in anger*) and occasionally appears in adjectival form (*sodden turf*).

Certainly, after William took the throne, the English dining table was never to be the same again. The Normans imported spices, foreign herbs, plants, and even animals, and they introduced to the English their tastes in food, their culinary methods, and their expressions for all of these. Consider the extent to which French changed the nature of medieval food terms. The French gave us *appetite*, *taste*, *victuals*, *sustenance*, and even the mealtimes themselves, such as *dinner*, *supper*, *feast*, *repast*, *mess* (now military), and *collation* (compare humble Anglo-Saxon *breakfast*). *Fish* is Anglo-Saxon, but *haddock*, *mackerel*, *sole*, *perch*, *bream*, *sturgeon*, *salmon*, *sardine*, and *oyster* are French. *Fowl* is Anglo-Saxon, but not *partridge*, *pheasant*, *quail*, *poultry*, *pullet*, *pigeon*. *Meat* is Anglo-Saxon, but *venison*, *beef*, *veal*, *mutton*, *pork*, *bacon*, *sausage*, and *tripe* are not; nor are the various cuts *loin*, *chine*, *haunch*, or *brawn*. When they're not food, the animals retain their Anglo-Saxon names: *sheep* and *lamb*, *cow*, *pig* and *swine*, and *deer*.

Dishes such as *soup*, *chowder*, *frumenty*, *pudding*, *custard*, *pottage*, *gruel*, *blancmange* (originally savoury), *fritter*, *rice*, and *pasty* are French. So are items such as *toast*, *biscuit*, *cream*, and *sugar*. *Salads*, *vegetables*, and *fruits* (all French) include *spinach*, *cabbage*, *cucumber*, *endive*, *lettuce*, *carrot*, *olives*, *cherries*, *pomegranates*, *prunes*, *lemons*, *oranges*, *grapes*, *dates*, *figs*, *raisins*, *peaches*, and *almonds*. And for afters, French has given us *desserts* and *confections*, comprising *tarts* and *tartlets*, *jellies*, *compotes*, and *treacle*, washed down with *claret* and *muscatel*. *Seasonings*, *sauces*, and *condiments* are French, as are *spices* and *herbs* such as *rosemary*, *cloves*, *thyme*, *mustard*, *coriander*, *chives*, *borage*, *sage*, *saffron*, *marjoram*, *cinnamon*, *nutmeg*, and *vinegar*. Even to cook, we employ French verbs such as *roast*, *boil*, *parboil*, *stew*, *fry*, *broach*, *blanch*, *grate*, *mince*, and *hash* (surviving in *hash browns* and, figuratively, in *rehash*); to serve, we use French crockery terms such as *goblets*, *saucers*, *cruets*, *platters*, and *plates*. As Albert Baugh and Thomas Cable observe, 'it is melancholy to think what the English dinner table would have been like had there been no Norman Conquest' (1993:178). And yet we must be careful not to exaggerate the impoverished state of English vocabulary before the arrival of the French. Many of these expressions would have been redundant borrowings, probably even more than we are aware of, since our knowledge of Old English is very limited.

Of course since medieval times, French has continued to contribute food terms, such as *omelette*, *caramel*, *cuisine*, *liqueur*, and *cognac*. And there have been many other contributors too. Spanish, Portuguese, Italian, German, Dutch, Persian, Arabic, Hindi, and Turkish have all left their mark on our food lexicon.

But moving closer to home, consider the impact of indigenous languages on NZ and OZ English. In both instances, we see a contact of unequal relationship, resembling that of Celtic and English (and Amerindian languages and English in North America). The borrowings are largely confined to three areas: native flora and fauna; place names and some other proper names; and aspects of the society and culture of the indigenous people. Table 6.1 gives examples from Maori and from Aboriginal languages. (Where possible, we have given the Aboriginal sources.)

Why do words die?

We've just seen the many ways in which English can extend its lexicon. But there are many ways in which we lose words too. Most of the time, we don't notice. Indeed, we only become aware of them when, for some reason, they make a reappearance. But dictionary-makers, of course, have to be more aware. They need to make decisions all the time about whether they classify a word as 'archaic' or 'obsolete', or even whether they'll bother to include it at all. It's a difficult decision: words may no longer be relevant for modern speakers, and yet we need to know them when reading texts from the past. As Dennis Baron (1989:122) has observed, an influential text such as the Bible can act as a kind of artificial life-support system for obsolete words. Let's begin by looking at what causes these words to drop out of use in the first place.

Obsolescence

Obviously, if objects, ideas, and institutions no longer form a part of speakers' mental worlds, then they will be forgotten. OZ and NZ English have lost many words to do with aspects of the natural landscape. *Brook*, *wood(s)*, *copse*, *thicket*, *spinney*, *meadow*, *common*, *moor*, and *heath* no longer form part of our everyday vocabulary, although of course we may be familiar with these terms from literature or through a

Table 6.1 Borrowings from NZ and OZ English

	NZ English	*OZ English*
Maori/Aboriginal life	haka, hangi, kumara, mana, marae, pa, poi, tapu, tiki, wahine, whare	boomerang (Dharuk), corroboree (Dharuk), waddy (Dharuk), woomera (Dharuk)
Flora	kauri, kowhai, manuka, matai, ngaio, nikau, punga, rata, rimu, toi-toi, totara	coolibah (Kamilaroi), jarrah (Nyungar), karri (Kalaaku), mulga (Yuwaalaraay), waratah (Dharuk)
Birds	kakapo, kea, kiwi, moa, pukeko, takahe, tui, weka	brolga (Kamilaroi), budgerigar (Yuwaalaraay), galah (Yuwaalaraay), kookaburra (Wiradhuri)
Fish and shellfish	mako, moki, paua, pipi, tarakihi, toheroa	barramundi (?), gilgie (Nyungar), luderick (Ganay), morwong (?)
Other animals	huhu, katipo, tuatara, weta	dingo (Dharuk), dugite (Nyungar), kangaroo (Guugu Yimighirr), quokka (Nyungar), wallaby (Dharuk), wombat (Dharuk)
Proper names	Maori, Pakeha, Aotearoa, Reinga, Eketahuna	Koori (Panyjima), one-third of Australia's place names

Source: Gordon & Deverson 1985:34–8; Thieberger & McGregor 1994

general knowledge of British English. This phenomenon may reflect the predominantly urban origin of Antipodean varieties of English, or the simple fact that these terms were inappropriate for the physical setting in which the early English-speakers found themselves.

In the area of food, lexical obsolescence is probably a matter of course. We no longer use words such as *pottage* 'porridge-like dish of vegetables and/or meat', *mortrews*, *buknade* 'pottages', *civet* 'stew', *frumenty*, *losyns* 'porridge-like dishes', *rapey*, *doucetes* 'desserts', and *letelorye* 'savoury custard'. The tendency in medieval times to macerate, smash into pulp, and spice food beyond recognition makes few of the dishes of that time appealing to modern palates. Clothing shows a similar high turnover of vocabulary. Sometimes lexical obsolescence can be revealing. The traditional vocabulary of sin and virtue provides us with interesting examples. Expressions such as *virtue*, *verity*, *temperance*, and *chastity* no longer form part of our active vocabulary, and this says much about changing mores and attitudes. (See later discussion on meaning change.)

Sound change

Words must have a certain phonetic saliency if they are to function as useful parts of the vocabulary. As we have observed in chapter 4, however, sound change is generally reductive, and the mutilation can be so bad that words become virtual fragments—for example, *ae* 'law', *ea* 'water', and *ig* 'island'. These words are no longer useful, except perhaps in the game of Scrabble, where knowledge of such words can prove invaluable. (Serious Scrabble players usually have a list.)

Intolerable ambiguity

It can happen, through change, that two originally distinct words come to have the same form but different meanings (that is, homophony). It can even happen that words with completely contradictory meanings collide in this way. Speakers may find this intolerable and end up ditching one of them. For example, in Old English, the two verbs *lǣttan* 'permit' and *lettan* 'stop, hinder' were originally distinct, but sound changes left them homophonous: *let* 'to permit' and *let* 'to stop'. The second *let* has now disappeared, except in relics such as *without let or hindrance.* The same thing happened with Old English *cleofian* 'to stick together' (compare related forms *glue* and *clay*) and *clēofan*, meaning 'split apart' (compare *cleaver* and *cleft*). Modern English *cleave* has both meanings, although the latter is more usual.

For ambiguity to cause problems, the words usually must belong to the same sphere of ideas and occur in similar contexts. But different contexts do not always ensure survival, especially in the case of taboo. The phonological collapsing of *arse* and *ass,* for example, caused considerable problems for the animal, which is now generally referred to as *donkey.* The Anglo-Saxon word *cunny* meaning 'rabbit' dropped out of use when it collided with the tabooed female body part *cunt.* In fact, speakers will often avoid expressions that are just phonetically similar to taboo terms. Many monosyllabic words beginning with [f] and ending in [k] have just dropped out of the picture.

Taboo

This leads us to consider the important contribution of **taboo.** We've all experienced a reluctance to talk directly about things that frighten us, embarrass us, or for some reason we just find difficult to discuss—taboo topics such as body parts, bodily functions and emissions, sex, sickness, disease, and death. They cover aspects of our lives that remind us that, whatever we may like to think, we are all firmly planted in nature. And to help us cope with the messy reality of life, we are provided with a linguistic escape hatch in the form of euphemism—or 'deodorant' language if you like.

Unfortunately, the protective magic of euphemism is only effective for a short time. Euphemisms will typically degenerate through contamination by the taboo topic. For example, words relating to sexual activity such as *copulation, orgasm, intercourse, ejaculation,* and *erection* were once general terms, but all quickly narrowed to the sexual sense alone. Hence the ever-changing chains of vocabulary items for words denoting taboo concepts. And the more severe the taboo, the longer the chain. Over the years, English has accumulated a staggering 2500 expressions for male and female genitalia (see Allan & Burridge 1991, chapter 4); taboo and euphemism are clearly potent forces for word loss and word addition.

Euphemism can even be found in our food terms. For example, NZ and OZ *lamb's fry* 'liver' disguises the fact that this dish involves sheep's liver (with unappetising thoughts of hydatid cysts); it nicely sidesteps the issue of what bits actually get fried. Then there are NZ *lemon fish* and OZ *flake* for 'shark'; for some reason, most of us experience a queasiness at the thought of eating shark. Who knows what new euphemisms will replace *beef* now that 'mad cow disease' has come to light.

No apparent reason!

We have to conclude this section by pointing out that many English words drop out of use for no obvious reason at all. It's curious why such an apparently useful word such as *gry* 'dirt under the finger nails' would disappear. And what about *horrorfiliation* 'goose bumps', *ugsome* 'horrid' or handy verbs like *groof* 'lie face down on the floor' (compare *groveling*), *apricate* 'bask in the sun', and *fibulate* 'perform the action of buttoning and unbuttoning'. Many of you have undoubtedly experienced at some time a sense of *velleity* 'mild desire but too slight to motivate any action'. How useful it would be to have a word to describe this feeling. The term *firkytoodling* seems to us a more inviting substitute for modern *foreplay*. But for some curious reason, these words, and hundreds of others, have just slipped quietly away.

SEMANTIC CHANGE

Remember back to chapter 2, when we talked about the arbitrary relationship between form and meaning. The simple fact that there's no connection between the shape of a word and its meaning means that either is free to change without affecting the other. We have already seen that sounds are in a constant state of flux, but this is just as true of meaning. To get an idea of just how weird and wonderful these changes can be, consider the following examples: *Black* derives from an original meaning 'white, shining, bright' and is historically related to words such as *bleach*, *blanch*, and even *bald*; *grammar* and *glamour* share the same source, as do both *cretin* and *Christian*.

Teenagers tell us that they use words such as *wicked*, *vicious*, *sick*, and even *rancid* and *putrid* to describe things that are really good. And if someone is particularly attractive, they are *scum*. In OZ English, *jack up* means 'to give in, to abandon a task', but in NZ it means the complete opposite 'to expedite, to arrange'. Clearly words change in extraordinary ways. Some even go full circle and come to be their own opposites. More than any other aspect of language, meaning is linked to the life and culture of speakers, and this creates a sort of human 'wild card' element.

Consequences of semantic change

To impose some sort of order, semantic changes have been classified into various types. The classification falls along two axes. First, words can change in **sense** (that is, what we understand as the actual 'meaning' of a word). Changes here are of three basic types: **broadening**, **narrowing**, and **shift**. Second, words can change in **connotation** (that is, any associations a word might have because of our ideas and experiences). Changes here are of two types: **deterioration** and **elevation**. Please note that such terms are just convenient name badges and have no actual explanatory value (as you might expect from the contradictory nature of the labels). To find out what motivates change, we have to look elsewhere, and this we do at the end of the chapter.

Broadening

Broadening involves an expansion of the contexts in which a word appears. (that is, the word means more than it did before). For example, our word *bludger*, meaning 'scrounger, some who lives off the efforts of others', used to refer specifically to those living off the earning of a prostitute. Another good example is the OZ and NZ extension of the word *bush* from its original meaning, 'shrub', in British English to mean a 'tract of land covered in natural vegetation', often *the bush*. In this way, *bush* has replaced words such as *copse*, *wood(s)*, *spinney*, and *thicket*, which are no longer relevant for our landscape. The word *creek*, when it came across from Great Britain, meant 'estuary, arm of the sea', but now refers much more widely to all types of water courses. *Paddock* was originally limited in the type of enclosure it referred to, but in today's Australia and New Zealand it covers a wide variety of enclosed land.

For a spectacular case of broadening, consider Antipodean *mob*. Originally from the Latin *mobile vulgus* 'rabble', the word extended in Australasian English to mean 'a body of animals or humans' (*a mob of cattle*) and now more generally to 'any quantity, number'. The following extract gives some idea of the flexibility of *mob* nowadays: 'There'll be mobs of water on the track, we'll get mobs of beef at the runs, the stage'll be mobs shorter, an' there'll be mobs better camping grounds... and of course we'll be able to take it mobs easier' (AND 1988).

A special case of broadening occurs when proper names are taken over to refer to the general class of phenomena (see pp. 124–5). The word *Claytons*, for example, was originally the name of a non-alcoholic whisky; you may remember it as 'the drink you're having when you're not having a drink'. This meaning has now been extended to refer generally to 'something that is illusory or exists in name only'. For example, OZ English isn't 'a Clayton's sort of English, a sort of colonial doggerel you speak when you cannot manage Standard Southern' (AND 1988).

Narrowing

Narrowing involves a reduction in the contexts in which a word appears. In short, the word comes to mean only a part of what it originally meant. It's more common than broadening, and many of the examples we gave at the start of this section included changes of this type. Other examples are easy to find. The word *liquor* once referred generally to 'liquid' but has now narrowed to 'alcoholic beverage'. It is interesting that our word *drink* appears to be heading in the same direction. For instance, if someone asked you how many drinks you'd had, they wouldn't be referring to soft drinks. In Australia this sense is being reinforced by the well-publicised campaign targeting drink drivers.

Narrowing often results when words are used in fixed situations where people share common interests and habits. For example, rural New Zealand and Australia have specific usages such as *station* 'extensive sheep- or cattle-raising establishment', *block* 'area of land', *run* 'large tract of grazing land', *to draft* 'to separate certain animals from the main body', and *to box* 'to mix animals accidentally'.

Taboo areas of vocabulary perpetually generate this sort of narrowing. For example, *liaison* was originally a seventeenth century cooking term. It referred to a binding agent for the thickening of sauces (French *lier*, meaning 'bind') and later broadened to any type of connection or cooperation. But nowadays when we talk about a *liaison*, it generally refers to 'an illicit sexual association'. Library liaison committees may become things of the past. As we've seen, taboo senses always dominate and eventually kill off other senses. People just won't risk being misunderstood.

Shift

Semantic shift entails the total alteration of the contexts. A word comes to mean something completely different from what it once meant. A *spell* earlier referred to 'a period of work', but now refers to 'a period of rest from work'. In this regard, it's interesting that the meaning of the word *sickie* appears to be shifting from 'a day's sick leave' to 'a day's leave you take when you're not sick' (aptly captured by Ron Tandberg, an Australian cartoonist, in the caption *Too crook to take a sickie*).

Another good example is the expression *dinkum*. A number of exotic etymologies have been attributed to this word, but in fact it's a good illustration that much of what we think is quintessentially OZ or NZ English can be traced back to eighteenth- or nineteenth-century regional British usage. In fact, our Antipodean varieties are often fossil-like, preserving usages that have long since disappeared elsewhere. Miners in Derbyshire used the word *dinkum* to mean 'hard work'. And from this sense of 'strenuous effort', the meaning then shifted to 'reliable, genuine, true'. Now as an adjective or adverb in phrases like *dinkum Aussie/digger* and *fair dinkum* it has gained much wider currency in Australia and New Zealand than it ever had in England (although it does have a rather dated feel to it now).

Changing values: elevation and deterioration

As a result of our beliefs, prejudices, and experiences, words take on emotive overtones that themselves are subject to change. Words can acquire favourable associations and pejorative associations.

Elevation can occur in two ways. First, unpleasant overtones can gradually erode away. Intensifying expressions such as *terribly*, *awfully*, *frightfully*, and *horribly* are particularly prone to this. These have lost their original strength and now mean little more than 'very' (witness 'contradictory' usages such as *awfully good* and our more colloquial versions such as *helluva/heck of a/hang of a good party*). Second, words can take on favourable overtones; they acquire a kind of 'semantic halo' (C. S. Lewis's term 1970). For example, the current egalitarian ideology has caused the elevation of terms such as *democracy* and *politician*, which previously were quite negative.

A more recent example is *attitude*. This is interesting because it's gone through a number of rapid changes. Originally a technical term meaning 'posture', it shifted to mean 'mental state or mode of thinking' (as implied by a person's physical position). It then deteriorated: *to have (an) attitude* came to mean 'a bad attitude or an attitude problem', something to be corrected by parents or teachers. More recently still, it has become positive again. It seems that this particular combination of aggression, insolence, and arrogance is now touted as a desirable quality.

More usually though, words take on negative overtones rather than favourable ones. Words to do with chance are particularly prone to this. For example, the noun *accident* once meant 'a chance event', and this is preserved in expressions such as *by accident*. However, through its association with misfortune, its meaning has narrowed to 'chance misfortune', as in *There was an accident*. OZ *mozz* (from Hebrew *mazzal*, meaning 'luck') shows a similar shift from 'luck' to 'bad luck', as in *put the mozz on (something)* meaning 'to put a jinx on (something)'. There is undoubtedly an interesting psychological basis to this sort of deterioration. Certainly, pessimism and prejudice have a role to play, as does taboo (see p. 133).

Why do words change their meanings?

There are many reasons why words change their meanings. For example, we can identify particular situations arising from the relationship between speakers and their world that will trigger certain changes. In the discussion below, we look at some of the most significant of these triggers.

Socio-cultural factors

Language of special groups

The relationship between special usage and general usage gives rise to many changes. Ordinary language is constantly borrowing terms from **specialist languages** or **jargons**. Sue Butler, the editor of the MD, describes the 'sudden transfer of computer jargon from the technicians and computer boffins to the non-technical and the struggling many' (1990:254). *Love is a warm boot* is a slogan that she doesn't understand entirely, and neither do we—but it sounds interesting. *Information overload* can happen to us all. People *interface* and *network* on a regular basis now. Even lecturers can be *user-friendly*. All these expressions have passed into everyday parlance. In each case, the original narrow specification has been lost and the term has expanded its meaning.

But the opposite can happen too. Specialist languages can borrow from ordinary language, and this has the effect of narrowing the meaning. Many of the terms we now associate with computer-speak actually derive from common usage in exactly this way. A *hacker* was (not surprisingly) a person who hacked things; the word was used for cut-throats and bullies. Nowadays it refers to someone who breaks computer security codes (more recently, any enthusiastic computer programmer or user). The verb *input* dates back to Middle English, when it had the meaning 'to impose'. *Interface* derives from a nineteenth-century noun meaning generally 'a surface where two portions of matter or space meet'. *Glitch* 'slippery place' entered English from Yiddish and was used in electronics well before it was picked up by the computer industry to refer to 'a bug' (probably influenced by *hitch*). It's interesting that these terms are now re-entering common usage and generalising from their specialised computer senses. *Glitches* now occur in all sorts of places, not just computer programs.

Subreption

Contrary to what you might think, **subreption** is not some kind of nasty disease. It simply refers to the process of external change, whereby objects, ideas, and institutions alter over time, but the names for them remain unchanged; it's as if the expressions outgrow their original meanings. Sometimes it involves a widening of the original meaning, but it may also involve a complete shift. In New Zealand and Australia, for example, referents for flora and fauna terms such as *birch*, *magpie*, and *bream* are completely different from their British counterparts. The original colonists retained the familiar names, perhaps out of a sense of nostalgia, and the meaning shifted accordingly.

Technological change causes many words to adapt in this way. The metamorphosis of the *pen* from a feather quill to the modern-day writing tool explains the shift from its original meaning ('feather'). The *visor* on a knight's helmet has become the shield of the modern-day crash helmet. Developments in telephonics have been considerable, and yet we continue to *dial* numbers on our push-button and touch-tone phones. We still listen for the *dial tone*.

Social change

As you might imagine, a close relationship exists between **social change** and semantic change. Any change in societal mores or attitudes will have semantic correlatives. Consider the shifts illustrated in the following modern 'success' terms. A number have lost their religious significance, but what else do they suggest about the nature of modern success?

celebrity	'a solemn (religious) ceremony' > 'popular public figure'	(secularised, trivialised)
charisma	'divinely conferred power' > 'popular aura'	(secularised, trivialised)
personality	'pertaining to the person' > 'celebrity'	(elevated)
image	'representation of person or thing' > 'cultivated favourable public reputation'	(elevated)
model	'representation of person or thing' > 'ideal representation' > ' sexual clothes-horse'	(elevated)

In a fascinating account of English vocabulary, Geoffrey Hughes (1988) offers many examples like these. All point to a culture that is becoming increasingly superficial and egotistical.

Our current obsession with modernity and youth is also apparent in the deterioration of words denoting 'old'. Words such as *geriatric* and *senile*, once respectful terms for one's elders, have become highly contemptuous in the twentieth century. To date, the word *senior*, as in *senior citizen*, has not yet acquired the same negative overtones, but it has lost its euphemistic sheen. Mind you, words for 'the young' are showing a turn for the worse too. Consider the pejorative associations attaching to words such as *yob(bo)* (originally backwards slang for *boy*), *juvenile*, *adolescent*, and even *youth*. Nowadays *youths* appearing in the newspaper are male and are generally up to no good. By comparison, *youthful* and *youngster* remain untainted. They have none of the hostility and aggression of the other terms, retaining the original innocence that all these words once had. Recent additions to the thesaurus under 'young person' such as *teds* (*teddy boys*), *bodgies*, *widgies*, *mods*, *rockers*, *punks*, and *skinheads* also reflect the deteriorating 'bloom of youth'.

Prejudice

The nasty sociolinguistic habit that we have of forming **prejudices** is responsible for long-term and widespread changes that affect, in particular, the value judgments attached to words associated with certain human groups. A case in point is what

C. S. Lewis (1970:21) dubbed 'the moralisation of status words'. Through what amounts to little more than snobbery, words denoting a certain rank or occupation come to refer to the (real or imagined) moral or intellectual qualities of the group. Witness the elevation of terms such as *noble* and *gentle*. Not all the nobility were honourable and magnanimous, nor were all gentlewomen and gentlemen docile and courteous. Yet these high moral qualities were conventionally attributed to people of this social status. Other examples include the elevation of *courteous* (< 'behaviour pertaining to the court'), *generous* (< 'of noble birth'), and *chivalrous* (< 'characteristic of the medieval knight').

By comparison, words denoting inferior social position are quick to become morally devalued. For example, *vulgar* meant simply 'pertaining to ordinary people', but soon came to mean 'offensively coarse, low'; *common* shows a similar shift. Throughout the ages, country people have been held in low esteem by the more influential classes, and this is reflected in the rapid pejoration of words such as *boorish*, *churlish*, *villain*, and *rustic* versus *urbane*.

Terms suggesting a lack of education also become terms of moral disapproval. *Lewd*, for example, originally meant 'uneducated' but deteriorated remarkably to 'stupid, worthless' and then 'indecent, lascivious'; compare *uncouth*, originally meaning 'unlearned'. But the educated aren't immune to this sort of pejoration either; *pedant* derives from the earlier meaning 'schoolteacher'. Equally disturbing is the way that words associated with women decrease in value. The shift is typically 'young woman' > 'promiscuous woman'. English *hussy* from *housewife* shows this, as do hundreds of others. By comparison, the terms for men remain remarkably stable.

Psychological factors

Psychological factors arise out of our mental make-up. For example, humans seem to be natural procrastinators—'why do today, what you can put off till tomorrow'. This probably explains the meaning shift from 'immediately' > 'soon' in words to do with punctuality. The word *anon* (now literary) used to mean 'at once', but by the late Middle English period had shifted to 'in a little while'. The expressions *soon* and *by and by* show the same shift, as do *presently* and *momentarily* in current OZ and NZ English. There are many psychological causes that we could look at in this section, but we will focus on two: emotion and taboo.

Emotion

> If all the year were playing holidays,
> To sport would be as tedious as to work
>
> William Shakespeare, *Henry IV, Part I*, I.ii.192

One very powerful stimulus for semantic change is feeling, or our desire to enhance expression and come up with innovative ways of saying things. One way that emotive force can be achieved is through **exaggeration**. We know it well from the highly charged language of abuse. Exaggeration is often used to magnify the offence (for example, attested pieces of OZ colour such as *You great prick! You rotten bloody mongrel bastard!*). It's also used to belittle a person, as in *You peabrain! You slimy little toad!*

But it seems that emotional extravagance of this kind inevitably goes hand in hand with semantic weakening, and overuse of such offensive language has the effect of bleaching terms of their taboo quality. A striking example is the so-called 'great OZ adjective' *bloody*. Once upon a time it was considered such 'a horrid word' that it was necessary to render it in print as *b——y*. After Eliza Doolittle's shocking outburst in Act III of *Pygmalion* ('Walk! Not bloody likely'), the press could do no more than just hint at it; it became 'the Unprintable Swearword', 'the Word', and 'Shaw's Bold Bad Word'. The word has now been emptied of its colour and force, and is little more than a variant of *very*.

Such expressive words inevitably wear out through use, becoming insipid, and alternative expressions have to be found. We've already seen how intensifiers such as *awfully* and *terribly* quickly lose their force and are replaced. The following words have also all seen their pejorative senses fade over time: *scamp* 'highway robber', *rascal* 'low, mean, dishonest person', *rogue* 'dishonest vagabond', *scoundrel* 'base, vile character', *scallywag* 'disreputable fellow, good for nothing', *naughty* 'depraved', and *mischievous* 'disastrous'. These were all strongly contemptuous at one time, but have now become mild terms of reproof; in fact, some are really quite playful. Even the term *ratbag*, once highly offensive, now pales in comparison with it modern relatives *scumbag*, *slimebag*, and *dirtbag*. It'll be interesting to see how these newer expressions fare over time.

Another way that speakers can achieve emotive force is by evoking certain images to describe their experiences. They might use a word in a figurative sense, and this sense then becomes one of its meanings. Sometimes the sources for these figures are obvious; things that are of interest to a society constantly crop up in the language expressions that speakers construct. Sports such as cricket, for example, have contributed a lot of the imagery in our everyday language. *It's not cricket* means 'it's not fair', and *to do something off your own bat* means 'to do something on your own, independently'. *People on a good wicket* could also be described as having *a fair innings*. But others not so fortunate might be *on a sticky wicket* 'facing a difficult situation'. People are *caught out* and *stumped*, if they are 'non-plussed or defeated'. And in Australia and New Zealand, things that are unreasonable are described as being *over the fence*. We can also *hit someone for six*, which means 'to overwhelm that person'. The idea here is perhaps that the blow you deal that person is as hard as the strike of the batsman hitting the ball way out past the boundary. But as these become everyday terms, the metaphors fade and lose their force. It's no longer obvious that we're dealing with the extension of a sporting term. This is true of expressions such as *aim* and *goal*, and even *tackling a problem*. These terms are no longer felt to be figurative; the figurative sense has become the conventional meaning. Expressions can even outlive the sports that gave rise to them. Many obsolete sports have become fossilised in now-dead metaphors; *pounce*, *reclaim*, and *lure* come to us from falconry.

Taboo

We've seen how taboo is an emotive trigger for word addition and word loss. It's also an important cause of meaning change. Euphemistic substitutes are not always novel expressions. They can be recycled from elsewhere in the language, and this invariably involves an adjustment of the original meaning (that is, new meanings for old expressions).

Striking examples occur in the area of mental illness. Like most stigmatising illnesses surrounded by fear and mystery, this has generated an impressive chain of euphemistic synonyms. For example, *insane* (Latin for 'not healthy') is now confined to 'mentally unsound' but originally had a much broader domain encompassing all bodily organs and their functions. Even the form *sane* has narrowed under the influence of *insane* to denote only a mental condition. The history of the word *deranged* illustrates a typical development for euphemisms. Originally from a verb meaning 'to disturb', it could be qualified with the modifier *mentally* to apply to people who were 'disturbed in the mind'. But once associated with mental illness, the word soon dropped the modifier and narrowed to the 'mad' sense alone. Compare *be/go mental* and *a mental patient*; clearly, *mental* no longer means 'pertaining to the mind'. Both *disordered* and *afflicted* are moving in the same direction. Even names for establishments accommodating mental patients show the same rapid deterioration and narrowing. Consider the clipping of *lunatic asylum* to *asylum*.

Linguistic 'contamination'

Semantic shifts can come about because of associations that words pick up from other words with which they are somehow connected. Although we've dubbed this '**contamination**', this doesn't mean that the value of the word has diminished in any way. We'll look at two types here: **folk etymology** (similarity of words) and **ellipsis** (proximity of words).

Folk etymology

Folk etymology, you will recall, stems from our desire to make familiar something that, for some reason, has become unfamiliar to us. It involves replacing opaque words or names (perhaps foreign in origin or just plain obscure) with something that is similar but more transparent. Essentially, what we're doing is making meaningless bits of language meaningful, and thereby furnishing words with a new etymology. Usually there's some semantic similarity between the expressions; (that is, the changes are semantically motivated). For example, the student in one of our classes who came out with *rope learning* for *rote learning* probably justified it on the basis of expressions such as *learn the ropes.*

Parts of words and phrases can be affected in this way too. For example, nowadays we're more likely to *wind our way home* than *wend our way home.* The verb *wend* 'to go' has dropped out of use (although it's preserved in *went*), so it's natural to replace it with something more familiar, and of course we can justify this because of the association of *winding roads*. Or take the expression *it augurs well* 'it promises a good outcome'. Nowadays, *augur* doesn't mean much; most of us have given up the habit of interpreting omens by the appearance of entrails or the behaviour patterns of birds. So it's understandable that we replace it with the more familiar *it all goes well.* Sometimes this process can be for humorous effect, as is probably the case with the slang expression *to cast nasturtiums (on)* 'to slander'. This is a remodelling of the phrase *to cast aspersions (on)*. The name for the orange-yellow flowers is probably more user-friendly than the word *aspersions*, but it creates a comic effect too.

In these examples, folk etymology has altered the form of a word without changing its meaning. Conversely, it can alter the meaning of a word without changing its form. In some cases, the meaning changes to such an extent that the word actually comes to be its own opposite. Consider *hoi polloi.* Originally Greek for 'the many', the word was borrowed by English to mean 'the masses'. But many of our students report that they have the opposite meaning for this word: 'aristocratic persons, the high born'. This shift has come about through association with *hoity toity* 'haughty'. Curiously *hoity toity* has itself undergone the same shift. It derives from the reduplication of the now obsolete verb *hoit* 'to behave boisterously'. *Hoity toity* originally described 'riotous behaviour', nothing like the meaning we have today. It then shifted to mean 'haughty' because it clashed with *haughty.* And now it's influencing *hoi polloi* in precisely the same way.

Ellipsis

It can happen that in expressions of two words or more, a word or words will drop out, and what's left of the expression then stands for the whole meaning (for example, *alarm* from *alarm clock*, and *life* from *life sentence*). In this way, adjectives can turn into nouns (*daily paper* > *daily*, and *private soldier* > *private*, for example). Sometimes the meaning changes are considerable, as is the case with end-clipped rhyming slang. For example, *Brahms* from *Brahms and Liszt* 'pissed, drunk', *rabbit (on)* from *rabbit and pork* 'talk incessantly', *Septic* from *Septic Tank* 'Yank'. Rhyming slang is a kind of verbal disguise (which is, of course, why it features in the language of euphemism and of the criminal underworld). The meaning derives from the unstated word that rhymes with the last part of the phrase (*Brahms and Liszt* = *pissed*). In these cases of ellipsis, however, the original significance is lost because the rhyme is clipped. The sense then transfers to the first part of the phrase, and we have a meaning shift. *Roast stop* only makes sense when you know that it derives from *Stop thief* = *beef* (originally 'stolen beef').

Something similar can occur in the process of narrowing with the loss of an original modifying word. The narrower context specified by the modifier becomes the norm, and the original wide significance is lost. No longer necessary, the modifier drops away. As we've already seen, this is a typical path for euphemisms: consider *funeral director* > *director* and *birth-control/contraceptive pill* > *pill* (as in *the pill is completely safe*). But it's not only in contexts of taboo that this takes place. Earlier we saw how *attitude* shifted to 'bad mental state': *He's got attitude.* Originally, this would have been rendered *He's got a bad attitude/an attitude problem*, but the negative sense came to dominate. Colloquial expressions such as *stuff* < *good stuff* and *shot* < *good shot* are examples of the same process.

The special case of metaphor

You've probably been struck by the pervasive force of metaphor in the processes discussed above. Our language is firmly founded in our perceptions and conceptions, and metaphor is a powerful agent for change. Earlier we referred to it explicitly as an expressive device, but it has many other roles too: a basis for the generalisation of specialist terms, a source for euphemism, and a basis for exaggeration or understatement.

Essentially, a **metaphorical change** is the transfer of meaning from one item to another item that is somehow associated. Metaphor always involves the comparison of two items, where there's a logical relationship of some sort—such as calling someone a *pig* or a *toad.* Such comparisons use salient characteristics of folk concepts about the appearance and/or behaviour of the animal, which is then attributed to the person. *A pig* is 'someone uncouth, slovenly' and *a toad* implies 'someone loathsome, sycophantic'. This involves a kind of analogy. If we say of someone *He's a pig*, we might want to convey a picture of someone totally disgusting in manner and character. Of course, taken literally, the statement is false; this person is not actually 'a pig'. But we're claiming that there is a semantic connection between this person (the figurative meaning) and a pig (the literal meaning). All the colour and the expressive force derives from this relationship.

One important type of metaphor is **synaesthesia** or association of senses (from Greek *syn* 'together' + *aisthesis* 'perception'). It can involve a transfer from sight to sound, from touch to sound, from sight and touch to intellect, and so on. Words for seeing, hearing, and touching can become terms to do with understanding: *I see* and *I hear you* for 'I understand (you)' or *He finally grasped it* for 'He finally understood'. Colours have strong psychological effects too, and this is exploited in figurative use. Words for brightness shift to become terms to do with intellectual ability, as in describing someone as *dull* or *bright*. Hue or colour words shift to become words expressing moods and moral qualities: *blue* has been associated with sadness since the seventeenth century, and we are still *singing the blues*; *yellow* is associated with cowardice, *green* with envy (or inexperience), *red* with anger, and so on.

Another important type of metaphor is **metonymy** or change by association (from Greek *meta* 'trans' + *onoma* 'name'). A word is extended to refer to something that is closely associated with the meaning of that word. For example, *pavlovas* and *sandwiches* get their names either from the inventors or from people associated with the items in some way. *Champagne* and *cologne* are goods named after their place of origin. Other examples include *spend a penny* for 'urinate' (from the days when toilets cost a penny to access); *go to bed* and *sleep with* for 'copulate'; and the practice of naming contraceptive devices as items of clothing—*caps*, *hoods*, *diving suits*, *shower caps*, *raincoats* (according to folk myth, men complain that wearing a condom while having sex is like 'showering in a raincoat'), *riding jackets*, and *gloves*.

An important subtype of metonymy is **synecdoche** or the relationship of part for whole. Something is named on the basis of its most prominent or salient part—for example, *silver* for 'cutlery' (originally made of silver), and *tit* for 'breast' (denoting the most tabooed part of the breast, the nipple). Synecdoche is often exploited in abusive language, as in calling someone a *prick*, and can be used for humorous effect—for instance, when the association is totally inappropriate, as in the Australian habit of naming people with red hair *Blue*. Examples of metonymy and synecdoche differ from the earlier examples of metaphor in that they don't evoke new associations but simply exploit those already existing between words that share a close logical relationship.

POINTS TO REMEMBER

- *Where do words come from?*
  Commonisations are proper names, place names and personal names that have entered the language as ordinary words.

Acronyms are words formed from the initials of other words.
Blends are words originating from two (or more) existing words.
Shortenings are clipped versions of longer words.
Compounds involve the combination of two or more free morphemes.
Affixations involve the addition of bound morphemes.
Conversions involve changes from one part of speech to another with no affixation.
Backformations remove affixes to derive new simple forms.
Borrowings are linguistic elements adopted from another language.

- *Why do words die?*
Obsolete ideas or objects will disappear.
Sound change can mutilate words to such an extent that they drop out of use.
Ambiguity can trigger the disappearance of a word.
Euphemisms typically become contaminated and are ditched.
- *Types of semantic change*
Broadening refers to the expansion of contexts in which a word can appear.
Narrowing refers to a reduction in the contexts in which a word can appear.
Shift entails the total alteration of the contexts.
Connotations arise through our beliefs, prejudices, and experiences; words can elevate and deteriorate.
- *Causes of semantic change*
Specialist languages can borrow from ordinary language, and terms from specialist languages can enter ordinary language.
Subreption is the process of external change ('old words in a new world').
Social change will always have semantic correlatives.
Prejudice is a powerful trigger for meaning change, as are psychological factors such as emotion and taboo.
Words can pick up associations from other words (through folk etymology and ellipsis, for example).
Metaphorical change involves the transfer of meaning from one item to another item that is somehow associated.

EXERCISES

1 Lexical addition

a The following are additions to the NZ and/or OZ lexicon. State the word-formation process that each illustrates. (Some of these appear in NZ and OZ slang dictionaries.)

Enzedder	'New Zealander'
grommet	'young surfer, skateboarder'
scuzz	'unpleasant person'
gonzo	'crazy person'
ear-bashing	'(lengthy) talk'
woop-woop(s)	'sticks, backblocks'
U-ey	'U-turn'

doona	'duvet, quilted eiderdown'
playlunch	'recreation snack'
bumbag	'small bag around the waist'
jandals	'thongs'
el cheapo	'of inferior quality'
shonk	'one engaged in illegal activities'
compo	'workers' compensation'
yowie	'mythical creature of South East Australia'
kumara	'sweet potato'
Nats	'National Party members'
guestimate	'rough estimate'
cereologist	'investigator of crop circles'
autochondria	'excessive concern for the health of one's car'

b Explain how the following new creations have arisen: *monokini* 'single-piece bathing suit', *dental floss kini* 'bathing suit held together by something resembling dental floss', *high-cut kini* 'knickers with a high waist band'. Can you think of others?

2 Borrowing

Maori and Australian Aboriginal loanwords sometimes undergo significant changes when they get adopted by English. Match the English words in the first and third columns with their Maori and Aboriginal sources in the second and fourth columns, and comment on any changes of form and meaning that have occurred in each case.

NZ	*Maori*	*OZ*	*Aboriginal*
cockabully/bully	pai	[within] cooee	garabara
hoot	tutu	humpy	waragal
biddy-bid(dy)	punga	gin	maiyal
bunger/bungie	utu	corroborree	kilaa
boohai/boo-eye	kuri	warrigal	gunya
puckeroo	kokopu	paddymelon	guwi!
goorie	Otakou	galah	yilimung
kit	Puhoi	kookaburra	guuguubarra
Otago	makomako	gunyah	wumara
cootie	pakaru	myall	giba
pie [in half-pie]	piripiri	hieleman	yumbi
matagouri	kete	[take to the] mallee	mali
toot	kutu	Woomera	dyin
mockamock/mocker	tumatakuru	gibber	badimalion

3 Linguistic fossils

The following show old meanings or actual words that have dropped out of use. Give the etymology of each italicised 'fossil'. Explain any meaning change that has taken place. Why do you think some speakers have now recast expressions such as *short shrift* and *let ball* to *short shift* and *net ball?*

bank *teller*
short *shrift*

kith and kin
neck of the woods
hem and *haw*
out of *kilter*
let ball (in tennis)
raring to go
new*fangled*
the exception which *proves* the rule
more haste, less *speed*
not a *whit*
at *bay*
to and *fro*

4 Semantic change

Find the etymology of each of the following 'OZisms' and 'NZisms'. Cite an earlier form and earlier meaning, and say what type of meaning change they illustrate. If you can, explain why they might have changed in this way. Comment on any that you consider obsolete or old fashioned.

crust	'job'
joker	'chap'
pongo	'person from the United Kingdom'
sport	'woman who accords sexual favours'
chiack	'to tease'
grog	'alcohol'
bail up	'to detain (in conversation)'
sook	'cry-baby'
gun	'expert'
scungy	'filthy'
rosella	'(type of) parrot'
rort	'act of fraud'
lay-by	'method of payment'
lurk	'occupation'
rapt	'overjoyed'
curly	'difficult (of questions, problems)'
bowser	'petrol pump'
financial	'paid up' (financial member)
cheerios	'cocktail frank-furters'
tail	'to dock lambs' tails'
tinny	'lucky'
white ant	'to undermine'
give someone curry	'to make some-one's life difficult'

5 Deterioration

Trace the history of *left, gauche,* and *sinister.* Now find as many expressions as you can that include the word *left* (*a left-handed compliment,* for instance) or that refer to 'left-handed people'. What view of left-handers is being presented here? By comparison, trace the history of *right, dexterity,* and *ambidextrous.* What sort of associations does *right* have in expressions such as *Right Reverend*? Think of others, and compare these with your findings for *left.*

6 Lexical and semantic change

The following is a medieval recipe for 'Departed' Creamed Fish. Identify words that no longer exist in ordinary language. Some may be preserved in specialist contexts or fixed expressions; explain these. Others may have changed their meaning. Give a brief sketch of their history and identify what types of meaning changes have taken place. Distinguish borrowed from native words. What generalisations can you make about the nature of the borrowings?

> To make mortrews [thick pottage] of fish. Take plaice or fresh merling and seethe it in fair water, and then take away the skin and the bones and press the fish in a cloth and bray it in a morter, and temper it up with almond milk, and bray powder of ginger and suger together and depart the mortrews in twain in two pots and colour that one with saffron and dress it in dishes, half of that one and half of that other, and strew powder of ginger and suger on that one and clean sugar on that other and mess it forth.

Recipe from Black 1992:74

7 Euphemism

Find as many 'linguistic fig leaves' as you can to replace the words below. Describe the word-formation process that each involves (for example, acronym, abbreviation, and so on).

a poor
b educationally dull
c to be fired from a job
d to die
e war
f toilet
g sexually transmitted disease
h copulate
i old person
j genitals (male and female)

8 Folk etymology

a On 9 November 1996 at 5.46 p.m., an ABC Radio cricket commentator was caught using the expression *one foul swoop*. What word should he have used here? Explain how this change occurs. Can you think of other examples?

b Examples such as *nasty ershems* (< *nasturtiums*) and *very coarse veins* (< *varicose veins*) are often heard in everyday speech. Some are probably deliberately humorous. Can you think of examples from your own experience?

7

Classes of Words

INTRODUCTION

In order to better understand how language works, let's look at the way that words are grouped into their various classes or categories. These are known as either '**word classes**' or '**parts of speech**'. They differ from language to language, although some, such as nouns and verbs, appear to be universal. Traditionally, eight parts of speech have been identified for English: verbs, nouns, adjectives, adverbs, pronouns, prepositions, conjunctions, and interjections. **Interjections** include items such as *hell! wow! psst!* and *shhh!*, and are peripheral to the language. We won't pay much attention to them here, but will instead add two other classes: determiners (traditionally included within the class of adjectives) and auxiliaries (traditionally included with verbs).

These classes fall into two main groups: **major** and **minor**. Major classes include lexical words: nouns, verbs, adjectives, and adverbs. These classes are open, meaning that they have a large and ever-changing membership. As the vocabulary needs of the society change, so new members are incorporated (in chapter 6, we saw how this happened). Minor classes, such as pronouns, prepositions, and conjunctions, include grammatical words; (that is, those words that help to build the grammatical structure of the language). They have few members and are not receptive to new ones. You only have to think of the difficulty that people have had trying to come up with a new non-gender specific pronoun to replace *he*—over sixty suggestions (including curiosities such as *thon*, *li*, and *ep*) and none successful. This doesn't, of course, mean that minor classes such as the pronouns are immune to change. In chapter 11, for example, we survey the massive changes that have occurred within the English pronoun system.

Intuitively you may know what many of these word classes are, and at some stage in your life you may have come across definitions such as the following:

- A noun is the name of a person, place, or thing.
- A verb is a doing word; it refers to an action.
- An adjective is a describing word; it modifies an object.
- An adverb is another describing word; it describes the time, manner, and place of an action.

These traditional definitions are based on meaning, and simple examples will illustrate just how inadequate these sorts of notional descriptions are. Compare the strings *my love of food* and *I love food*. Both instances of *love* express the same emotion of 'fondness, deep attachment' (as opposed to 'hatred'); yet one is a noun (although not a person, place, or thing) and one is a verb (although not an action). In the sentence *I am hungry/starving* the adjectives refer to a state of being, in much the same way as verbs such as *hunger* and *starve* do. And what about a word such as *am*? We know it's a verb, but surely not on the basis of its meaning. Clearly semantics is not a lot of help here. For one thing, the relationship between the form of a word and its meaning is just far too complex. In fact, what makes a noun a noun and a verb a verb is not their meaning at all; other aspects of their behaviour are more telling. As a final example, consider the following short text, and try to answer the questions underneath:

> This is one of the scrumpiest and most floptastical tapostrophies to be bunked when chumpets are in cropon. Chozzle the chumpets into boncy quimples. Scosh them though a croddle. Quank the flubback as murley as you can and cob it to the chumpets. Gungle bopplingly.
>
> What sort of tapostropy is it?
> What do you have to do to the chumpets?
> How do you gungle?

This is actually the beginning of a recipe for a capsicum salad. All we have done is changed the lexical words into nonsense ones. All the grammatically meaningful words and affixes are unchanged. The result is a syntactically well-formed sentence, which you could break down into its parts of speech. Because of this, you can actually make quite a lot of sense of the text, even though you haven't a clue what the nonsense words mean. Obviously, then, it is not meaning that is guiding you here.

We can classify all the items on the basis of their grammatical behaviour—that is, their shape (what endings they take, for example) and their position in the sentence. The first criterion has to do with word-form or morphology (in other words, the characteristic affixes that words take). Words of the same class will typically show the same morphological possibilities. Even though we don't know what *chozzle* means, as a verb it takes a characteristic range of inflections: *chozzle, chozzles, chozzled, chozzling*. And with the derivational suffixes *-er* and *-ment*, we can turn *chozzle* into nouns: *chozzler* 'someone who chozzles' and *chozzlement* 'a chozzled condition'. Nouns don't take these endings; neither do adjectives, prepositions, or adverbs. As an adjective, *scrumpy* takes two types of inflectional endings: *scrumpier* and *scrumpiest*. And we can turn it into an adverb with a derivational ending *-ly* or into a noun with *-ness*: *scrumpily* and *scrumpiness*.

Equally important is the second criterion: the syntactic behaviour of words. By this we mean where words position themselves in a sentence, and the sorts of elements that they can combine with. Words of the same class (such as *food, bread, meat, chumpet, tapostropy*, and *flubback*) will fill the same basic slots in the recurrent patterns of a language. Consider the distribution of words in the following sentences:

1	*2*	*3*	*4*	*5*	*6*	*7*	*8*
roast	the	red	capsicum	in	a	hot	oven
mix	a	green	tomato	with	the	fresh	basil
squash	the	fresh	garlic	through	a	metal	sieve
add	the	hot	basil	to	the	red	tomato
chozzle	a	scrumpy	chumpet	into	a	boncy	quimple

Note that there are regularities in the appearance of these words (that is, they show the same distributional possibilities). This is not a coincidence; it has to do with the strict organisational structure of English. The only way we can account for this is to assume that they belong to the same word class: verbs occur in column 1; nouns in columns 4 and 8; adjectives in columns 3 and 7; determiners in columns 2 and 6; and prepositions in column 5. Other words that can slot into these environments will prove to be members of the same classes. Can we say then that words of the same class are mutually substitutable? This is true, but only up to a point. As we will see in chapter 8, it turns out that members of the same word class do not behave identically. There are actually subclasses within these eight basic classes to account for the fact that we cannot say something like **Disappear the red capsicum into a hot oven* (the asterisk indicates that the sentence is unacceptable).

Return to the sample sentences above. Not only do the same types of words recur in the same columns, but you will see that they also occur in the same patterns. Sentences aren't just strings of words; together these words form structural units. These are **phrases**—groups of words that have some sort of grammatical relationship with one another (for example, the words in columns 2, 3, and 4 form a phrase, as do those in 6, 7, and 8). They are always named after the word that is the most important. This is called the '**head**', and all of the four major (open) word classes (nouns, verbs, adjectives, and adverbs) have corresponding phrasal classes: noun phrases, verb phrases, adjective phrases, and adverb phrases. The head is the core of the phrase. Take, for example, the phrase *stuffed tomato aux Herbs Shoreham-style* (a gloriously pretentious bit of restaurantese). The word *tomato* here is the head. It is the most important part, and all the others are somehow dependent on it. Not surprisingly, then, these are called '**dependents**'. They are subordinate elements, and they generally have a modifying or describing function. Unlike the noun *tomato*, elements such as *stuffed* and *aux Herbs* are completely optional. We can omit them without affecting the grammaticality of the sentence, as in *I like tomato.* Because the head may stand alone, this means that phrases may consist of only one word, and so *tomato* in *I like tomato* is both a noun and a noun phrase. You might think this odd, but as you will find in the next chapter, all the rules that apply to heads will also apply to their phrases, and so it is grammatically justified.

Note that although dependents are often grammatically optional, this is not always the case. Take the sentence *I am very fond of lamingtons.* The sequence *very fond of lamingtons* is a phrase (an adjective phrase, in fact). The head is *fond*, while *very* and *of lamingtons* are dependents. However, in this case only *very* is an optional dependent. The sentence *I am very fond* is ungrammatical. A feature of the adjective *fond* is that it requires a following phrase to complete it.

THE MAJOR WORD CLASSES

In the rest of this chapter we will examine each of the word classes and their corresponding phrases, paying particular attention to the properties of nouns and verbs. Before we do so, we need to stress that not all the members of a class will necessarily have all the identifying properties. Membership of a particular class is a matter of degree. There are prototypical examples of verbs that refer to an action, such as *jump*, and lousy examples, such as *beware*. In this regard, grammar is no different from the real world. There are prototypical vegetables, such as carrots, and not so 'vegetabley' vegetables, such as bean sprouts. There are exemplary mammals, such as dogs, and freakish ones, such as the platypus. It's a familiar story; throughout this book we keep having to admit to irregularity and fluidity in the categories we set up. Languages are not completely regular systems; they have these fuzzy edges, or as Edward Sapir so neatly put it, 'all grammars leak' (1921:38). But the leaky parts are the most interesting, as we hope you will come to appreciate.

Nouns

Semantic features

Typically nouns refer to objects (both physical objects and abstractions) and people. There are all sorts of ways that they can be classified. Do they exist in time or space? Are they living entities? A proper semantic classification is well beyond us here, but in the discussion below we will look at two important subclasses that have some bearing on the grammatical behaviour of nouns.

Morphological features

The properties that are traditionally associated with English nouns are **number**, **gender**, and **case**. These relate much more to earlier stages of English than to current English. Remember that Old English was a highly inflected language with a very elaborate system of suffixes on nouns, pronouns, verbs, adjectives, and even determiners (see chapter 11), and only traces of this system survive today. Only number and, to a very limited extent, case continue to be marked by morphological means.

Number is one of the most widespread categories in language, and most English nouns express number obligatorily in their morphology. The singular is unmarked (that is, it coincides with the lexical stem), while the plural carries a suffix *-s*. As we saw in chapter 5, however, there are many irregularities: some nouns mutate a vowel (*men*, *lice*); others add the suffix *-en* (*oxen*, *children*); and still others are syncretised with the singular (*sheep*, *fish*). A handful of nouns do not inflect for number at all (*rice* has no plural partner, for instance). Others are plural with no singular partner. You find ***dregs*** in the teacup, or ***greens*** on the plate, but you won't find a single ***dreg*** or ***green*** (although you might perhaps refer to an individual as ***a bit of a dreg***). Some nouns, such as *news*, look plural but are actually singular; others, such as *cattle*, look singular but behave as if they were plural. These nouns are simply exceptions.

Gender is a rather confusing term, but if you forget the sex associations and concentrate on its original meaning of 'class' or 'kind' (Latin *genus*), you will better understand its grammatical application here. It refers to a classification of nouns into groups for the purposes of agreement. It is a grammatical feature of nouns that also affects the form of other words in the sentence: its dependents. In Old English, all nouns fell into one of three genders or classes: masculine, feminine, and neuter. True, the classes might have roughly corresponded to the sex or sexlessness of objects, but not necessarily (in Old English, for example, 'woman' was masculine and 'girl' was neuter; see chapter 11). English has now lost this system of grammatical gender. It only has biological gender, and even then it only comes into play with the pronouns *he/him/his*, *she/her/hers*, or *it/its*.

Case involves grammatical markers (or inflections) that signal the relationship of nouns to each other and to the verb; in other words, they signal who is doing what and to whom. English doesn't really have case any more, although relics are preserved in the pronoun system (see p. 159 below). We now mark this sort of information via word order or prepositions. You may find that some grammar books, however, continue to recognise two cases for English. One, the 'common case', is used generally and is unmarked. The other, the 'genitive' or 'possessive case' is signalled by the ending *-s*. It codes a grab-bag of different relations between two nouns, including, of course, possession. For example, *the boy's photo* can be interpreted in a number of different ways: 'the photo of the boy'; 'the photo the boy owns'; 'the photo the boy took', and so on. Its status as a case marker, however, is questionable. Rather than attach to nouns, *-s* now actually attaches to the whole noun phrase; for example, you can say not only *the man's cheese* but also *the man in the moon's cheese* (in spoken varieties, even something like *the man I spoke to yesterday's cheese*). (How the case marker changed from a noun inflection to a noun-phrase clitic is a matter of hot debate; if you remember, inflections aren't supposed to be able to do this sort of thing.)

As far as derivational morphology goes, the most frequent noun-forming suffixes are *-ness* and *-ity* (adjective → noun) and *-er*, *-ee*, *-ation*, and *-ment* (verb → noun) (see Bauer 1983 for a fuller account).

Syntactic behaviour

Syntactically a noun is the head of a noun phrase (that is, the only or main word of a noun phrase), which can then function as the subject, direct and indirect object, and predicate complement. Take, for instance, the sentence ***Oil*** (subject) *gives* ***bread*** (indirect object) ***flavour*** (direct object). We will be discussing these various functions in the next chapter. As heads of noun phrases, nouns also occur with various kinds of dependents. These include adjectives, determiners, clauses, and even other nouns. While the majority precede the noun (as in the first three examples shown below), some can follow (as in the last two examples):

Adjective dependents	*simple white* bread
Determiner dependent	*the* dough
Noun dependent	*bread* rolls
Clause dependent	recipes *to make your own bread*
	recipes *that are perfect for bread and pasta*
Prepositional phrase dependent	recipes *for bread*

While noun phrases can consist of only a single noun (*recipes*, for example), they can also include a number of different pre- and post-modifying expressions (*some popular basic recipes for bread that use oil for a spongier texture*). You can probably see the potential for complexity here. First, there is theoretically no limit to the number of modifiers (although there is, of course, a practical limit: the speaker will probably run out of puff, and the audience most certainly will run out of patience). The following advertising slogan for Nuttall's Mintoes is a wonderful example:

> Why do you think we make Nuttall's Mintoes such a devilishly smooth cool creamy minty chewy round slow velvety fresh clean solid buttery taste?
>
> As quoted in Crystal 1995:22

Second, noun phrases can be linked to other noun phrases, and their modifiers can themselves be modified. We've created a text below that we think nicely illustrates the horrifying potential of this particular aspect of noun phrase modification.

> The induction of a soft elasticity into the bread dough and the promotion of a smooth and even texture in the end product can be achieved by the operation of enthusiastic kneading and in the initial stages of the procedure the addition of subtle flavoured oils together with sugar for assistance in the conversion of the flour's natural sugars into carbon monoxide.

In this syntactic nightmare, it is the structural complexity within the noun phrases that makes it so difficult to follow. Indeed most Plain English translations of the modern, 'super-literate' varieties of written English attempt to convert this kind of complex 'nouny' style into a more user-friendly 'verby' style. We will be looking at some examples of this in chapter 10.

Subclasses of nouns

Two distinctions that are relevant to the grammatical behaviour of nouns are the **proper/common** distinction and the **count/non-count** (or mass) distinction. First, proper nouns are the names of specific persons, places, and organisations. They are spelt with a capital letter and are usually not listed in any dictionary (for example, *Ian, Christmas, Parmenter*). What distinguishes these from common nouns is that they can stand alone and do not take the same array of modifying words. Generally speaking, they can't be made plural either. As we saw in chapter 6, however, proper nouns can sometimes convert to common nouns, and then their behaviour is no different from other common nouns.

The second distinction mentioned has to do with countability. Count nouns such as *lentil* and *noodle* can be interpreted as individuated entities and can therefore be counted. On the other hand, non-count nouns, such as *rice* and *bread*, are interpreted as indivisible masses of material. If we want to talk about one or more individual units, we have to resort to expressions such as *a grain of rice* or *a loaf of bread*. Non-count nouns are, therefore, usually treated as singular and are thus incompatible with quantifying expressions such as *a, many, those, three* (for example, we don't usually say **a bread* or **two breads*).

You might be wondering about special uses such as *This shop has a wide range of breads*. Indeed, much of the time, it does depend on context. For example, the word *pizza* in *Heather ate an entire pizza herself* is perceived to be a single unit and can be counted, whereas in *Heather shouldn't have eaten so much pizza*, it has an unbounded or mass interpretation. Even *essay*, which would normally be count, could in a special context be interpreted as mass—for example, *He talked of little else; for weeks we dined on nothing but essay*. What you must remember too is that languages do not necessarily see eye to eye as to whether nouns are individuated entities or groups of unindividuated entities. What is a count noun in one language may be a mass noun in another.

Verbs

Semantic features

In very general terms, verbs are those words denoting actions, processes, states, or events.

Morphological features

Verbs can also be readily identified in terms of their morphology; in fact, most morphological complexity in English is associated with the verb. In addition to derivational affixes such as *-ee*, *-er*, and *-ment* (verb → noun) and *-able*, *-ing*, and *-ive* (verb → adjective), the most distinctive property of the English verb is its ability to inflect. We need to consider certain verbal properties that are relevant in this regard (see Table 7.1).

Table 7.1 Verb forms in English

Verb categories	COOK	EAT	CUT
Finite forms			
Past tense	cooked	ate	cut
Present tense			
General	cook	eat	cut
Third person singular	cooks	eats	cuts
Non-finite forms			
Base form (infinitive)	cook	eat	cut
Present participle	cooking	eating	cutting
Past participle	cooked	eaten	cut

The first is **person**. English has three persons: first person (speaker), second person (person spoken to), and third person (person spoken about). The label 'third person' is a little curious. It can include semantically empty items such as *it*, as in *it is raining*, and inanimates, as in *the toast—it burnt*.

In English, person is closely bound together with a second property: **number**, which refers to the distinction between plural and singular. Traditionally, person and number are described as properties of the verb. More correctly, though, these apply primarily to nouns and only secondarily to verbs. The form of the verb is actually controlled by the person and number of its subject. For instance, *she* is third-person singular, and the verb takes its form from that—for instance, *she eats* but **you eats*.

Perhaps the most important of the verbal categories is **tense**. The term derives from Latin *tempus* 'time'. Basically it locates the time of an event relative to another event (either the time of speaking or something else). For example, in *I ate it yesterday*, the narrated event occurs before the time of speaking, whereas in *By the time I got there, the meal had already started*, the beginning of the meal is relative to my arrival. Tense is expressed by the verb via the usual sorts of morphological processes that we looked at in chapter 6: affixation, stem modification, and suppletion.

English has only two morphological tenses: **present** and **past** (for example, *he bakes* and *he baked*). The label 'present tense' is a misnomer, however, since it appears in so many contexts that don't actually deal with present time. (For instance, it occurs in timeless statements such as *Diet cures more than doctors*, and in eternal 'truths' such as *Lamingtons taste revolting*. It can also express future time in statements dealing with scheduled events such as *The restaurant opens next week*).

All verbs (apart from *be*) have two present-tense forms (third-person singular and general present for all other persons) but fall into one of three groups on the basis of their past-tense marking. The first group forms the past tense by adding the suffix *-ed*; the second changes the stem vowel; the third does not change. The first group, represented above by *cook*, is the largest, and any new verb entering English will fall into this group.

These three properties—person, number, and tense—define or restrict the meaning of the verb that is inflected. Verb forms that inflect for these properties are described as '**finite**', because they are limited (or made finite) with respect to person, number, and tense. For instance, *cooks* tells you that this is third-person, singular, and present (or, more correctly, that it agrees with a third-person singular subject). English also has three **non-finite** forms, which are not limited by inflection in this way. The first is the base or **infinitive** form. This is the basic verb form (coinciding with the lexical stem) and is what appears in a dictionary listing. The other two non-finite forms are the **present** and **past participles**. All three can combine with auxiliary verbs to create further distinctions of time (see section on auxiliaries on pp. 161–3).

If you examine Table 7.1, you will notice that many of the forms in all three groups are the same. As we mentioned in chapter 5, when two or more inflectional forms are identical in this way, it is described as '**syncretism**'. For example, the general present and the infinitive form are syncretised for all verbs except *to be* (see pp. 161–2). In the history of English, this sort of levelling out of forms has occurred on a massive scale. The last group of verbs is the most extreme. It shows syncretism of four forms.

Syntactic behaviour

The syntax of verbs is complex enough to warrant separate treatment, and we explore this in detail in chapter 8.

Adjectives

Semantic features

The core members of the class of adjectives typically refer to qualities or states (relating to factors such as shape, taste, size, colour, or judgments such as good/bad, pretty/ugly, and so on).

Morphological features

Typical adjectives are gradable or scalar, which means that they refer to properties or states that can be possessed in varying degrees. Most adjectives are therefore able to inflect for grade via a three-term system:

Absolute	tasty	good	old
Comparative	tastier	better	elder/older
Superlative	tastiest	best	eldest/oldest

Normally, the endings are *-er* and *-est* added to the lexical stem. But as you can see above, English also has some totally eccentric forms, such as *good–better–best* (remember these are called suppletive forms; see chapter 5). In some cases you also get a modification of the stem: *long–longer–longest* and *old–elder–eldest*. The sort of vowel mutation you find in *old* was once quite widespread, and forms such as *strong–strenger–strengest* and *long–lenger–lengest* were common. But now even *elder–eldest* has given way to *older–oldest* and is confined to special contexts, such as kin—*elder brother* for instance.

Not all adjectives carry these inflections, however. For one thing, they are going the way of the rest of our inflections, being replaced by free-standing forms (in this case, the quantifying expressions *more* and *much*). Rather than a neat, clean takeover, however, what we find is the usual messiness that we have come to associate with language change—although Laurie Bauer suggests that it's not as messy as is sometimes assumed (1994:51–61). Typically, it is adjectives of one syllable (but even not all of these) that are hanging onto the endings (*purer–purest*, for instance). Adjectives of three or more syllables have lost them and require *more* and *most* (for example, we don't say **beautifuller–beautifullest*). Adjectives of two syllables have a kind of split personality: some do; some don't; and some go both ways. Not all speakers will agree—for example, *tastier–tastiest* versus *more–most tasty*, but *?wickeder–?wickedest* versus *more–most wicked* (the question mark indicates a marginally acceptable form). (Bauer's account suggests that the suffixed comparison is being increasingly restricted to adjectives ending in *-y*, such as *tasty*, *yummy*, *spongy*, and so on).

The other difficulty here is that not all adjectives indicate degree in their basic sense; in other words, they are non-gradable and therefore won't take degree modification (for example, *pregnant*, *alive*, *dead*, *married*, *linguistic*, and so on). Sometimes you find that speakers will play with this property for a special, perhaps comical, effect. For instance, the adjective *Australian* is non-gradable. But to say *he's very Australian* invokes the caricature of the Australian ocker: a beer gut in shorts, singlet and thongs; cheerful, unpretentious, but without much between the ears.

As far as derivational morphology goes, there are a lot of suffixes that derive adjectives from nouns (for example, *-ful*, *-less*, *-ly*, *-y*, *-ish*, *-al*, *-ic*, and *-ese*) and a number from verbs (for example, *-able* and *-ible*).

Syntactic behaviour

Syntactically, adjectives are the head of adjective phrases, which have two important functions. Their first function is to act as modifiers within the noun phrase (the attributive function). As we discussed above, adjectives occur as preceding modifiers within noun phrases. Most adjectives will do this much (*a tasty but inexpensive dessert*). Adjectives may also follow the noun, especially indefinite nouns such as *anyone*, *someone*, or *anything* (*Anything tasty but inexpensive will do*). Linguistic curiosities in the legal world such as *the heir presumptive*, *court martial*, and *heir apparent* also show this less usual order, as do some everyday adjectives such as *the information available* and *the money due.*

The second important function of adjectives is to act as complements within the verb phrase (the predicative function). Typical adjectives can occur as part of the verb phrase after certain verbs (for instance, *the dessert was tasty but inexpensive* and *I made the dessert tasty but inexpensive*).

Central members within the adjective class, such as *tasty* and *expensive*, have both these functions, but English has plenty of examples of fringe-dwellers too.

Adjectives such as *awake, asleep, main, principal, mere, utter*, and *designate* are exceptional; see if you can work out why.

Adjectives themselves take a range of pre- and post-modifiers. Pre-modifiers are mainly intensifiers or degree expressions such as *more, most, almost, quite, rather, too, very, extremely*, and so on. Gradable adjectives typically take these kinds of modifiers. (We won't go into the question of whether or not something can be *rather* or *very unique*; as noted earlier, adjectives often show uses that lie beyond their central sense). Dependents that follow adjectives complete the meaning of the adjective. They can be whole clauses (*He was too hungry* ***to wait*** and *He was so ill* ***that he couldn't face dinner***, for example) or prepositional phrases (*I'm fond* ***of chocolate*** *but sick* ***to death of porridge***).

We've discussed the various adjective properties. Now let's apply them. Is the word *fruit* in *fruit cake* an adjective? Semantics doesn't help us out a lot here. *Fruit* appears to modify *cake*, but is it an adjective? Compare it with the modifying word *fruity* in *fruity cake*. Both words describe a property of the cake, but their grammatical behaviour reveals striking differences. *Fruity* behaves like an adjective; *fruit* clearly does not. Ask yourself:

- Are they gradable? (Compare **a very fruit cake* and **a fruiter cake* with *a very fruity cake* and *a fruitier cake*).
- Can they occur in a verb phrase? (Compare **The cake is fruit* with *The cake is fruity*).

Finally, if you are still unconvinced, try linking it with something that you know is a good example of an adjective, such as the word *rich* (you can only conjoin words that belong to the same part of speech with *and* or *but*). For instance, **a rich and fruit cake* sounds decidedly odd, whereas *a rich and fruity cake* is perfectly fine. The word *fruit* in this case is actually a noun. Most nouns in English can modify other nouns in this way. Though they might look like adjectives, they are not; they fail every adjective test. *Fruit* and *cake* could actually be said to form a noun–noun compound here. As we saw in the previous chapter, compounds comprise two or more roots, which can be spelt as one word or in a sequence, as in this case. Stress is sometimes helpful in identifying these compounds. You will notice that in *fruit cake* the stress is on *fruit*, whereas in *fruity cake* the primary stress falls on the noun *cake*.

Adverbs

Semantic features

The class of adverbs is a real mixed bag and is therefore a notoriously difficult class to define. Adverbs can range from the purely lexical to the grammatical, and can show diversity not only in meaning, but also in their grammatical behaviour. Perhaps what we might think of as prototypical adverbs fall closer to the more lexical end of the continuum. They can express information such as time, frequency, manner, and so on. These modify the meaning of the verb or the clause as a whole (*Mix* ***well*** and *Stir* ***frequently***). Other (more abstract) adverbs express the attitude of the speaker with respect to the degree of certainty or truth (***Probably*** *the bread won't rise*). They may also be emphatic (*I* ***just*** *know it won't rise*). Finally, as we saw, there are those adverbs that are used to intensify or modify the meaning of adjectives, which are sometimes called intensifiers, or degree adverbs (*It's really delicious*).

Morphological features

As far as inflectional endings go, adverbs fare rather badly. Many fall along some sort of scale and are therefore gradable, but they generally take *more*, *most*, and *much*, as in *more–most quickly*. Only a handful will inflect for grade. These include adverbs such as *well–better–best* and *soon–sooner–?soonest*.

As far as derivational morphology goes, a large proportion of adverbs are derived from adjectives with the *-ly* suffix (*fresh-ly*; *sparing-ly*). This is a highly productive suffix, but don't rely on it to tell you when you have an adverb. You might be caught out. For one thing, many adverbs don't have the ending (*soon*, *fast*, *often*, *nevertheless*), while there are adjectives that do (*user-friendly*, *deadly*, *beastly*). Other adverb-making suffixes include *-wards* and *-wise*.

Syntactic behaviour

Adverbs are the head of adverbial phrases and function as dependents of verbs, adjectives, other adverbs, and even entire clauses. For example:

Verb dependent	It cooked *quickly*.
Adjective dependent	The bread was *very* fresh.
Adverb dependent	It cooked *rather* quickly.
Clause dependent	*Surprisingly*, it turned out rather well.

The gradable adverbs take the same intensifiers or degree adverbs as adjectives (*too*, *rather*, *very*), but are otherwise limited in the range of modifiers they can take. Occasionally, they can take a following prepositional phrase (*Surprisingly for me, it turned out rather well*). (Note that adverbs of the connective type, such as *nevertheless* and *therefore*, can't take any modifiers at all).

THE MINOR WORD CLASSES AND SUBCLASSES

The minor classes, remember, contain the more abstract grammatical vocabulary, which is used to build structure and to show how the various parts of the sentence relate to one another. We will list them here with only very little discussion, since most of the detail will be covered in the following chapters.

Pronouns

Earlier we talked about the distinction between 'open' and 'closed' word classes: nouns belong to an open (major) class and pronouns to a closed (minor) class. The difficulty here is that pronouns are really a special type, or subclass, of noun, and this is problematic for any neat division into open and closed. Both nouns and pronouns have the same range of grammatical functions, such as subject, object, and so on. The main difference is that phrases headed by pronouns are more restricted with regard to the sorts of dependents that they can take; pronouns generally don't like being modified, and examples such as *silly me* and *poor you* are exceptional.

Basically, pronouns substitute for full noun phrases (from Latin *pro*, meaning 'for'). Consider the following short extract from the *Consuming Passions* cookbook: *Salt adds flavour but it retards the proving process... don't overdo it* (Parmenter 1992:9). It would sound curious indeed if Ian Parmenter were to repeat the full noun phrase here. Instead he uses the pronoun *it*. Pronouns can also indicate something actually present in the speech event: *That's going to burn!*

There are several different subclasses of pronoun.

Personal pronouns

Personal pronouns are the central class of pronouns. A quick glance at the pronouns from earlier stages of English (see chapter 11) will show that we have lost many of the original contrasts. Nonetheless, the properties of person, number, gender, and case are better preserved in the morphology of these pronouns than in that of nouns. They have distinctions in person (first, second, third); most contrast between singular and plural numbers; third-person singular distinguishes between male and female; and some preserve separate case forms for (roughly) subject and object functions (labelled '**subjective case**' and '**objective case**' in Table 7.2). The second person form *you* shows the greatest collapsing of forms or syncretism. Some varieties of rural British English have retained a *thou* series (*thou, thee, thine, thyself*) and OZ and NZ English (especially Maori English) have a plural form *youse*; compare the southern United States dialect forms *you-all* and *y'all*. Lorraine Johnston and Shelley Robertson (1993) mention that a three-way distinction is possible in Maori English: *you* (singular), *youse* (two), and *youse fullas* (more than two), as a carry-over from Maori. (See also chapter 12 for a discussion of the elaborate pronoun systems of Aboriginal Englishes.)

Table 7.2 Personal pronouns in English

	Subjective case	*Objective case*
First person		
Singular	I	me
Plural	we	us
Second person		
Singular/plural	you	you
Third person		
Singular		
Masculine	he	him
Feminine	she	her
Non-personal	it	it
Plural	they	them

Though, basically, first person refers to the speaker or writer, second person to the hearer or reader, and third person to third parties, the language has much more flexibility than this. Plural *we* can refer to the hearer in a sort of condescending 'hospitalese'—*Let's eat up our spinach now, shall we?* (you could imagine a nurse speaking to a elderly patient here). *You* can be used to refer to people in general (preferable in our varieties of English to the indefinite *one*)—*Chocolate is actually good for you*. In special cases of extreme politeness, third-person forms can be used to refer to the hearer (as a kind of distancing technique)—*If Madam so desires, she could have the pavlova without the whipped cream.* (Many languages conventionally use plural for a singular referent to indicate politeness—French *vous*, for example). *They* is used as a gender-neutral third-person singular pronoun—*If anyone wants, they can have pavlova with extra whipped cream.*

We often hear the argument that to use *they* in this way is grammatically incorrect because a plural pronoun shouldn't refer back to a singular word, but clearly this is linguistically unfounded. English has many examples in which pronouns depart from their central meaning for special uses; furthermore the form *you* is actually plural historically. The reflexive form *themself*, as in *Every student must do it themself*, is now common in both speech and writing here in Australia. This shows that singular *they* is already well incorporated into the system. (As a historical note, *themself* is an old form, which is making something of a comeback now.)

Indefinite pronouns

Indefinite pronouns express notions of definiteness or quantity, and comprise the largest group of pronouns. They fall into two types. One includes compounds consisting of two elements: *some-*, *any-*, *every-*, and *no-* with *-thing*, *-one*, and *-body*, as in *everything*, *everyone*, and *nobody*. The other group may appear alone or be followed by *of*. This group includes items such as *many*, *more*, *most*, *some*, *neither*, and so on. For most speakers of OZ and NZ English, *one* would be included here as an indefinite pronoun rather than as a personal pronoun; *One would prefer you didn't do that* sounds decidedly comical in our varieties of English, and forms such as *one's* and *oneself* are seldom heard.

Reflexive pronouns

These reflect (or are 'reflexes' of) noun phrases that occur elsewhere in the same clause. They all end in *-self* or *-selves*—for instance, *myself* is the reflexive form of *I*. Uses include:

Complement in clause or prepositional phrase	You have outdone yourself. She always cooked for herself.
Emphatic	Elspeth cooked that cake herself. Elspeth herself cooked that cake.

Reciprocal pronouns

There are only two reciprocal pronouns in English: *each other* and *one another*. They are used to express a two-way relationship.

Possessive pronouns

Not surprisingly, these express ownership. They occur as the head of a noun phrase—*This recipe is mine/yours/his*—and in terms of distribution, they parallel ordinary possessive noun phrases (compare *his* with *the chef's*).

Demonstrative pronouns

English has four demonstrative pronouns: singular *this* and *that* versus plural *these* and *those*. In their general sense, they relate to the orientational features of language.

In the example *This tastes better than that*, the two pronouns *this* and *that* contrast with respect to location—that is, near to speaker (*this*) and relatively distant (*that*). They are also used expressively to indicate dislike (***That** man!*), or at the start of a narrative to introduce a new topic (*Like I met **this** guy, you know*...).

Interrogative pronouns

These are used to ask questions of personal and non-personal nouns. The personal pronouns include *who* (subjective case), *whom* (objective case), and *whose* (possessive), although in OZ and NZ English, *whom* would be classed as an endangered species. Most of us would probably not be tempted to say ***Whom** did you give the recipe to?* (although admittedly some may still prefer to write the form). The pronouns *which* and *what* have only one form. *What* is non-personal (***What** did you cook?*) and *which* can be both personal and non-personal (***Which** is your brother? **Which** is your favourite recipe?*).

Relative pronouns

These pronouns are used to link modifying clauses (or relative clauses) to the head of the noun phrases: *This is the recipe **that** I always use*. They include *who*, *whom*, *whose*, *what*, and *which*. We look at relative clauses in some detail in chapter 9.

Auxiliaries

A subclass of verb is the so-called '**auxiliary**' (or 'helping') verb. The class falls into two main groups: **primary** auxiliaries (*be*, *have*, and *do*) and **modal** auxiliaries (*can*, *could*, *shall*, *should*, *will*, *would*, *may*, *might*, and *must*). These verbs all determine the inflectional form of the verb that follows them. Modal auxiliaries and *do* take the infinitive or base (*She will eat*; *Do eat!*); *have* and passive *be* take the past participle (*He has eaten*; *The pavlova was eaten*); and progressive *be* takes the present participle (*They are eating*).

Note that the primary auxiliaries can all be full (that is, lexical) verbs as well, in which case they are the main verb (sometimes the only verb) in the clause. The following pairs illustrate main-verb versus auxiliary-verb status for these three verbs:

Main verb		*Auxiliary verb*
Dinner *is* ready	*versus*	Dinner *is* cooking
That *does* the trick	*versus*	That *does* work well
She *has* my lemon zester	*versus*	She *has* stolen my lemon zester

As you can see from Tables 7.3 and 7.4 (p. 162), auxiliary verbs are distinctive in that they have negative as well as positive finite forms. Note that the verb *be* has extra person and number contrasts in the past and present tenses. Like a fossil, it preserves much of the original inflectional richness of Old English verbs. Remember that its irregularity (suppletion) is also because it is actually a collage of three, possibly four, different verbs (see chapter 5).

The characteristic verbal inflection is lacking in the modal auxiliaries. They are exceptional in having only finite forms (**to must* and **musting*) and yet do not contrast for person, number, or tense (**he musts* and **she musted*). Although, histori-

Table 7.3 Primary auxiliaries

	BE		
	Positive	*Negative*	
Finite forms			
Past tense			
First/third-person singular	was	wasn't	
General	were	weren't	
Present tense			
First-person singular	am	aren't (in questions)	
Third-person singular	is	isn't	
General	are	aren't	
	Base (infinitive)	*Present participle*	*Past participle*
Non-finite forms	be	being	been
	HAVE		
	Positive	*Negative*	
Finite forms			
Past tense	had	hadn't	
Present tense			
Third-person singular	has	hasn't	
General	have	haven't	
	Base (infinitive)	*Present participle*	*Past participle*
Non-finite forms	have	having	had
	DO		
	Positive	*Negative*	
Finite forms			
Past tense	did	didn't	
Present tense			
Third-person singular	does	doesn't	
General	do	don't	
Non-finite forms	*Base (infinitive)*	*Present participle*	*Past participle*
	do	doing	done

Table 7.4 Modal auxiliaries

	Positive	*Negative*
Finite forms	will	won't
	must	mustn't
	can	can't

cally, modals were ordinary lexical verbs, and pairs such as *will–would*, *shall–should*, *can–could*, and *may–might* were related by tense (that is, *will* was to *would* as *kiss* is to *kissed*), the relationship is no longer this straightforward. Over the years, these forms have gradually been going their own separate ways, and the original past-tense forms such as *would* and *could* are establishing their identity as modal verbs in their own right with their own meanings. There are only vestiges of contexts left in which they clearly function as past-tense forms, as in the context of reported speech (*I will cook you a pav* versus *I said I would cook you a pav*).

When we discussed verbs earlier, we mentioned the properties of the verb, such as person, number, tense, aspect, and mood. Whereas, in earlier stages of English, these were marked more by morphological means (that is, inflections), in Modern English the auxiliaries have taken over the expression of these grammatical properties, in particular the grammar of tense, aspect, and mood.

Tense

As mentioned earlier, English only has two morphological tenses: present and past. It has no future-tense ending. So how is future time marked? Present tense is often used in a future context, with or without a time expression such as *tomorrow*. However, future time can also be marked with the help of different modal auxiliaries, such as *will* and *shall*, followed by the base form of the verb. In OZ and NZ English, however, *shall* has now almost totally been replaced by *will* or more usually -*'ll* as in *She'll be right mate*. All signs are, however, that the 'future' marker of the future is gonna be *be* + *gonna* (< *be going to*) + the base form. Although still judged informal usage, it has now become quite common in very informal writing.

Aspect

In addition to temporal location (or tense), you may also want additional information about the action or event expressed by the verb. For example, is it well and truly over, or does it continue over an extended period of time? Is it a one-off thing, or does it happen again and again? These factors all have to do with what we call '**aspect**'. Aspect provides information in addition to the time reference. It looks at the kind of action that is involved and how it is distributed over time. There is a wide variety of possible distributions, but English has two main types of aspectual contrasts. Both are expressed with auxiliary verbs, and both combine freely with tense and mood.

The first is the **perfect aspect**. It is expressed by some form of the auxiliary *have* + the past participle of the following auxiliary or main verb. To understand the meaning of the perfect, compare the following two sentences.

I baked focaccia.	(simple past)
I have baked focaccia.	(perfect aspect)

Both events occur in the past, but the difference becomes obvious when you start combining them with time expressions such as *yesterday* or *this morning*.

> I baked focaccia yesterday.
> *I have baked focaccia yesterday.

In the first sentence, the action has an inherent completion point. It includes a point in past time, but excludes the present. In the second, the action is in the past but it continues up to the present—hence its incompatibility with *yesterday*. Perfect aspect has what is sometimes called 'current relevance'. This can mean many things. Perhaps it describes a situation that endures from some time in the past up to the present (*I have baked focaccia for years!*). Perhaps the effects of some past event still impact in some way on the present moment—*The bread has started browning* (in other words, turn the oven off now!). It can also be used to express new information or 'hot news', as in headlines or advertisements such as *Our new focaccia bread has arrived.* Sometimes it can be a combination of these different senses of current relevance (*Bloggs has scored a goal for the Eagles—oh, a most intelligent goal!*).

So far we have only considered the **present** perfect. The construction can also occur with the past tense or a modal indicating future time. The **past** perfect (or pluperfect) expresses past time, but in an earlier time frame; it is really a past in the past—a more distant past, which is relative to another past (*I turned the oven down, but by then it was too late: the focaccia had burned*). The **future** perfect (*will* + *have* + past participle) expresses that something will have been completed by a certain time in the future (*I will have finished the focaccia by then*).

The second aspect is the **progressive aspect**, and this is expressed by forms of the auxiliary *be* + the present participle of the following auxiliary or main verb (*I am zesting lemon*). As the name implies, it presents the situation as being in progress at a given time; it indicates duration. Not surprisingly, it is a favourite construction of sporting commentators (*Bloggs (is) trying to get the shot in*; *Bloggs (is) going forward*). You will find that some verbs, such as *know*, *think*, *understand*, *hate*, *love*, and *see*, don't happily combine with this aspect. These are stative verbs; that is, they refer to a state of affairs, rather than to an action or event (unchanging states can't be 'in progress', since they are static). Hence sentences such as **It is belonging to me* and **He is possessing a lemon zester* sound bizarre. However, when these verbs do actually occur with the progressive, then the situation is construed as having a more dynamic character and the subject is playing a much more active role in the event (for instance, *I taste salt* versus *I am tasting salt*).

The strong implication with the progressive is that something is taking place over a limited period of time and is therefore impermanent. Compare the following sentences:

They are baking focaccia.	(at present, limited duration)
They bake focaccia.	(permanent, non-progressive)

Although it is possible to get a habitual reading for the first sentence, the stronger implication is that this is a single occurrence; they may never bake focaccia again.

We'll just mention a third minor aspect: the **habitual**. This is constructed from the auxiliary verb *used to*, and the sense conveyed is habitual or of an event being characteristic of some period of time (specifically in the past). *Used to* is a curious auxiliary, as you can see by its form. It has developed from a main verb (meaning 'to follow a custom') and could once carry the full range of inflections. Here's a sixteenth-century example: *At dyner use not to drink syndry drinkes* (that is, 'don't mix your drinks'). In Modern English it appears only with the past-tense inflection (although our actual pronunciation is something like [ju:stə]) as in *they usta drink too much.*

Mood

Mood deals with the reality of an event or situation. There are two broad categories of modality: events can be **actual** or **non-actual**. While there is really only one way an event can be actual, there are many different ways it can be non-actual. It can, for example, be hypothetically possible, imposed on the speaker, desirable, or conditional on something else happening.

They are starving.	(actual)
They may/might/could/should/would be starving.	(non-actual)

Once upon a time, English distinguished between actual and non-actual events by morphological means. The so-called 'subjunctive' was a handy little verbal marker that could signal a speaker's doubt or uncertainty about the truth of the event. It expressed notions such as potentiality, contingency, hypothesis, conjecture, unreality, wishing, desiring, and even prohibition. With the exception of fossils such as *if need be* and *God bless you*, the job of the subjunctive has now been taken over by our modal auxiliary verbs.

In summary, it is possible to have as many as four auxiliaries in a single sentence, although this is unusual (*The roast must have been being cooked while the burglars were searching the house*). Of the four auxiliaries, the first is a modal, the second is the perfect aspect *have*, the third is the progressive aspect *be*, and the fourth is the passive *be*. (For a discussion of the passive, see chapter 10.) Table 7.5 illustrates some of the more commonly occurring combinations.

Table 7.5 Combinations of auxiliary verbs

		Auxiliary verbs		*Main verb*
modal			must	cook
(present) progressive			is	cooking
(present) perfect			has	cooked
(present) perfect progressive		has	been	cooking
modal + perfect		must	have	cooked
modal + perfect progressive	must	have	been	cooking

Some things to notice:

- There is always a main verb, and this is the last element.
- The order within the auxiliaries is fixed (modal + perfect *have* + progressive *be* + passive *be*).
- Each type of auxiliary influences the following auxiliary or verb in a kind of chain reaction: the modal triggers the base form; perfect *have* triggers the past participle; progressive *be* triggers the present participle; and passive *be* triggers the past participle (as in *The roast must have been being cooked, while the burglars were searching the house*).

Prepositions

Semantic features

The majority of prepositions express spatial relations: *at*, *in*, *on*, *under*, *over*, *to*, and so on. Some of these location markers have been recruited for a more grammatical function, taking over the roles of the disappearing inflections. For example, *to* not only indicates 'direction towards' but is also used to signal the infinitive form of the verb, as in *to give*. The preposition *of* once indicated 'away from' but has now come to mark possession, as in *the cover of the book.*

Morphological features

Prepositions can be simple (*to, from, of, with, by*) or complex (*in front of, on top of, outside of, because of, in addition to*). With the exception of a small handful of prepositions (for example, *near, nearer, nearest*), there is no inflectional and no derivational morphology to speak of.

Syntactic behaviour

Prepositions function as the head of prepositional phrases, which in turn function as modifiers or dependents of verbs, nouns, adjectives, or clauses:

Verb dependent	I always bake *in the morning.*
Noun dependent	Most plain flours are a mixture *of different wheat flours.*
Adjective dependent	Hard wheat flour is perfect *for bread and pasta.*
Clause dependent	*In my opinion,* there is no perfect recipe for bread.

Prepositions take following noun phrase dependents, as in *Soft wheat flour is better for pasties and puddings*. Unlike the classes we have just been looking at, however, they do not allow very much in the way of modification. Very occasionally you find degree modification with intensifying expressions such as *very much.* This is more usual when the preposition has a metaphorical sense rather than a literal sense, as in *He's very much on top of things* versus **He's very much on top of the house* (see Huddleston 1988:125).

Conjunctions

Conjunctions are items that link clauses or parts of clauses together. For the moment, we will just list the two different types of conjunctions without going into any detail, since they get separate treatment in chapter 9.

Coordinators link units that are of equal status in the sentence, such as two noun phrases, two clauses, and so on. The central coordinators are *and* (expresses addition), *but* (expresses contrast), and *or* (expresses alternatives), but they can also be reinforced with additional words (for example, *either...or, not only...but also, both...and*).

Subordinators also link units, but these do not have the same grammatical status. For example, one clause could be subordinated to another; in *It will be cooked, if it sounds hollow*, the subordinate clause is joined to the main clause by *if.* Some of the typical meanings expressed by subordinators include time, place, purpose, condition, reason, and 'concession'. There are more subordinators than coordinators, many consisting of more than one word. Common ones include *after, although, as, because, if, that, until, which, while*, and so on.

Determiners

Determiners are a new word class. Basically, what they do is express notions such as definiteness, quantity, number, and possession. In other words, they 'determine' what kind of a noun follows; is it definite or indefinite, count or mass, concrete or abstract? There are a number of subclasses.

Articles

The system of English articles is extremely complex. The meanings involved relate to notions of reference and are notoriously difficult to define. Basically, the **definite article** *the* signals that a noun phrase is definite, perhaps because it refers to something in the immediate context—*Have you put on **the** toast yet?*. Or it might refer back to an earlier noun—*Break in **the** eggs* (*the* here refers back to the 'three large eggs' specified earlier under ingredients). Or perhaps it refers to an object that has become part of our shared general knowledge (*I enjoy **the** cooking programs on television*). The **indefinite article** *a* is used when a noun has not already been specified (*He gave me **a** recipe for chocolate truffles*); it can refer also to a general state of affairs (*I'm learning to be **a** chef*). The absence of any article is common in idioms such as *do lunch, cook dinner, go to bed*, and so on.

Quantifiers

These are modifiers of the noun and express quantity or extent. They include words such as *all, few, little, much, several*, and *some* as well as phrases such as *a great deal of, lots of*, and *hardly any*. They also include more exact quantifying expressions such as numbers *one, two, three*, and so on. Note that quantifiers do not form a neat subclass of determiner. Some of these quantifying expressions actually occur before determiners (***all/both** the lemon zesters*), while others must follow (*the **many/seven** lemon zesters*). If they can't occur exactly where determiners do, then you're probably thinking (and rightly so) that they're not determiners. To be determiners, then, they should have the identical distribution to that of other determiners. For this reason, grammars often distinguish between pre- and post-determiners. But this introduces too much complexity for our brief treatment here.

Demonstratives, possessives, interrogatives, and relatives

We saw earlier that demonstratives, possessives, interrogatives, and relatives could be pronouns; that is, they can replace entire noun phrases. They also form natural subclasses of determiners. Like other determiners, they can occur right before the noun and can function (roughly) as modifiers of the noun (*those/my/which/whose eggs*). You could think of them as pronominal determiners.

And while we're on the subject of pronominal determiners, we should mention a curious inadequacy in the modern standard language with respect to relative pronouns functioning as determiners. Some time ago, we received an interesting enquiry from someone in the Original Juice Co. This person drew our attention to part of a sentence from The Australian Food Standards Code:

> Concentrated orange juice *whose* volume has been reduced by the removal of water to a volume not exceeding one half of the original...

It was the relative pronoun *whose* in particular that the person objected to. Many people dislike and therefore avoid *whose* when it refers back to something inanimate—in this case, orange juice. Yet the only alternative that Standard English can offer here is *orange juice, the volume of which has been reduced*, and most would agree that this construction is even more clumsy. However, colloquial English has come up with several ways around this problem—for example, *orange juice that its volume has been reduced* or, more usually, *orange juice thats volume has been reduced. Thats* uses the regular formation of the possessive by adding *-s* to the pronoun and arguably fills a gap in the standard language. But it's still some way off being accepted; most people are horrified when their attention is drawn to it.

POINTS TO REMEMBER

- Our vocabulary falls into various categories or classes. One type of category is word-based. Word classes or parts of speech include nouns, verbs, adjectives, and adverbs (major classes), and prepositions, conjunctions, determiners, pronouns, and auxiliaries (minor classes).
- Meaning provides a general characterisation of the central word-class members, but it is insufficient to characterise what part of speech or class a particular word belongs to. We need to take account of meaning (semantics), form (morphology), function, and distribution (syntax).
- We can never classify words in isolation, since so many belong to more than one part of speech. Because of their grammatical elasticity, English words must be taken in their grammatical context.
- A second type of category is phrasal. Phrases involve groups of words that have some sort of grammatical relationship with one another. They always contain a head (from which they take their name) and, optionally, one or more dependents.
- A useful test for determining the category of an item is coordination. Only words or phrases of the same class can be linked with conjunctions such as *and* or *but*. Find a prototypical class member and try joining it with the questionable word.
- Tense, aspect, and mood all specify different details about an event. Tense locates the event in time (relative to the time of the utterance or some other event); aspect characterises its distribution over time; and mood signals the actuality of an event. These three categories interact in subtle ways within our verbal system.

EXERCISES

1 Spot the word class

Rather than use nonsense words, we've indulged in some sesquipedalianism. Here is a text made up of inordinately long and unusual words. State the word class of each of the italicised words and substitute a current English word that makes sense. Explain how you decided on the word class in each instance; since the words are probably unfamiliar to you, you should be using grammatical cues to make your decision.

> She felt like a *groak* as the others *guttled* and *tippled* on *oenomel. Mephitically alliaceous, steatopygous, ventripotent fopdoodles* and *slubberdegullions*, she *mus-*

> *sitated.* She *piddled moliminously* at the *jejune* and *unsaporous* morsels on her plate. Dieting made her *egregiously pusillanimous*; she couldn't help it. It was a *niminy gulosity*—she knew it—but just the sight of them induced such an *increment* in her *recrement*, a *cupidity* that was altogether *ineluctable*: it was the bowl of *post-prandial* mints. It was those she *yissed*. She could do nothing but *gorm esuriently* at the bowl. *Peradventure*, she would find the strength to *repugn*, but it was doubtful. She *fibulated* nervously. They were so *gustful*, so richly *ambrosial*. She contemplated her *embonpoint*, but it was *nugatory*. She sensed an *ereption* coming on. And no one was there to *objurgate* and slap her *opisthenar*. The bowl of mints *evanesced* before her eyes. She leant back, loosened her *femoral integuments*, *pandiculated sumptuously*, and *ruminated* upon the *ineluctable costnung* of mints.

2 Word-class analysis

Classify all the words in the following extract from a *Vogue Entertaining* article into their respective word classes. Then give examples of any words that can function as another word class; for example, *barbecue* here is a noun, but it can also be a verb, as in *we barbecue regularly*.

> From the public coin-operated gas barbecues of Bondi to the balcony Webers of Fitzroy, from spit-roasted country-harvest Sundays to indoor chargrills that defy drizzle for convenient all-weather sizzle—we are returning to our roots, but with a swag of barbecue ideas that now span the globe. We have earned our searing stripes—we know the fire should be white with ash (when using coals) or down to a hot glow (when burning wood) before laying food on the grill; we don't stab and turn meat with forks which only encourages the juices to run out; we have gained the experience to test done-ness by prodding—the more give and spring a cut of meat has, the rarer it is. We have our long-handled utensils at the ready: tongs, an oiling and basting brush, a spatula for turning fall-apart foods, a quiver full of skewers for keeping vegetables and shellfish in line, and hinged frames to fit our favourite fish.

Adapted from 'Well Done!', *Vogue Entertaining*, February/March 1995:100

3 Mass and count nouns

State whether the italicised nouns are mass or count. Give evidence.

a Most of us are passionate about good *food*.
b *Rice* is a great food.
c When buying *garlic* and *onions*, make sure they are firm.
d Look for large *cloves* in the *garlic*.
e The *eggplant* and the *tomato* are really *fruits*.
f *Carbohydrate* exists as *starch* in vegetables, but as *sugars* in *fruit*.
g We need to watch our intake of saturated *fats*, *salt*, and *sugar*.

4 Adjectives

Australian and New Zealander teenagers have their own adjectives (many from the USA). For example:

> wicked ('good'), cool, budget ('uncool'), unreal ('absolute best'), grouse, daggy, sassy, babelicious ('blend of babe and delicious'), mega, bad ('excellent').

Which are gradable, ungradable, or both? If they can be both, give examples of each use and describe any differences in meaning. Which of these have inflectional forms for the comparative and superlative, and which require *more* or *most*? Do any use both constructions?

5 Adverbs and adjectives

Identify the adverbs in the following and say what each is modifying. Replace an *-ly* adverb with one without *-ly*, and replace an adverb without *-ly* with one formed with *-ly* (if necessary, change the meaning, but not the grammatical structure)—for example, *Elspeth ate quickly* > *Elspeth ate fast.*

a Pasta is wrongly regarded as a fattening food, but usually it's the sauce that's more fattening.
b Tinned tomatoes are very useful when cooking pasta sauces.
c I use oil almost exclusively. Naturally, it's always extra virgin olive oil.
d There is a widely held belief that pasta is cooked if it easily sticks to the wall.
e But really, you should just try it. It should still have a bite to it.

For each of the following italicised items, state whether it is an adjective or an adverb. Give evidence.

f She was cooking *better* than ever.
g The food became *better* as it went on.
h Can't you cook *better* than that?
i You'd *better* turn the oven off.
j I could make *better* ones myself.

6 Verb forms

Remember that there are six different forms for English verbs: third-person singular (*-s* form), general present, past, base form (infinitive), past participle, and present participle. Identify the form of each italicised verb below.

> Once upon a time, actually about two years ago, meat *meant* red flesh. While beef and lamb are *regarded* as red meat, pork is *being marketed* in Australia as 'the other white meat'. In response to the increasing health awareness of today's consumers, producers are *responding* with leaner cuts. Recipes are also being tailored in recognition of the need to *reduce* the fat intake of our daily diet.
>
> When *selecting* meat it has always *been* my view that it *pays* to *develop* a rapport with a good butcher, preferably one who *knows* and *cares* about cooking as well as about the meat he or she is *selling*. You can leave it to her or him to *select* the best cut.
>
> Fresh meat should *have* a clear pink or red colour without signs of grey or yellow. *Look* for cuts which *carry* the tick of approval from the National Heart Foundation.

Parmenter 1992:103

7 Auxiliaries

Auxiliaries allow *not* to contract with them, and some auxiliaries can themselves contract with the subject (for example *We are not cooking* → *We're not cooking/We aren't cooking*). Give the contracted forms of the following. If both contractions are possible, give both.

a Should not pasta be regarded as Italian?
b Not really, the origins of pasta are not known.
c They will not eat anything else.
d He would not eat anything else either.
e We are not sure when pasta is cooked.
f Do not they throw pasta against the wall?
g If it does not stick to the wall, it is not cooked.
h I have not tried this particular method myself.
i I had not been game before.
j I am not sure how reliable the method is.
k I would not try if I were you.

In our Antipodean varieties, many speakers prefer contractions such as *usedn't to*, but there is a lot of variation. How do you contract each of the following?

l may not
m need not
n used not to
o shall not
p might not
q dare not

How do you think the use of *of* as a non-standard form of the auxiliary verb *have* might have originated (for example, *He should of done it*)?

A new modal auxiliary, *better*, appears in colloquial varieties (*You better do it soon*). How can you account for the development of *better* into a full modal? How acceptable do you find the contracted forms with *not*, as in *You better do it soon, bettern't you?*

Look at the entry for *ain't* in some recent dictionaries. What do they say about the use of this form? What do you think about its use in your own variety?

8 Tense and aspect:

Identify the italicised verbs as present perfect, past perfect, present progressive, past progressive, present perfect progressive, or past perfect progressive:

a Some tycoons *are* regularly *eating* heavy four-course business lunches.
b Heather *was eating* her birthday cake with relish.
c She implied that sun-dried tomatoes *had* now *become* passé.
d She believes that she *has been enjoying* good health because of royal tennis.
e Until then, she *had been making* regular visits to health spas.
f Jake *has shown* evidence of the health advantages of a sedentary life.
g A confirmed couch potato, Jake *has* never *played* sport.

Make up a sentence using each verb below in the specified tense and aspect(s):

- enjoy (present perfect)
- find (past perfect)

- refuse (present progressive)
- convince (past progressive)
- go (present perfect progressive)
- win (past perfect progressive)

8

What's in a Sentence?

INTRODUCTION

In the previous chapter we concentrated on the ingredients of the sentence. Now we turn our attention to the way these ingredients combine to form sentences. The grammatical term ***sentence*** is probably very familiar to you. Yet adequately defining it is extremely difficult. One traditional definition is 'the complete expression of a single thought'. There are many sentences, though, that express a single thought, but would not generally be considered to be 'complete' as they do not contain a finite verb, for example.

Good luck!
Coffee?
Quiet!
G'day.

Conversely, there are many sentences that express more than one thought.

An optimist looks at an oyster and expects a pearl.
A pessimist does the same and expects ptomaine poisoning.

Anonymous, as quoted in Goode 1987:147

An alternate approach is to define a sentence in terms of its written form. For example, we could say that a sentence 'begins with a capital letter and ends with either a full stop, a question mark, or an exclamation mark'. However, many advertisements and newspaper headlines lack punctuation marks, and yet we can still tell when a sequence of words is a sentence, as in the following slogan from a sparkling wine advertisement:

IT'S OUT THERE POURING

Instead of trying to define a sentence, we take the approach of most modern grammars of English and focus on the way in which sentences are constructed. The study of the structure of sentences is called '**syntax**'. The major goal of syntax is to describe the form, positioning, and grouping of the elements that go into making up the different types of sentence structures.

In this chapter we begin by exploring what it means when we say that the sentences of English have structure, how we determine this structure, and how we represent it.

Next we consider some of the functions, such as subject and predicate, that syntactic units can perform in a sentence, as well as the patterns of basic English sentences. In the remainder of the chapter we look at the functions of the main types of sentences, such as declarative, imperatives, and interrogatives.

SENTENCE STRUCTURE

How do we know there is structure?

Sentences are constructed out of words, and whenever we put words together to form utterances or written sentences, we must do so in a systematic fashion. As we saw in chapter 7, words can only be grouped in certain arrangements, or structures, and we use these over and over again. For example, consider the following excerpt from an early Australian bush song that comments on rations provided by outback station owners:

> Ten pounds of flour, ten pounds of beef, some sugar and some tea,
> That's all they give to a hungry man, until the Seventh Day.
> If you don't be mighty sparing, you'll go with a hungry gut.
>
> Anonymous, 'The Old Bark Hut', as quoted in Goode 1987:23

As speakers of English we know that

*If you be don't sparing mighty, you'll go with a hungry guts

is not an acceptable alternative for the third line of the song. Not only is the order of the words **be don't sparing mighty* unacceptable, but we know that *hungry gut* can be preceded by *a*, whereas *hungry guts* cannot.

This illustrates that a sentence is not simply a random collection of words. Rather, the words are arranged in specific patterns, and we say that the sentence has a syntactic structure. As *don't be mighty sparing* and **be don't sparing mighty* showed, the words in a sentence occur in a particular order, and one aspect of syntactic structure is linear order.

Another aspect is that some of the words seem to belong together—that the words seem to work in groups. In our example above, if *gut*, which is singular, is changed to the plural *guts*, we get the unacceptable word sequence **a hungry guts*. This suggests that the use of *a* is dependent on *gut*, and that the group of words *a hungry gut* forms a phrase. We see, then, that a sentence can be divided into phrases, and this is another property of sentence structure.

In addition, groups of words form different kinds of phrases. What is wrong with **ten pounds of mighty sparing* (as compared with *ten pounds of coarse flour*) is that *mighty sparing* is a different type, or category, of phrase than *coarse flour*. So we need to include information about the category of a phrase as another property of the syntactic structure of a sentence.

Not only can the string of words in a sentence be divided into phrases of various categories, but these phrases can be further divided into smaller parts. Evidence of this aspect of syntactic structure is provided by sentences containing a phrase (rather than a single word) that is ambiguous. When this is the case, the sentence has more than one meaning, and we say that the sentence is an example of structural ambiguity, as in:

They ate more interesting delicacies at the next food stall.

The ambiguity of this sentence depends on the phrase *more interesting delicacies*, which can mean either:

a 'some additional interesting delicacies'
or
b 'some delicacies that are more interesting than the previous selection'.

This ambiguity reflects the fact that the same phrase has two different internal organisations, or structures. With the first meaning, *more* is modifying the phrase *interesting delicacies*, whereas, with the second meaning, *more interesting* forms a phrase that is modifying *delicacies*. The two different structures can be visually represented as:

a

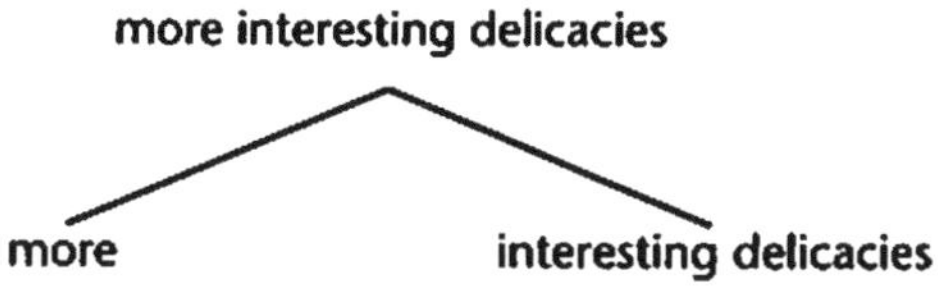

b

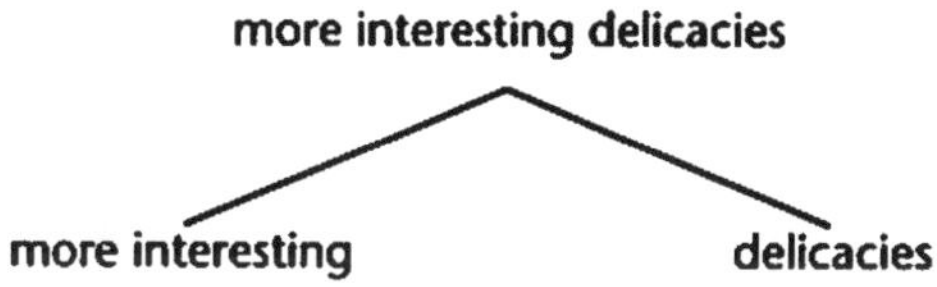

We observe, then, that the phrase *more interesting delicacies* can be divided in two different ways into smaller phrases. A sentence can be divided into phrases that are longer than a word but shorter than the entire sentence, and these phrases may be able to be further divided. Therefore, we can say that the syntactic structure of a sentence includes not only linear order and the grouping of words into structural phrases that can belong to different categories, but also hierarchical structure.

In the next three sections we consider, in more detail, the different kinds of phrases in syntactic structure, how to determine them, and how to represent them.

Constituents

It's usually easy to split a sentence into two phrases. Characteristically, the left phrase functions as the subject, while the right phrase functions as the predicate in that it describes the role of the subject in some event or state. For instance, the old adage

Too many cooks spoil the broth.

Balthazar Gerbier, *Discourse of Building* (1662), as quoted in Goode 1987:47

is a sentence, and it can be first divided into two phrases as follows:

too many cooks   spoil the broth

These phrases can be further divided, and we can represent the results in a branching diagram:

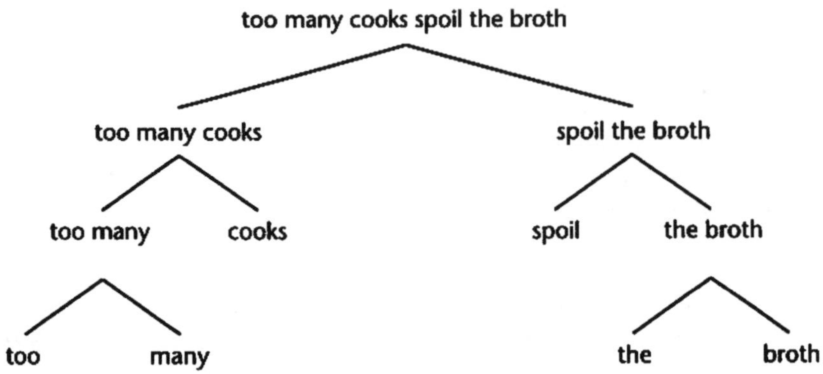

In analysing the structure of a sentence, each unit that is part of some higher unit is called a '**constituent**', and so the only unit that is not a constituent is the topmost one: the entire sentence. Determining the **constituent structure** of a sentence means, then, dividing a sentence into constituents, and then dividing these constituents into smaller constituents.

We will use a branching diagram like the one above to represent the syntactic structure of a sentence. Such a diagram is called a '**constituent structure tree**', although the 'tree' is upside down, with the 'base' at the top and the 'leaves' at the bottom. (Or is it right side up, with the 'base' at the top and the 'roots' at the bottom?) From either viewpoint, at each point where there is a 'branch', there is a group of words that form a constituent of the sentence. At the end of all the branches are the individual words that make up the sentence.

We can now formally define a phrase as a sequence of words that can function as a constituent in the syntactic structure of a sentence. A phrase, then, is a syntactic unit intermediate between a sentence and a word.

Sentence level	Too many cooks spoil the broth
Phrase level	too many cooks
Word level	cooks

In the next section, we focus on how to establish the various constituents in a sentence.

Determining constituent structure

If we were asked to give a constituent structure analysis of

They started to peel all the potatoes.

we would probably intuitively begin to divide it as follows:

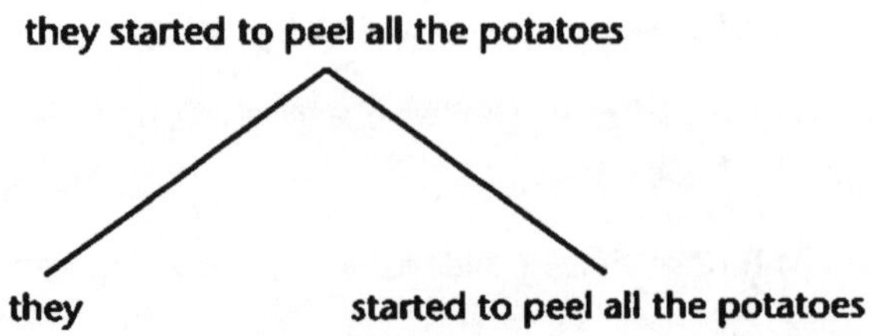

But within the constituent *started to peel all the potatoes*, it is not so clear how we would determine further constituents. Is *to peel all the potatoes* all one phrase, or should it be analysed as two?

a

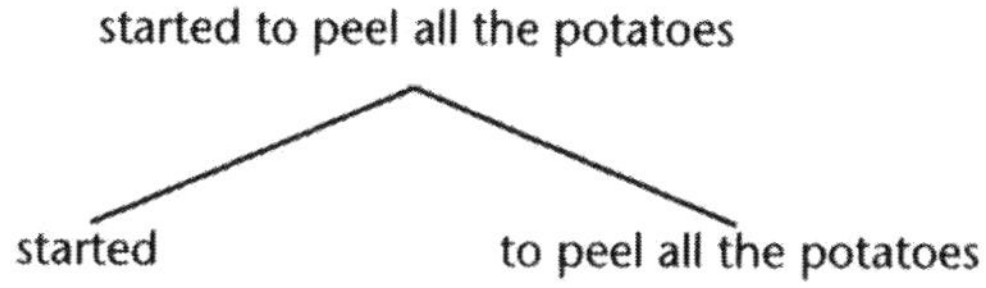

b

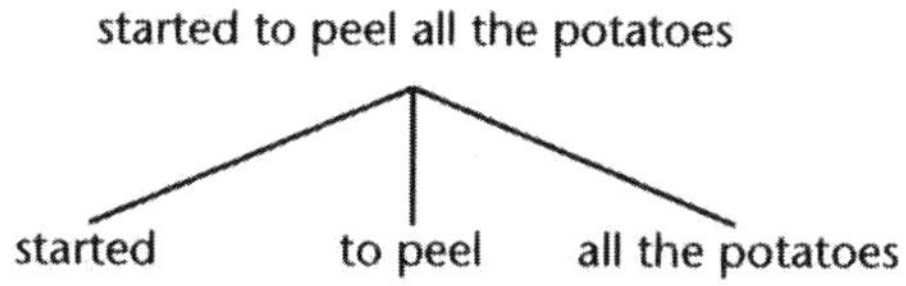

In order to decide between these two possibilities, we consider some criteria that help in establishing the constituent structure of a sentence.

Substitution

One way of determining whether or not a sequence of words forms a constituent is to try substituting a single word for the sequence of words. If the resulting sentence is acceptable (even though the overall meaning of the sentence may change), then the original sequence of words forms a syntactic unit or constituent. For example, in the sentence

> The name *beignet* (fritter) comes from *a Celtic word meaning swelling or tumour.*
>
> Alexandre Dumas (1802–70), *Dumas on Food,* as quoted in Goode 1987:224

we can substitute a single word such as *here* (or *this*) for *a Celtic word meaning swelling or tumour* and still have an acceptable sentence

> The name *beignet* (fritter) comes from *here/this.*

Alternatively an interrogative word such as *where* (or *what*) can be substituted, giving an echo question (this is discussed in more detail later in this chapter).

> The name *beignet* (fritter) comes from *where/what?*

On the basis of either of these substitutions, we can say that *a Celtic word meaning swelling or tumour* is a constituent and, thus, a phrase.

However, if we tried to find a single word to substitute for *comes from a* we would be unsuccessful. Since any potential substitutions would lead to unacceptable sentences, *comes from a* is not a constituent.

We can summarise this approach for establishing whether or not a sequence of words is a constituent as follows:

Substitution criterion

If you can replace a sequence of words in a sentence with a single word without changing the overall acceptability of the sentence, then that sequence is a constituent of the sentence.

Movement

A second approach for determining if a sequence of words is a constituent is to see if it can move about in the sentence as a unit. For example, in

> Fish and guests in three days are stale.
>
> John Lyly, *Euphues* (1580), as quoted in Goode 1987:52

the word sequence *in three days* can be moved to the beginning of the sentence indicating that it is a constituent.

> Fish and guests *in three days* are stale.
> *In three days*, fish and guests are stale.

We can formally state this test for 'constituency' as follows:

> **Movement criterion**
>
> If you can move a sequence of words from one position in a sentence to another without changing the overall acceptability of the sentence, then that sequence is a constituent of the sentence.

Conjoinability

The final approach for determining constituency that we explore here makes use of the observation that sequences of words that are constituents can be conjoined with *and*, but non-constituents cannot be conjoined. In the two examples below, the conjoined sequences of words are constituents or phrases.

> They live on *good food* and *fine words*.
> You cannot both *eat your scone* and *have it*.
>
> Anonymous, as quoted in Pescott 1994:34

However, as the next example illustrates, word sequences that are not constituents cannot be conjoined.

> **One plans the* and *the other cooks* the new menus.

To see how to apply this in determining constituent structure, let's consider the sequence *with coffee spoons* in the sentence

> I have measured out my life *with coffee spoons*.
>
> T. S. Eliot (1888–1965) 'Love Song of J. Alfred Prufrock', as quoted in Goode 1987:49

We can conjoin it with a sequence of words with a similar structure, as in:

> I have measured out my life *with coffee spoons* and *with chocolate eclairs*.

Since this is an acceptable sentence, we can conclude that *with coffee spoons* acts likes a constituent with respect to conjoinability.

This test can be summarised as:

Conjoinability criterion

If a sequence of words can be conjoined with one containing different words but the same internal structure, and if this gives an acceptable sentence, then that sequence is a constituent in the original sentence.

Now let's consider what these three criteria can show us about the constituent structure of *to peel all the potatoes.* Using the substitution criterion, we can replace the sequence of words with a single word, which suggests that it is indeed a phrase.

They started *to peel all the potatoes.*
They started *it.*

Similarly, we can move the whole sequence of words, which by the movement criterion also argues that it should be analysed as a constituent.

They started *to peel all the potatoes.*
To peel all the potatoes is what they started to do.

Finally, we can conjoin *to peel all the potatoes* with a sequence of words with a similar structure, which by the conjoinability criterion is further evidence that it is a phrase.

They started *to peel all the potatoes* and *to steam the vegetables.*

So, using the three criteria for determining constituent structure, we see that the correct structure for *started to peel all the potatoes* is

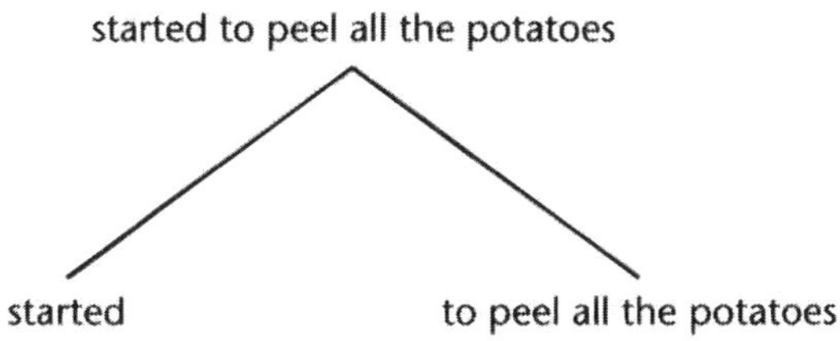

Phrasal categories

The next question to consider is just what kinds of phrases there are in a sentence. It turns out that each phrase in a sentence belongs to a particular category such as noun phrase (NP), verb phrase (VP), adjective phrase (AdjP), prepositional phrase (PP) or adverb phrase (AdvP). As we saw in chapter 7, these phrasal categories are named according to the most central word of the phrase (the head). For example, in the claim

Garlic defends the body against worms.

Adapted from Parmenter 1993:18

the phrase *defends the body against worms* is a verb phrase, *the body* is a noun phrase, and *against worms* is a prepositional phrase. Typically, a verb phrase contains a verb (such as *defends*), a noun phrase contains a noun (such as *body*), and a prepositional phrase consists of a preposition (such as *against*) followed by a noun phrase (such as *worms*).

This sentence also illustrates that a phrase can consist of a single word, such as *garlic* or *worms*. The reason we use the term *phrase* to cover such cases is that the single word can be replaced by a sequence of words without changing the acceptability of the sentence.

> *Lots of good strong garlic* defends the body against *worms, dysentery, typhoid, high blood pressure and even the common cold.*

What this indicates is that, in our example sentence, the single words *garlic* and *worms* are actually functioning as entire phrases. So we see that a phrase often, but not necessarily, consists of more than one word.

We can now add the phrase categories and streamline our constituent structure tree as follows:

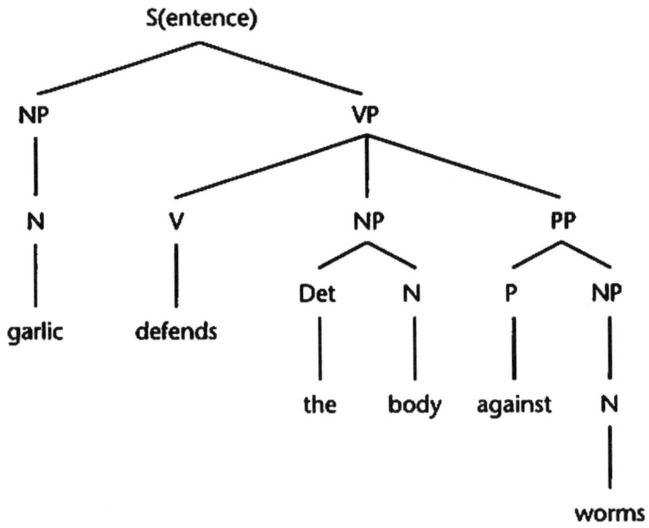

This constituent structure tree gives us the following information about the structure of the sentence:

- The entire sequence of words *garlic defends the body against worms* is a sentence ('Sentence', which dominates the whole word sequence, indicates this).
- The sentence consists of a noun phrase, *garlic*, and a verb phrase, *defends the body against worms*.
- The noun phrase *garlic* consists of a noun.
- The verb phrase contains a verb (*defends*), a noun phrase (*the body*), and a prepositional phrase (*against worms*), and so on.

To summarise, sentences do indeed have syntactic structure, and it is useful to describe the various aspects of structure in terms of constituent structure trees. As you have seen, a constituent structure tree provides the constituent or phrase structure of the whole sentence (that is, the groupings of words into syntactic units and their hierarchical structure), the phrasal category of each phrase (that is, what type each phrase is), and the word class of each word in the sentence. A tree does not, however, show information about the function of each phrase. Before we consider this, though, let's look in more detail at how to construct a constituent structure tree.

Phrase structure rules

Each of the sentences that we have looked at so far has been composed of two major constituents: a noun phrase followed by a verb phrase. This generalisation can be expressed in the form of a **phrase structure rule** (also called a '**constituent structure rule**'):

S(entence) → NP VP

This rule states that the constituents of a sentence are a noun phrase followed by a verb phrase.

If you look back at our constituent structure tree for *Garlic defends the body against worms*, you will see that there are other rules that reflect generalisations about the syntactic structure of English sentences. A noun phrase, for example, can consist of a determiner and a noun or just a noun, and this can be expressed as follows:

NP → (Det) N

The parentheses indicate that the determiner is optional.

Verb phrases can also be expressed by a phrase structure rule:

VP → V (NP) (PP)

Some of the possible verb phrases that are described by this rule are found in sentences such as:

Some of the dinner guests arrived.	(V)
The guests gathered in the dining room.	(V PP)
The hosts served some luscious finger foods.	(V NP)
They enjoyed the handmade chocolates after dinner.	(V NP PP)

And the structure of prepositional phrases can be described as:

PP → P NP

Together these four rules can be used to construct the constituent structure tree that was given for *Garlic defends the body against worms*, as well as a large number of other sentences. (Of course, they do not begin to account for all the possible sentence structures found in English.) In addition to being used to construct a constituent structure tree, they provide a sentence with a structural description (that is, the constituent structure and the constituent types of which the sentence is composed). In this way, phrase structure rules describe part of the syntax of English.

BASIC CLAUSES AND FUNCTIONS

We now move from structure to function, and consider the various roles that different phrases play in a sentence. What we see is that not only can each phrase be described in terms of its phrasal category (as determined by grammatical properties shared with other phrases), but it can also be described in terms of its **function** (as determined by the role it plays within the syntactic unit that contains it). In other words, a phrasal category is what a constituent is (for example, a noun phrase or verb phrase), whereas function is what a constituent does (for example, a subject, object, or predicate).

Why differentiate phrasal category and function?

We need to distinguish between what category a phrase belongs to and what function it performs, because most categories of phrases have a variety of different functions. For example, although subjects are frequently noun phrases, this does not mean that all noun phrases function as subjects.

Strong sauces overpower delicate fish.

Here both *strong sauces* and *delicate fish* are noun phrases, and yet the first functions as a subject, while the second functions as an object. So although both *strong sauces* and *delicate fish* belong to the same phrasal category, their functions differ according to their position in the sentence.

It is because of cases such as this—where there is a lack of one-to-one correspondence between function and phrasal category—that we need to maintain a consistent distinction between what a phrase is and what it does.

Basic clauses

The structure of most of the sentences that we have discussed so far has consisted of a noun phrase followed by a verb phrase. We need a term to describe sentences with this pattern and, as it is the most common sentence form in English, many grammars use *basic clause* for this purpose. A **basic clause** is structurally complete, and it is the smallest syntactic unit that is capable of being used completely independently in English. The following suggestions for decorating a pavlova are all basic clauses and share the same initial division between noun phrase and verb phrase, although they differ radically at a lower, more detailed, level within the hierarchical structure of the verb phrase.

Noun phrase	*Verb phrase*
Any kind of fruit	is good with pavlova.
You	can use fresh strawberries, bananas, kiwi fruit, peaches, or tinned pineapple or fruit salad.
Fresh fruit	should be sprinkled with lemon or orange juice before it is used on the pavlova.

Adapted from Omnibus Books 1991:27

In the remainder of this section we restrict ourselves to the basic clause. First we consider the different functions that a phrase can fulfil, and then, on the basis of these functions, we recognise the basic clause patterns that are determined by the different elements that can occur in the verb phrase.

Functions

As we have seen, the primary structural division within a basic clause is between the initial noun phrase, which we have informally said functions as the subject, and the verb phrase, which we have said functions as the predicate. The verb phrase always contains a verbal element that functions as the predicator. The verbal element may be accompanied by one or more phrases, and as we discuss in more detail below, these phrases may function as objects, predicate complements, or adverbials.

Before we look at each of these functions more fully, let us consider two other points. First, the functions or roles of subject, object, and predicate complement involve the different relations that the main noun phrases in a sentence can have with respect to the verb. These functions are sometimes referred to as '**grammatical relations**' because they are determined by the syntactic relationships between certain noun phrases and the verb.

Second, grammatical relations are only one way of looking at the functions of phrases in sentences. In chapter 10, when we consider how sentences 'go together' to constitute a discourse in speech and writing, we see that, in addition to functions within the sentence, phrases also have functions within the larger discourse, such as focus, topic and comment, and old versus new information.

Predicate and predicator

While we've already noted that the verb phrase in a basic clause functions as a predicate, we can now, more precisely, say that a **predicate** is a function that attributes properties to the subject by ascribing some property or role in the situation. For example, in

> The eye is bigger than the belly.
>
> George Herbert (1593–1633) *Jacula Prudentum*, as quoted in Goode 1987:11

is bigger than the belly is predicated of *the eye*.

What is the structure of the predicate? It is a verb phrase that can consist of simply a verbal element (predicates are in italics).

> The guests *are eating.*

Or it can be more complex.

> The guests *consumed the icky, sticky pudding with great delight.*

In all cases, however, the predicate contains a verbal element. Because the verbal element plays the most central role in clause structure and is obligatory in a basic clause, the term ***predicator*** (Pred) is used for the function of the verbal element. *Are eating* is the predicator in the first example above, whereas *consumed* is the predicator in the second.

Subject

Traditionally, the subject (S) has been described using meaning-based terms, such as 'what the sentence is about' or 'actor or performer of the action', but as we saw in chapter 7, meaning-based definitions are never adequate. For example, in *It is really raining hard*, the subject, *it*, doesn't fit either of these definitions. Instead, the notion of subject is best defined in terms of a cluster of structural features.

Basic position

The subject always precedes the predicator in basic clauses.

Subject	*Predicate*	
Absinth	*makes*	the heart grow fonder.

Adison Mizner, (1876–1933) *The Cynics Calendar*, as quoted in Goode 1987:230

Absinth	*makes*	the parts go stronger . . .

Jack Hibberd, *Odyssey of a Prostitute* (1983), as quoted in Goode 1987:230

Verb agreement

The subject determines whether the verb is singular or plural in the third person of the present tense.

Basil bruises easily.	(singular subject and verb)
Many herbs bruise easily.	(plural subject and verb)

Pronoun form

Some pronouns have a distinctive subjective case when used as a subject.

Subject		*Object*	
I	gave	*them*	my latest version of the recipe.
They	gave	*me*	their latest version of the recipe.

Obligatoriness

It is necessary to have a subject in basic clauses.

This recipe is based on the French Provencale daube.

Parmenter 1993:52

*Is based on the French Provencale daube.

Phrasal category

The subject is either a noun phrase (including single nouns and pronouns) or a subordinate clause.

Microwaves are not necessary for good cooking.	(noun)
I don't use white goods.	(pronoun)
That I don't expect others to have them is the reason.	(subordinate clause)

Adapted from Parmenter 1993:53

Object

The function of the object (O) has traditionally been ascribed to the noun phrase that is most affected by the action of the verb. In actual usage, though, objects cover a much wider range of semantic roles than simply the 'target' of the action.

We { cooked / bought / described / ordered / saw } the pavlova.

While the *pavlova* is directly affected when it is *cooked* or (to a somewhat lesser extent) when it is *bought*, it is not clear how it is affected when it is *described*, *ordered*, or *seen.*

Instead of attempting a meaning-based definition, we define object in terms of a cluster of structural features.

Passive

The object can be shifted to the front of a sentence to become the 'grammatical' subject in passive sentences.

(We discuss passive sentences in detail in chapter 10.)

We poured *the mixture* into the saucepan.
O

The mixture was poured into the saucepan.
S

Pronoun form

Some pronouns have a distinctive objective case when used as an object.

Subject		*Object*	
We	marinated	*them*	in a mixture of soy sauce and sesame oil.
They	served	*us*	next.

Basic position

The object usually follows the predicator in basic clauses.

You toss *the beef* in plain flour seasoned with a little pepper.

Phrasal category

The object is either a noun phrase (including single nouns and pronouns) or a subordinate clause.

We are cooking *chips.*	(noun)
You drain *them* next.	(pronoun)
Most outlets advertise *that they use cholesterol free oil.*	(subordinate clause)

In English the predicate can contain more than one object, and in these cases, two types of objects can be recognised: indirect object (iO) and direct object (dO).

I offered	*you*	*that recipe*	before.
	iO	*dO*	

An indirect object typically refers to an animate being that is the recipient of an action (here *you* is potentially the recipient of *that recipe*), whereas a direct object typically refers to the noun phrase directly affected by the action (here *that recipe* is what is being offered). When there is both an indirect object and a direct object present in a sentence, the indirect object comes before the direct object, as in the example above. And when both objects occur, it is the indirect object that can become the subject of a passive clause.

You	were offered that recipe before.
S	

In English we also usually have the option of expressing the indirect object in a prepositional phrase containing *to* or *for*, with a resulting change in word order.

I offered that recipe *to you* before.

We should note that many traditional grammars of English still refer to such a prepositional phrase as an indirect object, even though syntactically it behaves quite differently. For example, the prepositional phrase can't become the subject of a passive clause (**To you were offered that recipe before*).

Predicate complements

Like an object, a predicate complement is part of the predicate. However, unlike an object, a predicate complement does not pick out an entity that isn't already mentioned in the clause. Consider the following:

My favourite barbecued vegetable is *eggplant.*
I barbecued *eggplant.*

At first glance these sentences may not seem very different as they both have a verb followed by the noun phrase *eggplant*. However, the relationship between this noun phrase and the subject noun phrase is different in each case. In the first sentence, the two noun phrases are referring to the same entity, and *eggplant* is a predicate complement, whereas in the second sentence, the noun phrases are referring to two different entities, and *eggplant* is an object. The term *predicate complement* refers to the fact that the phrase is a 'complement' of the verb (that is, completes the verb), and that it is the key in 'predicating' or attributing something about the subject, rather than about the verb in the predicate.

English actually has two types of predicate complements: a **subject complement** (sC) and an **object complement** (oC). (In the example that we considered above, the noun phrase *eggplant* is a subject complement as it refers to the subject of the sentence.) The contrast between the two types of predicate complements is illustrated in:

My latest creation	is	*green bean supreme.*
S		sC

I called	*my latest creation*	*green bean supreme.*
	O	oC

In the first example, the predicate complement (*green bean supreme*) refers to the subject (*my latest creation*) and is thus a subject complement, while in the second example it refers to the object (*my latest creation*) and is thus an object complement.

In addition to this meaning-based definition, predicate complements have the following structural properties.

Basic pattern

A subject complement usually follows the subject and predicator. The form of the predicator contains a **copular** or 'linking' verb, such as *be, seem, appear, become*, or *remain*.

One of Indonesia's most popular rice dishes	is	*Nasi Goreng.*
S		sC

Parmenter 1993:14

An object complement usually follows the object.

Some people call	*coriander*	*cilantro.*
	O	oC

Passive

An object can be shifted to the front of a sentence to become the 'grammatical' subject in a passive sentence, but a predicate complement cannot.

The chef steamed	*the fresh spinach.*	>	*The fresh spinach* was steamed (by the chef).
	O		
The major ingredient was	*fresh spinach.*	>	**Fresh spinach* was been (by the major ingredient).
	sC		

(The parentheses indicate that a phrase is optional.)

Phrasal category

Predicate complements (either sCs or oCs) can be noun phrases, adjective phrases, or subordinate clauses.

Poached eggs became *their favourite food.*
NP/sC

These are *excellent.*
AdjP/sC

Poached eggs are *what they want for breakfast.*
subordinate clause/sC

They considered the egg *a perfect food.*
NP/oC

They found poached eggs *delectable.*
AdjP/oC

Number agreement

When the predicate complement is a noun phrase, it typically agrees in number with the entity it refers to.

The earliest *soup* was a thick cereal-based *pottage.* (singular)
The earliest *soups* were thick cereal-based *pottages.* (plural)

Adverbials

In the predicate, the phrases that may accompany the verbal element are of two general types: objects and predicate complements, on the one hand, and adverbials, on the other. The features that set an adverbial (A) off from the other elements of the predicate are:

Optionalness

An adverbial is more peripheral than an object or predicate complement, and it can be freely omitted from a clause. However, a clause either becomes unacceptable or its meaning changes significantly if an object or predicate complement is omitted.

We have propagated *thyme* *(any time of year).*
O *A*

*We have propogated (any time of year).

Flexibility of word order

An adverbial has a greater flexibility of word order than an object or predicate complement; by comparison, adverbials can be easily moved about in the sentence.

You place the rice balls into the steamer *very gently*.
You *very gently* place the rice balls into the steamer.
Very gently you place the rice balls into the steamer.

Number per clause

Adverbials are not restricted in number. A clause can only have one subject, one finite verb, one complement, and one or two objects, but there may be any number of adverbials.

The soup simmered	*slowly*	*on the stove*	*all day.*
	A	*A*	*A*

Phrasal category

Adverb phrases, prepositional phrases, subordinate clauses, and some noun phrases can function as adverbials.

Tarragon leaves should be dried *quickly*.	(AdvP)
The tarragon leaves infused the oil *with a splendid flavour*.	(PP)
I add a sprig of tarragon *before I roast the chicken*.	(subordinate clause)
I dried the tarragon leaves *last week*.	(NP)

Parmenter 1993:19

Range of meanings

Adverbials can have a wide variety of meanings, indicating factors such as manner, place, time, instrument, degree, and frequency.

We make homemade chips *quite often.*
(frequency)

They cook *in a couple of minutes.*
(time)

You should drain them *well* *on kitchen paper.*
(manner) *(place)*

We liked the homemade chips *enormously.*
(degree)

Clause patterns

Basic clause patterns

While a basic clause requires a subject and a predicator, the choice of verb largely determines what other phrases are used in the clause. On the basis of the functions of object (both direct and indirect) and predicate complement (both subject complement and object complement), we can recognise five basic clause patterns: **intransitive, transitive, di-transitive, complex-intransitive** (or copulative), and **complex-transitive**. (The term *complex-intransitive* was coined by Rodney Huddleston 1996.) Of these five clause patterns, the transitive is the most common, in terms of both the number of the verbs that enter into this pattern and the actual frequency of the pattern in spoken and written English. The term *transitive* captures the notion of transferring to, or affecting, an object.

To all of these patterns we can add additional optional adverbials. As we discussed in the previous section, adverbials are more peripheral than the other phrasal elements in the predicate, and verbs are not classified according to the type of adverbial they take, since adverbials supply additional circumstantial information (such as location, manner, attitude, and so on) and can appear with all verbs. (However, as we shall see in the next section, there are occasions where a particular verb requires an adverbial and its presence is obligatory in a clause.) In the following examples, the adverbials have not been italicised, and this reflects the fact that they are optional and can be removed without affecting the acceptability of the clause.

Intransitive

S + Pred

I	*can drink*	like a fish.
S	*Pred*	A

James Shirley (1596–1666) *Works*, as quoted in Goode 1987:235

Transitive

S + Pred + O

What use are cartridges in battle?

I	always	*carry*	*chocolates*	instead.
S	A	*Pred*	*O*	A

G. Bernard Shaw (1856–1950), *Arms and the Man*, as quoted in Goode 1987:222

Di-transitive

S+ Pred + iO + dO

Pat-a-cake, pat-a-cake, baker's man

[You]	*bake*	*me*	*a cake*	as fast as you can.
S	*Pred*	*iO*	*dO*	A

Anonymous, old nursery rhyme

Complex-intransitive

S + Pred + sC

Some circumstantial evidence	*is*	*very strong,*	as when you find a trout in the milk.
S	*Pred*	*sC*	A

H. D. Thoreau (1817–62), *Journal*, as quoted in Goode 1987:41

Complex-transitive

S + Pred + O + oC

Guns	*will make*	*us*	*powerful;*	*butter*	only	*makes*	*us*	*fat.*
S	Pred	O	oC	S	A	*Pred*	O	oC

Hermann Goering (1893–1946), *Broadcast* (1936), as quoted in Goode 1987:70

Adverbial complements

Most adverbials are peripheral to the structure of the clause, in that they represent additional information that can be left out without affecting the acceptability of the clause. There are some verbs, however, that require an adverbial. In these cases, the adverbial is closely related to the predicator, like an object or predicate complement, and we can label such a phrase an adverbial complement (aC). For example, in each of the following sentences, the prepositional phrase is obligatory and functions as an adverbial complement.

The proof of the pudding is	*in the eating.*
	aC

Cervantes (1547–1616), as quoted in Goode 1987:212

You place a layer of potato	*on a baking tray.*
	aC

Unlike the five basic clause patterns discussed above, there is no special label for this clause pattern or for those discussed in the next section.

Phrasal and prepositional verbs

There are two final types of verbs that we consider here: phrasal and prepositional verbs. As in the case of the adverbial complements discussed in the previous section, both of these types of verbs require particular elements to follow them in order to form a complete sentence.

A **phrasal verb** consists of a verb and an adverb particle, which function together as a unit. Often the unit takes on an idiomatic meaning (that is, a unique meaning that in no way derives from the sum of the parts).

The chef *threw down* the knife and yelled, '*Slow up!*'
The assistant chef *took off.*
The restaurant owner *backed up* the assistant chef.

With phrasal verbs that take an object, the particle can either precede or follow the object.

Drink *up* your milk quickly.
Drink your milk *up* quickly.

Although, it can only follow a personal pronoun.

Drink it *up* quickly.
*Drink *up* it quickly.

In contrast, a **prepositional verb** consists of a verb followed by a prepositional phrase, with the particular preposition that occurs determined by the verb in each case. Take *relied*, for example:

The chef *relied on* the assistant chef.

If you apply the constituent tests of movement and conjoinability, you will see that the preposition *on* forms a syntactic unit with the noun phrase *the assistant chef*, not with the verb *relied*. However, as shown by the unacceptability of

*The chef *relied in/by/at* the assistant chef.

the verb requires a particular preposition and for this reason is traditionally called a prepositional verb.

CLAUSE TYPE

There are four main types of clauses in English, which we can distinguish by the message that they are most typically used to convey: **declaratives** are used to make statements; **imperatives** are used to issue directives; **interrogatives** are used to pose questions; and **exclamatives** are used to make exclamatory statements.

And there are also a number of minor types of clauses, which include formulae for various social interactions (such as *How are you?*, *Wish you were here*, and *Bless you*) and imprecatives for cursing (such as *Piss on you!*, *Screw you!*, and *Get nicked!*).

Before we take a closer look at each of the four main types of clauses, though, let's consider the relationship between clause type and clause meaning.

Clause type and clause meaning

Traditionally, grammars of English have defined clause types in terms of their message or clause meaning, as we have informally given them above. While this works as a general definition, modern grammars recognise that the same clause type can, in actual use, convey a number of different clause meanings, depending on the context of use. For instance,

Dinner will be late.

can have the message (among others) of a warning, a promise, and a prediction.

Conversely, the same clause meaning can be achieved by using different clause types.

Shut the window!
I'm cold!

Would you (please) shut the window?
Aren't you cold?

While these examples vary in terms of politeness (and clause type), they all have the same clause meaning: a directive to close the window.

Labels such as 'declarative', 'imperative', 'exclamative', and 'interrogative' mark the clause type, whereas labels such as 'directive', 'statement', 'warning', 'question', and 'promise' mark the clause meaning. The important thing to remember here is that there is no one-to-one correspondence between clause type and clause meaning. As Table 8.1 illustrates, an imperative type of clause can express a number of different clause meanings.

Table 8.1 Examples of imperative clause types

Clause type: imperative	*Clause meaning*
Don't open the oven!	directive
Have a good time!	expression of good wishes
Sleep tight (and don't let the bedbugs bite).	leave taking
Watch your head!	warning
Have some cake.	invitation
Add the milk gradually.	instruction
Help me!	plea
Help yourself to some goodies.	permission
Let's see if the roast is done.	suggestion

Declaratives

The declarative is the most fundamental of clause types; basic clauses are always declarative. The primary clause meaning is to express statements that are either true or false, and in terms of syntactic structure, the clause contains a subject that precedes the verb. In casual conversation, though, the subject is sometimes omitted.

An empty stomach is a good political adviser.

Albert Einstein (1879–1955), as quoted in Goode 1987:23

(It) looks like a beaut.

Since we've already looked in close detail at the syntax of basic clauses, let's now move on to the structure of the more marked clause types.

Imperatives

The most central meaning of imperatives is to direct someone to do something. Structurally, imperatives have a verb in the base form; in other words, the verb carries no inflection.

Be brave!
Do it!
Eat a goldfish today.

Most imperatives have the second person pronoun as the 'understood' subject. With strong stress, though, the subject can be present.

You be Mother.

It is also possible to have a third person subject, as in:

Somebody get the cake out of the oven!
Nobody touch that pav!

Here, though, there is a hidden second person. In the first example, for instance, the implied subject is somebody among you all here. This becomes clear when we form an interrogative tag.

Somebody get the cake out of the oven, won't you?

Special types of imperative include negative and 'emphatic' imperatives, which are always formed with 'do'.

Don't be silly!
Do come to dinner tonight.

There is also a first-person imperative, which expresses a desire. It is formed with *let us*, which in casual speech is normally contracted to *let's* or even *'s*.

Let us pray.
Let's drink our cappuccinos outside.
'Sgo!

Interrogatives

While the primary function of all interrogatives is to ask questions, we can distinguish four different types based on the kind of reply that is expected and on how they are constructed.

Yes/no interrogatives

These are the most common type of interrogative and they seek an affirmative or negative reply. Structurally, the subject follows the auxiliary. However, if the corresponding declarative does not contain an auxiliary, then the appropriate form of the auxiliary *do* is added.

Are you going?
Did you sauté the mushrooms? (*Sautéed you the mushrooms?)

In addition, a yes/no interrogative can be formed from a declarative by using a rising intonation in speech or a question mark in writing.

You're going?
You sautéed the mushrooms?

Wh- interrogatives

These seek a reply from a wide range of information and begin with one of the interrogative words such as *who(m), which, whose, what, where, why*, or *how*. If the subject is not an interrogative word, then it follows the auxiliary, and the relevant form of the auxiliary *do* is added if there is no auxiliary.

> Who will be there?
> What did you eat? (*What ate you?)

Alternative interrogatives

The answer to this type of interrogative is one of the alternatives given in the question. Like the previous two types of interrogatives, the subject follows the auxiliary, and the auxiliary *do* is added if no auxiliary is present.

> Should we go to the Thai restaurant or the Vietnamese one?
> Did you say the fish is fresh or frozen? (*Said you that the fish is fresh or frozen?)

Sometimes an interrogative can be interpreted as either a yes/no or an alternative interrogative. For example, a 'party trick' that drives people crazy is to interpret *Would you like tea or coffee?* as a yes/no interrogative with an answer such as *Yes please*, rather than as an alternative interrogative with a more helpful answer such as *Tea please*. (Of course, one can play on the ambiguity, but not drive people up the wall, by answering something like *Yes please. Tea would be good.*)

Interrogative tags

This type 'tacks' the interrogative onto the end of a declarative clause and requests that the hearer express agreement or disagreement. The tag is formed by repeating the auxiliary (or adding the relevant form of the auxiliary *do* if there isn't an auxiliary) and then a pronoun version of the subject noun phrase.

> The hot chocolate is pretty hot, isn't it?
> She liked the liquorice, didn't she?

This is the most common type of interrogative tag and is called a reverse polarity tag, since the tag is negative if the declarative clause is positive and vice versa. Note that if the tag is negative, then the *not* is typically contracted with the auxiliary.

In speech, the intonation can be either rising or falling on the tag. The former indicates more doubt; the latter is more confirmation-seeking. In writing, the punctuation can indicate the difference. For example:

You're going, aren't you?	(I'm asking you.)
You're not going, are you!	(I told you so.)

Exclamatives

The clause meaning of exclamatives resembles that of the declarative, except that exclamatives are intended to be expressive or emotive, whereas declaratives are generally intended to be informative. The primary structural feature of exclamatives is that they begin with *how* or *what*.

> How over the top this dessert is!
> What a fine mess you've made!

They can also appear in a shortened form in which the subject and verb have been omitted.

How over the top!
What a fine mess!

In archaic and literary styles, as well as in mock-dramatic contexts, we also find examples where the auxiliary or verb comes before the subject.

How often *have I* cursed the day I met them!
What dreams *have I*!

In addition to using an exclamative clause, an exclamatory message can also be expressed by other means—for instance, with words such as *so*, *such*, and *remarkable*, or by appropriate intonation. But it is only in exclamative clauses that the exclamatory meaning is expressed by a grammatically distinct construction.

Echoes

All the clause types that we have discussed are mutually exclusive, in that any particular clause belongs to only one type. However, in conversation we find that any clause type can be echoed with the goal of confirming, questioning, or clarifying what has just been said. Echoes are commonly used for these purposes in police interrogations (for example, *You were where on the night of August the 13th?*)

There are two ways of forming echoes: a yes/no echo that uses a rising intonation (or a question mark in writing) and a wh- echo that uses an interrogative word to ask for a repetition of information.

Clause type	*Clause*	*Yes/no echo*	*Wh- echo*
Declarative	He gave it to Fred.	He gave it to Fred?	He gave it to who?
Imperative	Give it to Fred!	Give it to Fred?	Give it to who?

An echo is also a type of structure that is utilised in humour. In most 'Knock knock, Who's there?' jokes, the fourth line is a wh- echo of the third line.

Knock knock.
Who's there?
Doughnut.
Doughnut who?
Doughnut bother me with silly questions!

POINTS TO REMEMBER

- Syntax can be defined as the study of the structure of sentences.
- In analysing sentence structure, sentences are broken down into their component parts (called 'constituents').
- Structural ambiguity in sentences derives from different constituent structures.
- To determine constituent structure, three criteria can be used—substitution, movement, and conjoinability—and the resulting structure represented with a constituent structure tree.

- A phrase can be described as a sequence of one or more words that can function as a constituent in the syntactic structure of a sentence.
- A phrase needs to be described in terms of both its function and its phrasal category.
- A basic clause consists of a noun phrase that functions as a subject, and a verb phrase that functions as the predicate. In addition to a verbal element that functions as the predicator, the verb phrase may contain one or more phrases that function as objects (including direct and indirect), predicate complements (including subject complement and object complement), and/or adverbials.
- On the basis of these functions, five basic clause patterns (intransitive, transitive, ditransitive, complex-intransitive, and complex-transitive) and three special cases (adverbial complements, phrasal verbs, and prepositional verbs) can be established.
- In considering the different types of clauses in English, the structural clause type must be distinguished from clause meaning, which refers to the different types of messages that a clause can be used to convey.
- There are four main types of clauses in English that can be recognised in terms of syntactic structure and primary clause meaning: declaratives, imperatives, interrogatives, and exclamatives.

EXERCISES

1 Structural ambiguity

Paraphrase each of the following sentences in two different ways to show that you understand the ambiguity involved. Then explain the ambiguity in terms of syntactic differences, making reference to the constituent structure and grammatical terminology developed in this chapter.

a We have scrambled eggs for breakfast.
b Would you look after dinner, please.
c The gourmand ran down the restaurant.
d They are frying chickens.
e We saw the new snack bar on the train.
f The market sells a variety of hot chilli and spices.
g Grandma Possum cooked beautifully.
h The children took her chocolate chip cookies.

2 Determining constituents

Decide whether or not the italicised sequence of words in each of the following sentences is a constituent of that sentence. Justify your answer with evidence gained by applying the movement, substitution, or conjoinability criteria.

a *Other names for a hero sandwich* are submarine or sub, dagwood, grinder, and Hoagie.
b You have to be *a hero to eat one.*
c To assemble a hero sandwich, slice *one submarine roll* lengthways.
d *Butter cut* surface.
e Next, slather on *pickle of your choice.*
f *For best results,* try to pile up the meat, cheese, and salad in layers.
g To eat your creation, *unhinge the jaw.*

h Allow one clear *metre around you* for splattering.
i After a while, I remembered the sandwich on the plate *in front of* me.
j Everybody *needs a hero* sometimes.

Adapted from Greenwood & Pausacker 1995:166

3 Representing constituent structure

There are many varieties of tea, as well as many ways of marketing it. Give a constituent structure tree for each of the following phrases found in the tea section of a local market.

a Lady Grey tea
b choice small leaf
c distinctive flavoured tea
d finest quality herbal infusions
e oxygen bleached filter paper
f organically pure Ceylon tea
g richer blend mountain tea
h certified organically grown evening song tea
i All Rounder round tea bags
j wild raspberry naturally flavoured herbal tea

4 Phrasal category and function

Identify the phrasal category (NP, AdjP, PP, AdvP) and function (S, O, iO, dO, sC, oC, aC, A) of each bracketed phrase in the following sentences.

a [During the Ming Dynasty] [the whole coastal plain from Nanjing to the sea] became [a sort of aristocratic Disneyland].
b Vying with each other, [Imperial chefs] composed [dishes of refined elegance].
c [The noble ancestor of the now humble spring roll] originated [in Yangzhou].
d [It] was [a lacy-thin crêpe] [in those days].
e [The filling of finely shredded threads of the very first, tender vegetables to be picked in the spring] gave [the crêpe] [its name].
f [Hangzhou] is [famous] [for the real *haute cuisine* of the East].
g [Here] [the Ming emperors] built [their summer palaces, complete with artificial mountains, dwarf trees, and mirror lakes].
h [Without a doubt], [the palace cooks] grumbled [about their makeshift summer kitchens].
i By inventing such novelties as sizzling rice cakes, [they] kept [the bored exquisites reclining on embroidered silk in the pavilions] [amused].
j When making sizzling rice cakes, [the palace chefs] combined [hot, deep-fried rice crusts] [with sauced meat] [in a noisy, showy finale].

Adapted from Cullen 1995:50–1

5 Basic clauses and function

The following basic clauses have been analysed into constituents for you. Give the function of each constituent (S, P, O, iO, dO, sC, oC, A) and the basic clause pattern of each sentence (intransitive, transitive, di-transitive, complex-intransitive, complex-transitive).

a [Obviously] [people] [have been enjoying] [liquorice] [for quite some time] [now].

b [It] [was known] [in the region of Mesopotamia which is regarded as the cradle of civilisation].

c [Seven centuries before Christ] [physicians] [prescribed] [their Royal masters] [liquorice].

d [For Roman soldiers] [it] [was] [a thirst quencher].

e [Liquorice root] [was found] [in the recently opened tomb of King Tut].

f [Manuscripts of Buddhist origin dating from AD 360] [give] [us] [liquorice recipes for helping eye ailments, skin diseases, coughs and loss of hair].

g [In the middle ages] [it] [became] [very popular] [as a sweet medicine and general pick-me-up].

h [Historically] [some cultures] [considered] [liquorice] [a beautifying agent or an aphrodisiac].

i [Its soft eating and deliciously moreish characteristics] [have made] [our liquorice] [internationally famous].

j [After one taste] [you] [will understand] [liquorice's popularity for literally thousands of years].

Adapted from Darrell Lea Chocolate Shops (n.d.)

6 **Clause analysis**

For each pair of sentences, discuss the difference in structure between the two sentences using notions such as phrasal categories, functions, and clause patterns as appropriate.

a The take-away order appeared in a few moments.
The take-away order appeared a veritable feast.

b The casserole was bubbling.
The casserole was filling.

c The waiter brought in the chair.
The waiter sat in the chair.

d She turned up the burner.
She turned up the side street.

e The pizza delivery guy left some free garlic bread.
The pizza delivery guy left some time ago.

f We were waiting for an hour.
We were waiting for the pizza delivery guy.

g He has only made one souffle with the new kitchen whizz.
He has only made one souffle with macadamia nuts.

h They lived on junk food.
They lived on Melrose Street.

i The manager made the job applicant an offer.
The manager made the job applicant a chef.

j The new chef felt very proud.
The new chef felt a tap on the shoulder.

7 **Clause type**

Classify each of the following examples of advertising English with respect to clause type (declarative, imperative, interrogative, or exclamative) and suggest what clause meaning each would typically have.

- a Think once. Think twice. Think bike.
- b [Boing, Boing, Boing, Blleeaarrgghhhh!]
  Who ever heard of a kangaroo with travel sickness? (travel sickness tablets)
- c A Mars a day helps you work, rest and play.
- d How you can eat sunshine! (Kellogg's cereal)
- e Heineken refreshes the parts other beers cannot reach.
- f When it comes to the crunch, who can you turn to? (croutons)
- g Have a break, have a KitKat.
- h What's afoot in the world of fashion? (shoes)
- i Fosters, the Australian for lager.
- j Get strong. (Scrumpy Strong Cider)

8 Text analysis

The following dialogue is a segment from Kerry Greenwood and Jenny Pausacker's short story 'Afternoon Tea with Miss Marple' (1995:74–5), in which the detective is interviewing a murder suspect. The clauses are numbered and laid out with coordinating and subordinating conjunctions (which link them together) placed in columns on the left. (The way clauses are linked together and embedded in others is the focus of the next chapter.) For each of the italicised clauses, state whether it is declarative, interrogative, imperative, or exclamative. For each of the declaratives, identify the basic clause pattern, divide the clause into constituents, and give the function of each constituent (S, P, O, iO, dO, sC, oC, or A).

		Conjunction	*Clause*
a	i		*Come inside, Ma'am,*
	ii	and	*have a nice cup of tea*
	iii	while	*you tell me x*
	iv	x =	what you came here for.'
b	i		*Miss Marple sat in the cosy kitchen*
	ii	and	*[she] accepted a cup of strong tea.*
c	i		*Mrs. Crocker carried the kettle back to the stove*
	ii	and	[she] said over her shoulder:
	iii		'you don't want x
	iv	x =	to take any notice of our Joe.
d			*He's a good boy, really, in spite of his quarrelsome ways.*
e			He wouldn't hurt a fly.'
f	i		'I'm sure x
	ii	x =	he wouldn't,'
	iii		said Miss Marple gently.
g			*'Did he work for Mr. Blake-Harrington as well?'*
h			*The plump cook kept her back turned.*
i	i		'Only for a while,'
	ii		she said reluctantly.
j	i		*'Now, Ma'am, can I offer you some of my shortbread to go with your tea?*
k			*It's fresh out of the oven.'*
l			*Miss Marple shook her head.*
m	i		'Too kind of you—
	ii	but	that reminds me of my purpose in

	iii		coming here.
n	i		Your cream cakes—
	ii		*I've heard so much about them,*
	iii	and	my maid Gladys at home in St. Mary Mead has never been able
	iv		to bake a proper cream cake.
o			*Could I trouble you for the recipe?'*
p			*Mrs. Crocker's face cleared.*
q	i		She said:
	ii		'No trouble at all, Ma'am.
r			*I can copy it out for you right now.*
s			*Mr Blake-Harrington loved my cream cakes.*
t	i		*I left one for him on the very day*
	ii		*he died.*
u			A terrible tragedy, that was.
v	i		I can still hardly believe
	ii	that	*he's gone.*

9

'Conjunction Junction'

INTRODUCTION

In looking for sentences consisting of a basic clause, the cookery recipe seems a likely source as it represents a very formulaic type of instructional writing. It is usually presented in two sections: 'ingredients' and 'method'. Each item in the 'ingredients' section is a noun phrase, and the noun is frequently premodified (for example, *4 large eggs*). The 'method' section, on the other hand, consists of a series of sentences instructing how to make the dish. It seems reasonable to expect that the sentences would mostly be an imperative clause type and have a transitive clause pattern, given the semantic domain of cooking, with verbs such as *beat*, *blend*, *chop*, *cream*, *dice*, *grate*, *mix*, and *peel*. However, even when we looked at recipes in cookbooks for children (where we thought we would find the simplest of cookery writing), we found that the majority of sentences did not consist of a single basic clause. A typical example is the following passage, taken from the instructions for making the meringue for a pavlova in *The Grandma Poss Cookbook*:

1. Wash your hands and put on an apron.
2. Cut out a piece of brown paper large enough to cover the oven tray. Place a 20 cm cake tin face down on the paper and draw around it in pencil. Wipe over the circle on the paper with a pastry brush dipped in cooking oil.
3. Set the oven temperature at 120°C (250°F)

Omnibus books 1991:26

While all of these instructions are imperatives, only the third instruction consists of a single clause. All of the other sentences contain more than one clause. In the first instruction, for instance, there are two clauses—*wash your hands* and *put on an apron*—which are conjoined in a single sentence. In the last sentence of the second instruction set, the clause *dipped in cooking oil* modifies *brush*.

In this chapter, we explore how the basic clausal structures described in the previous chapter are joined in various ways to form **multi-clausal sentences**. We discuss the different relationships that exist between clauses, in particular the traditional distinction between coordination and subordination. The form and function of various subordinate clause types are considered, with a final section on clause combining and style.

SENTENCE TYPE

The types of sentences that we considered in the last chapter are what we call '**simple sentences**'. These consist of a single independent (or main) clause. What we are going to look at now are sentences consisting of a number of clauses. In such sentences, there are two kinds of relationships between the clauses: **coordination** (where the clauses are equal in status) and **subordination** (where a clause functions as part of another clause).

Compound sentences involve two or more coordinated clauses. Each coordinated clause is in angle brackets:

<Do not swill your soup> and <do not gobble your food>.
<Do not eat noisily> and <do not crunch bones in your teeth>.
<Do not throw bones to the dog> and <do not pick your teeth>.

Adapted from Anonymous, *Book of Etiquette* (China, c. 1000 BC), as quoted in Goode 1987:202

Complex sentences contain an independent clause and one or more subordinate clauses. Each subordinate clause is in square brackets.

He [who is master of his thirst] is master of his health.

Old French proverb, as quoted in Goode 1987:30

[To make good food go farther], eat less.

Australian Aboriginal proverb, as quoted in Goode 1987:18

The best way [to cook potatoes] is [to boil them in beer].

Francis Bacon (1561–1626) *Essays*, as quoted in Goode 1987:116

Compound-complex sentences are composed of two or more coordinated clauses and one or more subordinate clauses.

<Take fresh heart> and <never forget [that a warmed-up dinner is worth nothing at all]>.

Nicolas Boileau-Despréaux (1636–1711) *Le Lutrin*, as quoted in Goode 1987:196

Here the clause *that a warmed-up dinner is worth nothing at all* functions as the object in the clause *never forget that a warmed-up dinner is worth nothing at all*, which is coordinated with the clause *take fresh heart*.

In the following sections, we explore the relationships of coordination and subordination in more detail.

COORDINATION

Coordination implies the combination of equivalent structures; words, phrases, and clauses can be joined coordinately. Again, the coordinated elements are in angle brackets:

- words

<Promises> and <pie-crust> are made to be broken.

Jonathan Swift (1667–1745) *Polite Conversation*, as quoted in Goode 1987:87

- phrases

  Some of the best food I've eaten has come <from improvised kitchens> or <on picnics> where the only concession to the 20th century was an insect repellent.

  Parmenter 1993:53

- clauses

  <Drink provokes the desire>, but <it takes away the performance>.

  William Shakespeare, *Macbeth*, as quoted in Goode 1987:236

In the first example, two nouns (*promises* and *pie-crust*) are conjoined; in the second, it's two prepositional phrases (*from improvised kitchens* and *on picnics*); and in the third, it's two clauses (*drink provokes the desire* and *it takes away the performance*). The crucial thing is that the conjoined elements are equal in function and status.

As we noted in chapter 7, there are two types of common coordinators: coordinating conjunctions such as *and*, *but*, and *or* and correlating conjunctions such as *either...or, both...and*, and *not only...but also*. In the following directions from various recipes, the coordinators are in italics:

<Boil> *or* <steam> the rice.
<Carefully>, *but* <quickly>, turn over <plate> *and* <basin> so that the pudding may be released onto the serving plate.
Add *either* <a sprig of thyme> *or* <dried thyme>.
Sprinkle with *both* <the almonds> *and* <a little freshly grated nutmeg>.

With the coordinators *and* and *or*, more than two elements can be conjoined. In such cases, the coordinating conjunction normally only occurs before the last element.

Happiness is <a good bank account>, <a good cook> *and* <a good digestion>.

Jean Jacques Rousseau (1712–78), as quoted in Goode 1987:13

If you read this quote out loud, you will probably use a rising tone on all the conjoined elements except the last, which has a falling tone. In writing, a comma is usually used to separate all the conjoined elements except the last two, where in common practice, the comma is optional.

While the primary function of any coordinator is conjoining elements, the coordinator can actually express a variety of meaning relationships between the conjoined elements. For example, *and* can express a result.

I scoured the countryside *and* (as a result) found an assortment of wild mushrooms for the ragout.

It can order a sequence of events.

Roughly chop macadamia nuts *and* (then) lightly brown in pan.

It can encode a reciprocal relationship.

The waiter *and* bartender were hopelessly in love.

And, it can convey a sense of intensification

The dough rose higher *and* higher.

or continuous action

We stirred *and* stirred the sauce.

There are also several idiomatic uses of *and* that are quite common in informal speech (and often criticised as 'bad English'). In

They'll try *and*/to make it for dinner tonight.

and is functioning like the infinitive particle *to* (and has a sense of purpose), whereas in

This cake is *well and truly* done.
The icing was *nice and* sweet.

well and truly and *nice and* are functioning like the intensifying adverbs *really* and *very*. Finally, there is the curious use of *and* in expressions such as

There are cooks *and* (then there are) cooks.

meaning that some cooks are better or worse than others.

SUBORDINATION

Subordination implies the combination of clauses that are syntactically non-equivalent. In the opening sentence in the children's rhyme

There was an old woman who swallowed a fly.

the clause *who swallowed a fly* is called a **'subordinate'** (or **'dependent') clause**, and the clause *there was an old woman who swallowed a fly* is a **superordinate clause**. In this example, the superordinate clause is also a main or independent clause, as it can stand by itself. A subordinate clause is always part of another clause (while with coordination, we have joined clauses that are of equal status).

It is also possible for a clause to be subordinated within another clause, which is itself a subordinate clause. In the next extension of the rhyme

There was an old woman who swallowed a spider to catch the fly.

The clause *to catch a fly* is a subordinate clause in the superordinate clause *who swallowed a spider to catch the fly*, which is a subordinate clause of the superordinate or main clause *there was an old woman who swallowed a spider to catch the fly*. We can also use brackets as follows to show this structure:

There was an old woman [who swallowed a spider [to catch the fly]].

It's the ability to keep creating a longer and longer sentence by adding a new subordinate clause that underlies the fun of this type of rhyme. A rhyme such as this also nicely illustrates the creative aspects of language: that we can create a novel sentence by simply embedding a new clause within an existing sentence.

Typically, subordinate clauses are structurally different from main clauses. For example, they may be introduced by subordinators such as *that*, *if*, *whether*, *after*, *because*, *until*, *while*, and *although*, or by relative pronouns such as *who*, *whom*, *whose*, *what*, and *which*. They may have a base form of the verb. And the subject may be omitted, as in the subordinate clause *to catch the fly* (as compared with the main clause equivalent, *a spider caught the fly*), or the pronoun subject may have a non-subjective form, as in the subordinate clause in *I saw [her swallow a fly]*.

Not all subordinate clauses, however, are structurally different from a main clause, as the following illustrates:

I believe [she swallowed a fly].

Here the subordinate clause *she swallowed a fly* is identical in form to a main clause. In the example, it is a subordinate clause, in that it is functioning as the object within the superordinate clause.

In the rest of this section we survey the different types of subordinate clauses and the functions they serve.

Finite versus non-finite clauses

Virtually all main clauses are **finite**. As the term *finite* implies, this means they are limited by the person and number of the subject, and by tense. In contrast, subordinate clauses may be finite or **non-finite** (that is, not limited in this way). There are two criteria for distinguishing finite and non-finite subordinate clauses: verb form and form of a pronominal subject. In non-finite clauses, the verb form is a base form, or a present or past participle, whereas in finite clauses, it is usually present or past tense, but it can also be a base form. Consider the following:

Non-finite clause	*Verb form*
This is the best cheese *for her to try.*	base
They insisted on *him/his baking the bread longer.*	present participle
Bread is good *when eaten with cheese.*	past participle
Finite clause	
This is the cheese *that she wants.*	present tense
This is the cheese *that she wanted.*	past tense
They insisted *(that) he bake the bread longer.*	base

Some of you may find that the last sentence sounds very formal, and you may prefer *They insisted (that) he* ***bakes*** *the bread longer.* Others of you may find that it's this version that sounds odd. Variation of this sort is typical when you get a roomful of people from different backgrounds and may also be indicative of a change under way in the language.

No matter which version you prefer, the subordinate clause in this example is a finite clause. This becomes clear when we look at the second criterion, which is the form of the subject: if the subject of the subordinate clause is a pronoun that inflects for case, then it will be in the subjective case in a finite clause. Using this criterion we can distinguish the finite subordinate clause in the last example (where the subject *he* is subjective in form) from the non-finite subordinate clauses in the first and second examples (where the subjects *her* and *him/his*, respectively, are in a non-subjective form). The relationship between type of subordinate clause, verb form, and subject pronoun form is summarised in Table 9.1.

Table 9.1 Finite and non-finite subordinate clauses

Subordinate clause	*Verb form*	*Subject pronoun form*
finite	past or present tense base form	subjective case
non-finite	base form present or past participle	non-subjective case

Let's now focus on the different kinds of finite subordinate clauses.

Types of finite subordinate clauses

Traditionally, finite subordinate clauses were classified as 'nominal', 'adjectival', or 'adverbial' clauses, based on similarities between their function in the superordinate clause and the corresponding phrasal type that typically fulfils that function. In

Acorns were good *until bread was found.*

Francis Bacon (1561–1626) *Colours of Good and Evil*, as quoted in Goode 1987:68

the subordinate clause *until bread was found* functions as an adverbial in the superordinate clause, and this is a function often filled by adverbs phrases (AdvPs):

Acorns were good *then.*

To maintain the distinction between form and function that we made in the last chapter, we will follow several modern grammars of English and classify finite subordinate clauses according to their structural similarities with main clauses. In this approach we can recognise three types of finite subordinate clauses: **relative clauses**, **comparative clauses**, and **content clauses**.

Relative clauses

Relative clauses are typically constituents in a noun phrase. The term 'relative' highlights that the clause refers to the part of the noun phrase that precedes it, thus 'relating' the subordinate clause to the noun (or pronoun) that heads the noun phrase. A relative clause is 'introduced' either by a relative pronoun such as *who*, *whom*, *which*, *whose*, *where*, *when*, or *why* (and is sometimes preceded by a preposition), by the complementiser *that*, or by nothing at all. In the following sentences that we collected (or overheard) at a regional cheese fair, the relative clauses are in italics:

Here is the cheese-maker *who suggested the deep-fried Camembert with cranberry sauce.*
Show me the stall *where you found the Swiss cheese.*
Cheddar cheese is a hard cheese *that goes well with a hearty lunch.*
This stall sells the blue cheese *you like in salads.*

We can analyse a sentence with a relative clause as being derived from two sentences:

The cheese *that they gave us* will be fully ripened in about a week.
The cheese [they gave us the cheese] will be fully ripened in about a week.

In forming a relative clause, the 'introducing' word is often said to 'replace' the noun phrase in the relative clause that is identical to the one in the superordinate clause. In the example above, *that* is said to replace *the cheese* in the relative clause.

The sort of relative pronoun you use depends on the function of the replaced noun phrase in the relative clause and, in some cases, whether or not the reference is to a person. For example, when the reference is to a person (and sometimes other animates) *who* replaces a subject noun phrase and *who(m)* replaces an object noun phrase or the object of a preposition:

The person *who* is judging the dessert cheese platters has just arrived.
The person *who(m)* I will introduce you to has tried many of your recipes.

Whom is a remnant of the once much more extensive case system in English, which will be discussed in chapter 11. However, over the last two centuries, the overall use of *whom* has declined, particularly in speech and informal writing, and its decline is also more extensive in OZ, NZ, and American English than in British English. According to traditional grammar, *whom* should appear whenever it is the object of a verb or a preposition. Yet in common usage, *who* seems to be preferred unless it comes directly after a preposition.

They want someone *who* they can have confidence in.
They want someone in *whom* they can have confidence.

Which is used to replace a noun phrase that does not refer to a person and that is a subject, an object, or the object of a preposition in the relative clause.

This cheese has the nutty aftertaste *which* is characteristic of the best Brie cheeses.
Here are some of the many mouth-watering ways in *which* it can be served.

In the first example, *which* functions as the subject of the relative clause and, in the second, as the object of the preposition *in*.

As we have seen in some of the examples above, when the relative pronoun is replacing a noun phrase that is an object of a preposition, it is possible to include the preposition at the front of the relative clause (with the relative pronoun) or to 'strand' it at the end. Consider the stylistic differences between the first and second sentence in the pair below. As we discuss more fully in chapter 10, the choice between grammatical constructions is often a matter of matching the expression to the context of use.

I liked the cheese *to which* they awarded first prize. (formal)
I liked the cheese *which* they awarded first prize *to*. (informal)

Whose occurs when the replaced noun phrase is a possessive phrase.

We have met the cheese-maker *whose* cheeses won so many awards.
We have been to the dairy *whose* cheeses won so many awards.

As we discussed in chapter 7, some traditional grammars suggest that *whose* can only refer to animate noun phrases.

Where, *when*, and *why* 'replace' adverbs of place, time, and reason, respectively:

I liked the stall *where* you found the Swiss cheese.
I remember a time *when* you wouldn't touch that kind of cheese.

The word *that* was categorised as a subordinator in chapter 7, but it is a different kind from the others. It is usually called a 'complementiser' and can appear in relative clauses as well as in other contexts. Its function is to signal that what follows is a subordinate clause (for example, *We suspect that the dog ate all the donuts*). The idea of a complement is that it 'completes' another word or phrase; that is, a subordinate clause such as *that the dog ate all the donuts* may be thought of as completing the transitive verb *suspect*. In relative clauses, *that* can appear in many contexts as an alternative to one of the relative pronouns, as long as it is not functioning as a possessive noun phrase or the object of a preposition that hasn't been stranded. Let's revisit some of the examples from above:

They want someone *that/who* they can have confidence in.
This stall sells the blue cheese *that/which* you like in salads.
I liked the cheese *that/which* they awarded first prize to.
Tell me the reason *that/why* you liked it so much.

The choice of *that* instead of a relative pronoun seems to be largely a matter of individual style and the relative informality of the situation. We will consider the special case of *that* and *which* on p. 210.

It is also possible to omit *that* or a relative pronoun. Try omitting them from the examples above, and you should find that it is possible to delete the relative pronoun or complementiser, except when it functions as a subject. Although some dialects of English do allow sentences like the following:

There's a bloke at the door wants to buy your lemon zester.

To summarise, let's return to an earlier sentence and represent it as deriving from two sentences:

The person has tried many of your recipes.
I will introduce you to the person.

We can now see that there are five possible ways of producing a relative clause:

1 The person *to whom I will introduce* you has tried many of your recipes.
2 The person *whom I will introduce you to* has tried many of your recipes.
3 The person *who I will introduce you to* has tried many of your recipes.
4 The person *that I will introduce you to* has tried many of your recipes.
5 The person *I will introduce you to* has tried many of your recipes.

To complete our survey of relative clauses, let's consider the distinction English makes between restrictive or non-restrictive relative clauses. So far we have only been considering the more common of the two: restrictive relative clauses. This type contains information that forms an integral part of the message; it is a way of identifying the head of the noun phrase by restricting its denotation.

People who eat these things must be crazy.

Here not all people are said to be crazy—just those who would actually eat the items being discussed.

Non-restrictive relatives, on the other hand, provide extra information—information that is not necessary for the identification of the head of the noun phrase (in the next example, this is *Iron Goddess*).

> Our favourite tea is Iron Goddess, which has a rather ferrous flavour and is very strong.
>
> Greenwood & Pausacker 1995:32

Non-restrictive relatives are separated from the rest of the sentence by pauses in speech and, generally, by punctuation in writing.

The distinction between restrictive and non-restrictive relative clauses is clearly seen when you compare the two sets of examples below. In each pair, the first relative clause is non-restrictive, and the second is restrictive.

> Pavlovas, which are made of meringue, are fiendishly difficult to cook.
> ?Pavlovas which are made of meringue are fiendishly difficult to cook.

> Wine critics, who make pretentious claims, are justly snubbed.
> Wine critics who make pretentious claims are justly snubbed.

In the case of pavs, the restrictive relative clause is odd because it suggests that not all are made of meringue (some may be made of jelly, for example). In the second pair, on the other hand, the non-restrictive relative clause says that all wine critics are justly snubbed. Of course, by definition, pavalovas are made of meringue, and not all wine critics make pretentious claims.

Returning to the case of *that* versus *which*, many style guides and traditional grammars recommend using *that* for restrictive clauses and *which* (following a comma) for non-restrictive relative clauses. According to this recommendation, a 'that clause', such as

> I chose the first item on the desert menu that had chocolate in it.

conveys information that is essential to the meaning of the main clause (as this sentence demonstrates), whereas a '*which* clause', such as in

> I chose the first item on the desert menu, which had chocolate in it.

is used to convey additional information, which may be helpful but is not essential. Other than in publications with a house style, however, the choice of *that* or *which* is like that of the other relative pronouns: a matter of personal style and the relative informality of the situation.

Comparative clauses

A comparative clause is the type of subordinate clause that expresses the 'standard of comparison' in sentences where a comparison is made between two propositions. The comparative clause is italicised in each of the following examples.

> It tastes much better *than it looks.*
> This recipe isn't as hard *as that gourmet version (is).*
> Everything is functioning *as it should be.*

In the first example, 'how it tastes' is the proposition in the superordinate clause, and it is compared with 'how it looks', the proposition in the subordinate clause. In the second example, the degree of difficulty of a particular recipe is compared with how hard the gourmet version is, and in the third, the actual state of affairs is compared to how it should be.

Syntactically, a comparative clause is 'introduced' by *than* or *as*, and is often paired with a phrase in the main clause, such as the adverb phrase *much better* in the first example and the prepositional phrase *as hard* in the second. Compared with main clauses, comparative clauses are structurally incomplete: in each of our examples the comparative clause lacks a predicate complement.

Content clauses

Content clauses lack the distinctive structural properties of relative and comparative clauses. They are closest to main clauses, with the primary difference being that many content clauses are 'introduced' by a subordinator such as *after, although, as, because, if, that, until, while, whether*, although some content clauses are introduced by nothing at all and thus look similar to main clauses. In the following sentences, adapted from the collection of short stories in Kerry Greenwood and Jenny Pausacker's *Recipes for Crime* (1995:35, 124, 5, 18, 105, 13, 33), the subordinators are in bold and the content clauses are italicised.

> Their eyes glowed ***as** they described the treasure.*
> I came ***because** I suspected something.*
> ***Since** strychnine's effects are so instant,* it's a tricky poison.
> I was told ***that** you had amazing powers.*
> I think *someone moved the rock recently.*

Content clauses can be classified in terms of the four clause types found with main clauses: declarative, interrogative, exclamative, and imperative. In the examples above, the subordinate clauses are all declarative content clauses. Other than the possible presence of a subordinator, the structure of declarative content clauses is similar to that of declarative main clauses.

Continuing with our food and crime examples, let's consider the other clause types. The major differences between an interrogative content clause and an interrogative main clause are that, in a subordinate clause, a yes/no interrogative is introduced by the subordinator *whether* or *if*, and the subject does not follow the auxiliary.

> I was wondering ***whether/If** you could face breakfast now.*
> Could you face breakfast now?

Similarly, in a wh- interrogative content clause, the subject does not follow the auxiliary.

> He asked her *what she would like to eat.*
> What would she like to eat?

With exclamatives, the main and subordinate clause versions are normally the same.

> She noticed *how innocent the heir of the house looked.*
> How innocent the heir of the house looked.

The subordinate counterpart of an imperative main clause is called a '**jussive**'. The verb in a jussive content clause is in a base form, and the subject, if it is a pronoun, is in a subjective form.

> It is critical *that we be quiet.*
> The detective insisted *(that) they be questioned.*

Types of non-finite subordinate clauses

Non-finite subordinate clauses can be classified along two dimensions: according to the kind of verb phrase they contain and to whether or not there is an overt subject. Looking at the first dimension, we find that non-finite subordinate clauses can have either a base (that is infinitival) verb form, with or without the infinitival marker *to*, or a present participle or past participle verb form. Consider the following sentences, adapted from a discussion of the origins of the pavlova in G. A. Wilkes's *Exploring Australian English* (1993:64). The subordinate clauses are in italics:

- *to*-infinitival

> The pavlova appears *to have been invented independently in Australia and New Zealand.*
> New Zealand was first *to invent this dessert recipe.*
> *To make the 1927 New Zealand recipe,* you need a jelly mould.

- bare-infinitival

> Later New Zealand recipe books helped *establish the version of pavlova with cream and fruit.*

- present participial

> In 1926–27 and 1929, the ballerina Anna Pavlova toured Australia and New Zealand *leaving very impressed audiences.*
> *Garnishing the Australian pavlova with Kiwi fruit* is not a gesture of reconciliation.

- past participial

> Independently in 1935 at the Esplanade Hotel in Perth, Herbert Sachse produced a meringue dessert *named a pavlova.*
> *Served with cream and passion fruit and strawberries,* this has become a famous Australian delicacy.

Along the second dimension we find that some non-finite subordinate clauses contain an overt subject while others do not. All of the examples above are clearly subjectless. Returning to the discussion of pavlovas, in each of the following examples the non-finite subordinate clause is in italics and its subject is in bold:

> On April 22, 1981 the Australian media captured ***Al Grassby** launching a dry pavlova mix.*
> Some people remember ***his/him** declaring it National Pavlova Day.*
> He intended *for **the new product** to be a 'foolproof 50-minute pavlova'.*

Verbless clauses

In the last chapter, we briefly mentioned that there are various types of minor clauses, which include expressions such as

The hotter, the better
Two coffees, please
Down with the government!

What is common to each of these examples is the lack of a verb. Not surprisingly, such clauses are called '**verbless clauses**', and we find them in the class of subordinate clauses as well as main clauses. Consider the following subordinate verbless clauses, which are in italics:

At the height of the famine thousands were starving, *many of them babies.*
The displaced families walked for miles, *the younger children on their parents' backs.*

The relation between *many of them* and *babies*, and *the younger children* and *on their parents' backs*, is like that in the corresponding main clauses *Many of them were babies* and *The younger children were on their parents' backs*. Because we can generally infer the verb *be* in the corresponding main clause, these subordinate constructions are considered to be clauses, even though there is no verb present.

Functions of subordinate clauses

So far in our discussion of subordinate clauses, we have concentrated on the form of subordinate clauses and compared their structural similarities with main clauses. Turning now to the function of subordinate clauses in the superordinate clause, we find that subordinate clauses can replace the whole of any clause element except the verb. The grammatical function of a subordinate clause can always be tested using the technique of substitution: by replacing the clause with a simpler unit whose function is known (such as a pronoun, adjective, adverb, noun phrase, or prepositional phrase), the function of the replaced clause can be determined. Consider the following example, where the subordinate clause is in italics:

They wouldn't shout a round *if a shark bit.*
They wouldn't shout a round *ever.*

The adverbial function of the subordinate clause can be determined by replacing the clause with an adverb of time, such as *ever*. Here are examples of clauses as subject, object, predicative complement, and adverbial:

- clause as subject

  Naming it Tasmanian devil food cake was a clever idea.
  That was a clever idea.

- clause as object

  He doesn't enjoy *drinking with the flies.*
  He doesn't enjoy *it.*

- clause as predicative complement

  The tucker is *what they like the most.*
  The tucker is *beaut.*

- clause as adverbial

  The humble snagger comes into its own *when the barbie is lit.*
  The humble snagger comes into its own *then.*

We also find that subordinate clauses can function as modifiers in noun phrases, adjective phrases, and adverb phrases. Here they generally follow the head of the phrase. Once again, it's possible to use the substitution technique to replace the clause with a phrase, or sometimes even a single word, to help determine the function of the clause. In each of the following examples, the relevant phrase is bracketed, the head of the phrase is in bold, and the modifier is in italics:

- clause as modifier of noun within noun phrase

  A floater is [a **meat pie** *that is submerged in a sea of pea soup*].
  A floater is [a **meat pie** *extraordinaire*].

- clause as modifier of adjective within adjective phrase

  The kids were [**anxious** *to bite into their cut lunches*].
  The kids were [**anxious** *for lunch*].

- clause as modifier of adverb within adverb phrase

  They left [too **early** *to share some coldies*].
  They left [too **early** *for a beer*].

From these sets of examples, we see, then, that subordinate clauses share the same range of functions as phrases.

CLAUSE COMBINING AND STYLE

We can choose to write and speak in single-clause sentences or in highly complex combinations of clauses within a single sentence. There is no limit to the potential length or complexity of a sentence; you can always coordinate or subordinate another phrase or clause. The way we vary our use of English from one situation to another is part of what we identify as a person's 'style'. That is, different situations call for different ways of expressing the same thing, and how an individual speaker or writer chooses to express the relationships between words, phrases, and clauses make up part of that person's style. In this section, we're going to pre-empt some of the discussion in chapter 10, because we want to focus on how an understanding of clause structure and clause combining can be used in analysing the different styles of two English texts.

Consider first the following coffee ad, which illustrates several distinctive features of the style of language used in advertising:

This cup of coffee isn't for everyone.
It's for everyone who enjoys the aroma of coffee as much as the taste.
For you we offer the latest refinement to [brand name].
Our new enriched aroma has just been released.
We call it Enriched Aroma.
To us, it's a new way of retaining the airborne coffee scents within the coffee itself.
To you, it means a more pure, rich aroma in your cup.
Aroma you can literally breathe in.
And the taste?
It's the taste of the world's finest arabica beans, sourced from the highland plantations of Kenya, Brazil and Colombia.
The beans are blended and roasted by our master coffee makers in Switzerland, then freeze-dried to capture the original flavours.
And now, with our enriched aroma, the taste is even richer too.
Because we're always searching for ways to improve not only our coffee, but the whole coffee experience.

Advertisement in *Vogue Entertaining*, June/July 1995:9

The aim of the ad is to gain and maintain group loyalty to a certain brand of coffee by producing a particular effect on the reader. The ad appeals to the reader's emotions and seeks to establish a link between the newly improved brand of coffee and the sensory experiences of aroma and taste that make up an enjoyable and successful 'coffee experience'. While many aspects of the language contribute to the emotive power of advertising language (such as discourse strategies, which are discussed in chapter 10), let's focus here on some of the syntactic factors used to achieve the intended persuasive power of the ad.

If we look at the type of clauses that are used, for instance, we see that, apart from one question, the clauses are declarative-like statements. This gives an air of authority to the claims of the ad. Likewise, by blurring the distinctions that are usually found between speech and writing, the reader is given the feeling that those in the know are actually talking to them, suggesting and advising them of the merits of the brand of coffee, thus giving a spoken authority to the ad.

One way in which the spoken sense of the ad is created is by breaking the standard written conventions for structuring clauses into sentences. For example, mirroring spoken English, *and* introduces two of the sentences in the ad: *And the taste?* and *And now, with our enriched aroma, the taste is even richer too.* Similarly, commas and full stops are used to suggest the pauses of spoken English. To see this, try reading the ad out loud and mark where you tend to pause. Then note how the punctuation tends to correlate with the pauses. Using punctuation in this way leads to some clauses that are characteristically subordinate clauses being marked as sentences. The last sentence, for instance, consists solely of a finite subordinate clause, introduced by the subordinator *because*. The purpose of breaking the written conventions of sentence structure and punctuation is to make the reader hear the sound of spoken English.

Our second text is drawn from Laura Esquivel's *Like Water for Chocolate* (1993). This novel, which is set in Mexico, relates the bizarre history of the all-female De La Garza family. A recipe is used at the beginning of each chapter to reveal the chain of events experienced by the youngest daughter, who narrates most of the story. The passage given here is the opening paragraph of the book.

> Take care to chop the onion fine. To keep from crying when you chop it (which is so annoying!), I suggest you place a little bit on your head. The trouble with crying over an onion is that once the chopping gets you started and the tears begin to well up, the next thing you know you just can't stop. I don't know whether that's ever happened to you, but I have to confess it's happened to me, many times. Mama used to say it was because I was especially sensitive to onions, like my great-aunt, Tita.

The next paragraph tells how the violent tears from onion chopping resulted in the premature birth of Tita, the story's narrator.

By using square brackets for the subordinate clauses, angle brackets for the conjoined clauses, and bold for the coordinators, we can recast some of the sentences from the text to more clearly see the type of sentences that the author has used:

> *Take care [to chop the onion fine].*
> (complex sentence with main clause containing a subordinate clause)
> *[To keep from crying when you chop it (which is so annoying!)], I suggest [you place a little bit on your head].*
> (complex sentence with main clause containing two subordinate clauses)
> *<I don't know [whether that's ever happened to you]>,* **but** *<I have to confess [it's happened to me, many times]>.*
> (compound-complex sentence, with main clause consisting of two coordinated clauses, and with each of the coordinated clauses containing a subordinated clause)

Apart from the first sentence, the grammatical structure of the sentences is relatively complex. For instance, in the second sentence, the first subordinate clause, *to keep from crying when you chop it which is so annoying*, contains the subordinate clause *crying when you chop it which is so annoying*, which itself contains two subordinate clauses: *when you chop it* and *which is so annoying*.

Let's look now at how the clause and sentence structure of this opening paragraph contribute to its function of introducing Tita, the main character of the novel. We see that the paragraph begins with a relatively simple imperative, which introduces the topic of onions and directs the reader to finely chop them. From this we move to a declarative main clause, which gives advice on how to avoid crying when chopping onions, and then into the final three declaratives, which are statements. It is in these last three statements that the links are made between the person issuing the directive in the first sentence, the tears from chopping onions, and the introduction of the novel's primary narrator. The multiple layers of the onion and the multiple layers of the novel are nicely mirrored in the multiple layers of the sentence structure.

Our discussion of these two texts briefly highlights how important syntactic structure is in understanding different spoken and written styles of English. A knowledge of clauses and clause combining not only aids us in the study of style, but also makes us more aware of the choices that are available to us in our own speech and writing. We will explore this more fully in the next chapter.

POINTS TO REMEMBER

- A simple sentence contains a single independent clause; a compound sentence contains two or more coordinated clauses; a complex sentence contains an independent clause and one or more subordinate clauses; and a compound-complex sentence contains two or more coordinated clauses and one or more subordinate clauses.
- Coordination involves the combination of two or more elements—words, phrases, or clauses—that are equal in function and status.
- There are two types of coordinators—coordinating conjunctions and correlating conjunctions—of which only *and* and *or* are able to conjoin more than two elements. In addition to the primary function of conjoining elements, a coordinator can express a variety of meaning relationships between the conjoined elements.
- Subordination involves the combination of clauses that are syntactically non-equivalent. A subordinate clause is part of another clause: the superordinate clause.
- A subordinate clause can typically be identified by one or more of the following features: it is introduced by a subordinator or relative pronoun; it has no overt subject, or the pronoun subject has a non-subjective form; and/or it contains a non-finite verb. In some cases, though, a subordinate clause is identical in form to a main clause.
- While main clauses are generally finite, subordinate clauses may be finite or non-finite. The verb form and the form of a pronominal subject are the two criteria for distinguishing between finite and non-finite subordinate clauses.
- On the basis of their structural similarities with main clauses, finite subordinate clauses can be divided into relative clauses, comparative clauses, and content clauses.
- A relative clause is 'introduced' by a relative pronoun or the complementiser *that*, the choice of which depends on the function of the 'replaced' noun phrase in the relative clause and, with some relative pronouns, on whether or not the reference is to a person. Except when it functions as the subject of the relative clause, the relative pronoun or complementiser can be omitted.
- English distinguishes two types of relative clauses: restrictive relative clauses, which provide necessary information for identifying the noun phrase heading the relative clause, and non-restrictive relative clauses, which provide extra information about the head.
- A comparative clause is 'introduced' by *than* or *as* and expresses the 'standard of comparison' in sentences where a comparison is made between two propositions.
- Content clauses are 'introduced' either by a subordinator or nothing at all, and can be classified in terms of the four clause types found with main clauses: declarative, interrogative, exclamative, and imperative.
- Non-finite subordinate clauses are divided into four classes according to the kind of verb phrase they contain: *to*-infinitival, bare-infinitival, present participial, and past participial. In addition, some non-finite subordinate clauses have an overt subject, whereas others do not.
- One type of minor clause that can occur as a main clause or as a subordinate clause is the verbless clause. As the name indicates, such clauses lack a verb.
- Subordinate clauses share the same range of functions as phrases in that a subordinate clause can function either as a subject, object, predicative complement, or

adverbial within a superordinate clause or as a modifier in a noun phrase, adjective phrase, or adverb phrase.

- One aspect of exploring different styles of speaking and writing is considering the different ways people choose to combine clauses, ranging from single-clause sentences to highly complex combinations of clauses within a single sentence.

EXERCISES

1 Sentence type

Label each of the following sentences as 'simple', 'compound', 'complex', or 'compound-complex'.

> The secret of pavlova is in the cooking. The oven must not be too hot and it must not be too low. The dessert should end up crunchy on the outside without it being too browned. Beginners may need to practise a couple of times to master a good pav. You may find that you need to adjust your oven temperature as every oven is different.
>
> Adapted from Gaté 1996

2 Coordination

The following homilies are all quoted in *Early Settlers' Household Lore*, compiled by Loma Pescott (1994). Identify the conjoined elements and the coordinators in the following sentences. Indicate whether the conjoined elements are words, phrases, or clauses. If they are words, give their part of speech, and if they are phrases, give their category. Finally, indicate whether the coordinators are coordinating conjunctions or correlating conjunctions.

a You cannot both eat your scone and have it (anonymous).
b A place for everything and everything in its place (anonymous).
c Candy is dandy, but liquor is quicker (Ogden Nash).
d Eat, drink, and love; the rest's not worth a fillip (Lord Byron).
e Look after the pence and the pounds will look after themselves (anonymous).
f Eat at pleasure, but drink by measure (anonymous).
g Plain living is best for bodily health and mental comfort (anonymous).
h A good dinner sharpens wit and softens the heart (anonymous).
i Man is not what he eats, but what he digests (anonymous).
j Sit down and feed, and welcome to our table (William Shakespeare).

3 Relative clauses

Create relative clauses for each of the following sets of sentences by inserting the second sentence into the first as a relative clause. If there are any additional sentences, also insert them as relative clauses in the appropriate places. For each relative clause, indicate whether it is restrictive or non-restrictive (or ambiguously either), and whether or not it is possible to delete the relative pronoun or complementiser.

a The RAH (Real Aussie Hamburger) peaked around 1950.
The RAH (Real Aussie Hamburger) is the quintessence of Australian restaurant food.

b The RAH temple was Hamburger Max's.
Hamburger Max's was at St Kilda Junction in Melbourne.

c The bun was toasted.
The bun must be absolutely stale.

d Everything was cooked together on the same flat grill.
This contributed to the flavour.

e Lettuce, tomato, onions, and tomato sauce were piled on the toasted bun.
The lettuce was turning yellow.
The tomato was grilled to sogginess.
The onions were burned black.
The tomato sauce was always White Crow.

f The hamburger itself was a ball of meat.
The ball of meat was removed from the refrigerator with hands.
The hands' honesty was attested by a layer of black under the nails.

g The whole needed a crocodile's mouth to devour.
The whole was assembled with soggy, tinned beetroot.

h The RAH was memorable to eat, particularly in the area of the tie.
The RAH didn't drip so much as run.

Adapted from Peter Smark, 'Burger Bliss' (1985), as quoted in Goode 1987:207

4 Classification of non-finite subordinate clauses

The distinctive style of newspaper headlines is characterised by the widespread use of non-finite verb forms. The following headlines are taken from the 9 September 1996 editions of two New Zealand papers, the *Press* and the *Dominion.* Identify the non-finite subordinate clauses and classify them as *to*-infinitival, bare-infinitival, present participial, or past participial. Say whether or not each subordinate clause contains an overt subject.

a Many Christchurch voters fail to enrol
b Christchurch call to get tough with young offenders
c Otaki-Maori abandons races after inspecting course
d Kiwis given chance to fly over Antarctica
e Christchurch team to play for Bury
f Man jailed for knifing two Waikuku women
g Campbell keen to erase Paraparaumu memories
h Marist eager to bury bogey of Paremata
i Kiwi remains steady after ignoring Treasury update
j Candidate for NZ First quits, blaming Laws

5 Non-basic clauses

In this chapter, we said that main clauses are generally finite. However, newspaper headlines frequently provide exceptions to this observation, as is illustrated in the following examples taken from the 9 September 1996 edition of the *New Zealand Herald.* Recast each of the following headlines with a finite main clause and, using appropriate grammatical terminology, describe the features that make each of them a non-basic clause (that is, something other than a finite main clause).

- a Warm ocean to blame for big wet
- b Huge order for newly branded wool
- c Beef grading set to change
- d Wharf to get $1m revamp
- e The vote chase in the marginal seats
- f Jobless rise a setback as by election looms
- g Patients to go south for surgery
- h Backroom boys to fore
- i City planning small-minded
- j Optimistic figures boost for all parties' promises

6 Variation in English dialects

The following sentences illustrate variations in the usage of relative pronouns and subordinators across a number of dialects of English. All of these examples are considered to differ from 'Standard English'. Rewrite each of these sentences in 'Standard English' and describe, in grammatical terms, the differences between these dialect examples and 'Standard English' in their use of the relative pronoun or subordinator.

- a You could communicate with like a typewriter thing what does the Morse code (as quoted in Freeborn 1995:224).
- b There were a woman there as lives nearby in them there old houses (as quoted in Freeborn 1995:813).
- c We'll have trouble getting there without we stop for petrol (as quoted in Peters 1995:813).
- d The man what came to the door looked upset (as quoted in Peters 1995:805).
- e They asked me whom I thought was most suitable for the job (as quoted in Peters 1995:810).
- f So you come late, you don't know where to park (as quoted in Platt et al. 1984:126).
- g My father could hold his own with anyone down the mines at any job, which it was a pleasure when I followed to think of a history like that (as quoted in Freeborn 1995:224).
- h No, I don't think so my English is that good (as quoted in Platt et al. 1984:126).
- i They wanted it more than what I did (as quoted in Peters 1995:745).

Some grammars of English would classify the following sentence as non-standard. What is your opinion, and why? How would you analyse it in terms of the subordinate clauses we've discussed in this chapter?

- j She mustn't suffer the way her mother did (as quoted in Peters 1995:801).

7 Text analysis (1)

Identify the clauses in the following quotes by using square brackets for the subordinate clauses and angle brackets for the conjoined clauses. Also identify all the coordinators and subordinators. Then classify the form and function of all the subordinate clauses as fully as possible. Finally, determine whether each sentence is simple, compound, complex, or compound-complex.

- **a** Things sweet to taste prove in digestion sour (William Shakespeare, *Richard II*, as quoted in Goode 1987:15).
- **b** Early to bed and early to rise makes a man healthy, wealthy and wise (Benjamin Franklin, as quoted in Pescott 1994:115).
- **c** Never set an empty pot on the fire, hoping your neighbour will come and fill it (anonymous, as quoted in Pescott 1994:190).
- **d** If you carry out a blindfold test, you'll find that the beer snob is just as much a galah as the wine snob (Cyril Pearl, *Beer, Glorious Beer*, 1969, as quoted in Goode 1987:32).
- **e** Australian beer is one of Australia's national treasures. When the managing director of Fosters compared its taste to being kissed on the tongue by an angel, he was erring on the side of conservatism (Gareth Powell, 'There Are No Good Pubs in Australia', 1985, as quoted in Goode 1987:34).
- **f** To the table or to bed you must come when you are bid (Esquivel 1993:1).
- **g** Contrary to popular sentiment, I believe aluminium pans are less harmful to humans than an under-arm deodorant (Parmenter 1993:53).

8 Text analysis (2)

The following excerpt is from the preface to Greenwood and Pausacker's *Recipes for Crime* (1995:ix–x). Identify the conjoined elements and the coordinators in the following sentences, and indicate whether the conjoined elements are words, phrases, or clauses. Comment on the use of coordination and subordination, and on the sentence structure in this passage.

> But above all, fictional detectives are connoisseurs of food. It is as impossible to imagine Lord Peter Wimsey without his perfectly cooked *boeuf bourguignonne*, followed by austere black coffee served by his devoted manservant Bunter, as it is to imagine Hercule Poirot without his tisanes and *sirop de cassis*, Miss Marple without her cucumber sandwiches, or Inspector Maigret without the splendid cuisine of Madame Maigret to look forward to at the end of a day's work...
>
> Mind you, some detectives are equally notable for their total lack of interest in food. The old-style private eyes got by on a slug of rye and a knuckle sandwich, and the new women private eyes aren't much different...Cooking may be part of women's traditional role but clearly the female private eyes, and perhaps female detectives in general, relish the chance to get away from that stove and do a bit of sleuthing instead. Miss Marple might have knitted her own lacy shawls but she never, never baked her own scones.

10

Discoursing on Discourse

INTRODUCTION

In the last two chapters, we have explored some of the structural features of individual English sentences. For instance, we've seen that there is a subject and predicator in basic clauses, and that the subject precedes the predicator—that is, unless there is a special grammatical reason for putting it somewhere else (for example, in making interrogatives, exclamatives, and some types of subordinate clauses). But since sentences generally occur as part of connected speech and writing, and rarely in isolation, it's time to move beyond the humble sentence.

In this chapter, we examine the structural features of sequences of sentences within larger texts; in other words, we will be looking at how we, as speakers and writers, go about packaging our messages. This is **communicative structure**—the ways in which we distribute our bits of information in a text in order to provide the right sort of cues to help our audience interpret a piece of discourse appropriately. This has to do with choice. We are constantly drawing on the lexical and grammatical resources of our language for different expressive or communicational ends, choosing vocabulary items and constructions that are best suited for getting our message across. For example, the two sentences *The bread was baked by Heather* and *Heather baked the bread* don't differ in basic (or propositional) meaning. Which one we choose depends on what part of our message we want to highlight, what we think is most important, or even what we assume our audience already knows.

Our discourses are like stories. Any shifts in focus, changes of players, and beginnings and ends of scenes all need to be signalled. The ways in which we do this are collectively known as **discourse strategies**. They potentially involve all linguistic levels, including syntax (word order and special constructions, for example), morphology (specific markers), lexicon (expressions like *as for* and *well*), phonology (intonation and pausing, for instance) and even elements of body language (such as gesture and eye contact).

In the following section, we look at four basic principles for organising information in a sentence and some of the grammatical devices available for varying the information structure according to these principles. In particular, we will concentrate on those that use departures from basic clause structure to achieve these special communicational needs.

PRESENTING INFORMATION

End-focus: given information before new information

In writing and speaking, there are two basic kinds of information: **given** versus **new**. Given information is already familiar. It can refer to something that has appeared earlier in the text, or it can be given in the sense that it is common knowledge, perhaps privately or culturally shared. New information is what drives a discourse forward. It's where we expect our audience to pay special attention. To show the effect that these two types of information have on sentence structure, we've adapted part of a sentence from a story written by a little boy called JB.

> And the skull stood there with a dagger in his hand.
> And there stood the skull with a dagger in his hand.

Now the neutral or unmarked word order in English is more-or-less strict: subject + verb + everything else (SVX). The first sentence has this basic SVX order. But it was the order in the second sentence that JB chose in telling his story. The reason is simple. The end of the sentence is reserved for new and unexpected information, which in this case is *the skull with a dagger in his hand.* The first part of the sentence is reserved for old and unsurprising (that is, given) information. Once this extraordinary skull with the dagger in his hand is mentioned, then it is no longer the surprising bit of the message and can appear earlier.

We've taken the liberty of further adapting JB's story.

> To find a decent focaccia with sweet red capsicum was his one desire.
> His one desire was to find a decent focaccia with sweet red capsicum.

The skull is now established information; it is appropriate that it is replaced by the pronoun form *his* and is positioned early in the sentence, as in the second of the two examples above. The new information then follows. This is sometimes referred to as **end-focus**. As the position of the newest and most salient information, it's the end part of the sentence that really pushes the story forward. For this reason, it is important that we don't let our sentences fade off into nothingness.

A very effective trick often used by writers is to deliberately delay mention of the juicy bits right to the very last moment, as a way of further heightening our expectations. JB, even at the age of 7 years, was aware of this. His flare for the dramatic is evident from the original version of his opening sentence.

> And there at the door quivering all over with tremble stood the skull with a dagger in his hand.

JB has stacked up the adverbial expressions here, and this builds up the suspense. He's making you wait for the new information, and this gives it extra prominence.

We said at the outset that, when we speak or write, we are constantly choosing from the range of English's grammatical resources to achieve the appropriate communicational nuances for our message. For example, we saw in chapter 8 that indirect objects have the option of appearing immediately after the verb or in a prepositional phrase headed by *to* or *for.*

We gave the skull at the door the focaccia bread.
We gave the focaccia bread to the skull at the door.

Both sentences have the same basic meaning, but which construction we choose has to do with what part of our message we want to highlight, what we think is important, or even what we assume is already familiar to our audience. If it was assumed that we gave something to the skull and the focaccia bread was the new information, the context would favour the first sentence. However, a context in which the disposing of the focaccia bread was already known would favour the second version. In this case, *the skull* would be the point at which we expect people to pay special attention. New information appears in end position and therefore receives extra prominence.

Given information is typically much shorter than new. We simply don't need to include the same detail that we do if we are identifying something for the first time. One way we can minimise mention of it is via **proforms**. These are little words—for example, pronouns—that occur in the place of longer constructions (remember *pro* means 'for'). Have a look at the following extract, which deals with some of the joys of summer eating. Here the pronouns *it* and *its* replace the noun phrase *fresh fruit*. To keep repeating *fresh fruit* would be unnecessary, and would in fact sound quite odd.

Our recipe for summer: Take fresh fruit, serve *it*, preserve *it*, use *its* colour and eat *it* with abandon now that *it*'s at *its* best.

This and all the examples in the rest of this chapter
(unless otherwise specified) come from different issues of *Vogue Entertaining* 1995–96

Another way of giving old information less than full mention is by totally omitting it. This is called **'ellipsis'**. It just means we leave out that part of a sentence that is totally reconstructable from previous utterances, or that can simply be inferred from the context. For example, someone might ask you, 'Have you tried the focaccia?'. You might reply, 'No, I haven't'. But to reply, 'No, I haven't tried the focaccia bread' would sound most unnatural. Like proforms, ellipsis leads to economy and efficiency of expression. Our recipes are full of examples of this. In fact, recipes are almost formulaic in this regard, and allow ellipsis (for instance, of direct objects) that is not generally permitted in other types of writing. In the extract below, we've inserted a dash wherever elements have been omitted.

Heat the vegetable oil and when [—] hot, add the onions. Fry [—] until [—] golden and crisp. Remove [—] with a slotted spoon and drain [—] on paper towels, then set [—] aside.

Occasionally old information is *not* given this minimal treatment but is mentioned in full. The effect is usually to indicate contrast or some sort of emphasis. Look at the number of times Jill Dupleix mentions the word *oyster* in the following paragraph. Oysters and their sexy reputation are the focal point of this St Valentine's Day article.

It's *oysters*...Although *oysters* are farmed, they have a wildness that comes from ancient times. To pour an *oyster* down your throat, straight from its craggy, chalky shell, is to have exactly the same experience as a Roman of 2,000 years ago, feasting on a precious *oyster* transported from Britain, or a poor factory worker in Dickensian times, knocking back an ale and a dozen *oysters* because they were cheap and plentiful, or a Frenchwoman in a Parisian bistro eating one of the 1 billion *oysters* the French eat every year.

Dupleix 1996a

Cohesive texts: topic followed by comment

Old information frequently coincides with something called the '**topic**'. This is the part of the sentence that indicates what is being written or talked about. It's the perspective from which a sentence may be viewed. The rest of the sentence makes some sort of statement about the topic, and this is called the '**comment**'. In the natural order of things, the comment (providing the new information) follows on from its topic. Let's take a longer text, such as the following extract, to see just how this works. Ian Parmenter's sentences are clearly built upon a topic–comment frame, and in each instance, the most important information (here in italics) is reserved for the final part of each clause.

> Most of us are *passionate about good food* and when it comes to good food *Australia is certainly the place to be.* With our climate and soil types we are *able to produce the widest possible range of foods and beverages.* Our meats, fish and seafoods, fruit and vegetables, cereals, herbs and spices, wine and beer, even tea and coffee are *of a quality to rival the world's best.*

Parmenter 1992:6

What is new information in one sentence then becomes old and is taken up again at the beginning of the next sentence. The result is a kind of chain effect of old followed by new, and this arrangement is what gives the passage its coherence. Look how the whole passage just falls on its face when we reverse this order. There is no longer the clear topic–comment arrangement, and suddenly there's no common thread to follow; the whole point of the passage becomes lost.

> Passionate about good food most of us are and Australia is certainly the place to be when it comes to good food. We are able to produce the widest possible range of foods and beverages with our climate and soil types. Of a quality to rival the world's best are our meats, fish and seafoods, fruit and vegetables, cereals, herbs and spices, wine and beer, even tea and coffee.

Topic and *comment* are terms that refer to the informational aspects of sentence meaning. *Subject* and *predicate* (as you will remember from chapter 8) refer to grammatical constituents. More often than not, these things will coincide—the topic will be the subject and the predicate its comment—but not all the time. For example, one way English has of setting up the topic is by using expressions such as *considering*, *as for*, *with regard to*, *speaking of*, and so on. These are useful phrases for announcing the arrival of a new topic—the linguistic equivalent of a trumpet blast or fanfare.

As for its cancer-fighting properties, broccoli performs best against breast cancer.

A little later we look at other ways in which speakers and writers play around with topic–comment structure for creative effect.

Front-focus: initial position gives extra focus

We've just seen that ends of sentences are important for communication because they contain information of special significance. But beginnings of sentences can be positions of focus too. By bringing forward material that would usually be placed last, the effect is to give it much greater prominence. It's another way of gaining the audience's attention. Normally it's the subject that appears in initial position (ignoring conjunctions and short adverb phrases, which often precede the subject). This is the basic (or thematically neutral) word order for English. Arrangements that place something other than the subject in this position are therefore less usual and are more marked.

In a moment we will look at a number of strategies that English now has for moving something out of its usual place to initial position, but first have a look at the following sentences.

To us, it's a new way of retaining the airborne coffee scents within the coffee itself. *To you*, it means more pure, rich aroma in your cup.

Advertisement in *Vogue Entertaining*, June/July 1995:9

Of all the vegetables with life-saving properties, broccoli and the rest of the brassica family score highest.

All show different sorts of material occurring early in the sentence. This is an effective way of stating a contrast, as the first example shows. And it is frequently used to mark emphasis, as in the second example.

The principle of end-weight: 'heavy' elements come late

Length and complexity of material are obviously closely tied in with the informational aspects of sentence meaning. Syntactically complex or 'heavy' structures (those heavy with modifiers, for instance) typically appear late in a sentence. If they don't, the sentence becomes clumsy and is more difficult to process. This is known as the '**principle of end-weight**'. Constituents are usually 'heavy' when they contain more new information. So this arrangement coincides with the tendency for new information to follow given. Look at the amount of detail provided in the single constituent following the verb *are* in the example below.

There are *no boundaries to the imagination of this bright, quality-oriented food service company, whose legendary vanilla ice-cream is now a specialty at Sydney's revamped Capitol Theatre and The Opera House.*

When this principle is violated, the results are generally disastrous. Compare the pair of sentences below; the first is the original. It's easier to process than the second, which we have altered so that it no longer conforms to the expected arrangement of given–new information and end-weight.

1 Guests were soon soothed by the elegantly simple food, which included, naturally, whole suckling pig cut into pieces, spinach wrapped in cabbage, northern Chinese pork and vegetable dumplings and cold vegetarian summer rolls.
2 The elegantly simple food, which included, naturally, whole suckling pig cut into pieces, spinach wrapped in cabbage, northern Chinese pork and vegetable dumplings and cold vegetarian summer rolls soon soothed the guests.

DISCOURSE STRATEGIES

There is a long tradition in linguistics of using a movement metaphor when describing different kinds of discourse strategies in English. It's useful to assume, as we have been doing, that there is a basic English clause structure, from which speakers may deviate for the sorts of discourse reasons that we have been exploring here. In other words, speakers may 'move' items into other positions. This idea of movement, however, is not necessarily to be taken literally.

Movement that builds new structures

Once upon a time, English word order was much freer than it is today, and we explore this in more detail in the next chapter. In Old English, it was basically information structure that determined the position of elements. Flexible word order meant that elements could simply move around as required. In the modern language, however, the rise of strict SVX order has brought with it a potential conflict between grammar and discourse. How can we continue to accentuate and emphasise the crucial parts of our message? How can we get attention and create expectation within the confines of such rigid ordering conventions? In short, English grammar requires fixed word order, while discourse requires word order rearrangements for communicational and expressive ends. Who wins?

We have resolved this conflict by evolving a set of special devices, which somehow satisfy both conditions. For example, we now have at our disposal a number of what could be called 'subject-forming strategies'. These actually create new subjects and move what would normally be non-subject noun phrases leftwards into initial position. In addition, we have evolved elements called 'empty' (or 'dummy') subjects, such as *it* and *there*. These are meaningless words that simply function as subject place-holders. Both these developments allow movement of material without violating the requirement that every sentence has a subject, and that this subject appears in the left-most position in the sentence before the verb.

Passives: creating new subjects

Look at the sentence below. It shows the neutral SVX pattern with an actor or agent subject and a patient object (see chapter 8). This is the so-called '**active**' version.

Our master coffee makers in Switzerland	blend	the beans.
subject	*verb*	*object*
agent		*patient*

What the **passive** version of this sentence does is reverse this order, so that the original patient becomes the grammatical subject and the original agent gets moved into a prepositional phrase headed by *by*. The following passive sentence is the original version, which appears in an advertisement for coffee beans (in *Vogue Entertaining*, June/July 1995:9). (See chapter 7 for passive verb morphology.)

The beans	are blended	by our master coffee makers in Switzerland.
subject	*verb*	*adverbial*
patient		*agent*

The basic meaning remains more-or-less the same, but what appears in the focal position has been changed. In the advertisement, the constituent *the beans* is the given topic and is therefore the less informative part of the sentence. What the writer wants us to focus our attention on is *our master coffee makers in Switzerland*; hence, the passive construction allows this constituent to appear in the end focal position, appropriate to its new information status. Whether the writer uses the active or passive here is not a matter of 'grammar' but rather depends on the discourse context, and on considerations such as new versus old information, focus, and emphasis.

The passive lets us place in initial position the patient or what normally would be a direct object. It also gives us a means of emphasising the agent or subject by shifting it out of its usual position to end-focus. More often than not, though, the agent gets left out totally, and the whole focus shifts to the patient or recipient of the action. This can be because the agent is irrelevant information, or because it is already obvious, or even because it's undesirable to mention it (see later discussion of sportstalk and bureaucratese). Have a look at the following extract. Nearly all the verb forms are passive (in italics) and all are without agent phrases. Why do you think this is?

> At Armstrong's Tables of Toowong fat oysters *had been lifted* from their shells, and then *returned* onto a gently spiced cushion of noodles, *touched* with an olive oil, lemon and saltwater vinaigrette, and *topped* with a dollop of oscietra caviar. Linguini *had been tossed* in truffle oil, *studded* with shards of crisp asparagus, *topped* with a soft-poached egg and a generous slice of fresh, black truffle.

We can take it for granted that it's the chefs who are doing the lifting, returning, touching, topping, tossing, and studding. Here the passive enables the writer to omit uninformative (highly topical) elements, which would otherwise have to be stated in the active version.

Different semantic types as subjects

The conflict between strict SVX word order and discourse considerations has also partly been resolved by the fact that the subject-forming possibilities in English have become so much greater. We now allow more types of noun phrases to be subjects than we did before, and as subjects they can occupy sentence-initial position. It's not surprising that we had trouble coming up with a neat semantic characterisation of English subjects in chapter 8. Look at the range in the semantic roles of the following subjects; none are prototypical agents or actors.

This wine drinks well, and *the sweet* eats well too.	(patient)
The restaurant seats only 50 people.	(location)
Delia Smith's new cookbook has added 30 more recipes and *it* has already sold 40 000 copies.	(recipient, patient)
This pan will easily fry 5 or 6 large steaks.	(instrument)
Tomorrow promises a much more sumptuous repast.	(time)

Adapted from various issues of *Vogue Entertaining* 1995–96

English shows considerably more diversity than its Germanic relatives regarding what can appear as a subject. German, for instance, has tight restrictions: generally speaking, the subject must be an agent.

'Tough' movement

The semantic diversity of our subjects is also illustrated by something known as 'tough' movement. (We've used *tough* in our example to show you how the process got its name, but the procedure works just as well with other adjectives, such as *easy*, *interesting*, and *difficult*).

a It's really tough to find broccoli out of season.
b Broccoli is really tough to find out of season.

Sentence (a) is the basic version. In (b) the object *broccoli* in the second clause has been moved leftwards and turned into a new subject. We interpret (b) exactly like (a): what is tough is *to find broccoli out of season.* The difference between them is one of focus. Sentence (a) is the neutral version, and the 'tough' version is more marked: (b) is specifically a comment on broccoli.

Existentials

Sometimes the subject is completely new information, which we want to reserve for the end of the sentence, where it receives extra focus. We can do this by creating a dummy subject using the pronoun *there.* This then allows the understood subject, with all its new and exciting information, to appear later, giving it much greater prominence. *There* has no meaning. Its purpose is purely grammatical: to hold the place of the understood subject. For example:

There may still be some cloudiness remaining in the liquid.
[Some cloudiness may still be remaining in the liquid]

Parmenter 1992:63

The sentence in brackets is the basic version.

The reason we call the resulting sentence an '**existential sentence**' is because it expresses the existence of something, and this is often how new topics are introduced. It's the stock fairy-tale opener: 'Once upon a time there lived a king'. In the following, for example, Ian Parmenter is introducing us to the wonders of soups and sauces. He presents various soup stocks as new participants on the scene.

> There are four basic stocks: white, brown, fish and vegetable.

In our NZ and OZ varieties of English, there is good reason to assume that *there* is now the grammatical subject of the sentence. Although Ian Parmenter has kept the plural verb in the above example (to agree with *four basic stocks*), in spoken and more colloquial written varieties you would be more likely to hear *There's four basic stocks* (with a singular, usually contracted, verb). It's a construction widely condemned, but also widely produced. For example, the following was overheard being said of a curry laksa recipe: *There's loads of prawns, but she kind of skimps on the fish meat.* First position has such a strong association with subject in Modern English that it is hardly surprising that speakers are reanalysing *there* as the new subject pronoun.

Extraposition

As we saw in chapter 9, it is possible for the subject of a sentence to be an entire clause. What **extraposition** does is change the whole sentence around so that this subject clause appears in the end position. This is labelled 'extraposition' because the subject clause therefore appears *outside* its normal position. In place of the original subject, we insert the pronoun *it*. This is another dummy pronoun subject, a kind of place-holder, which anticipates the information coming up in the following clause. In the examples below, we have presented the non-extraposed counterparts in brackets.

> *It* is contentious *that searing meats seals in the juices.*
> [*That searing meats seals in the juices* is contentious]
> *It's* obvious *that a strong exhaust system will be required.*
> [*That a strong exhaust system will be required* is obvious]

The thematic motivation for this is the principle of end-weight (that is, the tendency for 'heavy' constituents to appear late in the sentence). The longer and more complex the subordinate clause, the more likely it is that extraposition will occur.

In the following example, the clausal subject is syntactically complex and highly newsworthy. Look how awkward the sentence becomes when the understood subject is not extraposed but is followed by its short and not terribly newsworthy predicate.

> It is curious enough *that oysters are hermaphrodites, with both male and female sex cells that mature at different times.*
> [?*That oysters are hermaphrodites, with both male and female sex cells that mature at different times,* is curious enough.]
>
> Dupleix 1996a

Cleft constructions

Clefting is another strategy to shift the focus of interest. It has the effect of 'cleaving' an original sentence into two clauses. There are two basic kinds of clefts: *it* clefts and *wh-* clefts.

Take the sample sentence *The restaurant at the Palace Hotel in Darlinghurst first gave Brian back his weekends.* This has its constituents in the basic unmarked word order. But let's say the writer wanted to focus on *the restaurant at the Palace Hotel in Darlinghurst* (which was, in fact, the case here). An *it* cleft has the effect of splitting off this constituent in order to give it prominence. Two clauses are formed: the first is introduced by a dummy subject *it* and a form of *be*, followed by the focused constituent, and the rest of the sentence is recast as a relative clause beginning with *that*. The clefted version, as it appeared in the magazine, was the following:

> It was *the restaurant at the Palace Hotel in Darlinghurst* that first gave Brian back his weekends.

The formula for forming an *it* cleft is straightforward: *It is/was X that [...]*. As with existentials and extraposition, the emphasis is thrown onto whatever follows the dummy subject and its verb (that is, X in the formula). As you can see above, *it* anticipates the new information after *be* (italicised in the above example). It's a way of getting our attention by delaying mention of what is of special significance.

Wh- clefting focuses on the significant information by using a clause with an introductory *wh-* word followed by either *be* or *do*. What follows the verb is then given extra prominence by virtue of being shifted into end position. For example, the *wh-* cleft version of the above sentence would read:

> What first gave Brian back his weekends was *the restaurant at the Palace Hotel in Darlinghurst*.

You can see that both types of cleft construction have the effect of bringing items into focus. They also assume a certain amount of background information. In this case, the article has already established the fact that Brian had been working hard and losing his weekends. Neither of the clefts would make a lot of sense, in this instance, unless the writer could assume that the reader was aware of this.

Movement that keeps everything intact

Processes such as those we've just seen not only shift things around, but they also change the grammatical functions of elements and build new structure. In the case of passives, for example, special verb morphology is added and something new becomes the subject. English also has other strategies, which simply shift items around but keep all the grammatical functions intact. In the written language, these are infrequent; with fixed word order, we simply don't have this sort of creative potential with our wording. However, these strategies can be found in spoken language, and we explore this difference later in the chapter when we compare spoken and written varieties of English. For the moment, let's look at some of the most important strategies.

Left-dislocation

Left-dislocation is a way of focusing a constituent, but without changing the grammatical functions. Again the movement metaphor is useful here. You simply move a constituent to the extreme left of the sentence, leaving behind some sort of proform copy in the gap left by the fronted constituent. An intonation break separates the fronted item from the rest of the sentence, and this has the effect of making it stand out even more. As the example below shows, subjects (whose basic position is initial anyway) can be given special emphasis this way.

> *Sorbet, kulfi (Indian condensed-milk ice-cream), Spanish fig ice-cream, watermelon sherbet—these* can transport you, to childhood and beyond.

The grammatical status of these various ice-creams has not changed: they still form the subject. All that changes is their position. In a sense, they have become detached from the rest of the sentence, separated by a distinct pause (indicated here by the dash). So it's different from, say, passives, which must change a constituent into a new subject in order to be able to front it. In writing, this construction is extremely rare, and it is heavily marked (we had to search high and low for this example). Speech, however, is built much more upon a topic–comment structure, and as we will soon see, left-dislocation structures like these are very common.

Fronting

Fronting is very similar to left-dislocation, except that no copy is left behind and the fronted constituent isn't set apart from the rest of the sentence in the same way. Items are simply fronted. We couldn't find any instances of fronting in our written sources. So we offer here a spoken language example, and one that we return to later in this chapter.

> *Zucchini* I hate!

Right-dislocation

This is the opposite strategy to left-dislocation, and involves moving something to the *end* of the sentence. If an item's usual position is early, then this has the effect of giving it extra focus by postponing its mention. Like clefting, extraposition, and existentials, **right-dislocation** introduces a pronoun, which in a sense announces what is coming up in the discourse. Unlike those other three constructions, though, the pronoun here is referential (and isn't just a place-holder). This can be a particularly effective way of building up expectations, as this next example shows.

> So sumptuous it curls around the spoon: chocolate sorbet and a meringue filled with licorice ice-cream.

Notice how the right-dislocated element is separated off from the rest of the clause by a distinct pause or punctuation.

Subject–verb inversion

We saw in chapter 8 how inverted subject–verb order is used for grammatical ends in the formation of questions. It can also be used for expressive ends. By shifting the subject out of its natural environment, it represents yet another way of shifting focus. In Old English, this inverted order had considerable dramatic force and was typical of lively narrative sequences. It has retained a kind of mock dramatic effect, as the example below shows. These constructions always involve a fronted phrase (often a directional adverbial) followed by an intransitive verb (often a verb of movement).

For example:

> The bush dinner draws to a close...Finally comes the haunting voice of the serene hostess Esther.

Here *comes* has shifted to precede the heavy subject *the haunting...Esther*. Examples such as this one echo literary favourites such as *Into the valley of death rode the six hundred.*

STYLES OF DISCOURSE: WHAT MAKES A VARIETY DISTINCTIVE?

Chapter 1 introduced you to the notion of language variation and discussed varieties of English associated both with user and with occasions of use. The chapters that followed investigated the structural properties of English, the last three concentrating on the basics of English grammar. This chapter has now introduced the notion of discourse—the grammatical analysis of stretches of language larger than just the sentence. We want to continue the discussion of discourse, but return to the question of variation—in particular, variation relating to the social use of language. Different situations call for different varieties. This is best exemplified by the different occupational 'dialects' (in other words, jargons peculiar to the activities of a trade, a profession, or some other group).

Too often these different occupational varieties are characterised solely in terms of their vocabulary. Probably this is because words are just so much more accessible to people. Certainly specialist terms are important to these varieties, but occupational dialects are more than simply esoteric vocabularies. They draw from inventories of style features at all levels of the language: phonology, discourse, grammar, even body language. Here we will concentrate on the grammatical features, and we'll show that the important grammatical choices we make about things such as the overall organisation of content are what help to make a variety distinctive. Of course, most of the linguistic features we'll look at occur in ordinary language too, but as with all stylistic varieties, it is the relative frequency and the special combination of these features that make a variety different from others.

Before we begin looking at these varieties, we need to identify a fundamental distinction, which will have an important bearing on the sorts of grammatical variation we find: language can be perceived and transmitted as speech or as writing. This is a rather obvious distinction, you might think, but one that is frequently overlooked.

Speech versus writing

A child who wanted to make quite clear her loathing of certain members of the vegetable world was recently heard to say the sentence *Zucchini I hate*. 'Is this a well-formed utterance of English?', you might be wondering. According to the norms of writing, it probably isn't. Unfortunately, people often equate 'normal' language with the written form, and common spoken features such as fronting (as in this example), ellipsis, and contractions are stigmatised.

Speech and writing are very different forms of communication, each with their own distinctive capabilities of expression and their own sets of 'rules'. (In fact, at one time in the history of English, speech and writing were so far apart that they even involved different languages: people spoke English, but most writing was done in Latin). Speech is not 'spoken writing', and writing is not 'speech written down'. To judge one in terms of the other is something like judging a pavlova in terms of whether it makes a good lamington or not—well, something like that.

Until now, the discussion of English grammar has been based largely on the formal, careful usage usually associated with writing. Let's turn our attention now to speech and what distinguishes it from writing. We will concentrate here on structural differences and ignore the very obvious formal differences, such as the fact that speech is produced orally and received by the ear, uses non-verbal features such as gesture and facial expression to communicate meaning, and so on.

To begin, compare the spoken and written versions of the blue-cheese butter recipe given below. The spoken version comes from a regular cooking program on the radio. The dialogue is between the radio show host, Doug Aiton (DA), and his invited guest, Jill Dupleix (JD). (Short pauses are indicated by (...). The italicised elements will be discussed below.)

Spoken version

DA: I'm delighted to see that this week we're talking about barbecues and you've got ten points *(...)* ten suggestions on how we can get away from burnt chops and sausages.

JD: Yeah, well I don't think that we all go and burn our chops and sausages. But it is a case where we *sort of* settle into a rut sometimes. *Hmm. (...)*

JD: I've got I've got ten terrific changes to ring on the lazy summer barbecue which are all *hmm (...)* printed out on the recipe but *er (...)* I'll just *sort of (...)* if we just meander our way through them.

DA: Yeah, let's do that. They look good; I've sneaked a look.

JD: Have you? Well, *the first one I want I love hmm (...)* when I'm grilling a steak, a really good steak, *I love (...)* I don't want to do too much to it, but I like sometimes at the end to just top it with a little disk of flavoured butter, like a blue cheese butter, not much, just enough to *sort of* capture that sizzle and give it a bit *of its (...)* of its own sauce as you eat it. And *that's an easy (...)* my favourite one is just beating let's say 100 grams of soft butter with a tablespoon of roquefort or gorgonzola cheese, a nice blue cheese, good quality, and a teaspoon of mustard to give it a bit of bite as well.

DA: What, a French mustard, French style mustard?

JD: Yeah, I can say that now Dijon mustard, that style of thing. I find the English a bit too harsh.

DA: So do I.

JD: And then I just put out a piece of silver foil. Bang your messy bit of beaten up butter on that and twist it up, roll it up into a log and twist the ends and *hmm (...)* bang that in the fridge or the freezer if *I'm* only got 5 minutes to spare. Then by the time the steak's done take it out and just slice it an' each little disk goes on each little steak and straight to the table.

Aiton & Dupleix 1996

Written version

A grilled steak and a baked potato are all very well, but how can you jazz up the last of our lazy summer barbecues? Here are ten delicious ideas.

1 Top steak with blue cheese butter: beat 100 g soft butter with tbsp of roquefort or gorgonzola cheese and tsp of mustard. When smooth place on silver foil and fold into the shape of a small log and chill. Unroll and slice, placing 1 slice on each steak while still hot from the grill.

Dupleix 1996b

Non-fluency features

Spoken language is spontaneous, with no time for planning, and is subject to instant feedback. The psycholinguist Jean Aitchison estimates that something like 40–50 per cent of the average utterance is silence (1983:231). Breathing pauses account for about 5 per cent of the gaps, and the rest are hesitation pauses. This is not surprising given all the things that are going on when we speak. While we talk, we have to monitor what we're saying to make sure that it is coming out as we intended and that our audience has understood it this way too. We also have to plan what it is we are going to say next. It's an impressive performance, although we don't tend to think of it this way because we take it so much for granted. Small wonder that some repairs and repetitions have to be made on the go, and there are occasionally hesitations, false starts, and fillers such as *hmm*, *err*, and *uhuh*. The above dialogue contains a number of these (in italics), although less than would be found in, say, an impromptu conversation between friends, which would be more 'off the cuff' (see exercise 6).

Warm 'fuzzy' features

Conversation is dotted with expressions such as *you know*, *I mean*, and *I think*, which are often mistakenly believed to belong to the non-fluency features just mentioned. But in this case, they're not meaningless little expressions that speakers use to fill in time while they plan what they're going to say next. Instead they have an important role in expressing social relationships, personal attitudes and opinions, and subtle nuances of meaning. Spoken interaction is much more personal than writing, and speakers continually make references to themselves and to their audience by using expressions such as these. They can have a complex effect on the utterance in which they occur. There are even interesting differences between the way women and men use them. (If you're interested in this, we recommend Holmes 1995, which looks generally at how the sexes express politeness and mostly uses data from New Zealand.)

In the spoken extract above, Dupleix achieves a friendly relationship with Doug Aiton and her listening audience through her informal vocabulary (*bang your messy bit of beaten butter*), but especially through her more personal references such as *let's say*, *sort of*, *just*, and *well*. Her written recipe, by contrast, is more formal, although admittedly has more evidence of her personality than more traditional-style recipes. Consider for a moment her use of *sort of* (italicised in the extract above). This is a typical hedging expression, which is used in informal contexts to reduce the force of an utterance. But here it does not express approximation or imprecision. (Janet Holmes, 1995:95–6, found more evidence of this particular function in men's speech.) It's used here to minimise the distance between the speaker and audience by modulating the authoritative tone and creating friendliness. Playing down expertise in this way is typical of women's speech.

Like the seasonings and flavourings essential to good food, these expressive fillers spice up a conversation, and without them, our speech would be very lifeless indeed. Of course, you can argue that, when they are too conspicuous, they become distracting and irritating. And this is true; don't overdo them. As the editors of *Vogue Entertaining* remind us, 'Nothing is more deadening to the tastebuds than a flavour repeated too often' (McCallum et al. 1986:11).

Ellipsis

Oral communication is usually face-to-face and can exploit the context of the interaction much more than writing can. Conversational dialogues such as the one given at the start of this section are full of examples of ellipsis. Speakers don't need to supply everything, and it would be irritating if they did. Most of us quickly grow bored with what we see as long-windedness. So subjects and verbs frequently get left out (*You hungry? Want some grub?*). Of course, they can always be 'recovered' from the context, and if the meaning should ever become unclear, the breakdown can easily be repaired. Writing, without the same immediate context, doesn't have this luxury and doesn't tolerate omissions to the same extent.

The difference doesn't leap out at you in the two extracts above, simply because of the formulaic language of recipes (as mentioned at the start of this chapter, part of the formula is ellipsis). For example, this written extract is missing direct objects (*unroll [—] and slice [—]*), determiners (*with [—] tbsp of roquefort*), and prepositions (*100 g [—] soft butter*).

Syntactic complexity

The concept of a sentence as we know it in written language is definitely 'fuzzy' in spoken language. For example, many of Dupleix's sentences don't fit nicely into the rules of English structure. Yet sentences like these are typical of speech and cause us no difficulty; in fact, most of the time they pass unnoticed. We must guard against viewing speech through the spectacles of writing.

One overall characteristic of speech is that it is grammatically less complex than writing (for example, it has less subordination in its clause structure). But of course, we must remember that presentation of information in these two mediums involves quite different skills. Speakers have available to them features such as intonation, stress, pitch, speed, silence, laughter, and voice quality, which all can be used to signal logical relations between clauses.

Presentation of information

Speakers can also manipulate word order to a much greater extent than writers can. Speech commonly shows the sorts of highly topic-oriented structures we looked at earlier, such as dislocation and fronting. It has a more expressive word order. Different sequences of noun phrases, for example, can be exploited to highlight or to contrast more salient information. On the other hand, writing has to resort to special constructions such as passives, clefts, and so on to encode differences within information structure.

The picture we paint here is that speech and writing form a straightforward dichotomy. However, some examples of spoken language—such as you might find in a well-planned lecture, for example—have many of the organisational features of written language. On the other hand, some examples of writing—a scribbled note to a friend or a message sent by e-mail, for instance—are much closer to speech. 'Chatting' on e-mail is like chatting on the telephone: people write very much as they speak. This type of language features ellipsis and the sorts of highly topic-oriented structures characteristic of spoken language. Some linguists have abandoned the general labels 'speech' versus 'writing', preferring instead 'planned' versus 'unplanned' discourse, since different types of speech and writing will show differing degrees of planning and formality. Either way, these labels imply two polar extremes. In reality, there are many intermediate varieties exhibiting features of both types of discourse to a greater or lesser extent.

Occupational 'dialects'

Now that we've identified these two general communicative modes, we will explore two of the occupational 'dialects' of English that feature prominently in the lives of most Antipodeans. The first is 'sports announcer talk', in this case the language of football commentary (we've picked Australian rules, but it could equally apply to rugby or soccer). The second is the particular brand of turgid, rather pedantic prose peculiar to government services, sometimes dubbed 'bureaucratese'.

We must emphasise that, although we use labels such as bureaucratese, legalese, and sportstalk as if they were discrete entities, these varieties are by no means fixed. They vary continuously in response to different factors, such as the relationship between the speaker or writer and audience, the setting, and whether a spoken or written medium is used. For example, legalese can occur in written documents such as statutes and wills, or less formally in briefs; it can be spoken in jury instructions, less formally in the examination of witnesses, and more informally still in conversations between lawyers. All these represent different styles of legalese.

Sportstalk: the poetry of football commentary

There are a number of special constructions that are particularly characteristic of this variety. In many ways, they can be regarded as linguistic antiquities, relic uses from the past that we tend now to associate more with the sort of literary ambition that we might find in poetry. The examples below are adapted from actual transcriptions of two games: Carlton versus Essendon and Footscray versus Essendon (Hyde et al. 1996:123–4).

Subject–verb inversion

First, there is the familiar inversion of subject and verb. We've seen it before as a literary device: a means of heightening expectation or a way of simply focusing the subject by shifting it out of its normal position. In the context of a football commentary, it can also function as a kind of stalling technique: a means of postponing mention of a player's name until the identity is known for sure.

> Here *comes Essendon*!
> Across the top of the pack *comes Kickett*, and Kickett has taken a magnificent mark!

Passive

The frequent use of passive is another handy delaying technique. Perhaps the football commentator can't yet identify the player who has unexpectedly stopped a kick. The passive provides some breathing space.

> Kick Daniher to the centre is well marked *by Young*.
> Ridley tried to hold it low down, couldn't do so, soccered on *by Wanganeen*, picked up though for Footscray and chipped out towards the boundary line, and eventually over *by Watts*.

Heavy noun-phrase modification

Football commentary is characterised by noun phrases that are heavy with modifiers, especially post-modifiers such as relative clauses, appositional noun phrases that restate the noun, and even postposed adjectives. The examples below are also unusual because of the number of modified proper nouns (see discussion of proper nouns in chapter 7).

> Symons *out-bustled* can't get into the contest for the Dons.
> Handpass to *the running* Doolan...
> Handpass backwards to the Axe *who pokes a kick onto the leading Grant.*
> Williams *for Essendon* beautiful smother.

Present tense

Football commentary is unusual in its use of the present tense. You might be thinking that this is hardly remarkable: present tense reports action happening at the time. But, in fact, if you recall the discussion of tense in chapter 7, present tense is rarely used now to report strictly present time. While Polonius might have asked of Hamlet, *What do you read, my Lord?* (William Shakespeare, *Hamlet*, 2.II.195) this construction now sounds very un-English. In ordinary language, it's usually used to report habitual actions, as in *I read cookbooks for pleasure*. The use of present tense in football broadcasting is another linguistic antiquity. It has considerable dramatic force and makes for particularly lively narrative sequences.

> West *goes* sideways, *finds* Ellis, who *chips* it on to Quill, who *pokes* it on.

Ellipsis

Also typical of football commentary is the use of ellipsis, or the omission of elements of sentence structure. The material can, of course, be immediately supplied by the context.

> Heeeading back into play, knocked out by Kernahan, went to Denim, sharked a beautiful left foot kick went straight into the hands of Symons. Red Symons on the backline. Someone went A over T.

Bureaucratese

At some stage in your lives you will no doubt have encountered the sort of incomprehensible language now usually dubbed 'gobbledygook'. We should point out here that the word *gobbledygook* has an interesting history. It was apparently originally coined by one Maury Maverick to describe the language of official documents produced in Washington, DC. He is quoted as saying 'People ask me where I got gobbledygook. I do not know. It must have come in a vision. Perhaps I was thinking of the old bearded turkey gobbler back in Texas, who was always gobbledy-gobbling and strutting with ludicrous pomposity. At the end of this gobble there was a sort of gook' (see Allan &Burridge 1991:196).

We encounter gobbledygook in many different domains: the law, linguistics, religion—even the world of food and wine. More usually though, it's a label used to describe the language of government (in other words, bureaucratese). There are many different features we could look at, and many different styles within bureaucratese, but we will concentrate on the grammatical complexity of written gobbledygook. It's the deadly combination of difficult syntax and esoteric vocabulary that makes bureaucratese at times so befuddling and so offensive to its readers. Not surprisingly, there has been a backlash against this sort of writing. Currently there are many social and political movements pushing for clear and simple English, particularly in laws, legal documents such as contracts, and government documents of all kinds. There are now 'Plain English' movements in Australia, New Zealand, the United Kingdom, and North America. (But this trend is by no means confined to the English-speaking world. In Sweden there is currently a strong push for comprehensible Swedish officialese in place of 'muddled Swedish', and in Norway for 'plain Norwegian for Bureaucrats'; in fact, parallel cries can be heard all over Europe. See Danat 1980:451f).

So let's look now at some of the grammatical features that have become the target of the cleaning-up activities of the various Plain English movements around the world. These movements have had great success in eradicating many horrors within official language; nonetheless, we should point out that we still frequently receive letters from people frustrated by a piece of virtually unintelligible writing that they have received from some government body. For this reason, we feel it's important to highlight what it is that makes gobbledygook so difficult to comprehend.

Bureaucratese is actually a variety of legal English and has a lot in common with it, but with one significant difference. A number of features that are functionally motivated in legalese have become more like ornamentation in bureaucratic language. (Mind you, we are probably being overly generous to legalese here. Many features, although historically motivated, have evolved into little more than conventionalised jargon markers of this variety too. They become part of the ritual magic of the legal process—the linguistic equivalents of the black gowns, the wigs, and the fanciful ceremonies of the courtroom.)

Lexical density: compounds and strings of synonyms

One striking feature of so much bureaucratic writing is its lexical density (in other words, the high proportion of lexical words to grammatical words). There are several contributing factors here. One is the propensity for compounding. Long complex strings such as *prototype crisis shelter development plans* and *young driver risk-taking research* are commonplace. The following gems were, in fact, nominees at the 1992 Doublespeak Awards; none of them were made up. Radio and television commercials have become *value minutes*; a United States Department of Energy nuclear fuel dump is *a monitored retrievable storage site*; electric fans are *high velocity multipurpose air circulators*; and Canadian politicians, we are told, engage in a little *reality augmentation* (they never lie) (Champaign-Urbana *News Gazette*, 20 November 1992). Of course, it's not just the process of compounding that turns these coagulated clumps of English into befuddling doublespeak.

Another reason for the density is the practice of stringing two, sometimes more, synonyms together. For example, United States park regulations warn us that:

> No person shall prune, cut, carry away, pull up, dig, fell, bore, chop, saw, chip, pick, move, sever, climb, molest, take, break, deface, destroy, set fire to, burn, scorch, carve, paint, mark, or in any manner interfere with, tamper, mutilate, misuse, disturb or damage any tree, shrub, plant, grass, flower, or part thereof, nor shall any person permit any chemical, whether solid, fluid, or gaseous, to seep, drip, drain or be emptied, sprayed, dusted or injected upon, about or into any tree, shrub, plant, grass, flower, or part thereof, except when specifically authorized by competent authority; nor shall any person build fires, or station or use any tar kettle, heater, road roller or other engine within an area covered by this part in such a manner that the vapor, fumes or heat therefrom may injure any tree or other vegetation
>
> As quoted in the Business Forms Management Association, *Plain English Manual*

Lexical density: nominalisation

Another thing that immediately strikes you about bureaucratic language is its excessive 'nouniness'. English also has the special ability to turn whole clauses into noun-like structures. For example, ***That the chefs use powdered eggs** is unexpected.* becomes ***The chefs' use of powdered eggs** is unexpected.* Prose that is heavily nominal in this way is more abstract; doing away with verbs means that we can also do away with subjects and objects. This means speakers and writers can be non-committal as to who is doing what to whom—a sneaky device, you are probably thinking, and one eminently suited to the language of government offices, where it can be desirable to conceal precisely this sort of information. Consider another version of this sentence. Throw in a few jargon nouns such as *utilisation* and some compounds, and you have an impressive piece of bureaucratese: *The utilisation of pulverulent egg products is contrary to expectation.*

In addition to the sneakiness of such prose, nominalisations have been shown in the psycholinguistic research of Robert Charrow and Veda Charrow (1979) to present significant processing difficulties for readers. Compare the following nominal version (a) with its more natural counterpart (b).

a in the event of default in the payment of

b if you don't pay what you owe

Grammatical complexity

Bear in mind that the average legal sentence contains fifty-five words. This is twice the number for scientific English and roughly eight times the number found in sentences in dramatic texts. In addition to length, sentences in legalese and its cousin bureaucratese are like onions: clauses embedded inside clauses embedded inside clauses. Here's some employment office jargon for you to decipher. It's the constant interruption of material that makes this piece so hard to follow. Try to identify the form and function of all the subordinate clauses as discussed in chapter 9.

> Unemployment benefit is not payable in respect of 13.2.56 to 17.2.56 which cannot be treated as days of unemployment on the ground that the claimant notwithstanding that this employment has terminated received, by way of compensation for the loss of the remuneration which he [sic] would have received for that day each of those days if the unemployment had not been terminated, payment of an amount which exceeds the amount arrived at by deducting the standard daily rate of unemployment benefit from two thirds of the remuneration lost in respect of that day each of those days.
>
> As quoted in McDougal 1985:3

Passives

A high frequency of passives, especially agentless passives, is also an earmark of this variety and one that distinguishes it from 'normal' discourse. There are two primary motivations here. First, doing away with agents is extremely useful for those occasions where it is again desirable to conceal this sort of information. In a sentence such as the following, it enables the writer to evade responsibility for the action. *The decision has been made* [but by whom?] *to continue the utilisation of pulverulent egg products by reason of a fund insufficiency.* Compare the more verbal equivalent of this: *We decided to continue to utilise pulverulent egg products because we don't have sufficient funds.*

Second, agentless passives can make even the most simple and mundane things sound complex and profound. They are also characteristic of the impersonal (some would say pretentious) style found in a lot of academic writing.

Negatives

Another hallmark of bureaucratese is the expression of an affirmative in terms of the negative of the contrary, as in *a not insignificant amount* or *not unnaturally.* (If you think that this needlessly complicates things, you're right. George Orwell's remedy for this affliction was to memorise the sentence 'A not unblack dog was chasing a not unsmall rabbit across a not ungreen field'.) (See discussion of this sort of understatement in Gowers 1975:73–4.)

The general stacking of negatives is a further feature of this variety, and one that has also been shown to cause difficulties for cognitive processing. This includes not only overt negative markers such as *not*, *never*, and *un-*, but also semantically negative words such as *default* and negative connectors such as *unless*. The following treasure comes from the Sales Act (Vic.). We've italicised the negative words.

> A term of a sale shall *not* be taken to *exclude, restrict* or modify the application of this Part *unless* the term does so expressly or is *inconsistent* with that provision.

To conclude, we offer you a carefully drafted departmental memo from the former City of Fitzroy in Melbourne. It contains a number of the features we've looked at. Combined they give the memo a legal air and lend a certain dignity and gravity to the problem of council rubbish collection.

> Refuse and rubbish shall not be collected from the site or receptacles thereon before the hour of 8.00 am or after the hour of 6.00 p.m. of any day
>
> As quoted in Pia Herbert, pers. comm., August 1989

Those of us who have the task of actually figuring out when we can put out our garbage are more likely to be impressed with a more mundane version, something along the lines of *We will collect your garbage between 8.00 a.m. and 6.00 p.m.*

We might just mention that the appearance of this memo coincided with the launch of the new Plain English version of the *Melbourne Metropolitan Planning Scheme*. This style of bureaucratic writing is clearly very ingrained.

Of course, all the features we've looked at occur in ordinary language too. But as with any style feature, it is a matter of relative frequency. In bureaucratese—as in other jargons, such as legalese, medicalese, educationalese, and even restaurantese—some peculiar lexical and grammatical features occur with much greater frequency than they would in other jargons or in everyday language. And in the case of bureaucratese, it's the combination of these features that can cause processing difficulties for a reader.

POINTS TO REMEMBER

- Communicative function involves the way sentences are packaged as messages within larger structures or discourses.
- Each element of an English clause appears in its neutral or basic position, unless there are special reasons for putting it somewhere else. Elements can deviate from this basic structure for expressive or communicational ends.
- Sentences can convey two kinds of information. The new, most salient information is what gains the audience's attention. The given information is familiar in the sense that it refers to something that has already appeared earlier in the text, or that is common knowledge.
- End-focus is when given (old, established) information comes before new (unpredictable, surprising) information. We usually arrange the information in our message so that what is most important comes towards the end.
- Topic–comment structure positions topical material early in the sentence, often to provide a cohesive link with what has preceded.

- Front-focus is when sentence-initial position is a focal point. Fronting an expression to this position gives it much greater prominence.
- End-weight is when longer, more complex structures are placed at the end of the sentence.
- Proforms are items that substitute for other constituents.
- Ellipsis is the omission of items in a sentence because they either appear elsewhere or can be reconstructed from the context.
- English has a number of discourse strategies that allow elements to deviate from their basic position. These can involve movement of material leftwards or rightwards. Some—such as left- and right-dislocation, subject–verb inversion, and fronting—simply shift material around. Others—such as passive, existentials, extrapostion, and clefting—alter the original grammatical relations.
- Different situations call for different varieties (for example, the jargons peculiar to the activities of a trade, a profession, or some other group). In addition to phonological, grammatical, and even paralinguistic differences (such as gesture), these occupational 'dialects' have distinctive discourse structures.
- Speech and writing are very different forms of communication, each with their own expressive capabilities.
- Features of football-speak include subject–verb inversion, passives, heavy noun phrase modification, present tense, and ellipsis.
- Features of bureaucratese include lexical density, grammatical complexity, passives, and a rich exuberance of negatives.

EXERCISES

1 Extraposition and clefting

For each of the following (made-up) sentences, write a paraphrase with extraposition. Which version sounds better?

a Whether you finish your meal or not is up to you.
b Why you made the linguini in truffle oil is entirely irrelevant.
c That responsibility for the disastrous hot treacle and fig pudding must be laid at the door of the short order cook is obvious to everybody.
d Who pays for my meal doesn't matter to me.

For each sentence, write the corresponding *it* and *wh-* cleft sentences, focusing on the italicised item.

e He was eating *my duck confit.*
f I decided to leave *after I sampled the porcini and potato 'cappuccino'.*
g They first tried braised veal shanks *in Wogga.*
h Did the restaurant open *in 1939*?
i *Thomas Crapper* invented the valveless water waste preventer.

2 Discourse strategies

In each of the following examples (from various issues of *Vogue Entertaining,* 1995–96), identify the special discourse strategy that has been used and give the basic version. Describe why you think the writer has used these techniques.

- a It's worth every moment, to create your own flavours—ours are a mixture of delectable old favourites and inventive tongue teasers.
- b Then there are fluid, enriching oil-based marinades: try a blend of sesame oil, Kikkoman soy sauce and grated orange rind for flavouring pork.
- c What's important with food is that it's easy and crisp and looks good.
- d Outstanding is Oceana, long a top-starred seafood restaurant.
- e Chins, wrists, elbows—we're up to our ears in sticky fingers.
- f And now, with our enriched aroma, the taste is even richer too.

3 Passive construction

Identify all the passive verb forms in the following extract (adapted from *Vogue Entertaining*, February/March 1996). Suggest why the writer has chosen the agentless passive for some.

- a Chefs for Queensland was formed by four of the state's most innovative and influential chefs.
- b Their impact on the industry has been highly praised.
- c The food that is offered by these chefs compares favourably with anything elsewhere in Australia.
- d Fat oysters had been lifted from their shells and then returned onto a gently spiced cushion of noodles.
- e The real strength of Chefs for Queensland is illustrated at the excellent 'Two Small Rooms' in Toowong. Here David Pugh turns out a trio of outstanding meat courses, which are inspired by new local products.
- f Pugh's baby racks of Gungel sucking-pig [*sic*] were served on an asparagus and leek risotto, and finished with a blackcurrant jus.
- g The state [of Queensland] is now a food destination to be taken very seriously, and enjoyed.

Make the following active sentences passive. Why do the passive versions sound better?

- h A puree of roasted pumpkin, baby spinach, and a Madeira jus complemented the dish.
- i Four of the newest luxury hotels hired her.

4 Bureaucratese

The following (adapted) chocolate-chip cookie recipe comes from Susan E. Russ (unpublished). First 'translate' it into the language more typical of an ordinary biscuit recipe. Then identify the combination of features that make the original such a successful piece of bureaucratic writing. As an alternative, find a recipe yourself and translate it into your best bureaucratese.

Total lead time: 35 minutes.

Inputs

1 cup packed brown sugar
½ cup granulated sugar
½ cup softened butter
½ cup shortening

2 eggs
½ teaspoons vanilla
2½ cups all-purpose flour
1 teaspoon baking soda
½ teaspoon salt
1½ ounce package semi-sweet chocolate pieces
1 cup chopped walnuts or pecans

Guidance

After procurement actions, decontainerise inputs. Perform measurement tasks on a case-by-case basis. In a mixing-type bowl, impact heavily on brown sugar, granulated sugar, softened butter, and shortening. Coordinate the interface of eggs and vanilla.

At this point in time, leverage flour, baking soda, and salt into a bowl and aggregate. Equalise with prior mixture, and develop intense and continuous liaison among inputs until well coordinated. Associate key chocolate and nut subsystems, and execute stirring operations.

Within this time frame, take action to prepare the heating environment for throughput by manually setting the oven-baking unit by hand to a temperature of 120 degrees Celsius. Drop mixture in an ongoing fashion from a teaspoon implement onto an ungreased cookie sheet at intervals sufficient enough apart to permit total and permanent separation of thoughputs to the maximum extent practicable under operating conditions.

Position cookie sheet in a bake situation and surveil for 8–10 minutes or until cooking action terminates. Initiate coordination of outputs with the cooling-rack function. Containerise.

5 'Plain English'

Examine the following examples and say why it is difficult to extract the information. Show how the original violates many of the discourse principles we have been looking at in this chapter. Also comment on the complexity with regard to clause structure and vocabulary. Translate each into a Plain English version. What has the rewritten version done to redress these problems?

a A New Zealand official made the following report, having surveyed a plot of ground for an athletic field:

> It is obvious from the difference in elevation with relation to the short depth of the property that the contour is such as to preclude any reasonable developmental potential for active recreation.

As quoted in Lutz 1989:125

b A memo from an office manager to the chief executive officer:

> Verbal contact with Mr X regarding the attached notification of promotion has elicited the attached representation intimating that he prefers to decline the assignment.

As quoted in Lutz 1989:125

c Subsection 27 (12) of the Companies (Acquisition of Shares) (Victoria) Code:

> Where an offeree who has accepted a take-over offer that is subject to a prescribed condition receives a copy of a notice under sub-section (10) in relation to a variation of offers under the relevant take-over scheme, being a variation the effect of which is to postpone for a period exceeding one month the time when the offeror's obligations under the take-over scheme are to be satisfied, the offeree may, by notice in writing given to the offeror within one month after receipt of the first-mentioned notice and accompanied by any consideration that has been received by the offeree (together with any necessary documents of transfer), withdraw his [*sic*] acceptance of the offer and, where such a notice is given by the offeree to the offeror and is accompanied by any such consideration and any necessary documents of transfer, the offeror shall return to the offeree within 14 days after receipt of the notice, any documents that were sent by the offeree to the offeror with the acceptance of the offer.

As quoted in Allan & Burridge 1991:199

d Entry in Sir Humphry Appleby's diary for Sunday 15 May:

> Sometimes one is forced to consider the possibility that affairs are being conducted in a manner which, all things being considered and making all possible allowances is, not to put too fine a point on it, perhaps not entirely straightforward.

Lynn & Jay 1988

6 Spoken language

The following dialogue is a genuine piece of spontaneous conversation between two friends. Describe the features that distinguish it from written English. Your answer should include factors such as vocabulary differences, non-fluency features (hesitations, fillers, false starts, and self-corrections), grammatical differences, and discourse structure (treatment of given and new information, and ellipsis). Before you tackle this, take note of the following conventions. The speakers are indicated with an initial. Each line represents one intonation unit. Continuing intonation units are marked with a comma, and final intonation units with a full stop or question mark. Simultaneous speech is indicated by two sets of parentheses (lines 4 and 5, for example). Pauses are marked by an ellipsis (three stops). Laughter is indicated in square brackets.

C Katherine said the food was,
C it was alright.
L Hayley enjoyed it,
L (the) food.
C (Yeah).
C An' I,
C I said to Mrs Boyle,
C something,
C she said about the pla-

C she said they were big plates an' a small meal.
C An' I said yeah,
C Katherine said the meal was small.
C Coz,
C forty five dollars or whatever it was,
L Yeah.
C I think the,
C ...some of the kids thought it was a bit expensive.
C I said,
C you pay for the venue,
C that's what you're paying (for).
L (Hmm).
C This is,
C it's all part of the atmosphere.
L We went to a restaurant night,
L Sis came out,
L but with another couple.
L And that was a place like that.
C Hmm.
L Stylish and grand piano,
C Hmm.
L pianist there playing and everything.
L Then she got the big plates an',
C Hmm.
L (where's) the food?
C ([laughter])
C A couple of snow peas arranged,
C in a nice,
L [laughter]
C pattern.
C Yeah.
C This,
C I said well it's a night.
C An' at least you can say you've been there.
L Hmm.
C But Judy said it would've been nice to be there in the day,
C because she said the gardens looked like they'd be beautiful,
C (down there).
L (Hmm).
C It would be great.
C She said you couldn't really see them,
C at night.
C So she said,
C she would've liked it to have been (in the) afternoon,

L (Yeah).
C which I think
C Naomi's was a lunch.
C I think.

Julie Reid, pers. comm., July 1996

7 Spoken relative clauses

At the end of the conversation in exercise 6, the following relative clause occurs:

C which I think
C Naomi's was a lunch.

This sort of relative clauses (dubbed 'the linking relative') is very typical of spoken English. Here are some others (provided by Julie Reid, pers. comm., July 1996):

> ...unless you get 88, which some universities are not going to give those marks.

Uttered by JB, La Trobe University

> ...going on his run in the Doncaster, which most of these couldn't get a run in the Doncaster

Heard at Caulfield races, 23 April 1994

> I'm taking them to Kangaroo Ground, which hopefully they won't have too much culture shock over there.

Uttered by Postgraduate student, La Trobe University

Describe how the formation of these relative clauses differs from that of the relative clauses described in chapter 9. Why do you think it is called 'the linking relative'?

8 Data collection

Tape part of a television or radio broadcast (approximately 2–3 minutes) of any sporting event. You could choose football, a horse race—any sport will do. Copy out the part you have taped. Identify those features that distinguish your transcription from 'normal' English discourse. Pay particular attention to lexical and grammatical features.

As an alternative to the above, try your hand at conversation analysis. Record about 2–3 minutes of a conversation between some of friends. (Make sure you get their permission first.) Transcribe using the conventions outlined in exercise 6. Identify those features that distinguish your text as spoken English, as opposed to written.

11

Structure across Time

INTRODUCTION

We have already seen that early English differs from the modern language in both sounds and vocabulary. There are also enormous differences in the way that words combine to form sentences. As we see in the following lines from a Middle English recipe for swan chowder, with a bit of phonological imagination all the words can be unravelled, but the way they're combined is quite strange.

> Cast þe flessh þerto ihewed & messe it forth with þe swan irostede. It schal beon god vor to eten.
>
> Recipe from Hieatt & Butler 1985

A literal rendition of this would be something like 'Cast the flesh thereto hewn & mess it forth with the swan roasted. It shall be good for to eat', or in other words, 'Add the minced meat and serve it up with the roasted swan. It'll be good to eat'.

While we obviously can't explore all of the developments in the structure of English here, what we will do is give some idea of how the distinctive character of Modern English developed, concentrating on the overall loss of inflections (including the levelling of case inflections, the collapse of gender distinctions, and loss of dependable subject agreement on the verb) and the gradual fixing of word order. As part of this we look at analogy, one of the major driving forces behind these changes, and also consider a more general question concerning the creation of grammar: where do the grammatical bits and pieces of English come from?

SYNTHETIC TO ANALYTIC: FROM OLD ENGLISH TO MODERN ENGLISH

The grammatical developments can be summarised by saying that English has shifted from what is called a '**synthetic language**', where inflections signal the relationships between words, to what is called an '**analytic language**', where this information is signalled by word order or function words like prepositions and auxiliaries. We will begin our story with the inflectional system of Old English.

The loss of inflections

To get an idea of the magnitude of the changes that have occurred, let's step back 1000 years to the time of Old English or Anglo-Saxon (roughly 450–1100). Here's some helpful advice from one of the medical collections or 'leechdoms' of the time.

Gif	*men*	***sio***	*heafodpanne*	*beo*	*gehlenced*	*alege*	***þone***
if	one	the	cranium	be	folded	lay	the

man	*upweard*	*drif*	*ii*	*stacan*	*æt*	***þam***	*eaxlum*
man	upwards	drive	2	stakes	at	the	shoulders

lege	***þonne***	*bred*	*þweores*	*ofer*	***þā***	*fet*	*sleah*
lay	the	board	across	over	the	feet	strike

þonne	*ariwa*	*on*	*mid*	*slegebytle*	*hio*	*Gæa*	*on*
that	thrice	on	with	sledge beetle	he	goes	on

riht	*sona*
right	soon

[If someone's head is fractured, lay the man supine, drive two stakes at the shoulders, then lay a board across his feet, then strike on it with a sledge hammer; he will come right at once.]

This and all other Old English medical texts and recipes in this chapter are from Cockayne 1865

Apart from the curious nature of the remedy (it's not easy to imagine how beating someone with a sledge-hammer would help to cure a fractured or 'folded' skull), there are additional curiosities of a linguistic nature in this text. One has to do with Old English noun phrases and relates to a property that we briefly discussed in chapter 7: **case**. In this particular text we have four different versions of what in Modern English would be rendered simply as 'the': *sio*, *þone*, *þam*, and *þa*. They differ in form because they represent different cases. Basically case involves changes to nouns and their modifying words in order to mark the relationship of these nouns to each other and to the verb of the clause. Some cases mark syntactic functions, such as subject and object, while others mark things such as possession and location. Table 11.1 indicates the four major cases of Old English (there was once an instrumental case too, but it disappeared very early). Those of you who speak Modern German were probably struck by its similarity to the Old English text above. Certainly the systems are very close, although the forms, of course, are quite different.

Table 11.1 Case system of Old English

Nominative	words referring to subject and predicate complements
Genitive	case of possession
Accusative	words referring to direct objects*; motion into
Dative	words referring to indirect objects; subjects of verbs of experience and feeling; motion towards

*Depending on the individual verb, some took objects marked in dative or genitive rather than accusative.

You might recall from chapter 7 that Old English had something called '**gender**'. Nouns fell into one of three genders or noun classes: masculine, feminine, and neuter. But it was even more complex than this. Within these three genders, nouns also fell into a number of different subgroups, or declensions, and this had a bearing on the endings they took. (We don't know why these different declensions existed; the motivation would seem to lie way back in Proto-Indo-European.) To give you some idea of the system at this time, Table 11.2 shows the sets of inflectional forms for just three nouns. Take particular note of the 'hound' forms, for these provided the pattern on which the modern system is based—(*hound*, *hound's*, *hounds*). (This is just an overview of the Old English inflectional system and is very sketchy. For those who are interested in the language at this time, we recommend you follow up on the further reading on Old English given at the end of this book.)

Table 11.2 Old English nouns

	hound (masculine)	*gift (feminine)*	*word (neuter)*
Singular			
Nominative	hund	giefu	word
Genitive	hundes	giefe	wordes
Dative	hunde	giefe	worde
Accusative	hund	giefe	word
Plural			
Nominative	hundas	giefa	word
Genitive	hunda	giefa	worda
Dative	hundum	giefum	wordum
Accusative	hundas	giefa	word

This system also had repercussions for modifying words such as adjectives and determiners, which had to agree with their head nouns in case, gender, and number (singular versus plural). Table 11.3 illustrates something of the complexity that existed at this time. It gives the forms for the definite articles or demonstratives in Old English; all of these now simply translate as 'the' or 'that' (depending on context). As you can see from this, the forms *sio/seo*, *þone*, *þam*, and *þa* from the text above represent 'nominative feminine singular', 'accusative masculine singular', 'dative plural', and 'accusative plural', respectively.

Table 11.3 Old English 'the' or 'that'

Singular	*Masculine*	*Feminine*	*Neuter*
Nominative	se	sēo	þæt
Genitive	a{s	alre	a{s
Dative	þǣm/**þām**	þǣre	þǣm/þām
Accusative	þone	þā	þæt
Plural	*All genders*		
Nominative	þā		
Genitive	þara/pǣra		
Dative	þǣm/þām		
Accusative	þā		

The complete disappearance of this case and gender system is a very significant change and one responsible for profound changes elsewhere in our grammar. Clearly the seeds for the collapse were already sown in this early period. As you can see from Tables 11.2 and 11.3, even at this time there was considerable levelling (or syncretism) of case markers—that is, different functions indicated by identical forms (see chapter 5). For example, many nouns had already lost the distinction between nominative and accusative for both singular and plural; the plural forms for the determiners already showed signs of collapse (there are only four distinct forms in the table above).

While we won't outline all the different processes that contributed to the disappearance of the inflectional system in English, we will mention just a couple of the most significant phonological changes that played a role in the syncretism (if you are interested in a fuller account, we recommend Allen 1995). Basically the loss of inflections is connected with the accent shift in early Germanic: what was once free word stress in Indo-European shifted to initial word stress in Germanic. With stress on the initial syllable, the case endings were harder to hear, and a number of reductive changes took place. Quite simply they began to erode away. One change affected vowels in final unstressed syllables (which included, of course, the case endings). These vowels all weakened to schwa: [a o u e] > [ə]. Another change was the loss of final [m] and [n] in the same syllables. This had a devastating effect on the case marking. Eventually final [ə] was also lost (although, of course, we keep it in our spelling). In relation to the 'hound' paradigm above, that leaves only two distinct forms: *hound* [haʊnd] and *hounds* [haʊndz].

As plausible as this scenario seems, phonology can't be the only motivating force here. German had strong syllable-initial stress; why didn't its case system erode away? In addition to phonological processes, contact with French- and Norse-speakers would certainly have had the effect of bringing about a speedier end to these inflections. When languages come into contact, grammatical stripping of this kind is a typical outcome. Some have even gone as far as arguing that medieval English underwent a kind of creolisation (see discussion in chapter 12).

Grammatical information previously signalled by the case system is now signalled via word order or function words such as prepositions. In basic clauses, the subject must appear before the verb, usually in initial position; the object typically follows. For example, in *The queen loved the chef* versus *The chef loved the queen*, it is the order that tells us who is loving who (whom). Our pronouns preserve something of the complexity of Old English. For example, ***She** loves **him*** and ***He** loves **her*** show different pronoun forms for the subjects (*she*, *he*) and the objects (*him*, *her*). But even these have changed beyond recognition. Compare Table 11.4 with the table of Modern English pronouns given in chapter 7. You might think pronouns are a relatively stable part of the language, but as you can see, it takes considerable linguistic imagination to construct the modern system out of what appears in Table 11.4.

All four noun properties (person, number, case, and gender) are well represented in the Old English pronoun system. Not all forms are distinctive though; already there is evidence of syncretism, with many forms having lost their distinctiveness (for example, dative and accusative).

Strikingly different is the number system, with a three-term contrast: singular, dual (signifying two persons), and plural. The fact that the dual pronouns were usu-

Table 11.4 Old English pronouns

Singular	*First person*	*Second person*	*Third person*		
			Masculine	*Feminine*	*Neuter*
Nominative	ic	þū	hē	hēo	hit
Genitive	mīn	þīn	his	hiere	his
Dative	mē	þē	him	hiere	him
Accusative	mē	þē	hine	hīe	hit
	(earlier mec)	(earlier þec)			
Dual	*First person*	*Second person*			
Nominative	wit ('we two')	git ('youse two')			
Genitive	uncer	incer			
Dative	unc	inc			
Accusative	unc	inc			
Plural	*First person*	*Second person*	*Third person (all genders)*		
Nominative	wē	gē	hīe		
Genitive	ūre	ēower	hiera		
Dative	ūs	ēow	him		
Accusative	ūs	ēow	hīe		
	(earlier ūsic)	(earlier ēowic)			

ally backed up by words such as *two* or *both* suggests, however, that these forms were probably already on their way out by this time. The distinction between the 'thou' and 'you' forms was originally one of number, but in late Middle English, and for some time after, the singular forms came to mark intimacy and the plural forms respect. In Modern English this has all collapsed, and all forms have been replaced by a single form *you* (of course, non-standard OZ and NZ English maintains a plural distinction with *youse*). Some of the other pronouns are totally unrecognisable. The original third-person plural forms were replaced by Norse forms, giving Modern English *they*, *them*, and *their*. The rise of *she* remains a linguistic mystery, although there seems no end to the interesting theories that linguists have put forward to account for its sudden appearance (see Crystal 1995:43 for some of these).

The four-case system has been reduced to two, although the current relics of the earlier nominative and dative forms behave quite differently now. Increasingly it has become position in the clause, rather than function, that dictates what form these pronouns take. Nominative pronouns (or what we called 'subjective') typically appear in absolute sentence-initial position, and the dative (or 'objective') has become a kind of default case, producing examples such as *You and **me** have to have a chat*, *Poor **me** will have to do it*; *bigger than **me*** (versus *bigger than I*), and *It is **me*** (versus *It is I*). (For discussion of curiosities such as *between you and I*, see chapter 2.)

The rise of fixed word order

Nowadays we have what we described in chapter 10 as **'grammatical word order'**, where the fixed order of items functions syntactically to indicate clause types and the grammatical relations expressed within them (such as subject and object). By contrast, Old English showed considerably more flexibility in its word order. In fact, all logically possible arrangements of subject, verb, and object appeared during that time. This doesn't mean, however, that word order was totally free. The Old English period was a time of '**expressive word order**', where the placement of elements was controlled by information structure and other contextual considerations (for example, given versus new information, what the speaker considers important, what the speaker wants to emphasise, and what she or he assumes the audience already knows; see chapter 10).

The following examples (a–h) give some idea of the possible variation at this time. To make things straightforward, we have considered only the order of the subject (S), the main verb (V), and everything else (X). As an interesting aside, you might notice that some of the subjects in the following examples (such as (a)) show dative marking. In Old English you could indicate that entities weren't wilfully involved in an event by placing them in the dative, instead of the expected nominative. Relics of this construction are examples such as *me thinks*.

With a couple of exceptions, which we have noted, the rest of the examples in this section come from a short extract of an exorcism of someone suffering from *ælfsogoþa* ('elf-sucked' or 'elf-hiccough'—some sort of nasty affliction caused by elf-possession, which some experts suggest was anaemia).

Main clauses showed predominantly verb-second order (that is, SVX and XVS).

a	*S*	*V*	*X*	
	him	*biþ*	*sona*	*sel*
	him	be	soon	well
	'He will soon be well'			

b	*X*	*V*	*S*	*X*			
	þonne	*meaht*	*þu*	*hine*	*gebetan*	*to*	*hwile*
	then	might	you	it	better	to	while
	'Then you can improve it for a while'						

Other minor orders included verb-third (XSV); verb-initial (VSX), which is a more expressive order often found in vivid prose; and verb-final or near-to-verb-final order (SXV(X)). Basically, verb-final order had a linking function and was common in coordinated clauses in sequence. (Examples (d) and (e) come from different medical texts; these minor orders are quite rare.)

c	*X*		*S*	*V*		*X*
	þone	*mon*	*au*	*meaht*	*gelacnian*	*æltæwlice*
	that	man	you	might	cure	completely
	'That man you might cure completely'					

d	*V*	*S*	*X*	
	gewitaþ	*he*	*sona*	*aweg*
	go	they	soon	away
	'They [the warts] will soon disappear'			

e	X		S	X		V
	yfelum	*deaþe*	*he*	*his*	*lif*	*geændaa*
	evil	death	he	his	life	ends

'He shall end his life by an evil death'

Subordinate clauses showed dominant verb-final (SXV) or near-to-verb-final order (this had the same cohesive function that we saw for linked main clauses; in other words, verb-final order signalled clauses that were bound contextually to other clauses).

f		S	X		V	
	Gif	*þu*	*þone*	*mon*	*lacnian*	*wille*
	if	you	that	man	treat	will

'If you wish to treat the person...'

It was also possible to find the subject and the main verb in sequence (SVX).

g		S	V	X
	Gif	*hit*	*biþ*	*wif*
	if	it	be	woman

'If it is a woman...'

Old English differed from Modern English also with respect to the order within complex verb units (in other words, where there was a main verb and one or more non-finite verb forms). In example (b), you can see that the main verb, *meaht*, is in second position and the rest of the verb unit, *gebetan*, comes later in the clause. This construction is sometimes called the 'verbal brace' because the 'verby' bits form a kind of bracket or brace around the other clause constituents, as in:

h		V	X		V
	ne	*meaht*	*hwaeþere*	*aeltaewlice*	*gelacnian*
	not	might	however	completely	cure

'Yet [you] cannot cure [it] completely'

All of these verb-final features are leftovers from the earlier times when verb-final order was more widespread. Evidence from early Germanic dialects suggests that the neutral unmarked order for both main and subordinate clauses in Proto-Germanic was more than likely verb-final.

The question now is: why should English have abandoned this earlier flexibility of word order in favour of a system of grammatically rigid SVX order? Again there is undoubtedly a complex of different interlocking factors involved. Some of these we will briefly sketch below.

Traditionally the fixing of word-order patterns has been attributed to the loss of a reliable case system in the language. Something is obviously going to have to replace this sort of collapsing inflectional system if the basic grammatical functions are to be signalled reliably, and grammatical word order is one such remedy. But it's probably not a straightforward matter of one disappearing and then the other stepping in to fill its shoes. The loss of case distinctions and the complementary fixing of word order are intimately connected processes and would most certainly have operated simultaneously in early English. A likely scenario is that the gradual erosion of morphological markings (through phonological processes) began to take place, creating a need in the language for some form of grammatical change if English was to continue to communicate effectively. Increasing reliance on word order then rendered these endings redundant, and this hastened their demise. So intricately linked are the processes that it probably doesn't make much sense to try to determine cause and symptom here.

In the texts we've been looking at, certain word orders were already clearly more important than others. Even 1000 years ago, the following constructions were emerging as clear favourites. (The subject, *him/he*, and the verb, *biþ/sy*, are italicised in each case.)

Main clauses	Sona *him biþ* hal	'soon he is well'
	Him biþ sona hal	'he is soon well'
	Sona *biþ him* hal	'soon is he well'
Subordinate clauses	...oþþæt *he* hal *sy*	'...until he well is'

These medical texts must come pretty close to the language that was spoken in Anglo-Saxon times. Being technical prose with little in the way of literary ambition, they provide some of our best evidence of a living, breathing speech community at that time. The alternative minor orders mentioned earlier were stylistic options and more the domain of the literary texts.

With the exception of XVS 'inverted order', which remains marked, these are the orders that eventually became fixed in main clauses (see chapter 10 for the use of inverted subject–verb order today). The association of verb-final order with subordination, however, is a striking difference. It has left no relics in Modern English (except for fossils in the form of compounds such as *typeset*, which show OV order; compare compounds such as *pickpocket*, which show VO order).

Planned versus unplanned discourse

Something we need to take into account here is the impact of the growing literary tradition within English. In the last chapter, we looked at some of the characteristics of the sort of unplanned discourse we associate with speech as opposed to writing. It's significant that many of the features of Old English we have just described—features like the flexibility of word order—still occur in the spontaneous spoken varieties of Modern English.

Of course, we will never know the exact relationship between Old English writing and its spoken equivalent. But we can probably safely assume that, 1000 years ago, the gap between writing and speech would not have been as great as it is today. Because there wasn't a widespread tradition of writing English at this time, people probably wrote very much as they spoke. Bear in mind, too, that the prohibitive costs involved in writing would certainly rule out careful planning—the countless rewritings, reworkings, and corrections that are now possible. At the time of the earliest English documents, the cost of a book was roughly comparable to the cost of a ship. Later English texts possess many more of the features that we now associate with relatively planned discourse, and more demonstrably planned writing. (See chapter 10 for discussion of planned versus unplanned discourse.) For example, the fixed word order of modern Standard English is more typical of the organisational features of writing.

In short, the differences we find between Old and Modern English syntax have undoubtedly been influenced by the emerging prose style and literary ambition over that period. Prestigious classical models would also have been influential. Remember that, for a long time, people had been speaking English but writing Latin. So when it finally came to writing English, many scribes tried to emulate what they considered to be good Latin style in their written English. The apex of this developing written tradition must surely be the highly 'syntactised' registers of those complex varieties such as legalese and bureaucratese, which we examined in chapter 10.

ANALOGY: REGULARISING THE IRREGULAR

We have seen how the reductive processes of phonological change were responsible for much of the simplification of our inflectional system. Another powerful force was a process called '**analogy**'. The term will not be new to you; throughout this book, we have been 'drawing (food) analogies' to help illustrate some of the concepts we have been presenting. The idea is this: we take something that we hope is familiar to you, and by showing its similarity to the new concept, this helps to make our point clearer.

Analogy in language operates in a very similar way. Basically, it is a process of pattern extension. One form becomes more like another form with which it is somehow associated. There are many different types of analogy, but all exploit this principle of resemblance between patterns in language. In chapter 6, for example, we saw analogy at work in the extension of active affixes to form new vocabulary items; for example, the spread of *-ccino* or *-chino* into new environments to create words such as *mugachino*, *frothachino*, and *bambinochino*. Analogy also works as a powerful force behind the spread of grammatical patterns in a language.

Verbs: 'well-hanged' versus 'well-hung'

You are probably familiar with analogy as it works in language learning. Learners encountering forms such as *chew–chewed* figure out that the past ending is *-ed* and then apply it to new verbs that they come across, such as *munch–munched.* In other words, *chew* is to *chewed* as *munch* is to *munched.* This is analogy. Speakers recognise the resemblance between these pairs and extend the pattern to new instances in order to form the past tense of unfamiliar verbs, such as *manducate–manducated.* Some of these generalisations will be correct and some of them won't. If you extend the pattern for the verb *eat*, for example, you arrive of course at *eated*, which is non-standard. If this were to be accepted, however, we would then have an instance of language change by analogy.

The thing about analogical change is that the outcome is the disappearance of irregular and exceptional forms. It is a kind of levelling process, whereby patterns of verbs, nouns, adjectives, and so on are neatened up. One very common type of analogy, illustrated above by *munch–munched*, can be expressed in terms of a proportional equation:

Analogy

X : Y as Z : Q

That is, the relationship between X and Y is the same as that between Z and Q.

Generalisation of -ed
chew : chewed *as* munch : Q (solve Q)
Q = munched

This very simple process has, in fact, been responsible for major changes in English verbs over the past 1000 years. Irregular verbs such as *eat–ate* were at one time much more common than they are today. In fact, they made up one of the two major verb classes in Old English. An inherited Germanic feature at that time was that verbs fell into either the 'strong' or the 'weak' verb class, depending on their past-tense and past-participle forms. The strong verbs comprised some seven subclasses, whose members all indicated a tense change by modifying their root vowel: *eat–ate–eaten.* Weak verbs signalled a tense change by the addition of some kind of dental suffix: *munch–munched–munched.* In chapter 7 we labelled the strong verbs 'irregular' simply because they make up the less numerous class now. Their takeover by the weak class (ironically the much stronger class, as it turns out) is a paradigm example of analogy at work.

Table 11.5 below gives some idea of the seven strong classes in Old English. There were four major parts of the verb: infinitive, past singular, past plural, and past participle. Out of these, you could then build the whole verb pattern by adding the necessary personal endings. There was considerable variation within each of these classes too, but we will spare you the gory details (see Lass 1994).

The past millennium has seen the slow but sure demise of this class, despite the valiant efforts of those within the 'Society for the Preservation of Old English Strong Verbs', who have tried to resuscitate forms such as *raught* for *reached* and *clomb* for *climbed.* Already suffering losses after the French invasion (with the disappearance of a lot of native vocabulary), the class continued losing more and more members to the weak class. By early Middle English, nearly half the original (approximately) 350 strong verbs had disappeared. In the course of Middle English some thirty more became obsolete, and during the sixteenth and seventeenth centuries about the same number again. There remain roughly sixty today, and many of them form part of our everyday vocabulary.

Table 11.5 The seven strong classes in Old English

Class		*Infinitive*	*Past (singular)*	*Past (plural)*	*Past participle*
1	'ride'	rīdan	rād	ridon	(ge)riden
2	'creep'	crēopan	crēap	crupon	cropen
3	'help'	helpan	healp	hulpon	holpen
4	'tear'	teran	tær	tǣron	toren
5	'speak'	sprecan	spræc	sprǣcon	sprecen
6	'go'	faran	fōr	fōron	faren
7	'fall'	feallan	fēoll	fēollon	feallen

Words used frequently stand out more clearly in speakers' minds and are often more successful in resisting this sort of analogical spread. Basic verbs such as *go*, *be*, and *get* are the real survivors, but even these have not remained completely intact. Many strong verbs have changed by analogy with other strong patterns: *slode* > *slid*; *slough* > *slew*; *clang*, *span*, and *stang* > *clung*, *spun*, and *stung*. Vowel variation within the past forms of individual verbs has also been levelled, with the singular past vowel usually winning out. We can therefore identify two instances in which analogy is at work:

- the movement of strong verbs over to the weak class
- the collapsing of distinct patterns within the remaining strong verbs themselves.

These analogical changes have been taking place gradually, and typically with a lot of messy variation. Often weak forms exist alongside strong forms for quite some time.

ached	oke
stepped	stope
climbed	clomb
shaved	shove
creped	crope
rowed	rewe
clawed	clew
laughed	low
yielded	yold

Sometimes the verbs diverge in function—for example, modern *shined* tends to be transitive (*I shined my shoes*) and *shone* intransitive (*The sun shone*). Some verbs undergo quite spectacular splits; for example, the three different verbs *owe*, *own*, and *ought* were all originally different functional forms of one and the same verb. Curiously, past participles of strong verbs are much more tenacious than the past-tense forms, particularly in their adjectival function. For example, you would talk about *a swollen head* but probably say *His head swelled when he heard the good news.* It seems that when some participles are regularised and acquire the normal *-ed* suffix, their adjective counterparts remain unaffected. It is as if these adjectives were stored in a different part of the brain as separate lexical entries and can therefore resist the analogy. We no longer even connect many of these adjectives with their original strong verbs. For instance, *straight* is the original past participle of *stretch*, and *wrought* (as in *wrought iron*) of *work*. Other examples include *cloven* (hoof) from *cleave*, and *molten* (lead, but not cheese) from *melt.*

Occasionally, it appears that the process is working in the opposite direction. Take, for example, the infamous *hanged* versus *hung*. According to most style or usage guides, the difference between these two forms lies in whether you are hanging a person or a thing. To hang a person is a method of execution. It takes the past form *hanged* (*He was hanged for drug trafficking*). To hang something takes the past form *hung* (*The New Zealand flag was hung from our balcony*). In reality, this distinction is rarely observed. For most people (including the present writers), *hung* is the all-purpose past, used as much to speak of people having *hung their suet pudding from the rafters* as of having *hung themselves from the rafters.*

In all the sources we checked, there were citations from around the world showing that *hanged* has clearly given way to *hung*. This is puzzling, given that *hanged* is the regular form, and in this case even the older form. The shift is apparently towards irregularity; but why? In fact, this is the regular process of analogy at work. For monosyllabic verbs whose stems end in a velar nasal [ŋ], the change to [ʌ] in the past has become quite productive, and the pattern has generalised to other contexts. Post-Old English converts include *fling–flung*, *string–strung*, and *ring–rung*. For analogy to work, all you need is some sort of productive morphological process.

The *hanged/hung* controversy is instructive in another respect. It often happens that older forms don't disappear entirely but enjoy something of an obscure afterlife. Sometimes they get relegated to marginal functions, or else they might survive as fossilised remains in certain fixed expressions. The reason why *hanged* survived for so long in the special context of execution was because the form continued to be used in legal English. We saw in chapter 10 how legalese, like some sort of gigantic linguistic fossil, preserves forms long since ousted from ordinary language. *Hanged* also survives in some informal idioms, such as *I'll be hanged if*...But note that in more modern idioms it is *hung* that wins out; you can't, for example, say someone is *well hanged*, only *well hung*.

Nouns: the story of *-s*

Another spectacular example of analogical change in English is the spread of plural *-s*. In Old English there was no plural ending as such. The various noun classes certainly had different endings or vowel changes to indicate plural, but these were conflated with the properties of case and gender. Take another look at Table 11.2 (p. 251). By Middle English, this elaborate system of noun endings was already completely obliterated. We can illustrate the changes with the example below. As you can see in Table 11.6, this was the first time that plural was represented directly in the morphology of English. Case and gender were no longer distinctive, but there still remained a number of competing plural endings across the different classes of nouns: *scip–scipu*, *gear–gear*, *hand–handa*, *ēage–ēagan*, *hund–hundas*, and so on. These various expressions of plural were then ripe for change, and sweeping analogical changes took place, finally ridding English plurals of all this variation.

Table 11.6 The development of plural *-s* from Old to Modern English

	Old English	*Modern English*
Singular		
Nominative/Accusative	hund	hound
Dative	hunde	
Genitive	hundes	hound's
Plural		
Nominative/Accusative	hundas	
Dative	hundum	hounds
Genitive	hunda	

Once more we see the spread of one particular suffix at the expense of all others—in this case *-s* (from the original masculine *hund* 'hound' class). But it was touch and go as to whether or not the *-s* would win out as the plural ending. The other hot favourite (especially in the south) was *-en*. For a while it looked as if we would be forming our plurals today with this suffix (for instance, *shoe–shoen*, *knee–kneen*, *eye-eyen*, and so on). But by the end of the fourteenth century, *-s* had won out and had been extended to all plural forms.

These plural variations are inherited features from Germanic, and it's interesting that the other Germanic languages show similar sorts of analogical extensions, but with different suffixes emerging as dominant (*-en* in Dutch and -[vowel] *r* in Scandinavian languages). Only German seems to have maintained something of the original variation.

This touches on a real problem for analogy: how can we figure out which of the patterns will survive and be extended? Frequency certainly has something to do with it, but it's not the whole story. In the case of our plural ending, it's probably the additional support of the Anglo-Norman plural *-s* that helped to tip the scales in favour of *-s*.

It's small wonder that Jean Aitchison (1991:146) describes analogy as a kind of 'tidying up process'. It really does seem to step in and clean up areas of messy variation and irregularity that might exist in a language. It's clearly a very strong force at work in language change, but it is problematic. For example, we can't predict when it will occur or, when it does, what direction it will take (in other words, which new patterns will and won't be accepted). Some linguists have attempted to come up with generalisations (see McMahon 1995:80). Two overall tendencies emerge:

- The clear and systematic marking of grammatical categories such as tense and number is preferred.
- These categories tend to be expressed by a single marker, not by multiple markers.

GRAMMATICALISATION: CREATING GRAMMAR

So where do items such as auxiliary verbs, prepositions, conjunctions, definite articles, and negators come from? How do case, tense, and aspect markers evolve? These are the grammatical bits and pieces of a language, and as we hinted earlier in chapter 5, all grow out of the ordinary lexicon of a language. This is **grammaticalisation**, or the creation of grammar. Linguists studying grammaticalisation examine the lexical sources that give rise to grammatical forms and constructions, as well as the events that take place as the items become more grammatical (See chapter 5 for a discussion of the grammaticality cline.)

Are all lexical items eligible for grammaticalisation? Could a word such as *lamington* ever evolve into an indirect object marker? Probably not. Those lexical items that get recruited for grammatical service are generally drawn from the most basic vocabulary. They are culture independent (unlike *lamington*), and refer to the most fundamental of human experiences and activities. Accordingly, they typically have more general meanings, which is why they are used more frequently and in a wide range of contexts. For example, verbs such as *devour*, *munch*, and *gorge* have such specific meanings and accordingly restricted contexts of use that they would be unlikely recruits for grammatical marking. Compare these with a general verb such as *eat*.

As we will see, the metamorphosis from lexicon to grammar is itself made up of a parcel of closely interrelated processes occurring at the semantic, grammatical, and phonological levels. To illustrate, we offer a 'potted' history of English negation.

Because of its expressive nature, negation is an aspect of language that is prone to rapid change, and the history of English offers us a spectacular illustration of this.

Modern English, as you know, negates by placing *not* or *-n't* directly after the auxiliary verb. If there is no auxiliary, then a kind of 'dummy' auxiliary *do* is needed to support the negator. For example:

I will not/won't cook stuffed tomato aux Herbs Shoreham-style.
I do not/don't cook stuffed tomato aux Herbs Shoreham-style.
*I cook not stuffed tomato aux Herbs Shoreham-style.

But let's again step back 1000 years to the time of Old English (450–1100) to see how people negated then. Here is one suggested use for radishes from the tenth century.

Wiþ	*wif*	*gemædlan*	*geberge*	*on*	*neahtnestig*	*rædices*	*moran*
against	woman	madness	eat	on	nightfasting	radish's	root

þy	*dæge*	*ne*	*mæg*	*þe*	*se*	*gemædla*	*sceþþan*
that	day	**not**	may	you	the	madness	bother

'Against a woman's mad behaviour: eat some radishes before breakfast [literally during nightfasting] and that day the madness cannot bother you'

As we see here, Old English typically negated by placing a negative adverb *ne* before the finite verb (here *mæg*). Also common at this time was multiple negation, whereby *ne* was supported by one, perhaps even more, additional negative words. Here is some more dietary wisdom from the tenth century.

Georne	*is*	*to*	*wyrnanne*	*bearneacnum*	*wife*
earnestly	is	to	warn	pregnant	woman

þæt	*hio*	. . .	***ne***	*swines*	*flæsc*	*ete*	***ne***	***naht***	*fættes*
that	she	. . .	**not**	swine's	flesh	eat	**nor**	**nothing**	fat

ne	*druncen*	*gedrince*	*ne*	*on*	*weg*	***ne***	*fere*
nor	drunkeness	drink	nor	on	road	**not**	travel

'A pregnant woman is to be earnestly advised that she eat no pork or anything fatty, [that she] not drink to intoxication or travel by road'

Læcas	*lærdon*	*þæt*	***nan***	*man*	*on*	*þam*	*month*	***ne***
leeches	taught	that	**not-one**	man	on	that	month	**no**

drenc	***ne***	*drunc*	*Of*	*mete*	*y*	*sigge*	*þat*	*to*
drink	**not**	drink	of	food	I	say	that	to

hym	*þat*	*is*	*of*	*an*	*hot*	*&*	*moiste*	*complexioun*
him	that	is	of	a	hot	and	moist	complexion

be	***no***	*manere*	*weye*	***ne***	*scholde*	***noght***	*be*	*gessen*	*flesch*
be	**no**	manner	way	**not**	should	**not**	be	eating	flesh

'Physicians taught that no one in that month should drink a potion'

In Middle English (1100–1500), multiple negation was still the norm. One fourteenth-century text warns of the serious consequences of wine.

þere	***nys***	***noþynge***	*þat*	*so*	*sone*	*smyteþ*	*with*
there	**not-is**	**nothing**	that	so	soon	smites	with

grevaunce	*þe*	*hed*	*oþere*	*þe*	*synwe*	*as*	*wyne*
grievance	the	head	or	the	sinews	as	wine

'There isn't anything which damages the head or the sinews as quickly as wine'

This and all other Middle English and Early New English etiquette texts in this chapter are from Furnivall 1868

By this period, a serious rival to preverbal *ne* had appeared on the scene. This was *nogt* or what was eventually to become our modern *not* and *-n't*. (It began life as one of the extra reinforcing expressions—originally Old English *ne-a-wiht*, 'not-ever-anything'—and its use was emphatic in origin.)

Of	*mete*	*y*	*sigge*	*þat*	*to*	*hym*	*þat*
of	food	I	say	that	to	him	that

is	*of*	*an*	*hot*	*&*	*moiste*	*complexioun*
is	of	a	hot	and	moist	complexion

be	***no***	*manere*	*weye*	***ne***	*scholde*	***noght***	*be*	*gessen*	*flesch*
be	**no**	manner	way	**not**	should	**not**	be	eating	flesh

'Of food I say that those who are of a hot and moist complexion should in no kind of way be eating meat'

During the Middle English period, however, *noght* lost its emphatic quality and, together with preverbal *ne*, emerged as the normal expression of negation. This is sometimes called 'embracing negation', because these two negators snugly wrapped themselves around the verb (for example, *hyt* ***ne*** *swellyþ* ***noght***, meaning 'it **not** swells **not**').

During this period, *not* also started to appear all alone. The following comes from the same fourteenth-century text as the two previous examples.

And	*if*	*þat*	*he*	*mygte*	***not***	*absteyen*	*him*	*fro*
and	if	that	he	might	**not**	abstain	him	from

fleisch	*geve*	*him*	*fleisch*	*of*	*smale*	*chickenes*
flesh	give	him	flesch	of	small	chickens

'And if he can't hold himself back from meat, give him meat from small chickens'

By the end of this period, preverbal *ne* had disappeared, and single postverbal *not* had established itself as the preferred negator. We are talking about Standard English here, of course. Non-standard varieties of both OZ and NZ English (as well as other Englishes) maintain multiple negation as the norm (for example, *I never eat no dinner*).

Here are some examples from the sixteenth century that show the various negative patterns available:

I *would not* that you should observe a certaine houre, either for dinners or suppers.

One and the same order of diet *doth not* promiscuously agree with all men.
Drinke *not* above four times.

Things are looking more familiar, but the third example shows that there are still interesting differences. In Modern English, we need the support of *do* here (for instance, *Do not drink*). Although auxiliary *do* was available to speakers at this time, it wasn't until roughly 1900, that it became obligatory in negation if there was no other auxiliary present. The origin of this *do* is disputed, and it won't concern us here; suffice to say that it is another example of grammaticalisation at work, its source being the lexical verb *do* 'to make, perform'. The rise of 'dummy' *do* has been a significant development in the way we negate.

To summarise, the history of English negation looks something like this:

preverbal negation *ne* > embracing negation *ne–not* > postverbal negation *not*

We can describe the different types of changes that have taken place as follows. These are all predictable changes associated with grammaticalisation.

Semantic changes

With grammaticalisation, words lose their more concrete lexical meanings and take on much more general or abstract meanings. And the more general they become in their meaning, the more frequently they're used. The full expression *ne-a-wiht* shifted from the literal meaning of 'not ever anything' to a general expression of negation. You can compare some of the extra reinforcing expressions we find in Modern English negation: *I don't care **a bit***, which shows the start of this kind of generalisation, as *bit* derives from the lexical item *bite*.

Phonological reduction

When words become more grammatical, they typically become unstressed; consonants and vowels reduce. Put simply, the words shorten. *Bit*, with its short vowel, already shows signs of this kind of reduction. In the case of *not*, what was formerly a three morpheme item (*ne+a+wiht*) is now an unsegementable unit *not*, and *-n't* in normal speech. In fact, in most rapid speech, *not* disappears entirely. Like the 'Cheshire Cat's grin', only the shadow remains in the form of nasalisation. For example, *It can't be done* [ɪt kæ̃: bi dʌn]. The linguist Jim Matisoff has captured this process by which grammatical morphemes are reduced to such an extent that all of their segmental phonemes disappear; he has dubbed it appropriately 'cheshirisation'.

Grammatical words are used more than lexical words, and this increased frequency also contributes to the reduction process. We always reduce the most frequently used forms. Think of all the grammatical elements in English. They're all short. They are also the less informative bits of a message, and for that reason too they are short; as we discussed in chapter 10, there is an iconic relationship between informativeness and size.

Structural changes

Grammatical words can't be stressed; they can't be modified, and we don't move them around for special focus as we do lexical words. As they become fixed in position, and as they reduce in size, so they become increasingly dependent on surrounding material, eventually even fusing with it. The development *not* > *-n't* shows nicely this transition from full word to clitic (to affix) (see also chapter 5).

So what is the current state of affairs regarding *not?* Linguists such as Paul Hopper and Elizabeth Traugott (1994), who work in the area of grammaticalisation, emphasise the perpetual tug of war between, on the one hand, creativity and expressiveness (that is, a speaker's introduction of new and innovative ways of saying things) and, on the other hand, routinisation (that is, a speaker's tendency to reduce the speech signal—through compacting, reduction, and boundary obliteration—as in Old English *neawhit* 'not-ever-anything' > *noght* > *not* > *-n't*). Given the significance of negation, Modern English *-n't* is clearly ripe for renewal.

There are many likely contenders for the job. One is the adverb *never* (literally, 'not ever'), which has become common in OZ and NZ English (and varieties elsewhere) as the general expression of negation (*I never ate it*, meaning 'I didn't eat it'). Another candidate involves a group of concrete nouns used to express minimal quantities when combined with negation. They are typically emphatic (for example, *I didn't drink* ***a drop***; *He didn't get* ***a spot*** *of praise*; *I couldn't walk* ***a step***; *I didn't eat* ***a crumb***; *It didn't hurt* ***a bit***; *I don't give* ***a damn***). All are reminiscent of the early days of *not*, and any one could potentially evolve into a negative marker.

As Hopper and Traugott point out, there is nothing intrinsic in their meaning that predicts their development into negators, but it is rather the way they combine with negators in discourse that determines this particular development. Any one could start expanding its contexts, although as we implied above, one likely contender is *bit*. It is already showing signs of semantic and phonological change and has started to generalise into other contexts, no longer being confined to verbs of eating, as in examples such as *It didn't hurt a bit*; compare *a crumb*, which can only be used with verbs of eating (**It didn't hurt a crumb*).

In teenager slang, there is a curious development in negation; it takes the form of post-sentential negation, as in *You're a terrific cook—not* ('You're not a good cook at all'). This is still a rather faddish construction and is limited in contexts of use. But you should be on the lookout for these kinds of constructions, as they often provide the basis for real change in the language. Mind you, in this case it is extremely rare for free-standing negators to appear well after the verb. Post-sentential negation will likely remain a fashion item of teenspeak.

In OZ English, it has even been suggested that *pig's arse* is a potential new negator (we owe this observation to Bill McGregor). Certainly, the expression is used to reinforce negation (in the same way as concrete nouns such as *spot*, *crumb*, and *bit*) and has even expanded its contexts in a way that suggests incipient grammaticalisation (as in *Pig's arse I did it!*). But it is a long way from a general negator. Its taboo quality means that it is unlikely to ever gain the currency needed to start the grammaticalisation ball rolling. A more likely candidate is *no way* (as in *No way I did it!*).

Being a very expressive area of language, negation is particularly driven by fashion and the continual search for novelty—much like food preferences really. In the languages of the world, we find a rapid and constant turnover of negators.

POINTS TO REMEMBER

- In Old English, nouns, pronouns, adjectives, and determiners inflected to signal gender, number, and case. Verbs inflected for person, number, tense, and mood. We have now lost most of these inflections.
- The Old English period represents a time of expressive word order, when the placement of elements was controlled by information structure and considerations such as old versus new information, what speakers consider important, what they want to emphasise, and so on. This has been replaced by grammatical word order, where the fixed order of items functions syntactically to indicate clause types and the grammatical relations expressed within them (things like subject and object).
- These changes can be summarised as a shift from a synthetic character, where the relationships between words are indicated primarily by their inflectional forms, to an analytic character, where these relationships are indicated by word order and grammatical (or functional) words such as auxiliaries and prepositions.
- The process of analogy is a powerful force in grammatical change. While it does not create new grammatical forms, it is responsible for the spread of already existing forms; in other words, it is a kind of tidying-up or levelling process, whereby irregular patterns and exceptional forms become regular.
- Grammaticalisation is the creation of grammar. It refers to the transition of morphemes from a lexical to a grammatical status. Grammaticalisation itself is made up of a parcel of closely interrelated processes, occurring at the semantic, grammatical, and phonological levels.
- The history of English negation from *ne-a-wiht* 'not ever anything' to Modern English *not* and *-n't* follows along the paths of grammaticalisation, showing the expected semantic generalisation, phonological reduction, and the eventual shift from free to bound status.

EXERCISES

1 Old English word order

There are considerable differences in word order between Old and Modern English. For each of the following examples, describe how the word order departs from that of the present day. (Any of you with tired, swollen eyes might also like to try the 'live crab' remedy.)

Ealdes	*mannes*	*eagan*	*beoþ*	*unscearpsyno*
old	person's	eyes	are	unsharp

þonne	*sceal*	*he*	*þa*	*eagan*	*weccan*	*mid*	*gnidingum*	*mid*	*gongum*
then	should	he	the	eyes	arouse	with	rubbings	with	walkings

He	*sculan*	*nyttian*	*lytlum*	&	*hiora*	*heafod*	*cemban*	&	*wermod*	*drincan*
They	should	eat	little	&	their	heads	comb	&	wormwood	drink

ærþon	*hie*	*mete*	*þicgean*
before	they	food	take

Wiþ	*aswollenum*	*eagum*	*genim*	*cucune*	*hrefn*	*ado*	*þa*	*eagan*	*of*
against	swollen	eyes	take	alive	crab	do	the	eyes	off

&	*eft*	*cucune*	*gebring*	*on*	*wætre*
and	afterwards	alive	bring	into	water

&	*do*	*þa*	*eagan*	*þam*	*men*	*on*	*sweoran*
and	do	the	eyes	the	one	on	hang

þe	*him*	*þearf*	*sie*
to-whom	him	need	be

'An old person's eyes are not sharp sighted. Then he is to arouse his eyes with rubbings, with walkings. And they are to use foods sparingly and comb their heads and drink wormwood before taking food. For swollen eyes take a live crab, remove the eyes, and afterwards put it alive into water, and hang the eyes around the neck of anyone who has need of them'

2 From Old to Modern English

The following short extracts deal with a similar theme: hair care and etiquette. Each is taken from a different period of English, and as you work your way through, the language should become more and more familiar (the first text is from Cokayne 1865; all other texts in this exercise are from Furnivall 1868). Describe how the English from each period differs from Modern English. Concentrate on grammatical differences such as word order, word endings, clause linking, and so on. (You may find the ingredients of these tonics a little odd, but the reasoning at this time was quite simple: bees are hairy creatures and therefore promote hair growth; ants' eggs are bald and therefore work to prevent unwanted hair.)

a Old English (tenth century)

Gif	*mannes*	*feax*	*fealle*	*...*
if	mann's	hair	falls	...

Wiþ	*þon*	*gif*	*man*	*calu*	*sie*	*Plinuis*	*se*	*micla*	*læce*
against	that	if	one	bald	is	Pliny	the	great	physician

segþ	*þisne*	*læcdom:*	*Genim*	*deade*	*beon*	*gebærne*	*to*	*ahsan*	*&*
says	this	leechdom:	take	dead	bees	burn	to	ashes	and

linsæd	*æc*	*do*	*ele*	*to*	*on*	*þæt*	*seoþe*	*swiþe*	*lange*	*ofer*
linseed	also	do	oil	to	on	that	boil	very	long	over

gledum	*aseoh*	*þonne*	*...*	*smire*	*mid*	*æfter*	*baþe*
coals	strain	then	...	smear	with	after	bath

Wiþ	*þon*	*þe*	*hær*	*ne*	*weaxe*
against	that	that	hair	not	grows

æmettan	*ægru*	*genim*	*gnid*	*smit*	*on*	*þa*	*stowe*
ants	eggs	take	rub	smite	on	the	place

ne	*cymth*	*þær*	*næfre*	*ænig*	*feax*	*up*
not	come	there	never	any	hair	up

'If a man's hair falls out...In case one is bald, Pliny the great physician gives this treatment: Take dead bees, burn to ashes and also linseed, add oil to that, cook for a very long time over coals...anoint with it after a bath. In order that the hair may not grow; take ants eggs, rub them up, smudge on the place; never will any hair come up there'

b Middle English (fourteenth century)

Whanne	*a*	*mannes*	*heeris*	*fallib*	*awei*
when	a	man's	hair	falls	away

so	*in*	*vnkyndeli*	*tyme*	*as*	*þe*	*while*	*he*	*is*	*young*
so	in	unkindly	time	as	the	while	he	is	young

þan	*make*	*him*	*a*	*baþ*	*&*	*anoynte*	*him*	*wiþ*	*chamomile*
then	make	him	a	bath	and	anoint	him	with	chamomile

and	*wiþ*	*bittir*	*almondis*	*&*	*wiþ*	*oile*	*maad*	*þerof*
and	with	bitter	almonds	and	with	oil	made	therefrom

'When a man's hair falls out in such an unkindly time as when he is young, then make him a bath and anoint him with chamomile and with bitter almonds and with oil made from that'.

c Middle English (mid-fifteenth century)

Pike not youre nose ne that hit be droppynge with no peerlis clere, sniyff nor snitynge [blow] to lowd lest youre souerayne [master] hit [it] here [hear]. Put not youre handes in youre hosen youre codware for to clawe [don't claw your cods].

d Late Middle–Early New English (sixteenth century)

After you have euacuated your bodye, & trussed your poyntes, kayme your heade oft, and so do dyuers tymes in the day. And wasshe your handes & wrestes, your face, & eyes, and your teeth with colde water.

e Early New English (seventeenth century)

When you have apparelled your selfe hansomely, combe your head softly and easily with an Iuorie combe: for nothing recreateth the memorie more.

After the body is well clothed, kembe your head wel with an Iuory comb, from the forehead to the backepart, drawing the comb some forty times at the least; then wash all the instruments of the sences, as the eies, the ears, the nostril, the mouth, the tongue, the teeth.

f Early Modern English (nineteenth century)

While waiting at dinner, never be picking your nose, or scratching your head, or any other part of your body; neither blow your nose in the room; if you have a cold, and cannot help doing it, do it on the outside of the door; but do not sound your nose like a trumpet.

3 New strong verbs

Some new strong forms have appeared over the years. These represent the analogical extension of some common strong verb patterns. Try to figure out which of the original strong verbs are behind the new strong formations below. Say which of these are now in standard use. (You may find it necessary to consult a grammar of English such as Quirk et al. 1985, where the different classes of irregular verbs are outlined.)

a	wear	wore	worn
b	spit	spat	
c	stick	stuck	
d	fling	(?flang)	flung
e	string	strung	
f	dive	dove	
g	strive	strove	
h	drag	drug	
i	squeeze	squoze	
j	sneeze	snoze	
k	think	thunk	
l	clink	clunk	
m	ring	rung	
n	bring	brang	brung
o	skim	skum	
p	skin	skun (in the context of skinning a rabbit)	

4 False analogies

Consider the past tense forms of the following verbs:

Present	*Past*
speak	spoke
seek	sought
reek	reeked

Why do you think we can understand a child who says *I speaked; I seeked* but not one who says *I spought; I rought* on analogy with *seek*, or *I soke; I roke* on analogy with *speak*? What about colloquial OZ and NZ *I snuck* in place of *I sneaked*? Why is this problematic?

5 Backformation

The analogical spread of the plural *-s* has been a real success story—so successful, in fact, that even the *-s* on the end of some noun stems has been 'wrongly' interpreted as a plural and a new singular then 'backformed'. Identify the source of the backformations in the following words. (For more on backformation, see chapter 5.)

a gentry
b asset
c caterpillar (additional changes here)
d eave
e sherry
f marquee 'tent'

Why do you think some people have been heard to say things like *This is a very nice hoe* (meaning 'stocking') or *You'll find this a very elegant pant*?

The following words appear to illustrate a related, but quite different, process. Using a dictionary, give the history of these words, and then describe the process of word-formation that is involved. Explain how this process has occurred.

g truce
h chicken
i (one) sixpence
j chess
k (one) dice
l lettuce
m chintz

6 Exceptions to the rule

Why are the following examples exceptional in the way they form their plurals? Why do you think they go against the expected pattern?

a Maple Leafs 'Canadian ice-hockey team'
b pink foots 'a type of bird'
c Mickey Mouses 'easy courses'
d still lifes 'paintings of inanimate objects'
e flatfoots 'policemen'
f sabertooths 'a type of tiger'

The following show both regular and irregular forms. Can you identify a pattern? What do the forms have in common?

	Regular	*Irregular*
g	weaved (through traffic)	wove
h	halfs (as in *rounding up the halfs*)	halves
i	gooses 'a heavy smoothing iron used by tailors'	geese
j	mouses (of a computer)	mice
k	wolfs 'agressive men'	wolves
l	badder 'tougher'	worse

/ **7 Grammaticalisation in Tok Pisin (New Guinea Pidgin)**

In Tok Pisin, the form *save* as an independent verb means 'to know'.

Em	*i*	***save***	*kukim*	*kaikai*	*bilong*	*ol*	*Yuropen*
s/he	[particle]	know	cook	food	of	all	Europeans

'She knows how to cook European foods'

It can also be used to mark habitual action; (that is, that something is done regularly). With this meaning, it is usually reduced to the unstressed form *sa*.

Mipela	*ol*	*Papua*	*Niugini*	*i*	***sa***	*kaikai*	*kaukau*
we	all	Papua	New Guineans	[particle]	[habitual]	food	sweet potato

long	*nait*
at	night

'We Papua New Guineans usually eat sweet potato at night'

a How would you describe what is happening in the language? What sort of change is this? (Your answer should include some details about pronunciation, meaning, and grammar.)
b Can you account for the meaning change 'to know' > 'to do something regularly'?
c Can you give one other example of this type that has occurred, or is currently occurring, in English?

8 **Grammaticalisation in Kriol (northern Australia)**
In Kriol, *gotta* has a variety of functions. For each of the following functions:

- Explain the grammatical function of *gotta* in each of these examples.
- Explain what is it about the semantics of *get* that makes it an appropriate candidate for each of these functions?
- Can you see any potential for misunderstanding between a speaker of Kriol and a speaker of Standard English?

a If you kick him here you gotta kill'im.
'If you kick it there, you will kill it.'
b They gotta get the crowbar, they gotta get it out.
'They have to get the crowbar; they have to get it out.'
c One big plate gotta three little candle.
'A big plate with three little candles.'
d Sometime they killim gotta gun and gotta net.
'Sometimes they kill it with a gun and with a net.'
e You gotta tape us?
'Will you tape us?'

12

English Globe-Trotting

INTRODUCTION

One consequence of the worldwide spread of English is the mushrooming of hybrid varieties of English. A favourite illustration of ours comes from the label on a tin of snails. The label is in two languages: French and, well, we'll leave you to decide what this is.

> **Instruction:** To hold one box, open at cooling.
> **Preparation of Farce (for one dozen):** With 5 g of parsley, to join 4 g of garlic, 1 g of shallot, 4 g of salt, one prim of pepper, the half of one nut. To hew him and to mix at 50 g of butter very fine. To drain the put in the shells, to furnish of farce clase-border, to passt at over hot one quarter time about.

One can't help but think that this is evidence of some cunning plan (perhaps hatched by the Académie Française) to get back at English for all the borrowings (thefts?) during the Norman Conquest and for the present storming of the French lexicon with English words.

What it does make clear is that a singular designation of English is no longer adequate to describe a language that now involves almost every linguistic area in the world. Terms such as *Modern Englishes*, *World Englishes*, and *New Englishes* (as well as *Spanglish*, *Frenglish*, and *Anglikaans*) are needed to cover the varieties that have sprung up as a consequence of this expansion of English beyond its original mother-tongue country.

In this chapter we look at these different Englishes, as well as the overall effect on English of globalisation (the rise of 'the global village')—for instance, with respect to current advances in communication technology, such as e-mail English. We also consider the implications of the worldwide marketing of English (for example, the export of OZ English in books, dictionaries, and even 'soapies' such as 'Heartbreak High' and 'Paradise Beach'). English has become a commodity to be promoted and sold, and the market-place is fiercely competitive.

GLOBALISATION AND ENGLISH AROUND THE WORLD

The world is becoming increasingly global in orientation, and this process of globalisation is having many effects. The most dramatic involve the spread of worldwide communication networks and media, the internationalism of products and consumerism, massive flows of people (including tourists, refugees, and migrants), and the recognition that environmental issues must be addressed globally. In short, people talk of 'a global village'. This global village demands a *lingua franca*, or common language. Although most agree that this will be English, the question is: what kind of English?

The global takeover by English probably began as early as 450 years ago with its initial spread towards Wales and Scotland. Since that time, English has been slowly but surely bulldozing its way to becoming the language of the world—and now even the language of space and cyberspace. It is important to emphasise that the extraordinary 'success' of English is not on account of any inherent linguistic superiority. All along the way, English has been piggybacking on the British Empire and, more recently, on American cultural and economic imperialism. When a language dominates in this way, it is never for linguistic reasons.

The world's population is approaching six billion, and a staggering proportion of this six billion are already regular users of English. Braj Kachru, a scholar of global Englishes, discusses these users of English in terms of three concentric circles (see Figure 12.1).

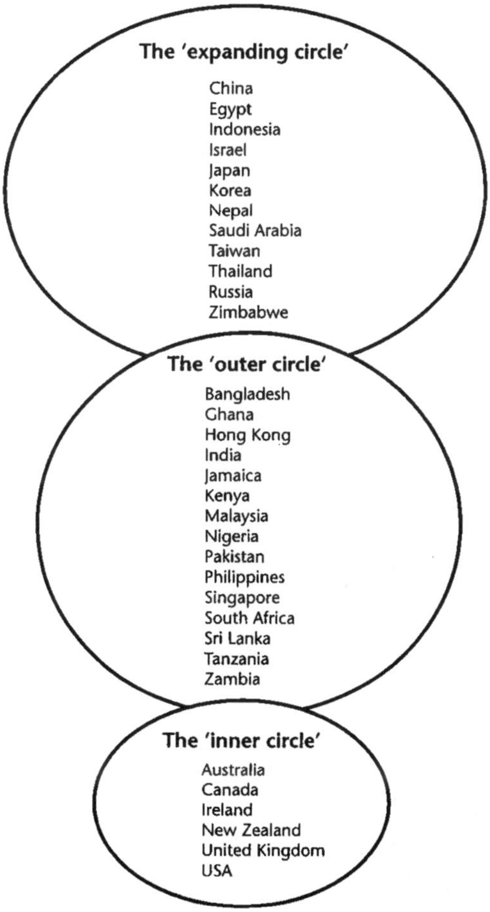

Source: adapted from Kachru 1992:233.

Figure 12.1 The spread of English worldwide

These circles reflect the historical spread of English from the United Kingdom, as well as the current sociolinguistic status of English within each region. The 'inner circle' refers to the 350 million or so speakers of English as a native language (or ENL) and includes countries such as the United Kingdom, the USA, Ireland, Canada, New Zealand, and Australia.

The 'outer circle' refers to the 300 million or so regular users of English as a second language (or ESL) and includes Singapore, Malaysia, India, the Philippines, and Hong Kong. The use of English in these settings stems originally from colonial times, and English continues to play an important role in government, the courts, higher education, the media, and other public domains. Depending on the country, English may be one of the official languages, it may be recognised as an official second language, or it may have no official status.

The third 'expanding' circle refers to the huge and steadily growing numbers of consumers of English, who frequently use it as their international language, both in work and in play—the so-called speakers of English as a foreign language (or EFL). This circle includes Indonesia, Thailand, China, Japan, Taiwan, Saudi Arabia, and Russia. Unlike the outer circle, English is taught here as a foreign language and does not have its roots in colonisation, nor does it have any official status in these countries. The number of English-users here is probably about a billion, but it's hard to estimate, since the demand for English is growing so rapidly. Berlitz International, the world's largest language school, says that 70 per cent of the five million lessons it gives each year are for English (compare around 6 per cent for French and less for Spanish).

Figures are also hard to estimate because we are potentially dealing with such a wide range of abilities, from fully competent speakers to those millions of semi-speakers with just a smattering of English (for example, the street urchin who knows just enough to con a few dollars out of the unsuspecting tourist, the foreign pop group who compose and record in English, and even those in the audience who sing the lyrics of these songs but otherwise speak little English). These people may not have full command of English, but the fact that they speak it at all is significant for what it tells us about the status of English in the world today.

The circles aren't as clearly defined as our descriptions suggest. In places like Malaysia and South Africa, for example, the sociolinguistic situation is complex, involving both second- and foreign-language features. However, this sort of representation does allow us to distinguish some of the different historical and sociolinguistic factors involved in identifying where English is spoken.

THE TWO FACES OF GLOBALISATION: CONFORMITY AND DIVERSITY

Recent trends in globalisation indicate that there are two distinct effects of the global village. On the one hand, what we see is a worldwide levelling of difference: the disappearance of local identifiers has produced a conformity or uniformity at the global level. This is evident in many different areas, not simply language. Take the example of our cities. A rise in urban tourism has brought with it a conscious 're-imaging' of cities by the fashionable 'image consultants' of the modern urban-planning world. This is meant to attract tourist dollars, which in turn is expected to generate employment and potential investment. While the intention of these re-imaging and marketing strategies is exciting diversity—something new and distinct—paradoxically, the outcome is a levelling of difference. Australian tourism academic Michael Hall (1997) describes how the removal of local identifiers has introduced a monotonous conformity, as cities are pushed into a kind of ideal mould of 'the international city'.

On the other hand, in reaction against increasing global conformity, there has also been a growth spurt of local identifiers, which has meant increased diversity at the local level. What amounts to a celebration of difference and otherness is evident, for example, in the blossoming of local activity in traditional communities—communities once 'submerged' but now re-emerging in postcolonial societies. In New Zealand, a clearly identifiable Maori subculture is finding new ways to express its identity and distinctiveness in writing, broadcasting, and films. Similarly, in Australia, Aboriginal peoples are using distinctive art forms to achieve new recognition, a new visibility.

Language has two distinct functions. The primary, or orthodox, function is to facilitate communication. The other is to promote identity, or in-group solidarity, to preserve a group's uniqueness or to establish its presence. When we trace the movement of English around the globe, we see both the communicative and solidarity functions of our language reflected in the competing homogenising and differentiating pressures of globalisation. The global village wants a uniform world language; individual nations want a national voice.

Global conformity: World English

English is the most 'successful' language in the history of the world. Hand in hand with this success is an inescapable decline in linguistic diversity. One of the effects of the worldwide movement of English and its use as an international language is the widespread linguistic destruction that has followed in its wake. We are referring here to the death, or near death, of so many indigenous languages in those places where English has taken root. Local languages are disappearing at an alarming rate (for example, American Indian, Celtic, Austronesian, and Australian Aboriginal languages). Even in those places where they appear healthy, the high status of English suggests that their survival is precarious. In the report *The Land Still Speaks* (McKay 1996), it is estimated that, at the present rate of destruction, only 10 per cent of the world's languages will still be spoken in the year 2100. Of course, not all the blame falls on English: the spread of other European languages such as German, French, and Spanish, as well as non-European languages such as Chinese and Indonesian, has been at the expense of many local languages too. Nonetheless, English language dominance has caused the highest rate of destruction of endangered languages.

The carnage is very apparent, even on our own doorstep. By the 1980s, the number of Maori-speakers was already as low as 12 per cent of the total Maori population (which in turn is only 12.5 per cent of the total New Zealand population). And the situation may get even bleaker for Maori. For one thing, the remaining speakers are bilingual Maori and English, and most are middle-aged or older. In addition, all indications are that English is intruding increasingly into what were originally Maori domains (even the formal domain of the *marae,* the grounds of the meeting house where ceremonial speeches are made; see Benton 1991:217). In fact, very few contexts remain where Maori is the natural means of communication. Over and over again, we see language-spread leading to language-shift and then language-death. For Maori, vigorous efforts are now being made to reverse this trend through, for example, the *Te Kohanga Reo* ('language nests' for children) and *Kura Kaupapa Maori* (Maori language medium schools). The initial results have been very positive for the individuals involved in programs such as these, and they are being used as models in other places throughout the world. However, only time will tell how successful they will be in reversing the overall trend towards language-death.

The effect of English (and the English-based creoles it has spawned—see below) on Aboriginal and Torres Strait Islander languages in Australia has also been devastating. The following shows the approximate numbers of dialects, languages, and language families at the time of earliest European contact (figures based on Eagleson et al. 1982:31).

Dialects	500–700
Languages	200–250
Families	26–29

Only a small number of these original languages remain today, and few can boast of healthy numbers; of the ninety surviving languages, only about twenty are still robust (for example, Warlpiri, Arrente, and Western Desert, each with about 3000 speakers; see Schmidt 1990).

Even those languages that appear to be holding their own against English have not escaped completely. Another effect of the dominance of English has been the convergence of many of these languages towards English in their structure. This 'Englishisation' (or probably more accurately 'Europeanisation', since it involves the spread of other European languages as well) is another aspect of the creeping homogeneity within the world's languages. It's a kind of structural compromise; non-Indo-European languages (like those of Austronesia and Aboriginal Australia) are losing what makes them distinctive.

As the need for international intelligibility increases, a loss of diversity is also apparent within the English language itself. Global opportunities such as trade, international travel, satellite broadcasting, the superhighway, world press, world stock markets, and multinational corporations are changing the concept of the English speech community beyond recognition. No longer are we simply looking at a group of people bound together because they live close by and speak the same language. Millions of people from around the world, both native and non-native users of English, are communicating on a daily basis. Three-quarters of the world's mail is written in English. Eighty per cent of the information stored on the world's computers is in English. Over two-thirds of the world's scientists read English. Air traffic controllers use English.

We all now operate in a diversified environment, where speakers from all three circles—inner, outer, and expanding—are constantly mixing and mingling. A Thai will use English with business contacts from Indonesia, Singapore, China, or Germany. Indians from Delhi have to do business with Japanese, Australians, and Turks. Newfoundlanders from Canada must be able to make sense of someone from Jamaica,

Ireland, or Wellington. And so it goes. Inevitably the need to understand and to be understood is giving rise to a kind of 'World' or 'International English', one stripped of its local identifiers, with a core of common vocabulary, grammar, and spelling.

But what will World English look like? There are two obvious possibilities. On the one hand, a currently existing variety could emerge as the world's standard. The two main contenders come from the inner circle: British English and American English. British English might have a better toe-hold because it has historical priority, having traditional links with places such as Singapore, Malaysia, and Brunei. But then again, American English has greater political and economic clout. America is also a very successful exporter of its culture. Television programs, films, music, advertising, food, and drink are producing a mass culture that is very much American in its orientation. Americans own the seven top communications and computer companies in the world. These factors all help to promote American English as the dominant language of the global village.

The other possibility is that no single variety will be allowed to dominate. Rather, the various Englishes will all merge to produce a hybrid variety that is different from any other. We've seen this kind of levelling effect before. In chapter 2 we described how countries such as Australia, Canada, and New Zealand experienced a melting-pot effect, whereby the different accents, vocabulary, and grammatical features of the original varieties of English underwent a kind of blending process in the new environment. The end result was a remarkably homogenous language, but one distinct from any of the previously existing varieties.

In trying to figure out which of these two outcomes is more likely, it is useful to examine the forces at work in international marketing. English is now clearly a product to be sold and to be promoted. Both British English and American English are, of course, the main competitors in the linguistic market-place, but Australasian English is securing a foothold, especially within the ASEAN (Association of South East Asian Nations) countries. Australia already carries out a significant amount of direct language teaching in Indonesia, although in other regions, especially those with traditional links with the United Kingdom and the USA, the Englishes of these two dominant countries have a much more stable foothold. Australia and New Zealand lack the prestige of the United Kingdom and the USA, but they have the advantage of geographical proximity and can exploit what, at least at the moment, appears to be a favourable image. For visiting Asian students, for example, they are generally seen as offering a convenient, pleasant, and safe location to learn English. To give you some idea of the money already involved, in 1992 Australia made about $500 million from English language teaching within the country, and an estimated $1 billion when we factor in what these students brought into the country at the time (Bennett 1994:25). Australian English is clearly a valuable national resource, comparable to wheat, iron ore, and coal. It's already a big money-earner.

But it's not your true blue Aussie or dinky-di Kiwi English that is valuable here. The sort of English that is more saleable in these regions is not the locally home-grown variety, but one with much more international appeal: a World English if you like, from which the 'differences' have been removed. For instance, these buyers don't want a distinctly Australian English or New Zealand English dictionary—such as ACOD, DNZE, or MD—but an English dictionary that can pass itself off internationally

(Oxford University Press, Longman, and Chambers already offer this). After all, people in this region don't just interact with those from the inner circle; they need to communicate with English-speakers from all over ASEAN and the rest of the world.

Let's consider what an internationalising of English down under would entail.

The 'commodification' of English: exporting OZ English

Kirsten Tilgals (1995) has written about the difficulty of exporting Australian produced books overseas. She uses the example of one publishing company, Lansdowne Press, and, in particular, the marketing of *50 Ways,* one of its most successful series of cookery titles, which is sold in Australia, the United Kingdom, the USA, South Africa, Hong Kong, and Singapore. (The international market for cookery books is apparently huge, and Australian food photography and food know-how is widely sought after.)

Lansdowne constructs its cooking books with an overseas market in mind from the beginning. But because it's dealing with non-fiction, a number of problems arise. Take the example of a cookbook such as *50 Ways with Fish.* For a start, different countries have different names for the same kind of fish. Even within countries, there can be a lot of regional variation; a fish called the *orange roughie* in Victoria is the *red roughie* in western Tasmania and the *pineapple dory* in eastern Tasmania (although some fishmongers now appear to be making an attempt to standardise these names). Now if this were fiction, where you don't need to get the sense of every word, a reader would hardly be aware of these differences, or would just simply pass over them. In a text of instruction, however, where complete communication is necessary, a glossary of terms or even footnotes would be required. But there are other lexical complications too. Americans wouldn't swallow any shellfish recipe that referred to *Balmain bugs*. Bugs mean only one thing to an American. (You might compare your own reaction to a recipe for *Battered Slugs*; even if you were told that a slug in this instance was a type of root vegetable and not the slimy creature in the garden, would the recipe be any more appealing?). For a British reading audience, though, it's the vegetable accompaniments that cause the most problems. They would want to rename *eggplant* 'aubergine', *snowpeas* 'mange tout', *zucchini* 'courgette', and *shallots* (or *eschalots* if you live in Sydney) 'spring onions' (in the USA these would become 'scallions', 'green onions', or 'bunch onions'; the confusion this little vegetable causes is huge). Then there's the problem of differences in spelling. Do you use *-our* or *-or*; *-ize* or *-ise*; *-er* or *-re*? Is it *traveling* or *travelling*; *focused* or *focussed*?

Here's what a recipe might look like, written to suit American, British, Australian, and New Zealand readers:

> For an entree/main course, serve lamb with ears/cobs of corn and a Caesar salad made from 1 head romain/cos lettuce, 2 slices/rashers of broiled/grilled bacon, and 2 hard-cooked/hard-boiled eggs.
>
> Wrap lamb cutlets/chops in parchment/baking-paper or (aluminum/aluminium/tin) foil with a little broth/stock to cut down on calories/kilojoules. Bake on an oven tray/baking sheet at 350°F/175°C/Gas Mark 4 for 30 minutes.

You are probably wondering: why not simply print different editions for each country, changing the language appropriately? As Tilgals points out, the answer to this question is, of course, cost: the advantages of 'going international' would be totally lost.

One solution is to put aside localisms and aim for something that reflects an internationally based culinary language, not a nationally based one—a variety that is regionally neutral in grammar, vocabulary, spelling, and punctuation. Words that are demonstrably different, for example, and have no ready equivalents elsewhere (like American *pot roast*, Oz and NZ *damper*, and English *kipper*) would have to go.

In the world of global epicureanism there are already signs of a generic food language emerging. It's not a French-based variety (despite the old prestige of French in this area), but one that has a distinctive American flavour. With the egregiously successful globe-trotting 'gastronomy' of fast-food giants such as McDonald's and KFC, this will hardly come as a surprise. For example, according to the McDonald's Corporation's 1995 *Annual Report*, Big Macs are sold in an astonishing 18 380 stores around the world, covering eighty-nine countries and bringing in annually $29.9 billion. All over the world you can find *french fries*, *pan pizza*, *hot waffles*, *hot dogs*, *thick shakes*, *burgers to go*, *sodas*, *hash browns*, *potato wedges*, and *donuts*.

Given the dominant presence of American English in the global market and the sheer fact that there is a reading audience of about 250 million people in the USA, it is no small wonder that Lansdowne Press is under pressure to 'go American' in their so-called international cooking books. Clearly, American English is already in a good position to act as the model for a new World English, outstripping even British English in international clout. At this stage, it looks like any 'exporting of English from down under' will entail a hefty dose of Americanisation.

World English: whose accent?

As we discussed in chapter 2, Standard English is really a matter of grammar, vocabulary, spelling, and punctuation, but it can be spoken in a wide variety of different accents. If you read newspapers around the English-speaking world or use e-mail, bulletin boards, list-servers, or electronic 'conversation' programs, you can probably believe that a fairly uniform world standard is imminent, at least in writing. But the notion of a world standard in pronunciation is a little trickier. Could there ever be a totally uniform, regionally neutral accent for English? Or will there always be two main models: British Received Pronunciation and General American? Again we can turn to the export of Australian English overseas for some insight here.

Linguist Fran Gleeson (1995) examined two Australian soap operas with respect to the way they sought to represent Australian English to their respective audiences. The first series, 'Heartbreak High', was conceived exclusively for the local audience. It represents the face of globalisation that favours diversity and the expression of identity. The second, 'Paradise Beach', was conceived from the outset with an overseas market in mind and was exported to many countries including networks in North America, parts of Western Europe, Asia, South America, and New Zealand. It represents the face of globalisation that favours uniformity and the removal of difference.

'Heartbreak High' had members of various immigrant groups playing the leading roles, and their English reflected the different ethnic mixes. The language is noticeably Australian, with general, broad, and ethnic broad accents represented (see chapter 3 for a discussion of these accents). It also depicts fairly representative teenspeak, with plenty of colourful slang and colloquial pronunciations (for example, *it just sucks*, *y' little bugger*, *y' slope head*, *I don't believe that crap*, *little Johnny copped one in the guts*, *oh get nicked*, *just wrack off*, *the old perv*, *'sgo!*, *shoulda rang*, *d'you wanna hang out together*, and *stay outa my face*). The way the characters interact is also clearly Australian in terms of naming and addressing conventions and general communicative style.

'Paradise Beach', on the other hand, appeared to aim for a kind of English that would guarantee intelligibility to foreign audiences. Gone are the markers of OZ English. Gone are local references, slang, and colloquial pronunciations. Un-Australian lexical items, such as *the perfect chilli dog* and *to chill out*, are included in their place. The accents are definitely tempered. They range from general to cultivated, with a distinctive American flavouring added (for instance, /r/ after all vowels, flaps instead of stops, and some obvious General American vowels). But most striking of all are the carefully enunciated pronunciations, and the avoidance of the casual patterns characteristic of natural connected speech. Take, for example, the lack of vowel reductions in unstressed syllables, the lack of contractions (pronouns and auxiliary verbs appear in their full forms, for instance—*I have been nearly 20 years in this business*), and the lack of assimilation of sounds occurring in sequence. This is not ordinary, casual, quick, everyday speech. And it's certainly not the colloquial speech of people whose lives centre around the casual beach world of the Gold Coast. What it appears to represent is a kind of regionally neutral accent—an oral standard if you like—aiming to appeal to a wider audience than just the locals. It would be interesting to examine New Zealand's 'Shortland Street' to see if it has undergone any linguistic metamorphosis since it went international.

We probably shouldn't make too much of these findings; after all, *Paradise Beach* was axed in 1994. But they are suggestive at least of where global English might be heading in terms of pronunciation. Again, it's a kind of blending effect, but with a hefty dash of American thrown in. Any nation seeking to put forward its own identity is going to have to climb out of this global melting pot somehow.

Local diversity: striving for identity

You would be justified in thinking that, with all this cross-fertilisation and levelling of difference, English loses a lot of its richness and vitality. There's a blandness that creeps into the language when it loses its individuality in this way. In chapter 1, we saw how language can be a potent symbol of a group's identity, whether it be professional, social, regional, ethnic, or national. We express solidarity through accent, vocabulary, grammar, and communicative patterns (or ways of speaking). Not surprisingly, then, in the face of globalism, countries often seek to assert a separate national and political identity with their own distinctive English.

To explore how the pressures towards global conformity are 'impacting' on the desire for local diversity, let's first see what's happening within the inner circle nations, which traditionally have been associated with English.

Native Englishes: case study of Americanisms 'down under'

Even within countries that are traditional bases for English there is considerable linguistic diversity. The different mixes of original dialects, the different dates of settlement, the different settlement patterns, and contact with the different indigenous languages have meant that varieties growing up in places such as Australia, New

Zealand, Canada, the USA, and South Africa are already quite distinct. The physical separation from other English-speaking regions has allowed this distinctiveness to flourish. The term ***Native Englishes*** is often used to describe these established dialects of English.

The effects of globalisation are contributing to this diversity by fostering new, socially defined ethnic variation in these places. Massive flows of people, including tourists, refugees, and migrants, have produced an unprecedented intermixing of people and cultures. Clearly culture and language at the local level have been changed irrevocably by this 'inter-national' movement of people. And as each individual group seeks to assert its own identity, different ethnic varieties of English can become an important means of signalling the group boundaries. As we saw in chapters 1 and 3, Italian or Greek features in a group's English can be potent markers of that group's ethnicity. The new local ethnic diversity found in these Migrant Englishes is in sharp contrast to the levelling processes occurring globally.

Another consequence of the rise of the global village is that Native Englishes such as NZ English and OZ English are now much more open than ever before to global influence. And as we've discussed, there is a pervasive American dimension to much of what is global; in fact, sometimes it is rather difficult to maintain a clear distinction between globalisation and American cultural imperialism.

To bring the discussion closer to home—what exactly is the impact of American English on our Englishes down under? Given the global presence of the USA as a cultural and political superpower, and given the inevitable loosening of ties between the United Kingdom and its former Antipodean colonies, it would be surprising if there weren't some sort of linguistic steamrolling going on. The 'Americanisation' of OZ or NZ English is a frequent topic in the papers these days, and reactions are generally hostile. Newspaper headlines such as 'Facing an American Invasion' go on to 'condemn this insidious, but apparently virile, infection from the USA'. (See Gordon & Deverson 1989:77–81 for an excellent collection of letters to the editor on exactly this issue. Although these date from 1941, the same sentiments are echoed in such letters today.) Normally easygoing, Australians and New Zealanders rail against 'horrid Americanisms'. Talkback callers vent their spleen on air, blaming their pet hates on the USA (whether they are actually Americanisms or not.). But are we really facing an American infiltration of our English?

When we look at the particulars of the complaints, we see that all aspects of the structure of English are felt to be under siege. Certainly, some American imports can be phonological—for example, features of stress (*prim**a**rily* instead of ***pri**marily*) and voicing of inter-vocalic /t/ (where *latter* and *ladder* become similar in pronunciation). However, since examples such as these illustrate natural phonological changes, it is difficult to establish the exact role of American influence here. Imports can also be grammatical, although these are few in number—for example, verbs such as *to protest* and *to appeal (something)* with direct objects are replacing the expressions *to protest against* and *to appeal against (something)*, as in *to appeal (against) the decision.* But once again we might be dealing with independently motivated change rather than direct borrowing.

The high visibility of spelling is what probably helps to intensify the widespread perception of American influence. Although our spelling conventions derive traditionally from the British, the technological presence of the USA means this is an area of rapidly growing American influence. But we can't necessarily attribute all these spellings to postwar American imperialism. As Pam Peters points out (1992:22), major urban newspapers in Melbourne, for example, have endorsed 'American' *-or* spellings in place of English *-our* for many decades (for example, *honor/honour*). In fact, over the years *-or* spellings, along with a number of others, have been alternatives in many English-speaking places around the world. Probably where the USA is having an effect is in successfully promoting one of the two alternatives. This would also account for the increasing preference for *-ize* over *-ise* (although this spelling is not an American invention either; like so many so-called 'Americanisms', it originated in the United Kingdom).

Most of the complaints centre around vocabulary. Certainly words are very accessible to people, and lexical influence will usually be the most conspicuous. Lexical invasion may also be feared because it is seen as 'the thin edge of a wedge'. To try to assess just how valid the reports of an American takeover of our lexicon are, we surveyed just one small area of the lexicon: the world of gastronomy. A comparison of everyday Australian, New Zealand, British, and American cooking terms and expressions is revealing. It suggests that, in this realm, at least, the reports of a takeover are clearly exaggerated.

As we saw in our earlier discussion of the export of OZ English in cookbooks, there are certainly differences between these four countries. However, a closer look reveals that OZ and NZ usage still appears to align much more frequently with British usage than American usage. The examples in Table 12.1 are typical. However, there are a few clear exceptions where the American term is preferred in Australia or New Zealand (or both) (see Table 12.2). Occasionally both American and British usage coexist, as shown in Table 12.3. But there are also cases where the preferred Antipodean usage differs totally from both American and British usage, as Table 12.4 illustrates.

Table 12.1 Similarities between Antipodean and British food terminology*

	OZ and NZ	*British*	*American*
Equipment/cooking expressions	frying pan	frying pan	skillet
	greaseproof paper	greaseproof paper	wax paper
	grill	grill	broil
Ingredients	beetroot	beetroot	beets
	bicarbonate of soda	bicarbonate of soda	baking soda
	caster sugar	caster sugar	granulated sugar
	cornflour	cornflour	cornstarch
	crystalised fruit	crystalised fruit	candied fruit
	desiccated coconut	desiccated coconut	shredded coconut
	essence	essence	extract
	glacé cherry	glacé cherry	candied cherry
	icing sugar	icing sugar	confectioners' sugar
	self-raising flour	self-raising flour	all-purpose flour with baking powder
	wholemeal flour	wholemeal flour	wholewheat flour

*Although we did survey speakers about these cooking expressions (and those in Tables 12.2–12.4 as well), inevitably there will be individual variation; if you do disagree with these judgments, we would be very happy to hear from you.

Table 12.2 Similarities between Antipodean and American food terminology

OZ	*NZ*	*British*	*American*
eggplant	eggplant/aubergine	aubergine	eggplant
snow pea	baby pea/snow pea	mangetout	snow pea
zucchini	zucchini/courgette	courgette	zucchini

Table 12.3 Antipodean food terminology that reflects both British and American usage

OZ	*NZ*	*British*	*American*
tin/can	tin/can	tin	can
patty pan/muffin tin/patty tin	patty pan/muffin tin	patty tin	muffin tin
tomato puree/paste	tomato puree/paste	tomato puree	tomato paste

Table 12.4 International differences in food terminology

	OZ	*NZ*	*British*	*American*
Equipment/cooking expressions	crushed (but not of meat)	crushed (but not of meat)	minced	pressed
	seeded (or stoned)	seeded (or stoned)	stoned	pitted
Ingredients	capsicum (or pepper)	green/red pepper	pepper	bell pepper
	cream	cream	single cream	light or coffee cream
	flour	flour	plain flour	all-purpose flour
	lemon cheese/butter	lemon honey/cheese	lemon curd	lemon spread
	mince meat	mince meat	hamburger steak	ground beef
	pickled pork	pickled pork	gammon	ham steak
	stock cube	stock cube	bouillon cube	broth cube

It would seem that our Antipodean varieties of English are in no immediate danger of being overwhelmed by American English. Grammatical and phonological transfers are still very slight. Most influence involves vocabulary, and this may even be increasing in some contexts. We've already seen that, in the fast food area, American imports are very evident. But even if the borrowings flood in, is this really such a terrible thing? After all, English is a language that has already borrowed from a staggering 120 different languages. When the borrowings have occurred well and truly in the past, however, no one so much as bats an eyelid. Recall the monumental changes from Old to Middle English. If King Alfred had had the chance to read the language of Chaucer, he would have been horrified by the changes—an astounding 10 000 words from French and the decimation of the inflectional endings for nouns. (So considerable were these changes that some linguists even challenge the continuation of Old to Middle English, arguing for creolisation during the Middle Ages.)

But English survived. In fact, it did more that just survive. Most of us now speak with pride about the richness and the versatility of our language, especially its wealth of terms. In truth, hostility towards American usage is not generally based on genuine linguistic concerns, but reflects much deeper social judgments. It is a linguistic insecurity born of the inescapable dominance of the USA as a cultural, political, and economic superpower. *French fries*, *hash browns*, and *potato wedges* are merely symbols of this American hegemony, but they're easy targets for this anti-American sentiment.

New Englishes: case study of the 'Indianisation' of English

Wherever English put down its roots, it was greatly influenced by the cultures and languages it came into contact with. For example, in India it encountered a range of Indic, Dravidian, Munda, and Tibeto-Burman languages. The emerging contact Englishes have become so distinct in grammar, vocabulary, pronunciation, and conventions of use that they are now labelled **'New Englishes'**. Examples include Singapore English, Malaysian English, Hong Kong English, and Indian English. These Englishes are acquiring new speakers at such a rate that they are outstripping the inner circle of Native Englishes in numbers.

English is now the official or co-official language in more than seventy-five countries; they include places with colonial associations with the United Kingdom or the USA, as well as those without these traditional links. The rise of new varieties in these regions has played a major part in English attaining the status of a global language. It's also likely that these varieties will have a significant role to play in shaping the future world standard.

But the global growth of English is not always viewed as beneficial. As we discussed earlier in this chapter, the expansion of English has, repeatedly around the world, occurred at the expense of one or more local indigenous languages. Often, though, a distinctive New English has emerged from the period when English was still a second language in contact with the indigenous language. These new multicultural identities for English mean that, despite the irrevocable loss of the indigenous languages, at least some linguistic diversity has remained.

But even when the use of English is not threatening existing local languages, its presence may generate antagonism. In India, for example, the role of English in relation to Hindi and other regional languages is an ongoing source of tension and conflict. At the national level, its status is currently that of an 'associate' official language alongside the official language, Hindi. In the 1960s the bitter conflicts over the roles of English, Hindi, and regional languages in the national language policy led to the 'three language formula'. What this policy endorsed was the official use of either English or a local state language, which in the north is generally Hindi and in the south a regional language.

One of the facets of the conflict has been that nationalistic movements have wanted to reject English as an official language, because of its associations with colonial history; the idea is that the basis of an independent government is a national language, and that this language should not be the one of the former colonisers. But how much is it still the language of the former British Empire? And just how much has English been 'Indianised' to become a distinct national voice? These questions have resulted in great polemics in recent years. Read what literary critic K. R. S. Iyengar has to say on the subject:

> Indian writing in English is but one of the voices in which India speaks. It is a new voice, no doubt, but it is as much Indian as others. The point is controversial, and is reflected in controversies in other parts of the world, where the growth of the English language is perceived as a threat as well as a blessing. There is no doubt, however, about the emerging structural identity of Indian English, or about the growth of a recognized body of Indian English literature.
>
> 1962:3

There are a number of linguistic factors that contribute to this 'Indianisation' of English. First, Indian English shows distinct characteristics in its sound system, including unaspirated voiceless stops /p t k/ and a series of retroflex consonants (sounds made with the tip of the tongue curled away from the alveolar ridge) in place of the usual alveolar series. In addition, Indian English differs strikingly from other varieties of English with respect to stress, intonation, and rhythm.

There are also markedly distinctive features of grammar. The transfer of features from the first language has resulted in differences in interrogatives (no subject–auxiliary inversion, as in *What you would like to eat?*), in tag questions (invariant tags, as in *He isn't going there, isn't it?*), in count-mass noun distinctions (*We ate fruits*), and in progressives forms (*Rama is having two houses*). Vocabulary differences include substantial lexical borrowings from Indian languages, such as *durzi* 'tailor', English archaisms such as *tiffin* 'lunch', (from English *tiff* 'to sip, drink'), and large numbers of hybrid forms, such as *janta meals* (*janta* means 'the people').

Other Englishes: case study of Aboriginal English and Kriol

Any discussion of English diversification must include the contribution of the many (roughly sixty) English-based pidgin or creole varieties dotted round the world. Because of their unique development, they are often labelled as '**Other Englishes**'. To trace this development, let's start with the pidgin Englishes.

Generally speaking, a **pidgin** is a type of makeshift language that springs up when English-speakers, for instance, come into contact with speakers of different linguistic backgrounds. Trading is a typical setting in which pidgins evolve, and this commonly happened along the trade routes during the sixteenth and seventeenth centuries. For this reason, we find many pidgins along the coastlines of Asia, Africa, and the Caribbean. But a pidgin can evolve wherever speakers of different linguistic backgrounds come together and need to talk. For example, in the pearling fisheries around Broome in Western Australia and around Thursday Island, pidginised forms of Malay were used during the early part of this century. Broome Pearling Pidgin is now extinct.

In the formation of a pidgin, there are always two (or more) languages that are involved, but the pidgin takes one language, usually the socially dominant one, as its point of origin. It's this language that contributes most of the vocabulary. In this way, English forms the basis of many of the Pacific and West African pidgins. Traditionally, people thought of these languages as simply debased forms of English, and they used derogatory labels such as 'broken English', 'monkey-talk', 'impoverished English', even 'lingual bastardisation' and 'gibberish'.

This 'me Tarzan, you Jane' image of pidgins is totally inaccurate. Pidgins clearly have their own grammars; they are not simply 'broken' Englishes. However, they do differ from Standard English in a number of respects. For a start they aren't anybody's first language. In a speaker's linguistic provisions, a pidgin could be said to provide the emergency rations for use when the speaker ventures outside his or her usual speech community. Because pidgins are only used in limited contexts, they can make do with reduced vocabularies, and need to be far less complex and flexible in their structures. English-based pidgins are syntactically and morphologically much simpler than the variety of English on which they are based. Because they are so restricted in their contexts of use, they also lack the range of stylistic variation characteristic of a normal language. Finally, pidgins are typically short-lived. If the contact ceases, the pidgin dies. It might also be abandoned by its speakers, who chose to speak the source language.

If the situation stabilises, however, and the contact continues, there can be a very different outcome. All sorts of interesting linguistic things happen then, as the makeshift pidgin metamorphoses into a fully fledged **creole**. (Be careful though, people may continue to refer to the new creole as a pidgin, even though it has become a mother tongue.) These creole varieties cluster in three main areas: the Caribbean, West Africa, and the West Pacific. They include Bislama (Vanuatu), Krio (Sierra Leone), Tok Pisin (Papua New Guinea), Gullah (spoken by African Americans in Florida and the Sea Islands), Costa Rican Creole, Jamaican Creole, and Kriol (northern parts of Australia).

In theory, determining when a pidgin ends and a creole begins is straightforward. As soon as children in a community are brought up speaking the pidgin as their first language, it becomes a creole. Quite simply, a creole is a nativised pidgin. The linguistic reality, however, is another matter; linguistically it is impossible to say where the boundary lies. As soon as the pidgin becomes a first language, there follows a speedy elaboration of grammar and vocabulary, as the language expands beyond its original very limited context of use. The changes are massive and rapid, as the pidgin becomes a fully fledged and dynamic language, able to serve its speakers in all kinds of settings and circumstances. This process is called '**creolisation**'. But even before it is a first language, a pidgin can develop a highly elaborated structure (close to that of a creole), if it is used for a number of different purposes.

As we will see below, with increased formal education and emphasis on schooling, the creole can also move gradually more and more in the direction of the standard language, literally doing itself in by massive convergence and borrowing. In other words, over time an English-based creole can become more and more like Standard English. It is a kind of 'language suicide', although its more official title is '**decreolisation**'.

Because Other Englishes play such an interesting role in the worldwide spread of English, we've included here a brief account of the structural features of a typical creole. Creoles, even those from unrelated language mixes, will share many of these basic features.

Clearly, both Australia and New Zealand offer situations where English comes into close contact with other languages. Since European contact, Aboriginal Australia and

Maori New Zealand have seen members of several language groups living in the same community and interacting daily. In Australia, pidgins based on English appeared not long after the arrival of the Europeans. The pidgin varieties became increasingly important for contact, not only between Aboriginal-speakers and English-speakers, but also as a *lingua franca* between speakers of different Aboriginal languages.

It has long been observed that linguistic change follows closely on the heels of drastic social upheaval. We see a striking illustration of this in the evolution of creoles. Needless to say, the extreme disruption that followed the arrival of the Europeans with the movement of people to mission stations, pastoral properties, and towns meant that Aboriginal people of different linguistic groups were thrown together much more. Although there had always been widespread bilingualism among adults, it wasn't adequate to cover communicative needs in these new settlements, where children of different linguistic backgrounds were thrown together and where there was continued unequal interaction between Aboriginal- and English-speakers. Because of this, pidgins fulfilled definite communicative needs. Out of these, creoles evolved in the Kimberley Region, the Roper River area, and parts of North Queensland. These various English-based creoles have much in common, but they also show some regional differences too. These differences depend on the Aboriginal languages represented in the community where the pidgin originated and also on influences from other pidgins and creoles brought into Australia from the outside.

In New Zealand the situation was somewhat different. As Ross Clark (1979) documents, in the early nineteenth century a 'foreigner-talk' system known as South Seas Jargon was used in various parts of the Pacific, primarily between European whalers and indigenous crew members, some of whom were Maori. In New Zealand this jargon developed into Maori Pidgin English, which was used for early contact between Maoris and Pakehas (or Whites). Unlike Australia, however, this pidgin never stabilised enough to evolve further. For one thing, in New Zealand there was only ever a single indigenous language, so there was never a need for a *lingua franca* between indigenous groups as there was in Australia. The historical records also suggest that the most common pattern was for English-speakers to learn enough Maori to communicate. As a result, New Zealand Pidgin was short-lived. For this reason, our brief look at creole structure will focus on an Australian variety of creole, called Kriol. It has more than 20 000 speakers. (But see chapter 1 for discussion of Maori English).

First, where does Kriol fit in with Aboriginal English? The trouble is that names like these never refer to a single clearly defined dialect. Just as the labels OZ English, NZ English, and American English refer to clusters of (more-or-less) mutually intelligible speech varieties, these are also just convenient umbrella terms to cover the many different varieties of English and creole English that Aboriginal people speak. In fact, the situation is even more complicated here because of something called a '**creole continuum**'. Varieties of 'Aboriginal English' range from something that is virtually identical to Standard Australian English in everything but accent, through to pure creole, which is so remote from Standard Australian English as to be mutually unintelligible (see chapter 2 for a discussion of the dialect/language distinction). Of course, in between these two polar extremes, you find a whole range of varieties. Generally speakers have command of a number of these varieties, and they move along the continuum according to the situation and the audience.

Let's concentrate for a moment on what makes Kriol a variety distinct from Standard Australian English. There are, of course, many vocabulary differences: some words are borrowed directly from Aboriginal languages; familiar-looking English words can have quite different meanings, such as *dust* 'to overtake on a road', and words can change in function, such as *lie* in *We lie-don't look* 'we pretended not to look' (see Eagleson et al. 1982 and the Further Reading for a full account of creole features).

In addition to vocabulary differences, these creoles have their own grammatical and semantic properties, which are different from those of the base language, English. Below we have listed some of the most striking grammatical features of Kriol. The closer the variety is to the creole end of the continuum, the greater the number of these features. Many of them are shared with other creoles; some are found in other non-standard dialects:

- Simplified tag questions such as *isn't it*, *init*, *ini*, *ana* and *na* function as invariable tags, taking the place of standard tags such as *weren't they* and *didn't she*, as in *You're going, isn't it?*
- Noun suffixes such as plural and possessive are often omitted (*two big turtle* and *my cousin bike*, for instance). In northern areas, possessives are sometimes marked with *bilong* or *blo*, as in *woman bilong friend* 'friend's woman'.
- *He* or *'e* tends to be used as a general third person singular, as in *this old woman he started packing up.* (Note the presence of a subject pronoun after the subject noun phrase, which is a feature of other non-standard varieties of English.)
- In creoles in the Kimberleys and other Northern areas, there is an elaborate pronoun system, which distinguishes dual and plural, as well as inclusive and exclusive first person:

yuntupala	'you two'
yupala	'you (more than two)'
minyu	'me and you'
mintupala	'the two of us, excluding you'
wilat	'several of us, including you'
mela/mifella	'several of us, excluding you'

  Personal pronouns can be used as possessive pronouns, as in *dey teacher* (for 'their teacher').
- In some creoles, especially those in rural areas of Western Australia, there are interesting differences in the positioning of noun modifiers such as adjectives. If there are several modifiers, one usually precedes the noun and the others follow. The pronoun form *one* is often added to the modifiers that follow, as in *we get five sheeps fat one.*
- Doubly marked comparatives and superlatives are common, as in *more longer.* In central and east Kimberleys, numerals and adjectives often appear with the suffix *-pala* or *-pela* (a feature of many other creole varieties), as in *twopela chasing around.*
- Prepositions are frequently omitted (*I'm gonna go Melbourne*, for instance). In the Kimberleys, as in other Northern creole-speaking areas, *la* or *longa* marks a variety of locational relationships: *I gotta go la* [to] *Ruby Plains*, *they tell you story night time longa star* [by the stars].

- Future tense is marked with auxiliary *gonna* or else *gotta* (this also has a locational sense 'by' or 'with'), as in *All the kid gotta go bogie-bat gotta bus* 'all the kids will go swimming by bus'.
- Auxiliary *bin* is used in the Kimberleys, in desert regions, and along the north-west coast as the regular marker of past tense, as in *water bin take me 'way.*
- As is typical of many non-standard British and American English dialects, third-person *-s* marker is omitted: *When Christmas come, he still live in that house.*
- In northern Kriol-speaking areas, there is a strong tendency to mark transitivity by adding *-im* to the verb roots: *I bin eatim up goanna.*
- Also in some northern varieties of Kriol, continuous aspect is distinguished from non-continuous aspect with the suffix *-bat* (from *'bout, about)* as in *Don't you lookim batim* 'don't keep looking at me'.
- Auxiliary *do* is used to signal tense distinctions, as in *When you sing, they do dance* (here *do* is not emphatic as it would be in Standard English).
- There is a huge range of different negative constructions, many shared with other non-standard varieties, as in *'e never even die* (here *never* means 'not') and *I never see no spirits.*
- Main and auxiliary verb *be* is often omitted, as in *Dey too small* and *We just playing.*
- As is typical of many non-standard varieties, subject–verb agreement is lacking, as in *I don't know where I were born.*

When you see creoles like this one written down, it is tempting to think of them simply as forms of English. But remember, they are really different languages with quite different grammars, and when spoken among fluent creole-speakers, they are mutually unintelligible with Standard English. Symbolically too, it's important to emphasise their linguistic distinctiveness. As languages in their own right, as distinct from English, creoles such as these have become an important means of signalling their speakers' cultural and social identity. In this way, Kriol is now an important part of these speakers' Aboriginality.

WHAT DOES THE FUTURE HOLD?

As we have seen, there are two competing pressures on our globe-trotting language. One relates directly to the communicative function of language. As the world becomes more global in outlook, the need for some kind of worldwide *lingua franca* becomes more pressing. Certainly, the future of English as the Esperanto of the global village looks secure, but we are still a long way from any real global standard. The melting pot metaphor suggests the various Englishes will go through a general levelling process to produce a uniform and regionally neutral grammar, vocabulary, spelling, pronunciation, punctuation, and communicative style. But the technological and cultural clout of the USA suggests there is a pervasive American dimension to World English too.

The other pressure currently working on English relates to its solidarity function. The desire for difference and the attendant fear of these homogenising forces at work will ensure that linguistic diversity will continue to thrive at the local level. World

English will bind members of the international community together, but individual nations will continue to assert their identity via their own distinctive Englishes. These regional varieties, left to their own devices, will be able to diverge even more dramatically to develop more individual character. It's conceivable that they may even become mutually unintelligible.

In short, English is an agent of both conformity and diversity in the world. The outcome will likely be, as David Crystal (1995) and a number of others have envisaged, a more universal 'bidialectism' or 'tridialectalism'—in other words, an ability to use two or three dialects of a language. Already many speakers of English are bidialectal. For example, they can be native speakers of a non-standard regional dialect and have learnt the national standard as a second variety in school. For many of these bidialectal speakers, tridialectalism will become the norm. Those participating in an international culture will be able to shift from their local dialect or national standard to the international standard.

The future of English is undoubtedly a promising one. The global success of English means exciting diversity for the language too. But the triumph of English comes at considerable cost. For speakers of dying languages, it has meant a vital part of their cultural and social identity has just disappeared. For linguists, it has meant important linguistic systems have vanished forever.

POINTS TO REMEMBER

- Recent trends in globalisation indicate two distinct effects of the global village: while there is greater conformity appearing at the global level, diversity continues to thrive at the local level.
- The worldwide spread of English illustrates the different effects of these homogenising and differentiating forces. Globalisation requires international intelligibility (a global uniform standard). The preservation of national identity, however, fosters diversity (distinctive Englishes).
- Speakers who are traditionally associated with English belong to the 'inner circle' and are speakers of English as a native language (ENL). Native Englishes include Scottish English, American English, NZ English, and OZ English.
- Speakers of so-called 'New Englishes' belong to the 'outer circle' and are regular users of English as a second language (ESL). Included here are Singapore English, Malaysian English, Indian English, Nigerian English, and Hong Kong English.
- The growing numbers of speakers of English as a foreign language (EFL) belong to the 'expanding circle' of nations, including China, Egypt, Japan, Indonesia, Thailand, Saudi Arabia, and Taiwan.
- So-called 'Other Englishes' refer to English-based pidgin and creole varieties around the world. These varieties aren't degenerate forms of 'broken' English. They have their own grammatical and semantic properties and are the result of the contact of English with other languages.
- Despite the massive loss of indigenous languages around the world, some linguistic diversity has been maintained by the development of these Other and New Englishes.

- The global spread of English is not always welcome, as, for example, when English is seen as the language of the coloniser, or when the local voice is perceived to be threatened through lexical invasion.
- Aboriginal English is not a single homogenous entity but forms a creole continuum of speech varieties ranging from pure creole (Kriol) to forms close or identical to Standard Australian English.
- The form that World English will most likely take is a variety that is regionally neutral in grammar, vocabulary, spelling, and punctuation, but with a strong 'dollop' of American thrown in.

EXERCISES

1 **Why English?**
What would you say to someone who told you that English had achieved its worldwide status because of its intrinsic linguistic features (in other words, because English is more logical, is inherently more beautiful, and has a richer vocabulary than other languages)? What types of evidence would you present?

2 **Vocabulary: Americanisms**
Make a list of words connected with the take-away food industry. How much of the vocabulary has its origins in North America? Can you suggest why this is? Can you think of other areas where America has had an impact on our vocabulary and general idiom? Do you think this enriches our language, or is the language worse off?

3 **Singapore English**
Rhymes that work in one variety may not work in another. The following verses are taken from poems by Singaporean Mohammad Ibrahim (1980, as quoted in Brown 1988:136–7). The rhyming scheme in (a) is A A B B, while in (b)–(e), it is A B A B. Pick out each of the rhyming pairs and give the phonetic symbol for the 'rhymed' vowel in each word. Identify those pairs that don't rhyme in your dialect (but that do in Singapore English).

a When Nature sleeps and the world is almost still,
Oh, my darling, you don't know how I really feel.
So, if you love me as you know I love you too,
Remember that my love is for no one else but you.

b When my baby starts to bawl,
I'm the one who must get up,
To soothe that pink, living doll,
Who is our first little pup.
When my baby starts to bawl,
Because his diaper is wet,
Though he wakes up one and all,
I've to attend to the brat...

c The Angel at the window stood,
Through which the bright moonbeams shone;
He was in a deep pensive mood;
It was long before the dawn.

d With thunderin' hooves and lots of dust,
That makes me cough and makes me cuss,
The Stagecoach come a-rushin' past,
But 'tis only the kids' school bus.

e But I would have gone on and on,
And am glad myself I've checked,
For to me now it's clearly shown,
I myself am not perfect!

4 Indian English

The following sentences illustrate some of the typical characteristics of Indian English. State how the grammatical features of each sentence differ from those of Standard English.

- **a** Do not throw litters [rubbish] on the street.
- **b** What do you want to eat? Meat is there; vegetables are there; bread is there.
- **c** I am here since two o'clock.
- **d** When you will arrive, please visit me.
- **e** She was having many houses.
- **f** Yesterday's lecture has lasted three hours.
- **g** Who you have come to see?
- **h** I asked him where does he work.
- **i** You are going home soon, isn't it?
- **j** I want that you should leave.

5 New Englishes in writing

The following passage from Amos Tutuola's *The Palm-Wine Drinkard* (1952:8) is an example of Nigerian English.

> When it was early in the morning of the next day, I had not palm-wine to drink at all, and throughout that day I felt not so happy as before; I was seriously sat down in my parlour, but when it was the third day that I had no palm-wine at all, all my friends did not come to my house again, they left me there alone, because there was no palm-wine for them to drink.

Identify what is distinctive about the variety of English used in this passage. Why do you think the writer might deliberately seek a local flavour here? Do you see a possible tension between reflecting the local variety of English and maintaining comprehension for a wider reading audience?

6 Australian Kriol

The following sentences illustrate some of the typical characteristics of Kriol. State how the vocabulary and grammatical features of each sentence differ from those of Standard English. Identify which of these features might be found in more colloquial varieties of English. (Note that close translations have been supplied, with grammatical morphemes in capitals).

a	*Wi*	*bin*	*mekim*	*big*	*ampi*
	we	[past]	make [+ transitive]	big	humpy

'We made a big humpy [hut, shelter]'

b

I	*bin*	*faindim*	*im*
I	[past]	find [+ transitive]	him/her/it

'I found him/her/it'

c

Im	*kukimbat*	*dat*	*kanggaru*
he/she	cook [+ trans + continuous]	that	kangaroo

'He/she is cooking that kangaroo'

d

Mi	*na*	*laikim*	*go*	*la*	*kul*
I	[negative]	like [+ trans]	go	[location]	school

'I don't like going to school'

e

Dat	*san*	*blo*	*mai*	*sista*	*im*	*lib*	*la*	*Sydney*
that	son	[possession]	my	sister	he	live	[location]	Sydney

'My sister's son lives in Sydney'

f

Im	*blakpala*
he	black [+ adjective marker]

'He's black'

g

Dey	*bin*	*go*	*indid*
they	[past]	go	[tag question]

'They went, didn't they?'

h

An'	*mela*	*new*	*teacher*	*gotta*	*come*
and	our	new	teacher	[future]	come

'And our new teacher is going to come' (*mela* means 'several of us excluding you')

i

Dad	*did*	*get*	*two*	*turtle*
Dad	[do]	get	two	turtles

'Dad got two turtles'

j

E	*bin*	*wipeim*	*gotta*	*tissue*
he	[past]	wipe [+ trans]	with	tissue

'He wiped it with a tissue'

7 Kriol: a threat?

Many people—both Aboriginal and non-Aboriginal—consider Kriol varieties to be a threat both to indigenous Aboriginal languages and to Standard English. Why do you think they believe this? What are your reactions—do you think they are justified in their objections to Kriol?

8 Tok Pisin text

The following conversation in Tok Pisin (Papua New Guinea) illustrates some typical creole features. Read through this text from Tom Dutton's *A New Course in Tok Pisin* (1985) and make a list of the non-standard features in the vocabulary (that is, any unfamiliar vocabulary), word-formation, and grammar.

Mi inap	*I've had enough*
Mem i go lukim Wana, wantok bilong em. Nau tupela i kaikai i stap.[1]	Mem goes to see Wana his wantok [mate]. Here the two of them are at table.
Wana: Yu laikim sampela mo—rais, pis, banana samting?	Would you like some more—rice, peas, banana or something else?

Mem: Nogat. Mi inap long kaikai.[2] Mi pulap.	No thank you. I've had enough. I'm full.
Wana: Oloman, yu inap long kaikai a? Yu no kaikai bikpela. Yu man o yu manki?	Gosh, you've had enough have you? You didn't eat very much. Are you man or boy?
Mem: Nogat, kaikai i winim[3] mi.	No, there's more food there than I can eat.
Wana: Tasol, planti i stap	But there's still plenty.
Mem: Mi save. Tasol mi pulap pinis.[4]	I know. But I'm full.
Wana: Oke, mi wokim ti. Yu laikim sampela?	Okay, I'll make some tea. Would you like some?
Mem: Gutpela. Nek bilong mi i drai.	Thank you. I am thirsty.

1 The verb *stap* means 'to be in a place, to exist, to remain' (it doesn't mean 'stop'). The *i* is a particle that belongs to the verb.

2 The noun *kaikai* means 'food'. *Long* is a kind of all-purpose preposition.

3 The verb *winim* means 'to beat, to be better than' (note the suffix *-im*).

4 *Pinis* indicates that the action is finished, completed (from *finish*).

Glossary

abbreviations words that are formed by the initials of words that, unlike **acronyms**, cannot be pronounced as words. *BO* 'body odour' and *CIA* 'Central Intelligence Agency' are examples of abbreviations.

accent a kind of pronunciation associated with particular groups of speakers.

acronym a word formed by the initials of other words—for example, *Anzac* 'Australian and New Zealand Army Corps' or *scuba* 'self-contained underwater breathing apparatus'.

active the most common type of 'grammatical voice', whereby, in **transitive** clauses, the actor or agent occurs as the **subject** of the **clause** and the patient occurs as **object**—for example, *The dog chased the cat*. See also **passive** voice.

actual mood a grammatical **mood** that is used to refer to events or activities that have actually taken place, or are actually taking place, in reality.

adjective a **word class** that typically refers to qualities or states. In English, some adjectives can be **inflected** for degree (for example, *tasty*, *tastier*, *tastiest*). Adjectives occur as modifiers of noun phrases (*a tasty dinner*) and as **complements** of verb phrases (*that dinner was tasty*).

adjunct an omissible element in a grammatical construction.

adverb a **word class** that typically refers to time, frequency, manner, and so on. Many (but not all) adverbs are **derived** from **adjectives** with the **suffix** *-ly*. Adverbs occur as the **heads** of adverbial phrases that function as **dependents** of **verbs, adjectives**, other adverbs, and entire **clauses**.

adverbial a **phrase** (adverb phrase, prepositional phrase, **subordinate clause**) that is optionally included in the **predicate**. Features include flexibility of word order, **number** per **clause** (no restriction on number), and a range of meaning (manner, place, time, frequency, and so on).

affixation the addition of **affixes** to **roots** or **stems**.

affix a **bound morpheme** that is attached to a **root** to form a word.

affricate a sound produced by first making a complete closure or **stop** in the oral cavity, which is then slackened and released as a **fricative**.

allomorphs variant sequences of sounds found in actual speech that represent the same **morpheme**. For example, the **indefinite article** {A} has two different allomorphs: [ə] (which occurs before **consonants**) and [ən] (which occurs before **vowels**).

allophones the different ways in which a **phoneme** can actually be pronounced under different circumstances.

alveolar a sound produced using the tip or the blade of the tongue and the **alveolar ridge**.

alveolar ridge a bony ridge found between the back of the teeth and the **hard palate**.

analogy a process of pattern extension, whereby a form becomes more like another form with which it is somehow associated. A powerful force in grammatical change, analogy works to remove irregularity—for example, the spread of plural *-s* at the expense of other endings.

analytic language a language in which words tend to have very little **inflection** and in which grammatical relations are shown mainly by word order.

Anglo-Saxon another name for **Old English**.

anticipatory assimilation what occurs when a sound becomes more like a sound that follows it, as when *handbag* is pronounced as *hambag*.

aphesis the loss of an unstressed **vowel** from the beginning of a word.

apocope the loss of a final **vowel**.

approximant a sound produced when two speech organs come very close to each other, but not so close that an audible turbulence is produced. The initial sounds of *you*, *woo*, and *roo* in the speech of OZ and NZ English speakers are examples. Some linguists also classify **laterals** as approximants.

articles an encoding of the notions of definiteness and indefiniteness. English has a **definite article** (*the*) and an **indefinite article** (*a*).

aspect a notion referring to the kind of action expressed by a **verb**, and to how the action is spread over time. English expresses (via **auxiliaries**) **perfect** and **progressive aspects**, as well as **habitual aspect**.

assimilation the modification of a sound so that it becomes more like a nearby sound.

auxiliaries a group of **verbs** that are used to support **non-finite** forms of main verbs, and that are **inflected** for **person**, **number**, and **tense**—for example, *was* in *I was running* and *could* in *I could have gone*. See also **primary auxiliaries** and **modal auxiliaries**.

back vowels **vowels** produced with the tongue retracted back in the mouth.

backformation the formation of a new word by the removal of an imaginary **affix**—for example, the reinterpretation of the word *pease* (once a singular **noun** with just one **morpheme**) as a plural **count noun** *pea-s*.

basic clause a structurally complete **clause**, consisting of a **noun phrase** followed by a **verb phrase**. It is the smallest syntactic unit that can be used completely independently in English.

bilabial a sound produced using both lips.

blends words originating from the contraction of two or more other words—for example, *chortle* from *chuckle* and *snort*.

borrowing the addition of a new word or other element to a language by recruiting it from some other language.

bound morphemes **morphemes** that cannot appear on their own as words but that must co-occur with other morphemes to form words. See also **free morphemes**.

bound roots **roots** that can only occur in conjunction with other **morphemes**—for example, *-ceive* in *receive*, *perceive*, *conceive*, and so on.

broadening the change in meaning of a word so that it refers to a wider variety of things than it originally did. For example, *bludger* used to mean 'someone living off the earnings of a prostitute', but it now refers to any 'scrounger'.

case a grammatical category associated with **nouns**, which bear **inflections** showing the relationship of the noun to other nouns and to the **verb** in a **clause**, or in other words signalling who is doing what to whom. Case only plays a peripheral role in the **pronouns** of Modern English (for example, *she* is in the subjective case and refers to the person doing something in a **basic clause**, while *her* is in the objective case and in canonical clauses refers to someone who has something done to her). In **Old English**, case was a much more important grammatical category, and all nouns were marked for case.

central vowels **vowel** sounds produced with the tongue held in a central position (that is, neither forward nor back) in the mouth.

clause a structural unit that is larger than a **phrase** and that may either constitute a **simple sentence** or be a **constituent** of a **multi-clausal sentence**.

cleft sentence a **sentence** in which a single **clause** has been split into two sections for the purpose of focus—for example, *It was the whisky that made him ill* (compare *The whisky made him ill*).

clitics items that are neither fully **bound** nor fully **free morphemes**. While **phonologically** bound in the sense that they attach to other words, they are grammatically free forms in the sense that they correspond to elements that are independent words—for example, *-'nt* in *isn't*.

coda any **consonants** within a **syllable** that follow the **nucleus**.

cognates linguistic forms that are derived historically from a common source.

comment the part of a **sentence** that says something about the **topic** of a sentence.

common nouns **nouns** that can co-occur with modifiers within the noun phrases that they head. This is a subcategory of nouns distinct from **proper nouns**.

commonisation the historical process whereby **proper nouns** become **common nouns** over time—for example, in Australia and New Zealand, the use of the name *Sheila* to refer to any woman or, in Australia, the use of the brand name *esky* to refer to portable coolers known as *chilly bins* in New Zealand.

communicative structure the ways in which the pieces of information in texts are organised.

comparative clause a **subordinate clause** that expresses the 'standard of comparison' in **sentences** in which a comparison is made between two propositions. For example, *he does* is the comparative clause in *She runs much faster than he does*.

compensatory lengthening a process whereby, as a **consonant** is deleted, a neighbouring **vowel** is lengthened as if to take up the space once occupied by the consonant.

complement an obligatory element in a grammatical construction.

complementary distribution the situation in which two similar **phones** only ever occur in different contexts within the words in which they are found.

complex sentences **sentences** containing an independent **clause** and one or more **subordinate clauses**.

complex-intransitive a term applied to **verbs** and **clauses** that must take a **subject complement**—for example, *an engineer* in *Mary is an engineer*.

complex-transitive a term applied to **verbs** and **clauses** that must take both an **object** and an **object complement**—for example, *me sick* in *Jeffrey makes me sick*.

compound sentences **sentences** involving two or more coordinated **clauses**.

compound-complex sentences **sentences** consisting of two or more coordinated **clauses** and one or more **subordinate clauses**.

compounds words that consist of two or more **roots** (for example, *blackbird*).

conjoin see **conjunctions**.

conjoinability a test for **constituent structure** whereby, if a sequence of words can be **conjoined** with one containing different words but the same internal structure, and if this gives an acceptable **sentence**, then the original sequence of words is a **constituent**.

conjunctions the **word class** that is used to link **clauses** or parts of clauses. **Coordinators** such as *and* and *but* link units that are of equal status, while **subordinators** link units, one of which is subordinate to the other—for example, *after*, *since*, *because*.

connotation associations of a word or other linguistic expression.

consonants sounds produced when airflow through the mouth is obstructed in some way— for example, by closing the lips or moving the tongue across the airway to block the flow.

constituent a linguistic component that is a part of some larger unit.

constituent structure a hierarchical linguistic structure in which **constituents** join together to make further constituents of a higher level and so on.

constituent structure rules see **phrase structure rules**.

constituent structure tree a diagram representing **constituent structure**, depicting it as a tree with branches showing each of the **constituents**.

contamination a **semantic shift** that comes about through the close associations one word has with other words.

content clause a kind of **subordinate clause** introduced by **subordinators** such as *after*, *because*, *whether*, and so on. For example, *because she forgot the eggs* is a subordinate content clause in *The souffle didn't rise because she forgot the eggs*. Content clauses more closely resemble main clauses than do many other kinds of subordinate clause.

conversion the **derivation** of words that have different **word class** membership without any **affixation**—for example, *swim* (**noun**) from *swim* (**verb**). Conversion is sometimes called 'zero affixation'.

coordination the relationship between two **constituents** of the same sort that are joined together by means of a **coordinator** to create a complex construction of the same sort as the **conjoined** elements.

coordinators a type of **conjunction** used to link **clauses**, **phrases**, or words that are of equivalent status (for example, *and* and *or*).

copular verb a **verb** such as *be*, *seem*, *appear*, *become*, or *remain* that 'links' the subject complement in a complex-intransitive clause.

correspondences see **sound correspondences**.

count nouns **nouns** that can be **inflected** for **number**—for example, *cup* (singular) versus *cups* (plural). See also **non-count nouns**.

creole a **pidgin** that has acquired native speakers.

creole continuum the range of language varieties between a pure **creole** and the Standard language found in places where **decreolisation** is occurring.

creolisation the speedy elaboration of vocabulary and grammar that occurs when a **pidgin** becomes a **creole**.

declarative a type of **clause** typically used to make statements. See also **exclamative**, **imperative**, and **interrogative**.

decreolisation a process of linguistic change whereby, under the influence of increased exposure to formal education and mass communication, a **creole** becomes more and more like the Standard language on which it was based.

definite article a type of **determiner**. The definite article *the* occurs in noun phrases, and its use signals that the **noun** it determines is definite, perhaps because it has already been referred to or because it is something well known to both speaker and hearer. See also **indefinite article**.

demonstrative pronouns in English, the forms *this*, *that*, *these*, and *those*, which refer to things by pointing to their location in time and/or space—for example, *this* 'near speaker' versus *that* 'away from speaker'. Demonstratives are also used as **determiners**.

dental a sound produced using the tongue tip between the teeth, or the tongue tip or blade close behind the upper teeth.

dependent optional elements within a **phrase** that are dependent on the **head** of that phrase. For example, *very* is an optional element in the adverb phrase *very quickly* and is dependent on the **adverbial head** of the phrase, *quickly*.

dependent clause see **subordinate clause**.

derivation the creation of new **lexemes** by adding **derivational morphemes** to a **stem**.

derivational morphemes **morphemes** that, when added to **stems**, can change the meaning of the **derived** form and create new **lexemes**.

descriptive rule a statement about language that aims to characterise objectively how people speak. See also **prescriptive rule**.

deterioration a process whereby words take on negative overtones. For example, *accident* once meant simply 'chance event', but now it refers to 'chance misfortune'.

determiners a **word class** that expresses notions such as definiteness, quantity, **number**, and possession. A variety of different subclasses of determiners are found in English: **articles**, **quantifiers**, and **demonstrative**, **possessive**, **interrogative**, and **relative pronouns**.

dialect a language variety associated with a particular group of people (for example, a regional, ethnic, or socio-economic group) and characterised by a distinct vocabulary and grammar.

dialect chain a series of different **regional dialects** that are all mutually intelligible with their immediate neighbours, but where the dialects spoken at each end of the chain are not mutually intelligible.

diphthong a sound that is produced as a sequence of **vowels**, with a movement of the tongue from one position to another.

discourse strategies the ways in which speakers vary the linguistic constructions they use in order to show shifts in focus, change in players, beginnings and ends of scenes, and so on.

dissimilation the modification of a sound so that it becomes less like a neighbouring sound.

di-transitive a term applied to **verbs** and **clauses** that must have two **objects** (a direct object and an indirect object) as with verbs referring to transfer of possession. For example, in *I gave the book to Mary*, *the book* is the direct object and *Mary* is the indirect object.

echo the repetition of any **clause** type for the purpose of confirming, questioning, or clarifying what has just been said. For example, *Roscoe ate the quark* can be echoed *Roscoe ate the quark?* (yes/no echo) and *Who ate the quark?* (wh- echo).

elevation a process whereby words take on positive overtones. For example, *democracy* used to have quite negative overtones, while modern Western ideology gives it positive overtones.

ellipsis the omission of items in a **sentence**, either because they appear elsewhere or because they can be reconstructed from context (in other words, old information). It is also a process whereby, in expressions of two or more words, one or more words drop out, and what's left of the expression stands for the whole thing—for example, *alarm* from *alarm clock*.

end-focus the situation in which **new information** is presented at the end of an utterance.

end-weight the principle whereby the most complex components of a **sentence** are introduced at the end of a sentence.

epenthesis the addition of sounds, as when a word such as *umbrella* gets pronounced in **non-standard** varieties of English as *umberella*.

epenthetic change a historical process whereby a variant pronunciation of a word involving **epenthesis** becomes the normal way of pronouncing a word.

euphemism any sweet-sounding, inoffensive expression that is substituted for one that is thought to be offensive—for example, *pass away* for 'die'. The term derives from the Greek meaning 'speaking fairly'. See also **taboo**.

exaggeration the persistent use of particular words, leading to the meanings of these words becoming weakened. For example, in OZ and NZ English, words such as *bloody* and *bastard* have become much weaker through widespread use.

exclamative a type of **clause** typically used to make exclamatory statements. See also **declarative, imperative, interrogative.**

existential sentence a **sentence** that expresses the existence of something by using the 'dummy subject' *there*, as in *There is a fly in my soup*.

expressive word order a grammatical system found in languages such as **Old English**, in which **inflection** is used to signal **grammatical relations** such as **subject** and **object**, and word order can be manipulated for expressive means.

extraposition a construction whereby a **clause** that would usually be a **subject** occurs instead at the end of a **sentence** and the subject position of the sentence is occupied by the 'dummy subject' *it*, as in *It is wonderful that champagne is available to drink.*

finite a form of a **verb** that has been **inflected** for **person**, **number**, and **tense**. See also **non-finite**.

finite clause a **clause** containing a **finite** verb.

First Germanic Consonant Shift see **Grimm's Law**.

folk etymology a rewriting of the history of a word in some way in order to make previously meaningless parts of the word meaningful. For example, folk etymologies can be used to create new **morphemes** where they did not originally exist, as with the restructuring of the word *crayfish*, which was originally the **borrowed** French word *crévisse* and had nothing to do with *fish*.

free morphemes **morphemes** that can occur on their own as words. See also **bound morphemes**.

free variation the situation in which two different sounds may occur in the same context without signalling any difference in meaning.

fricative a sound produced when two speech organs come close enough together to partially block the airflow and create a turbulence in what we can hear.

front vowels **vowel** sounds produced with the tongue positioned relatively forward in the mouth.

fronting the movement of an element to the front of the **sentence** for the purpose of focus—for example, *Zucchini I hate*. See also **left-dislocation**.

gender a grammatical category associated with **nouns**. In linguistics, gender does not necessarily refer to sex, but simply to the classification of nouns into groups for purposes of agreement, as, for example, **dependents** having to agree in gender with their **head** noun. **Old English** had three grammatical genders—masculine, feminine, and neuter—but these have been lost from Modern English.

geographical dialects see **regional dialects**.

Germanic a language family consisting of English, German, Dutch, Swedish, and a variety of other languages such as Icelandic and Friesian, which are all descendants of **Proto-Germanic**.

given information information that is already familiar to a hearer, either because the information has already been presented earlier in a text or because the information is already a part of the hearer's background knowledge.

global English a term used to refer both to the spread of English into parts of the world where English was not traditionally used and to the creation of new varieties of English in these places.

glottal sounds produced using the space between the **vocal folds**.

grammatical morphemes **morphemes** that have purely grammatical meaning and that do not refer to anything in the real world. See also **lexical morphemes**.

grammatical relations notions such as **subject** and **object**, which describe the functional relation between noun phrases and the **verbs** they occur with.

grammatical word order a grammatical system found in languages such as Modern English, where fixed word order within a **clause** is used to signal **grammatical relations** such as **subject** and **object**.

grammaticalisation a cover term for a number of different historical changes that work together to create new grammatical forms and constructions. Through grammaticalisation, **morphemes** or combinations of morphemes shift from a lexical to a grammatical function, with changes occurring at the semantic, **phonological**, and grammatical level.

Great English Vowel Shift a series of historical sound changes that took place between **Middle English** and early Modern English whereby five of the long **vowels** of Middle English shifted up a position in height and the two long high vowels became **diphthongs**. See also **pull chain** and **push chain**.

Grimm's Law a set of rules devised by one of the famous Grimm brothers (who also wrote many fairy stories) that explain some of the most important sound changes that occurred in the **Germanic** languages and that help to define the Germanic languages as a distinct subgroup of the Indo-European language family. Proto-Indo-European (PIE) voiceless **stops** became voiceless **fricatives**, voiced stops became voiceless stops, and 'breathy voiced stops' became voiced stops in Germanic.

habitual aspect an **aspect** encoded (in English) by the form *used to*, which conveys the idea that some activity was carried out habitually over a period of time—for example, *I used to drink too much*.

haplology the loss of an entire **syllable** from a word.

hard palate a bony partition found in the front part of the roof of the mouth, providing a partition between the oral and the nasal cavities.

head the central, obligatory element within a **phrase**, which may have a number of optional **dependants** associated with it. For example, the **noun** *raisins* is the head of the noun phrase *more plump juicy raisins*.

high rising intonation an intonational pattern characteristic of the speech of many OZ and NZ English speakers, whereby statements have an **intonation** that rises at the end rather than falling, similar to the intonation often found at the end of yes/no questions.

high vowels **vowel** sounds produced with the tongue raised relatively high in the mouth.

homographs words that are written the same way but that are pronounced differently—for example, *read* in *I read a book yesterday* and *I read a book every day.*

homonyms words that belong to different **lexemes** but that are pronounced and written the same way—for example, *bank* in *the bank one deposits money in* and *the bank of a river*.

homophones words that belong to different **lexemes** and that are written in different ways, but which are pronounced in the same way—for example, *wait* and *weight*.

idiolect variation within a language that is associated with individual speakers.

imperative a type of **clause** typically used to issue directions or commands. See also **declarative, exclamative, interrogative**.

indefinite article a type of **determiner**. Indefinite articles *a* and *an* are used when the **noun** with which they occur has not already been specified. See also **definite article**.

indefinite pronouns **pronouns** that express notions of definiteness or quantity and which come in two major types in English: **compounds** with elements such as *some-* (as in *something*) or *any-* (as in *anyone*), and words that either occur alone or are followed by *of* (as in *many* and *most*).

infinitive the base form of a **verb**, uninflected for **person**, **number**, or **tense**. This is the form occurring in dictionaries and preceded by *to*, as in *to eat*.

infixes **bound morphemes** that occur within the **root** to which they are attached. They are only found in English as intensifiers in **non-standard** forms, such as *bloody* in *fanbloodytastic*.

inflection the creation of different grammatical forms of a **lexeme** by the addition of **inflectional morphemes** to a **stem**.

inflectional morphemes **grammatical morphemes** that signal grammatical relationships and do not change the **lexeme** of the form to which they are attached.

interjections **word classes** that do not enter into syntactic relationships with other elements and have a purely expressive function—for example, *Yuk!*

interrogative a type of **clause** typically used to ask questions. See also **declarative, exclamative, imperative**.

interrogative pronouns **pronouns** used to ask questions about the identity of people or things—for example, *who, what, which*.

intonation the pattern of pitch changes characteristic of an utterance.

intransitive a term applied to **verbs** and **clauses** that cannot take an **object** noun phrase.

jargon a specialised language variety used by a particular social group or within a particular field of expertise.

jussive the subordinate counterpart of an **imperative** main **clause**. The **verb** is in a base form, and the **subject**, if it is a **pronoun**, is in a subjective form. For example, *that she be on time* is the jussive in *it is critical that she be on time*.

labiodental a sound produced using the lower lip and the upper teeth.

lag assimilation the modification of a sound so that it becomes more like a sound that precedes it, as when *seven* is pronounced as *sevem*.

larynx a valve sometimes called the 'Adam's apple' or 'voice-box', which is located above the trachea or wind-pipe. All air coming up from the **lungs** passes through an opening in the larynx called the glottis, along the sides of which are found two small muscular folds called the '**vocal folds**' or sometimes 'vocal cords'.

lateral a sound produced by forming a partial closure with the tongue, so that air can still flow between one or both sides of the tongue and the area of the mouth where the partial closure is made. In English, the only lateral is [l], formed in the **alveolar** region.

left-dislocation a strategy for focusing an element of a **sentence** by 'shifting' it to the front of the sentence and leaving some sort of **proform** copy of the element in its usual position—for example, *That curry you cooked, it was fantastic!* See also **fronting** and **right-dislocation**.

lexeme a term referring to individual vocabulary items, which may encompass more than one word form—for example, the lexeme EAT may involve a number of different word forms, such as *eat*, *eats*, *ate*, and so on.

lexical diffusion the gradual progress of a sound change through the vocabulary. At first only a few words are affected (typically common-usage words); then large numbers of words take up the change.

lexical morphemes **morphemes** that refer to things in the real world. See also **grammatical morphemes**.

lingua franca a medium of communication for people who have different first languages. English is rapidly becoming a global *lingua franca*.

low vowels **vowel** sounds produced with the tongue held low in the mouth and normally with the mouth held fairly widely open.

lungs the organs of breathing, which act as a power source for all of the sounds of English.

major word classes in English the major word classes are **nouns**, **verbs**, **adjectives**, and **adverbs**. These **word classes** have many members and are continually expanding as new words are added to the language.

mass nouns see **non-count nouns**.

metaphor a figure of speech whereby the use of a word is extended beyond its primary meaning to describe something that shows some similarity. For example, by calling someone a 'pig' we are saying that there is a semantic connection between the person (the figurative meaning) and a pig (the literal meaning). See also **metonymy**, **synaesthesia**, **synecdoche**.

metaphorical change a historical change in meaning, whereby what was a metaphorical use of a word becomes part of its meaning. One common area of metaphorical change in most languages is that of body part terms that take on new meanings—for example, *head* in *the head of a table*, *the head of an organisation*, *the cylinder head in an engine*, and so on.

metathesis the swapping in order of adjacent sounds.

metonymy a type of **metaphor** involving the extension of a word's meaning so that it refers to something closely associated with the original meaning of the word—for example, using the term *champagne* to refer to a type of wine produced in the Champagne district of France.

mid vowels **vowel** sounds produced with the tongue held at a mid-level height within the mouth.

Middle English a language ancestral to Modern English that was spoken in England about 500 years ago.

minimal pairs two words that differ only in the pronunciation of one sound in the same position within each word, as in *pat* and *bat*.

minor word classes the minor word classes of English include classes such as **pronouns, prepositions**, and other grammatical words. These **word classes** are typically 'closed', in that they only have a small number of members and are typically resistant to incorporating new members.

modal auxiliaries a group of **auxiliaries** that express things such as ability and permission, that have no distinctions for **person, number**, and **tense**, and that co-occur with the **infinitive** forms of main **verbs**—for example, *can*, *could*, and *might*.

mood a grammatical category dealing with the reality of an event or situation. Two broad categories of mood, **actual mood** and **non-actual mood**, are characteristically distinguished in English through the use of **modal auxiliaries**.

morph the actually occurring sequences of sounds to which meaning attaches. See also **allomorphs** and **morpheme**.

morpheme the smallest meaningful units of a language, more than one of which may sometimes occur within a single word. A morpheme may be represented in actual speech by a number of different **allomorphs**.

movement a test for **constituent structure** whereby, if a sequence of words can be shifted from one position in a **sentence** to another without changing the overall acceptability of the sentence, then that sequence may be seen as a **constituent**.

multi-clausal sentence a **sentence** consisting of more than one **basic clause**.

narrowing the change in meaning of a word so that it refers to a narrower range of things. For example, *liquor* once referred to 'any liquid', but now it generally refers to 'alcoholic beverages'.

nasal a sound produced with the **velum** lowered so that air can escape through the nose.

Native Englishes the established **dialects** of English spoken in places where native speakers of English have lived for a long time and distinct varieties of the language are spoken—for example, Australia, New Zealand, the United Kingdom, Canada, the USA, and South Africa. See also **New Englishes** and **Other Englishes**.

New Englishes varieties of contact English spoken in places such as India, Singapore, Hong Kong, and Malaysia, where the use of English is increasing very rapidly and distinct varieties of the language are emerging. See also **Native Englishes** and **Other Englishes**.

new information information, presented in a text, that is not familiar to a hearer until the point of its introduction.

nominalisation the process of creating a **noun** from some other part of speech—for example, *sweet* + *ness*. It also includes the process of turning whole **clauses** into noun phrases. For example, *that the chefs use powered eggs* becomes *the chefs' use of powered eggs*.

non-actual mood a grammatical **mood** used to refer to events and activities that, for some reason, have not taken place or are not taking place in reality. Non-actual mood can occur for a variety of reasons: perhaps the event referred to will occur in the future; perhaps it did not occur (negative); or perhaps the speaker is uncertain whether it occurred or not.

non-count nouns **nouns** that are interpreted as indivisible masses of material and that cannot normally be pluralised, as with *rice*. They are also called 'mass nouns'. See also **count nouns**.

non-finite forms of a **verb** that have not been **inflected** for the grammatical categories of **person**, **number**, and **tense**. In English, non-finite verb forms are **infinitives** and the **present** and **past participles**.

non-finite clause a **clause** (usually a **subordinate clause**) in which the main **verb** has a **non-finite** form—for example, *This is the best cheese for her to try*.

non-standard varieties or **dialects** other than **Standard English**.

nouns the **word class** that typically refer to objects (both physical objects and abstractions). Among many other properties, English nouns typically **inflect** for **number**, and occur as the **heads** of noun phrases with **determiners**, **adjectives**, and so on as **dependents**.

nuclear syllable the **syllable** within an utterance that receives the greatest prominence through carrying the major pitch change.

nucleus the central peak of a **syllable**, usually consisting of a **vowel**, but sometimes consisting of one of the **consonants** /l/, /r/, or a **nasal**.

number a grammatical category associated primarily with **nouns**. Most nouns are unmarked in the singular and marked with *-s* in the plural. **Verbs** must agree in number and **person** with their **subjects**.

object a **constituent** of a **clause**—either a noun phrase or a **subordinate clause**—that normally follows the **predicator** in **basic clauses** and that can be made the **subject** of a clause if the clause is made **passive**.

object complement a noun phrase, adjective phrase, or **subordinate clause** that is like an **object** in that it is included in the **predicate**, but unlike the object in that it refers to an entity already mentioned in the clause. In the **sentence** *I called my latest creation green bean supreme*, the object is *my latest creation* and the object complement is *green bean supreme*. See also **subject complement**.

objective case the typical form a **pronoun** takes when it is functioning as the **object** of a **verb**. See also **case** and **subjective case**.

obsolescence the loss of words, usually because the things they refer to are no longer of great importance to speakers of a language.

Old English a language ancestral to Modern English that was spoken about 1000 years ago.

onomastics the study of the origins and use of **proper nouns**.

onset any **consonants** within a **syllable** that precede the **rhyme**.

oral a sound produced with the passage of air flowing exclusively through the oral cavities.

Other Englishes the language varieties called **pidgins** and **creoles**, which are partially based on English but which have radically different grammatical structures from **Standard English**. See also **Native Englishes** and **New Englishes**.

palatal sounds produced using the front of the tongue and the **hard palate**.

palatalisation the label given to the process whereby a following **front vowel** (for example, [i] or [e]) or the **palatal approximant** ([j]) conditions a change in the preceding sound so that it too receives a palatal pronunciation, as when *can't you* is pronounced as [kantʃu].

palato-alveolar a sound produced using the blade of the tongue and the back of the **alveolar ridge**.

parts of speech see **word classes**.

passive a kind of 'grammatical voice' where, in **transitive** clauses, the patient occurs as the **subject** of the **clause** and the actor or the agent is introduced by the preposition *by* or is left out of the **sentence** altogether—for example, *Plenty of simple, beat-the-clock recipes are included by the authors* or *Plenty of simple, beat-the-clock recipes are included*. See also **active** voice.

past participle a **verb** form commonly ending in *-en* or *-ed* (for example, *eaten* or *sweated*) that refers to events that have been completed. It must be supported by an **auxiliary** when it is used as the main verb in a **sentence**.

past tense the **tense** used to refer to an event that occurred before some other event (often the time of speaking).

perfect aspect an **aspect** expressed by some form of the **auxiliary** *have* and the **past participle,** which is used to indicate that an action or activity has been or will be completed, as in *I have eaten*.

person a grammatical category associated primarily with **nouns**, consisting of first person (the speaker), second person (the person spoken to), and third person (the person or thing spoken about). **Verbs** must agree in person and **number** with their **subjects**.

personal pronouns these **pronouns** refer simply to the **person** and **number** of the referent. Many of the English personal pronouns have special forms depending on whether they occur as **subjects** (for example, *they*) or **objects** (for example, *them*).

phone a term referring to actual units of speech as produced by speakers.

phoneme the abstract, distinctive sound units within a language.

phonesthemes sound sequences that, while not **morphemes** in themselves, are still associated with particular meanings—for example, *-ump* meaning 'heavy fall' in *bump, dump, thump*, and so on. They occur either at the beginning of words (*tw-, gl-, fl-*) or their **rhymes** (*-ash, -ump, -itter*).

phonetics the study of the way we make, transmit, and receive speech sounds.

phonology the study of the sound systems and patterns that occur in a language.

phonotactic constraints language-specific rules that describe the allowable sequences of **phonemes** found within **syllables** or words.

phrasal verb a **lexeme** consisting of a **verb** and an **adverb** particle that function together as a unit—for example, *look up* and *run over*.

phrase structure rules sometimes called 'constituent structure rules', these describe the **constituent structure** of **phrases**. For example, the phrase structure rule VP → V (NP) (PP) says that a verb phrase consists of an obligatory **verb** optionally followed by a noun phrase and a prepositional phrase (the parentheses indicating an optional **constituent**). Further phrase structure rules will describe the constituent structure of noun phrases and prepositional phrases as well as those of other constituents.

phrases groups of words that are smaller than a **clause** and that behave as a structural unit, named after the **head** or the word that is most important within the phrase. For example, noun phrases have **nouns** as their heads, verb phrases have **verbs** as their heads, and so on. A head may have a number of **dependants** associated with it.

pidgin a kind of make-shift language that springs up when speakers of different languages come together for a period of time and need to talk. Historically, pidgins typically sprang up along trade routes and in places where indentured labourers or slaves who originally spoke other languages came together. In forming a pidgin, two (or more) languages are involved, but the pidgin takes one language, usually the socially dominant one, as its point of origin. In this way, English forms the basis of many of the Pacific and West African pidgins. See also **creole**.

polysemy the relationship between the different but related meanings of the same **lexeme**—for example, *foot* in *the foot on someone's body* and *the foot of a mountain*.

possessive pronouns **pronouns** that are used to express ownership, or some other close relationship between two things—for example, *mine*, *hers*, and so on.

predicate the verb phrase in a **basic clause**. The predicate attributes something to the **subject** by ascribing some property or role in the situation.

predicator the function performed by the **verb** in a **basic clause**.

prefixes **bound morphemes** that precede the **root** to which they are attached—for example, *un-* in *uncooked*.

prejudice preconceived opinion or bias, which can result in changes in the meanings of words. For example, many words relating to the upper classes have become words referring to good qualities, while words relating to the lower classes have become words referring to bad qualities; compare *noble* with *boorish,* which was originally a term for a country person.

prepositional verb a **verb** followed by a prepositional phrase, with the particular **preposition** that occurs determined by the verb. For example, in *she relied on the chef*, the preposition *on* forms a syntactic unit with *the chef* but is determined by the verb *rely*.

prepositions English prepositions are used for a variety of semantic purposes, often to refer to spatial relationships—for example, *behind* and *in front of*. They can also be used to indicate the grammatical role of a noun phrase in a **sentence**. For example, *by* marks the logical **subject** of a **passive** clause. Prepositions occur as the **heads** of prepositional phrases, which can serve a variety of grammatical functions within a **clause**.

prescriptive rule a statement about language with authoritarian intent, which aims to tell people how they should speak or write 'properly'. See also **descriptive rule**.

present participle a **verb** form commonly ending in *-ing* (as in *eating*) that refers to events that are in progress. It must be supported by an **auxiliary** when it is used as the main verb in a **sentence**.

present tense the **tense** often associated with events occurring at the present time, but also used to refer to timeless truths, as in *Elephants are big*, or scheduled events that are due to occur in the future, as in *The show opens next week*.

primary auxiliaries a subgroup of **auxiliaries** consisting of the **verbs** *be*, *have*, and *do*. These verbs may also occur as main verbs.

proforms small words, such as **pronouns**, that can replace longer constructions when the information provided by the longer construction is **given information**.

progressive aspect an **aspect** with a form of the **auxiliary** *be* and the **present participle**, which is used to indicate that some event or activity was or is still in progress—for example, *I am eating*.

pronouns a **minor word class** which can be used in the place of full noun phrases. A variety of sub-groups of pronouns are found in English: **personal pronouns**, **indefinite pronouns**, **reflexive pronouns**, **reciprocal pronouns**, **possessive pronouns**, **demonstrative pronouns**, **interrogative pronouns**, and **relative pronouns**.

proper nouns **nouns** that are the names of specific persons, places, and organisations. They are spelt with an initial capital letter, are not normally able to be pluralised, and are not able to co-occur with the same range of modifying words as **common nouns**.

prosodic features **phonological** properties that are not a part of individual segments or **phonemes** but that are features of **syllables**, words, and **phrases** They include **tempo**, loudness, and **stress**, and are sometimes called 'suprasegmental features'.

Proto-Germanic the **proto-language** once spoken by the ancestors of English and other **Germanic** languages such as German, Dutch, Swedish, and so on.

proto-language an ancestral language that, over time, can develop sufficient differences in its varieties that these different varieties of the same language eventually become distinct languages that are no longer mutually comprehensible.

pull chain one possible explanation of how the **Great English Vowel Shift** and other changes of this nature occurred. According to this explanation, one **vowel** moved position, leaving a space for another vowel to move into, which in turn left another space, and so on.

push chain one possible explanation of how the **Great English Vowel Shift** and other changes of this nature occurred. According to this explanation, one **vowel** encroached on the territory of another, pushing it towards the space occupied by another vowel, and so on.

quantifiers modifiers of **nouns** that express quantity or extent, such as *all*, *few*, *little*, *lots of*, and so on.

reciprocal pronouns in English, the forms *each other* and *one another*, which are used to express a two-way relationship between different referents.

reduplication a process whereby all or part of a **stem** is repeated in order to derive a new word, as in *goody-goody*.

reflexive pronouns **pronouns** ending in *-self* or *-selves*, which reflect noun phrases found elsewhere in a **clause**—for example, *myself*, *yourselves*, and so on.

regional dialect the **dialect** spoken by the inhabitants of a particular region.

relative clause a **clause**, usually introduced by a **relative pronoun**, that occurs as a **constituent** of a noun phrase and provides further information about the **head** noun.

relative pronouns **pronouns** that are used to link **nouns** with the **relative clauses** that modify them—for example, *who* in *the man who I saw yesterday*.

rhyme that part of the **syllable** that consists of the **nucleus** and the **coda**. It is the linguistic unit that has the property of rhyming in, for example, poetry and rhyming slang.

right-dislocation a construction whereby something that would usually occur early in a **sentence** is not mentioned until the end of the sentence. A **proform** is found in the position that the element would usually be expected to occupy—for example, *It was very tasty, the dog curry I ate on holiday*. See also **left-dislocation**.

roots single **lexical morphemes** that form the core of a word and to which **bound morphemes** can be attached.

rounded a sound (usually a **vowel**) produced with rounded lips.

Second Germanic Consonant Shift a historical process of sound change undergone by German, but not any of the other **Germanic** languages. In this process, Germanic [t] became [s] in German; Germanic [k] remained [k] initially but became [x] elsewhere; and Germanic [p] became [pf] initially but [f] elsewhere in

German. Other Germanic languages such as English and Dutch retain the original Germanic sounds.

semantic change a change in the meaning of words. For example, in modern teenage-speak, words such as *wicked* and *sick* refer to positive attributes.

semantic shift a change in meaning whereby a word refers to something completely different from what it once referred to. For example, a *spell* once referred to a period of work, while now it refers to a break from work.

semi-vowels **consonants** produced with relatively unimpeded airflow through the mouth and sounded continuously. In English, the semi-vowels are the sounds found at the beginning of the words *wet* and *yet*.

sense the meaning of a word.

sentence the largest unit of structure in terms of how the grammar of English is organised. Traditionally, a sentence is thought of as a 'complete expression of thought'. However, many sentences—such as *G'day!*—express a single thought but would not be considered to be 'complete' as they do not contain a **finite verb**.

shortenings abbreviated versions of longer words—for example, *bus* from *omnibus*, or *uni* from *university*.

simple sentence a **sentence** consisting of a single **clause**.

social change changes in social mores can often be responsible for shifts in the meanings of words. For example, many words that once had religious overtones—such as *charisma* (originally 'divinely conferred power')—have now lost their religious significance.

social variation differences in **dialect** associated with groups of people sharing similar social characteristics. Such differences may be based on socio-economic class, ethnicity, gender, and sexual orientation, among other factors.

soft palate see **velum**.

sound correspondences in languages descended from a common **proto-language**, we often find that the **phonemes** of one language have systematic correspondences with the phonemes of another. For example, we find that German [pf] (at the beginning of a word) and German [f] (elsewhere in a word) systematically occur in positions where English and Dutch have [p]. These are sound correspondences.

specialist languages see **jargon**.

spelling pronunciation sound changes that have occurred as a result of speakers shifting their pronunciation of a word to make it more consistent with its spelling.

Standard English the **dialect** of English originally spoken in London and the Central Midland region of England, which has gained more prestige than other dialects and which is often associated with education and higher income groups.

stem modification modification of sounds in a **stem** in order to create words with either new grammatical meanings or new lexical meanings—for example, *foot–feet* and *sale–sell*.

stems constructions consisting of one or more **morphemes** to which an **affix** is attached. For example, the **root** *cook* is also the stem to which the **suffix** *-ed* can be added to create the word *cooked*, but the multimorphemic *cooked* is the stem to which the **prefix** *un-* can be added to create the word *uncooked*.

stop a sound produced by completely blocking off airflow through the oral cavity.

stress a term used for a **syllable** that is given prominence in a word or **phrase**.

subject an element of a **clause**. In a **basic clause** the subject is an obligatory noun phrase, which precedes the **predicate**, and with which the **verb** must agree in **person** and **number**.

subject complement a noun phrase, adjective phrase, or **subordinate clause** that is like an **object** in that it is included in the **predicate**, but unlike the object in that it refers to an entity already mentioned in the **clause**. In the **sentence** *She is a teacher*, the subject complement is *a teacher*. Subject complements occur with **copular verbs** such as *be*, *seem*, *appear*, and so on. See also **object complement**.

subject–verb inversion a **discourse strategy** that moves the **subject** out of its normal environment for the purpose of focus—for example, *Out will come beef dusted with Japanese pepper*.

subjective case the typical form a **pronoun** takes when it is functioning as the **subject** of a **verb**. See also **case** and **objective case**.

subordinate clause a **clause** that occurs as a **constituent** of another clause.

subordination the relationship between two **clauses** whereby one clause is a **constituent** of another clause.

subordinators a type of **conjunction** used to link grammatical units that are of unequal status—for example, *after*, *because*, and so on.

subreption a process of **semantic change** whereby objects, ideas, and institutions change over time but the words that refer to them remain the same. For example, a *torch* was once 'a flame on the end of a stick' and now it generally refers to what Americans call '*flashlights*'.

substitution a test for **constituent structure** whereby, if a sequence of words in a **sentence** can be substituted by a single word without affecting the overall acceptability of the sentence, then that sequence of words is a **constituent**.

suffix a **bound morpheme** that follows the **root** to which it is attached—for example, *-ed* in *cooked*.

superordinate clause a **clause** that contains a **subordinate clause**.

suppletion the situation where two forms of the same **lexeme** have no obvious relationship in the actual form they take—for example, *go–went*. This situation arises when two historically unrelated paradigms merge, and almost invariably affects frequently occurring words.

suprasegmental features see **prosodic features**.

syllable an element of speech consisting of one or more **phonemes** (usually including a **vowel** as its **nucleus**) that acts as a rhythmic unit.

synaesthesia a type of **metaphor** involving the association of **senses**—for example, *I see* for 'I understand'.

syncope the loss of **vowels** occurring in the middle of words.

syncretism what is said to occur if the same word form is used to represent different grammatical meanings of the same **lexeme**—for example, when *cut* is the general **present-tense** form as well as the **past-tense** form and the **past participle** of the **infinitive** *cut*.

synecdoche a type of **metaphor** involving the relationship of part for whole. Something is named on the basis of its most prominent or salient part—for instance, *silver* for 'cutlery'.

syntax the study of the structure of **sentences**.

synthetic language a language in which **inflections** on words carry most of the weight in signalling **grammatical relations**, and in which word order is not very important.

taboo as originally **borrowed** from Tongan, taboo is prohibited behaviour—in particular, behaviour believed to be dangerous to certain individuals or to the society as a whole. Traditionally tabooed expressions are avoided because they are thought to be ominous or evil. English taboo terms, however, are avoided because their use is regarded as distasteful within a given social context; these taboos rest on traditions of etiquette. Taboo topics include things that frighten us, embarrass us, or for some reason we find difficult to discuss. See also **euphemism**.

tempo the speed at which we speak.

tense a grammatical category associated with **verbs**. It locates the time of one event with respect to the time of another event (often the time of speaking).

topic the part of a **sentence** that indicates what is being talked or written about.

'tough' movement a construction in which, for the purpose of focus, a noun phrase moves out of the **complement** clause of an **adjective** such as *tough* and becomes the **subject** of the higher **clause**. For example, *It's really tough to find broccoli out of season* becomes *Broccoli is tough to find out of season.*

transitive a term applied to **verbs** and **clauses** that must take an **object** noun phrase.

tune the pitch change pattern associated with a particular utterance. See also **intonation**.

umlaut a type of **assimilation** whereby a **vowel** in a word assimilates towards a vowel in a following **syllable**.

unrounded a sound (usually a **vowel**) produced with unrounded lips.

use-related variation differences in the variety of language used that are associated with the occasion of use.

user-related variation differences in the variety of language used that are associated with the person speaking.

velar a sound produced using the back of the tongue and the **velum**.

velum sometimes called the 'soft palate', the velum is a muscular flap forming the back half of the roof of the mouth. When the velum is raised, air can only escape through the mouth and we produce an **oral** sound. When the velum is lowered, air is allowed to pass through both the mouth and the nasal cavities, and we produce a **nasal** sound.

verbless clauses a minor **clause** type in which the clause contains no **verb**, as in *the bigger, the better*.

verbs the **word class** generally referring to actions, processes, states, and events. In English, verbs are readily identified as the word class that is **inflected** for **number**, **person**, and **tense**.

vernacular another word for **non-standard** varieties of English.

vocal cords see **vocal folds**.

vocal folds commonly called the 'vocal cords', these are small folds of muscle found alongside the glottis. The vocal folds remain relaxed while we produce **voiceless sounds** and they vibrate when we produce **voiced sounds**.

voiced sounds sounds that are produced with taught, vibrating **vocal folds**. In English, these sounds include all of the **vowels**, all of the **nasals**, and sounds such as [v, z, b, d, g].

voiceless sounds sounds that are produced with relaxed, non-vibrating **vocal folds**. These sounds include [f, s, p, t, k].

voicing assimilation this process occurs when a normally voiceless sound gets voiced because of **voiced sounds** in the neighbourhood, as when the [t] in a word such as *atom* gets pronounced more like a [d] because it is flanked by **vowels**.

vowels sounds produced when airflow is unimpeded through the mouth.

word the smallest unit of language that can be used alone as a complete utterance, that can have pauses around it in connected speech, and that is separated by spaces in written language.

word classes sets of words sharing many linguistic features, such as the kind of **inflection** possible, syntactic distribution, and so on. Word classes are sometimes called 'parts of speech' and include classes such as **nouns** and **verbs.** See also **major word classes** and **minor word classes**.

zero-affixation see **conversion**.

Further Reading

The following lists of references are designed to guide you in your further reading. Rather than list these chapter by chapter, we have organised them according to the various topics covered within the chapters. We have only included short references here; full citations can be found in the References.

GENERAL REFERENCES ON LANGUAGE

The following references deal with various aspects of language, including historical and sociolinguistic aspects: Aitchison 1983, Aitchison 1991, Bloomfield 1933, Bolinger 1975, Crowley 1997, Holmes 1992, Hopper & Traugott 1993, Lyons 1968, McMahon 1995, Sapir 1921, and Trudgill, 1995.

GENERAL REFERENCES ON ENGLISH

These are general introductions to English structure and history: Bolton 1982, Crystal 1995, Lass 1987, and McArthur 1992.

ENGLISH GRAMMARS AND STYLE GUIDES

These present outlines of Modern English structure and selected usage issues: Crystal 1984, Freeborn 1995, Huddleston 1984, Huddleston 1988, Kaplan 1995, Kuiper & Allan 1996, Lass 1987, Leech & Svartvik 1994, Murray-Smith 1990, Peters 1995, Quirk & Greenbaum 1973, Quirk, Greenbaum, Leech, & Svartvik, 1985, and Wardhaugh 1995.

HISTORY OF ENGLISH

These outline details of the general history of English and change within specific areas: Aiken 1930, Allen 1995, Barber 1993, Bauer 1994, Baugh & Cable 1993, Bean 1983, Blake 1996, Dennison 1995, McCrum, Cran, & MacNeil 1991, Myers & Hoffman 1979, Pyles & Algeo 1993, Samuels 1972, Smith 1996, and Strang 1974.

OLD AND MIDDLE ENGLISH

These focus specifically on different aspects of Old and Middle English: Blake 1992, Hogg 1992, Jones 1972, Lass 1994, Mitchell & Robinson 1992, Partridge 1982, and Quirk & Wrenn 1955.

EARLY NEW AND PRESENT-DAY ENGLISH

These focus specifically on aspects of Early New and present-day English: Barber 1976, Görlach 1991b, Lass (in press), and Romaine (in press).

PRESCRIPTION AND THE RISE OF STANDARD ENGLISH

These cover standardisation and issues to do with prescriptivism; see also titles listed under 'History of English': Bolton 1966, Cameron 1995, Freeborn 1992, Milroy & Milroy 1991, and Shopen & Williams 1980.

OZ ENGLISH

These cover different aspects of OZ English; see also titles listed under 'Aboriginal English': Baker 1970, Bennett 1994, Bradley 1989, Bradley 1991, Bradley, Sussex, & Scott 1989, Cheshire 1991, Cochrane 1989, Collins & Blair 1989, Gupta 1995, Horvath 1985, Hornadge 1989, Mitchell & Delbridge 1965, Newbrook 1992, Peters 1992, Romaine 1991, Tilgals 1995, Turner 1966, Wilkes 1993,

Note that two wonderful, up-to-date sources on the use of English in Australia are the newsletters *Ozwords* (published by the Australian National Dictionary Centre, Australian National University, and Oxford University Press) and *Australian Style* (The Dictionary Research Centre, Macquarie University). See also the various proceedings of the Style Council (The Dictionary Research Centre, Macquarie University) and the series *English World-Wide*.

ABORIGINAL ENGLISH

These cover varieties of Aboriginal English ranging from Standard Australian to Australian Creole English; see also titles listed under 'Australian English': Cheshire 1991, Eagleson, Kaldor, & Malcolm 1982, Harkins 1994, Koch 1985, McKay 1996, Schmidt 1990, and Walsh & Yallop 1993.

NZ ENGLISH

These cover different aspects of New Zealand English; see also titles listed under 'Maori English': Bartlett 1992, Batterham 1995, Bauer 1979, Bauer 1992, Bayard 1995, Bell & Holmes 1990, Britain 1992, Cheshire 1991, Gordon & Deverson 1985, Gordon & Deverson 1989, Gordon & Maclagan 1989, Gordon & Maclagan 1990, Holmes 1994, Holmes & Bell 1993, Maclagan 1975, Maclagan & Gordon 1996, Smith 1993, and Turner 1966.

Note that an excellent, up-to-date source on the use of English in New Zealand is the series *New Zealand English Journal* (formerly *New Zealand English Newsletter*, published by the Department of English, University of Canterbury, Christchurch); see also the series *English World-Wide*.

MAORI ENGLISH

These cover different aspects of Maori English; see also titles listed under 'NZ English': Benton 1991, Clark 1979, Clark 1991, Johnston & Robertson 1993, and King 1993.

GLOBALISATION AND ENGLISH WORLDWIDE

These focus on globalisation and the international spread of English; see also references on 'Regional Variation' below: Bailey & Görlach 1982, Burchfield 1994, Crystal 1997, Gleeson 1995, Hall 1991, Pennycook 1994, and Pennycook 1995. See also the series *English World-Wide.*

REGIONAL VARIATION

These describe aspects of regional varieties of English; see also titles listed under 'Globalisation and English Worldwide', 'South Asian Englishes', and 'Pidgin and Creole Englishes': Algeo (in press), Cheshire 1991, De Klerk 1996, Gass & Lefkowitz 1995, Görlach 1991a, Görlach 1994, Graddol et al. 1996, Hughes & Trudgill 1979, Kachru 1986, Todd & Hancock 1986, Trudgill 1986, Trudgill 1994, Trudgill & Hannah 1994, and Viereck, Scheider, & Görlach 1984. Note that the De Klerk and Görlach publications above contain useful bibliographies.

SOUTH ASIAN ENGLISHES

These deal specifically with New Englishes in South Asia: Foley 1988, Iyengar 1962, Kachru 1983, Kachru 1992, Nihalani, Tongue, & Hosali 1970, and Platt, Weber, & Ho 1984.

PIDGIN AND CREOLE ENGLISHES

These deal specifically with Other Englishes; see also 'Aboriginal English' for Kriol references: Dillard 1972, Dutton 1985, Roberts 1988, Romaine 1988, and Todd 1984.

SOCIAL VARIATION

These deal with various aspects of social variation: Labov 1966, Labov 1972, Leith 1983, Machan & Scott 1992, Milroy 1980, Romaine 1982, Trudgill 1974, and Trudgill 1975.

LANGUAGE AND GENDER

These deal with linguistic differences between both heterosexual and homosexual men and women, and with how language represents them: Banks & Mulder 1996, Cameron 1992, Chesebro 1981, Coates 1997, Crawford 1995, Dynes 1985, Gaudio 1994, Graddol & Swann 1989, Holmes 1995, Miller & Swift 1991, Pauwels 1987, Poynton 1985, Risch 1987, and Rodgers 1972.

ENGLISH SOUNDS AND SPELLING

These cover English phonology and issues to do with spelling; see also 'History of English', 'OZ English', and 'NZ English': Carney 1994, Catford 1988, Clark &

Yallop 1995, Haas 1969, Katamba 1989, Ladefoged 1993, Lieberman & Blumstein 1988, and Roach 1983.

ENGLISH VOCABULARY

These deal with aspects of English words, past and present, as well as with word formation: Allan & Burridge 1991, Ayto 1993, Baron 1989, Bauer 1983, Bauer 1988, Bauer 1993, Burchfield 1989, Butler 1990, Denning & Leben 1995, Hughes 1988, Katamba 1994, Lewis 1970, Lutz 1989, Partridge 1970, and Serjeantson 1935.

ENGLISH DISCOURSE AND STYLE

These deal generally with aspects of stylistic variation and discourse: Biber 1988, Charrow & Charrow 1979, Crystal 1980, Crystal & Davy 1969, Danet 1980, Freeborn 1996, Freeborn (with French & Langford) 1986, Halliday 1985, Kuiper 1996, Ochs 1979, and Shopen & Williams 1981.

References

ACOD. See *The Australian Concise Oxford Dictionary*.

Aiken, Janet 1930, *English Past and Present*, Roland Press, New York.

Aitchison, Jean 1983, *The Articulate Mammal*, Universe Books, New York.

—— 1991, *Language Change: Progress of Decay*, Cambridge University Press, Cambridge.

Aiton, Doug & Dupleix, Jill 1996, *Doug and Jill's Summer Barbecue*, transcript of radio interview, ABC Radio 3L0, 20 February.

Algeo, John (ed.) (in press), *The Cambridge History of the English Language*, vol. 6, *English in North America*, Cambridge University Press, Cambridge.

Allan, Keith 1995, *Language in Australian Society*, unit study guide, Department of Linguistics, in conjunction with the Distance Education Centre, Monash University, Melbourne.

Allan, Keith & Burridge, Kate 1991, *Euphemism and Dysphemism: Language Used as Shield and Weapon*, Oxford University Press, New York.

Allen, Cynthia 1995, *Case Marking and Reanalysis: Grammatical Relations from Old to Early Modern English*, Clarendon Press, Oxford.

AND. See Ramson, W. S. 1988.

The Australian Concise Oxford Dictionary 1992, ed. J. M. Hughes, P. A. Michell, & W. S. Ramsom, 2nd edn, Oxford University Press, Melbourne.

Australian Style, The Dictionary Research Centre, Macquarie University, Sydney.

Ayto, John 1993, *Euphemisms*, Bloomsbury Publishing, London.

Bailey, Richard W. & Görlach, Manfred (eds) 1982, *English as a World Language*, Cambridge University Press, Cambridge.

Baker, Sidney 1970, *The Australian Language*, Sun Books, Melbourne.

Banks, Julie & Mulder, Jean 1996, *What Did I Say? Using Non-Discriminatory Language*, University of Melbourne, Equal Opportunity Unit, Melbourne.

Barber, Charles 1976, *Early Modern English*, Deutsch, London.

—— 1993, *The English Language: A Historical Introduction*, Cambridge University Press, Cambridge.

Baron, Dennis 1989, *Declining Grammar: And Other Essays on the English Vocabulary*, National Council of Teachers of English, Illinois.

Bartlett, Christopher 1992, 'Regional Variation in New Zealand English: The Case of Southland', *New Zealand Newsletter*, no. 6, pp. 5–15.

Batterham, Margaret I. 1995, 'There is Another Type Here': Some Front Vowel Variables in New Zealand English, unpublished PhD thesis, Department of Linguistics, La Trobe University, Melbourne.

Bauer, Laurie 1979, 'The Second Great Vowel Shift?', *Journal of the International Phonetic Association*, vol. 9, pp. 57–66.

—— 1983, *English Word-Formation*, Cambridge University Press, Cambridge.

—— 1988, *Introducing Linguistic Morphology*, Edinburgh University Press, Edinburgh.

—— 1992, 'The Second Great Vowel Shift Revisited', *English World-Wide*, vol. 13, no. 2, pp. 253–69.

—— 1993, 'Un-Bloody-Likely Words', in Laurie Bauer & Christine Franzen (eds), *Of Pavlova, Poetry and Paradigms: Essays in Honour of Harry Orsman*, Victoria University Press, Wellington, pp. 70–7.

—— 1994, *Watching English Change*, Longman, London.

Baugh, Albert C. & Cable, Thomas 1993, *A History of the English Language*, 4th edn, Routledge, London.

Bayard, Donn 1995, *KiwiTalk*, Dunmore Press, Palmerston North.

Bean, Marian C. 1983, *The Development of Word Order Patterns in Old English*, Croom Helm, London.

Bell, Allan & Holmes, Janet 1990 (eds), *New Zealand Ways of Speaking*, Multilingual Matters, Clevedon.

Bennett, Bruce 1994, 'Exporting Australian English', in Pam Peters (ed.), *The National Language*, Proceedings of Style Council 94, The Dictionary Research Centre, Macquarie University, Sydney, pp. 124–40.

Benton, Richard A. 1991, 'Maori English: A New Zealand Myth?', in Jenny Cheshire (ed.), *English Around the World: Sociolinguistic Perspectives*, Cambridge University Press, Cambridge, pp. 187–99.

Biber, Douglas 1988, *Variation Across Speech and Writing*, Cambridge University Press, Cambridge.

Black, Maggie 1977, *A Heritage of British Cooking*, Charles Letts & Co., London.

—— 1992, *The Medieval Cookbook*, British Museum Publications, London.

Blake, N. F. (ed.) 1992, *The Cambridge History of the English Language*, vol. 2, *1066–1476*, Cambridge University Press, Cambridge.

—— 1996, *A History of the English Language*, London, Macmillan.

Bloomfield, Leonard 1933, *Language*, Holt, Rhinehart & Winston, New York.

Bolinger, Dwight 1975, *Aspects of Language*, 2nd edn, Harcourt Brace Jovanovich, New York.

Bolton, W. F. 1966, *The English Language: Essays by English and American Men of Letters 1490–1839*, Cambridge University Press, Cambridge.

—— 1982, *A Living Language: The History and Structure of English*, Random House, New York.

Bowden, Ros & Bunbury Bill 1990, *Being Aboriginal: Comments, Observations and Stories from Aboriginal Australians*, ABC Books, Sydney.

Bradley, David 1989, 'Regional Dialects in Australian English Phonology', in Peter Collins & David Blair (eds), *Australian English: The Language of a New Society*, University of Queensland Press, St Lucia, pp. 260–70.

—— 1991, '/[ae]/ and /a:/ in Australian English', in Jenny Cheshire (ed.), *English Around the World: Sociolinguistic Perspectives*, Cambridge University Press, Cambridge, pp. 227–34.

Bradley, David, Sussex, Roland, & Scott, Graham (eds) 1989, *Studies in Australian English*, Department of Linguistics, La Trobe University, Melbourne.

Britain, David 1992, 'Linguistic Change in Intonation: The Use of High Rising Terminals in New Zealand English', *Language Variation and Change*, vol. 4, pp. 77–104.

Brown, A. 1988, 'Vowel Differences between Received Pronunciation and the English of Malaysia and Singapore: Which Ones Really Matter?', in Joseph Foley (ed.), *New Englishes: The Case of Singapore*, Singapore University Press, Kent Ridge, pp. 129–47.

Burchfield, Robert W. 1989, *Unlocking the English Language*, Faber & Faber, London.

— (ed.) 1994, *The Cambridge History of the English Language*, vol. 5, *English in Britain and Overseas: Origins and Development*, Cambridge University Press, Cambridge.

Butler, Susan 1990, 'Recent Additions to the Australian Lexicon', in Pam Peters (ed.), *Australia into the Nineties*, proceedings of Style Councils 90 and 91, The Dictionary Centre, Macquarie University, Sydney, pp. 254–66.

Buzo, Alex 1994, *Kiwese: A Guide, A Ductionary, A Shearing of Unsights*, Mandarin, Melbourne.

Cameron, Deborah 1992, *Feminism and Linguistic Theory*, 2nd edn, Macmillan, London.

— 1995, *Verbal Hygiene*, Routledge, London.

Catford, J. C. 1988. *A Practical Introduction to Phonetics*, Clarendon Press, Oxford.

Carney, Edward 1994, *A Survey of English Spelling*, Routledge, London.

Charrow, Robert P. & Charrow, Veda R. 1979, 'Making Legal Language Understandable: A Psycholinguistic Study of Jury Instructions', *Columbia Law Review*, vol. 79, pp. 1306–74.

Chesebro, James (ed.) 1981, *Gay Speak: Gay Male and Lesbian Communication*, Pilgrim Press, New York.

Cheshire, Jenny (ed.) 1991, *English Around the World: Sociolinguistic Perspectives*, Cambridge University Press, Cambridge.

Clark, John & Yallop, Colin 1995, *An Introduction to Phonetics and Phonology*, 2nd edn, Blackwell, Oxford.

Clark, Ross 1979, 'In Search of Beach-La-Mar: Towards a History of Pacific Pidgin English', *Te Reo*, vol. 22, pp. 3–64.

— 1991, 'Pidgin English and Pidgin Maori in New Zealand', in Jenny Cheshire (ed.), *English Around the World: Sociolinguistic Perspectives*, Cambridge University Press, Cambridge, pp. 187–213.

Coates, Jennifer (ed.) 1993, *Women, Men and Language*, 2nd edn, Longman, London.

— 1997, *Language and Gender: A Reader*, Blackwell, Oxford.

Cochrane, G. R. 1989, 'Origins and Development of the Australian Accent', in Peter Collins & David Blair (eds), *Australian English: The Language of a New Society*, University of Queensland Press, St Lucia, pp. 177–86.

Cockayne, Oswald (ed.) 1865, *Leechdoms, Wortcunning, and Starcraft of Early England*, Longman, Green, Longman, Roberts & Green, London.

Cockx-indestege, Elly 1971, *Eenen Nyeuwen Coock Boeck*, Guido Pressler, Weisbaden.

Collins, Peter & Blair, David (eds) 1989, *Australian English: The Language of a New Society*, University of Queensland Press, St Lucia.

Crawford, Mary 1995, *Talking Difference: On Gender and Langauge*, Sage, London.

Crowley, Terry 1997, *An Introduction to Historical Linguistics*, 3rd edn, Oxford University Press, Auckland.

Cutts, Stephen P. 1992, 'The Deviant Phonology of Several Warner Bros Cartoon Characters', *California Linguistics Newsletter*, vol. 23, no. 2, Spring–Summer, pp. 37–8.

Crystal, David 1980, 'Neglected Grammatical Factors in Conversational English', in S. Greenbaum, Geoffrey Leech, & Jan Svartvik (eds), *Studies in English Linguistics for Randolph Quirk*, Longman, London, pp. 153–66.

— 1984, *Who Cares About English Usage?*, Penguin Books, Harmondsworth.

—— 1995, *The Cambridge Encyclopedia of the English Language*, Cambridge University Press, Cambridge.

—— 1997, *English as a Global Language*, Cambridge University Press, Cambridge.

Crystal, David & Davy, D. 1969, *Investigating English Style*, Longman, London.

Cullen, Paul 1995, *Cook's Tour: A Haphazard Journey from Guangzhou to Dublin and Back Again*, Allen & Unwin, Sydney.

DAC. See Wilkes, Gerald Alfred 1985.

Danet, Brenda 1980, 'Language in the Legal Process', *Law and Society Review*, vol. 14, no. 3, pp. 445–564.

Darrell Lea Chocolate Shops (n.d.), *The Story of Liquorice*, pamphlet.

De Klerk, V. (ed.) 1996, *Focus on South Africa*, John Benjamins, Amsterdam.

Denning, Keith & Leben, William R. 1995, *English Vocabulary Elements*, Oxford University Press, New York.

Dennison, David 1995, *Historical English Syntax*, Longman, London.

Dillard, J. L. 1972, *Black English: Its History and Usage in the United States*, Random House, New York.

DNZE. See Orsman, Harry 1997.

Dupleix, Jill 1996a, 'The Lovin' Spoonful', *The Good Weekend Magazine*, 10 February, pp. 57–8.

—— 1996b, *Doug and Jill's Summer Barbecue*, information sheet provided by ABC Radio 3L0, 20 February.

Dutton, Tom 1985, *A New Course in Tok Pisin*, Pacific Linguistics, Canberra.

Dynes, Wayne R. 1985, *Homolexis: A Historical and Cultural Lexicon of Homosexuality*, Gay Academic Union, New York.

Eagleson, Robert D., Kaldor, Susan, & Malcolm, Ian G. 1982, *English and the Aboriginal Child*, Curriculum Development Centre, Canberra.

Esquivel, Laura 1993, *Like Water for Chocolate*, Transworld Publishers, London.

Foley, Joseph (ed.) 1988, *New Englishes: The Case of Singapore*, Singapore University Press, Kent Ridge.

Freeborn, Dennis (with Peter French and David Langford) 1986, *Varieties of English: An Introduction to the Study of Language*, 2nd edn, Macmillan, London.

—— 1992, *From Old to Standard English*, Macmillan, London.

—— 1995, *A Course Book in English Grammar: Standard English and the Dialects*, 2nd edn, Macmillan, London.

—— 1996, *Style: Text Analysis and Linguistic Criticism*, Macmillan, London.

Furnivall, Frederick (ed.) 1868, *The Babees Book, The Bokes of Nurture of Hugh Rhodes and John Russell*, published for the Early English Text Society, Trübner and Co., London.

Gass, S. & Lefkowitz, N. 1995, *Varieties of English*, University of Michigan Press, Ann Arbor, Mich.

Gaté, Gabriel 1996, *Pavlova Recipe*, information sheet provided by ABC Radio 3LO, 22 August.

Gaudio, Rudolf P. 1994, 'Sounding Gay: Pitch Properties in the Speech of Gay and Straight Men', *American Speech*, vol. 69, no. 1, pp. 30–57.

Giles, Howard 1977, *Language, Ethnicity and Ingroup Relations*, Academic Press, London.

Gleeson, Fran 1995, *The Impact of Globalisation on the Representation of Australian English*, unpublished Masters dissertation, Department of Linguistics, La Trobe University, Melbourne.

Goode, John 1987, *Bubble and Squeak: A Collation of Culinary Quotes*, Lothian, Melbourne.

Goode, John & Willson, Carol 1987, 'Hair of the Dog or Prairie Oyster: Name your Antidote', in John Goode, *Bubble and Squeak: A Collation of Culinary Quotes*, Lothian, Melbourne, p. 22.

Gordon, Elizabeth & Deverson, Tony 1985, *New Zealand English: An Introduction to New Zealand Speech and Usage*, Heinemann, Auckland.

— 1989, *Finding a New Zealand Voice*, New House Publishers, Auckland.

Gordon, Elizabeth & Maclagan, Margaret 1989, '*Beer* and *Bear*, *Cheer* and *Chair*: A Longitudinal Study of the Ear/Air Contrast in New Zealand English', *Australian Journal of Linguistics*, vol. 9, no. 2, pp. 203–20.

— 1990, 'A Longitudinal Study of the "Ear/Air" Contrast in New Zealand Speech', in Allan Bell & Janet Holmes (eds), *New Zealand Ways of Speaking*, Multilingual Matters, Philadelphia, pp. 129–48.

Görlach, Manfred 1991a, *Englishes: Studies in Varieties of English 1984–1988*, John Benjamins, Amsterdam.

— 1991b, *Introduction to Early Modern English*, Cambridge University Press, Cambridge.

— 1994, *More Englishes: New Studies in Varieties of English 1988–1994*, John Benjamins, Amsterdam.

Gowers, Sir E. 1975, *The Complete Plain Words*, Penguin Books, Harmondsworth.

Graddol, David & Swann, Joan 1989, *Gender Voices*, Blackwell, Oxford.

Graddol, David, Leith, Dick, & Swann, Joan 1996, *English: History, Diversity and Change*, Routledge, London.

Greenwood, Kerry & Pausacker, Jenny 1995, *Recipes for Crime*, McPhee Gribble, Melbourne.

Gupta, Anthea Fraser 1995, 'Markets for Australian English', in Pam Peters (ed.) *Australian English in a Pluralist Society,* Proceedings of Style Council 95, The Dictionary Research Centre, Macquarie University, Sydney, pp. 188–94.

Haas, William (ed.) 1969, *Alphabets for English*, University of Manchester Press, Manchester.

Hall, Michael 1997, 'Cultural Tourism and Urban Imaging', in Kate Burridge, Lois Foster, & Gerry Turcotte (eds), *Canada and Australia: Towards a Second Century of Partnership*, Carlton Press, Ottawa, pp. 287–304.

Hall, Stephen 1991, 'The Local and the Global', in A. D. King (ed.), *Culture, Globalization and the World System: Contemporary Conditions for the Representation of Identity*, Macmillan Education, London, pp. 67–80.

Halliday, Michael A. K. 1985, *Spoken and Written Language*, Deakin University Press, Geelong, Vic.

Harkins, Jean 1994, *Bridging Two Worlds: Aboriginal English and Crosscultural Understanding*, University of Queensland Press, St Lucia.

Harmer, Wendy 1995, 'Wounded by a Glance', *The Good Weekend Magazine*, 13 May, p. 16.

Hieatt, Constance B. & Butler, Sharon (eds) 1985, *Curye On Inglysch: English Culinary Manuscripts of the Fourteenth Century*, published for the Early English Text Society, Oxford University Press, London.

Hogg, Richard M. (ed.) 1992, *The Cambridge History of the English Language*, vol. 1, *The Beginnings to 1066*, Cambridge University Press, Cambridge.

Holmes, Janet 1992, *An Introduction to Sociolinguistics*, Longman, London.

— 1994, 'New Zealand Flappers: An Analysis of T Voicing in New Zealand English', *English World-Wide*, vol. 15, no. 2, pp. 195–224.

— 1995, *Women, Men and Politeness*, Longman, London.

Holmes, Janet & Bell, Allan 1993, 'On Shear Markets and Sharing Sheep: The Merger of EAR and AIR Dipthongs in New Zealand English', *Language Variation and Change*, vol. 4, no. 3, pp. 251–73.

Hopper, Paul & Traugott, Elizabeth Closs 1993, *Grammaticalization*, Cambridge University Press, Cambridge.

Hornadge, Bill 1989, *The Australian Slanguage*, Mandarin, Melbourne.

Horvath, Barbara M. 1985, *Variation in Australian English: The Sociolects of Sydney*, Cambridge University Press, Cambridge.

Huddleston, Rodney 1984, *Introduction to the Grammar of English*, Cambridge University Press, Cambridge.

—— 1988, *English Grammar: An Outline*, Cambridge University Press, Cambridge.

—— 1996, Grammar of English, course conducted for the Australian Linguistic Institute, Australian National Univeristy, Canberra, 1–12 July.

Hughes, A. & Trudgill, Peter 1979, *English Accents and Dialects*, Edward Arnold, London.

Hughes, Geoffrey 1988, *Words in Time: A Social History of the English Vocabulary*, Blackwell, Oxford.

Hyde, Michael, Kesselschmidt, Johnny, & Mason, Mary 1996, *Englishworks 3*, Cambridge University Press, Melbourne.

Iyengar, K. R. Srinivasa 1962, *Indian Writing in English*, Asian Publishing House, Bombay.

Johnston, Lorraine & Robertson, Shelley 1993, '*Hey, You!*: The Maori–NZE Interface in Sociolinguistic Rules of Address', *Te Reo*, vol. 36, pp. 115–27.

Jones, C. 1972, *An Introduction to Middle English*, Holt, Rinehart & Winston, New York.

Kachru, Braj B. 1983, *The Indianization of English: The English Language in India*, Oxford University Press, Delhi.

—— 1986, *The Alchemy of English: The Spread, Functions and Models of Non-Native Englishes*, Pergamon, Oxford.

—— 1992, 'The Second Diaspora of English', in Tim William Machan & Charles T. Scott (eds), *English in Its Social Contexts: Essays in Historical Sociolinguistics*, Oxford University Press, New York, pp. 230–52.

Kaplan, Jeffrey P. 1995, *English Grammar: Principles and Facts*, Prentice-Hall, Englewood Cliffs, NJ.

Katamba, Francis 1989, *An Introduction to Phonology*, Longman, London.

—— 1994, *English Words*, Routledge, London.

King, Jeanette 1993, 'Maori English: A Phonological Study', *New Zealand English Newsletter*, no. 7, pp. 33–47.

Koch, Harold 1985, 'Non-Standard English in an Aboriginal Land Claim', in J. B. Pride (ed.), *Cross-Cultural Encounters: Communication and Miscommunication*, River Seine, Melbourne, pp. 176–95.

Kuiper, Koenraad 1996, *Smooth Talkers: The Linguistic Performance of Auctioneers and Sportscasters*, Lawrence Erlbaum Associates, Mahwah, NJ.

Kuiper, Koenraad & Allan, W. Scott 1996, *An Introduction to the English Language: Sound, Word and Sentence*, Macmillan, London.

Labov, William 1966, *The Social Stratification of English in New York City*, Center for Applied Linguistics, Washington, DC.

—— 1972, *Sociolinguistic Patterns*, University of Pennsylvania Press, Philadelphia.

Ladefoged, Peter 1993, *A Course in Phonetics*, 3rd edn, Harcourt Brace Jovanovich, Fort Worth, Tex.

Langacker, Ronald W. 1977, 'Syntactic Reanalysis', in Charles Li (ed.), Mechanisms of Syntactic Change, University of Texas Press, Austin, pp. 57–139.

Lass, Roger 1987, *The Shape of English: Structure and History*, Dent, London.

— 1994, *Old English*, Cambridge University Press, Cambridge.

— (in press), *The Cambridge History of the English Language*, vol. 3, *1476–1776*, Cambridge University Press, Cambridge.

Lauder, Afferbeck 1981, *Let's Stalk Strine: A Lexicon of Modern Strine Usage*, Ure Smith, Sydney.

Leech, Geoffrey & Svartvik, Jan 1994, *A Communicative Grammar of English*, 2nd edn, Longman, London.

Leith, Dick 1983, *A Social History of English*, Routledge & Kegan Paul, London.

Lewis, C. S. 1970, *Studies in Words*, Cambridge University Press, Cambridge.

Lieberman, Philip & Blumstein, Sheila 1988, *Speech Physiology, Speech Perception, and Acoustic Phonetics*, Cambridge University Press, Cambridge.

Lindgren, Harry 1969, *Spelling Reform*, Halstead Press, Sydney.

Lodge, David 1989, *Nice Work*, Penguin Books, London.

Lutz, William 1989, *Beyond 1984: Doublespeak in a Post-Orwellian Age*, National Council of Teachers, Urbana, Ill.

Lynn, Jonathan & Jay, Anthony 1988, *Diary 1989 of Sir Humphry Appleby*, Doubleday, Sydney.

Lyons, John 1968, *Introduction to Theoretical Linguistics*, Cambridge University Press, Cambridge.

McArthur, Tom (ed.) 1992, *The Oxford Companion to the English Language*, Oxford University Press, Oxford.

McCallum, June, Lockhart, Carolyn, & Campbell, Joan (eds) 1986, *Vogue Entertaining*, Octopus Books, Sydney.

McCrum, Robert, Cran, William, & MacNeil, Robert 1991, *The Story of English*, revised edn, Faber & Faber and BBC, London and Boston.

McDougal, Keith 1985, *Linguistles*, La Trobe Linguistics Society, Melbourne.

Machan, Tim William & Charles T. Scott (eds) 1992, *English in Its Social Contexts: Essays in Historical Sociolinguistics*, Oxford University Press, New York.

McKay, Graham 1996, *The Land Still Speaks: Review of Aboriginal and Torres Strait Islander Language Maintenance and Development Needs and Activities*, prepared for the Australian National Board of Employment, Education and Training, AGPS, Canberra.

Maclagan, Margaret A. 1975, 'Thoughts on New Zealand English', *The New Zealand Speech Therapists' Journal*, vol. 30, no. 1, pp. 6–10.

Maclagan, Margaret & Gordon, Elizabeth 1996, 'Out of the AIR and into the EAR: Another View of the New Zealand Dipthong Merger', *Language Variation and Change*, vol. 8, 1996, pp. 125–47.

McMahon, April 1995, *Understanding Language Change*, Cambridge University Press, Cambridge.

The Macquarie Dictionary 1997, 3rd edn, ed. A. Delbridge, J. R. L. Bernard, D. Blair, P. Peters, & S. Butler, The Macquarie Library, Macquarie University, Sydney.

MD. See *The Macquarie Dictionary*.

Miller, Casey & Swift, Kate 1991, *Words & Women*, 2nd edn, Anchor Press, New York.

Milroy, James & Milroy, Lesley 1991, *Authority in Language*, 2nd edn, Routledge, London.

Milroy, Lesley 1980, *Language and Social Networks*, Blackwell, London.

Mitchell, Alexander George & Delbridge, Arthur 1965, *The Pronunciation of English in Australia*, revised edn, Angus & Robertson, Sydney.

Mitchell, Bruce & Robinson, F. C. 1992, *A Guide to Old English*, 5th edn, Blackwell, Oxford.

Montagné, P. 1961, *Larousse Gastronomique*, The Hamlyn Publishing Group, London.

Murray-Smith, Stephen 1990, *Right Words: A Guide to English Usage in Australia*, Penguin Books, Melbourne.

Myers, L. & Richard Hoffman 1979, *The Roots of Modern English*, 2nd edn, Little, Brown & Co., Boston.

The New Shorter Oxford English Dictionary on Historical Principles 1993, ed. Lesley Brown, 2 vols, Clarendon Press, Oxford.

New Zealand English Journal (formerly *New Zealand English Newsletter*), Department of English, University of Canterbury, Christchurch.

Newbrook, Mark 1992, 'Unrecognised Grammatical and Semantic Features Typical of Australian English: A Checklist with Commmentary', *English World-Wide*, vol. 13, no. 1, pp. 1–32.

Nihalani, P., Tongue, R. K., & Hosali, P. 1970, *Indian and British English: A Handbook of Pronunciation and Usage*, Oxford University Press, Delhi.

NSOED. See *The New Shorter Oxford English Dictionary on Historical Principles*.

OAWD. See Purchase, Shirley 1997.

Ochs, Eleonor 1979, 'Planned and Unplanned Discourse', in T. Givón (ed.), *Syntax and Semantics 12: Discourse and Syntax*, Academic Press, New York, pp. 27–42.

OED. See *The Oxford English Dictionary*.

Omnibus Books 1991, *The Grandma Poss Cookbook*, Omnibus Books, Adelaide.

Orsman, Harry 1997, *Dictionary of New Zealand English: A Dictionary of New Zealandisms on Historical Principles.* Oxford University Press, Auckland.

The Oxford English Dictionary 1989, prepared by J. A. Simpson & E. S. C. Weiner, 2nd edn, 20 vols, Clarendon Press, Oxford.

Ozwords, The Australian National Dictionary Centre, Australian National University with Oxford University Press, Melbourne.

Parmenter, Ian 1992, *Consuming Passions*, National Heart Foundation, Sydney.

—— 1993, *Bon Appétit*, Gore & Osment Publications, Sydney.

Partridge, Astley Cooper 1982, *A Companion to Old and Middle English Studies*, Deutsch, London.

Partridge, Eric 1970, *Slang Today and Yesterday*, 4th edn, Routlege & Kegan Paul, London.

Pauwels, Anne (ed.) 1987, *Women and Language in Australian and New Zealand Society*, Australian Professional Publications, Sydney.

Pawley, Andrew 1995, Some Characteristics of Tasmanian Vernacular English, paper presented to the Australian Linguistic Society National Conference, Australian National University, Canberra, September.

—— forthcoming, 'Gender Assignment to Inanimate Nouns in English: Tasmanian and Other Cases', in Nick Enfield (ed.), *Ethno-Syntax: The Embodiment of World-View in Grammatical Constructions*, Cambridge University Press, Melbourne.

Pennycook, Alastair 1994, *The Cultural Politics of English as an International Language*, Longman, Harlow, UK.

—— 1995, 'English in the Word/The World in English', in J. Tollefson (ed.), *Power and Inequality in Language Education*, Cambridge University Press, New York, pp. 34–58.

Pescott, Loma 1994, *Early Settlers' Household Lore*, Ballarat Historical Park Association, Ballarat, Vic.

Peters, Pam 1992, 'American and British English in Australian Usage', in Pam Peters (ed.), *Style on the Move*, Proceedings of Style Council 94, The Dictionary Research Centre, Macquarie University, Sydney, pp. 20–30.

—— 1995, *The Cambridge Australian English Style Guide*, Cambridge University Press, Melbourne.

Platt, John, Weber, Heidi, & Ho, M. L. 1984, *The New Englishes*, Routledge & Kegan Paul, London.

Poynton, Cate 1985, *Language and Gender: Making the Difference*, Deakin University Press, Geelong, Vic.

Puchase, Shirley 1997, *Oxford Australian Writers' Dictionary*, Oxford University Press, Melbourne.

Pyles, Thomas & Algeo, John 1993, *The Origins and Development of the English Language*, 4th edn, Harcourt Brace Jovanovich, San Diego.

Quirk, Randolf & Greenbaum, Sydney 1973, *A University Grammar of English*, Longman, London.

Quirk, Randolf, Greenbaum, Sydney, Leech, Geoffrey, & Svartvik, Jan 1985, *A Comprehensive Grammar of the English Language*, Longman, London.

Quirk, Randolf & Wrenn, C. L. 1955, *An Old English Grammar*, Methuen, London.

Ramson, W. S. (ed.) 1988, *The Australian National Dictionary*, Oxford University Press, Melbourne.

Reid, Julie 1997, Relatives and their Relatives: Relative Clauses in Conversational Australian English, PhD thesis, Department of Linguistics, La Trobe University, Melbourne.

Risch, Barbara 1987, 'Women's Derogatory Terms for Men: That's Right 'Dirty' Words', *Language in Society*, vol. 16, pp. 353–8.

Roach, P. J. 1983, *English Phonetics and Phonology: A Practical Course*, Cambridge University Press, Cambridge.

Roberts, Peter A. 1988, *West Indians and their Language*, Cambridge University Press, Cambridge University Press.

Rodgers, Bruce 1972, *The Queen's Vernacular: A Gay Lexicon*, Straight Arrow, San Francisco.

Romaine, Suzanne (ed.) 1982, *Sociolinguistic Variation in Speech Communities*, Edward Arnold, London.

—— 1988, *Pidgin and Creole Languages*, Longman, London.

—— (ed.) 1991, *Language in Australia*, Cambridge University Press, Cambridge.

—— (ed.) (in press), *The Cambridge History of the English Language*. vol. 4, *1776–Present Day*, Cambridge University Press, Cambridge.

Samuels, M. L. 1972, *Linguistic Evolution: With Special Reference to English*, Cambridge University Press, Cambridge.

Sapir, Edward 1921, *Language*, Harcourt, Brace & World, Inc., New York.

Schmidt, Annette 1990, *The Loss of Australia's Aboriginal Heritage*, Aboriginal Studies Press, Canberra.

Serjeantson, Mary S. 1935, *A History of Foreign Words in English*, Routledge & Kegan Paul, London.

Shakespeare, William 1987, *King Henry IV, Part I*, ed. David Bevington, Clarendon Press, Oxford.

Shopen, Timothy & Williams, Joseph M. 1980, *Standards and Dialects in English*, Winthrop Publishers, Cambridge, Mass.

—— 1981, *Style and Variables in English*, Winthrop Publishers, Cambridge, Mass.

Smith, Diana 1993, 'Teenage Slang in New Zealand', *New Zealand English Newsletter*, no. 7, pp. 25–8.

Smith, Jeremy 1996, *An Historical Study of English: Function Form and Change*, Routledge, London.

Strang, Barbara M. H. 1974, *A History of English*, Methuen, London.

Thieberger, Nick & McGregor, William 1994, *Macquarie Aboriginal Words: A Dictionary of Words from Australian Aboriginal and Torres Strait Islander Languages*, The Dictionary Research Centre, Macquarie University, Sydney.

Tilgals, Kirsten 1995, 'Adapting Aussie Books for Overseas Markets', in Pam Peters (ed.), *Australian English in a Pluralist Society,* Proceedings of Style Council 95, The Dictionary Research Centre, Macquarie University, Sydney, pp. 175–82.

Todd, Loreto 1984, *Modern Englishes: Pidgins and Creoles*, Blackwell (in association with Deutsch), Oxford.

Todd, Loreto & Hancock, I. F. 1986, *International English Usage*, Croom Helm, London.

Trudgill, Peter 1974, *Social Differentiation of English in Norwich*, Cambridge University Press, Cambridge.

—— 1975, *Accent, Dialect and the School*, Edward Arnold, London.

—— 1986, *Dialects in Contact*, Blackwell, Oxford.

—— 1994, *Dialects*, Routledge, London.

—— 1995, *Sociolinguistics: An Introduction to Language and Society*, Penguin Books, Harmondsworth.

Trudgill, Peter & Hannah, Jean 1994, *International English: A Guide to Varieties of Standard English*, 3rd revised edn, Edward Arnold, London.

Turner, George William 1966, *The English Language in Australia and New Zealand*, Longman, London.

Tutuola, Amos 1952, *The Palm-Wine Drinkard*, Faber & Faber, London.

Vaughan, Marcia 1989, *The Wombat Stew Cookbook*, Ashton Scholastic, Sydney.

Viereck, Wolfgang, Scheider, Edgar W., & Görlach, Manfred 1984, *A Bibiography of Writings on Varieties of English 1965–1983*, John Benjamins, Amsterdam.

Walsh, Michael & Yallop, Colin (eds) 1993, *Language and Culture in Aboriginal Australia*, Aboriginal Studies Press, Canberra.

Wardhaugh, Ronald 1995, *Understanding English Grammar: A Linguistic Approach*, Blackwell, Oxford.

Wickham, Lesley n.d., *The Ultimate Book of Kitchen Hints*, Bay Books, Sydney.

Wilkes, Gerald Alfred 1993, *Exploring Australian English*, ABC Books, Sydney.

—— 1996, *A Dictionary of Australian Colloquialisms*, 4th edn, Oxford University Press, Melbourne.

Winter, Jack 1994, 'How I Met My Wife', *The New Yorker*, 25 July, p. 82.

Acknowledgments

We would like to offer special thanks to Margaret Batterham, Barry Blake, John Bowden, David Bradley, Sue Butler, Hilary Chappel, Peter Clarke, Imants Dizgalvis, Bruce Donaldson, Christina Eira, Janet Fletcher, Margaret Florey, Lorna Gelbert, David Howes, Rodney Huddleston, Maris Lakis, Terry Laidler, Sandra Masel, Ng Bee Chin, Eve Oakley, Pam Peters, Janet Perkins, Allison Pritchard, Julie Reid, Deborah Staunton, Tonya Stebbins, Lesley Stirling, Catherine Travis, Alastair Ussher, Bryce Weber, Gerald Wilkes, Angelika Zimmerman, and the listeners of 3LO, who provided us with so many wonderful examples.

Most importantly, we would like to highlight our 'inner circle' of supporters: Cam, Ross, Elspeth, and Heather. Their contribution and our gratitude defies any attempt at conventional written expression.

As we mentioned in the Preface, we firmly believe that the language that is used in the examples should be English as it is actually spoken and written. Accordingly, we are indebted to the many people whose speech we have (surreptitiously) eavesdropped on. With our publisher, we would also like to thank the following copyright holders for permission to reproduce numerous extracts and examples: **ABC Books** for extracts from Ros Bowden & Bill Bunbury, *Being Aboriginal: Comments, Observations and Stories from Aboriginal Australians*, and from G. A. Wilkes, *Exploring Australian English*; **ABC Radio 3L0** for extract from Jill Dupleix, *Doug and Jill's Summer Barbecue*, and from Gabriel Gaté, *Pavlova Recipe*; **The Age** for extracts from various articles; **Allen & Unwin** for extract from Paul Cullen, *Cooks Tour: A Haphazard Journey from Guangzhou to Dublin and Back Again*; **Angus & Robertson** for extract from Alexander George Mitchell & Arthur Delbridge, *The Pronunciation of English in Australia*, revised edn; **Asian Publishing House** for extract from K. R. Srinivasa Iyengar, *Indian Writing in English*; the **Australian National Dictionary Centre** for extract from *Ozwords*; **Ballarat Historical Park Association** for extracts from Loma Pescott, *Early Settlers Household Lore*; **Black Swan Books, Transworld Publishers (Aust.) Pty Ltd** for extracts from Laura Esquivel, *Like Water for Chocolate*; **Blackwell** for extract from Geoffrey Hughes, *Words in Time: A Social History of the English Vocabulary*, and from David Graddol & Joan Swann, *Gender Voices*; **British Museum Publications Ltd** for extracts from Maggie Black, *The Medieval Cookbook*; **Business Forms Management Association** for extract from *Plain English Manual*; **Cambridge University Press** for extracts from W. F. Bolton, *The English Language: Essays by English and American*

Men of Letters 1490–1839, from David Crystal, *The Cambridge Encyclopedia of the English Language*, from Barbara Horvath, *Variation in Australian English: The Sociolects of Sydney*, from Michael Hyde, Johnny Kesselschmidt, & Mary Mason, *Englishworks 3*, and from Pam Peters, *The Cambridge Australian English Style Guide*; **California Linguistics Newsletter** for extract from Stephen Cutts, 'The Deviant Phonology of Several Warner Bros Cartoon Characters'; **Charles Letts & Co.** for extract from Maggie Black, *A Heritage of British Cooking*; **Condé Nast Publications Pty Ltd** for extracts from various issues of *Vogue Entertaining* 1995–96; **Curriculum Development Centre** for extracts from Robert Eagleson, Susan Kaldor, & Ian Malcolm, *English and the Aboriginal Child*; **Darrell Lea Chocolate Shops** for extract from *The Story of Liquorice*; the **Dictionary Research Centre, Macquarie University**, for extract from Susan Butler, 'Recent Additions to the Australian Lexicon', and from Nick Thieberger & William McGregor, *Macquarie Aboriginal Words: A Dictionary of Words from Australian Aboriginal and Torres Strait Islander Languages*; **Doubleday, Transworld Publishers (Aust.) Pty Ltd** for extract from Jonathan Lynn & Antony Jay, *Diary 1989: Secretary of the Cabinet, Yes, Prime Minister, Sir Humphrey Appleby K.C.B.*; **Faber & Faber Ltd** for extract from Amos Tutuola, *The Palm-Wine Drinkard*; **The Good Weekend Magazine** for extract from Wendy Harmer, 'Wounded by a Glance'; **Elizabeth Gordon** for extract from personal communication; **Gore & Osment Publications Pty Ltd** for extracts from Ian Parmenter, *Bon Appétit with Ian Parmenter*; **Guido Pressler** for extract from Elly Cockx-indestege, *Eenen Nyeuwen Coock Boeck*; **Heinemann** for extracts from Elizabeth Gordon & Tony Deverson, *New Zealand English: An Introduction to New Zealand Speech and Usage*; **Pia Herbert** for extract from personal communication; **La Trobe Linguistics Society** for extract from Keith McDougal, *Linguistles*; **Matthew Leditschke** for extracts from personal communication; **Language Variation and Change** for extract from David Britain, 'Linguistic Change in Intonation: The Use of High Rising Terminals in New Zealand English'; **Little, Brown & Co.** for extract from L. Myers & Richard Hoffman, *The Roots of Modern English*, 2nd edn; **Lothian Publishing Company Pty Ltd** for extracts from John Goode, *Bubble and Squeak: A Collation of Culinary Quotes*; **Mandarin, a part of Reed Books Australia**, for extract from Alex Buzo, *Kiwese, A Guide, A Ductionary, A Shearing of Unsights: New Zealand-speak Made Easy*; **Macmillan** for extracts from Dennis Freeborn, *A Course Book in English Grammar: Standard English and the Dialects*, 2nd edn; **McPhee Gribble, Penguin Books Australia Ltd**, for extracts from Kerry Greenwood & Jenny Pausacker, *Recipes for Crime*; **National Council of Teachers** for extract from William Lutz, *Beyond 1984: Doublespeak in a Post-Orwellian Age*; **National Heart Foundation in association with ABC Enterprises** for extracts from Ian Parmenter, *Consuming Passions: Cooking with Ian Parmenter*; **New House Publishers** for extracts from Elizabeth Gordon & Tony Deverson, *Finding a New Zealand Voice*; **The New Yorker** for extract from Jack Winter, 'How I Met My Wife'; **Patrick Nilens** for extract from personal communication; **Octopus Books Pty** for extract from June McCallum, Carolyn Lockhart, & Joan Campbell, *Vogue Entertaining*; **Omnibus Books** for extracts from Omnibus Books, *Grandma Poss Cookbook*; **Oxford University Press Australia and New Zealand** for extracts from Terry Crowley, *An*

Introduction to Historical Linguistics, 3rd edn, and from G. A. Wilkes, *A Dictionary of Australian Colloquialisms*; **Oxford University Press, New York**, for extracts from Keith Allan & Kate Burridge, *Euphemism and Dysphemism: Language Used as Shield and Weapon*; **Oxford University Press, Oxford**, for extracts from Constance B. Hieatt & Sharon Butler (eds), *Curye On Inglysch: English Culinary Manuscripts of the Fourteenth Century*, and from Braj Kachru, 'The Second Diaspora of English', in Tim William Machan & Charles T. Scott (eds), *English in Its Social Contexts: Essays in Historical Sociolinguistics*; **Pacific Linguistics, Department of Linguistics, Research School of Pacific Studies, the Australian National University**, for extracts from Tom Dutton, *A New Course in Tok Pisin (New Guinea Pidgin)*; Andrew Pawley for extracts from unpublished work; **Penguin Books Australia** for extract from David Lodge, *Nice Work*, and from Stephen Murray-Smith, *Right Words: A Guide to English Usage in Australia*; **Julie Reid** for extract from personal communication; **Routledge** for extracts from Albert Baugh & Thomas Cable, *A History of the English Language*, 4th edn; **Routledge & Kegan Paul** for extracts from John Platt, Heidi Weber, & M. L. Ho, *The New Englishes*; **Susan Russ** for extract from personal communication; **Singapore University Press** for extract from Adam Brown, 'Vowel Differences between Received Pronunciation and the English of Malaysia and Singapore: Which Ones Really Matter?', in J. Foley, *New Englishes: The Case of Singapore*; **Ivan Uemlianin** for extract from personal communication; **Ure Smith Pty Ltd** for extract from Afferbeck Lauder, *Let's Stalk Strine: A Lexicon of Modern Strine Usage*; the **Washington Post** for quotation from Laurence Urdang; **Malcolm Whiffin** for letter to Peter Clarke.

Every effort has been made to trace the original source of all copyright material reproduced in this book. Where the attempt has been unsuccessful, the authors and publisher would be pleased to hear from the copyright holder concerned to rectify the omission.

Index